The Test of Love

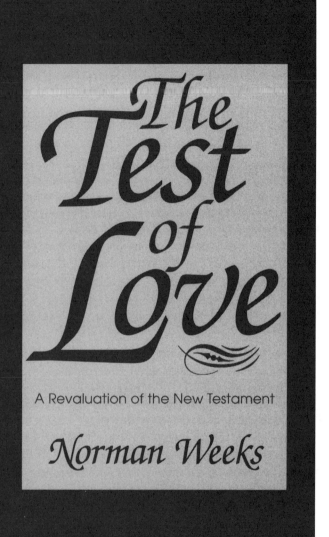

The Test of Love

A Revaluation of the New Testament

Norman Weeks

Prometheus Books • Buffalo, New York

To the Memory of Bertrand Russell

Published 1992 by Prometheus Books

96 95 94 93 92   5 4 3 2 1

Library of Congress Cataloging-in-Publication Data

Weeks, Norman.
The test of love : a revaluation of the New Testament / by Norman Weeks.
        p.   cm.
Includes bibliographical references and index.
ISBN 0-87975-741-8
1. Bible. N.T.—Controversial literature. 2. Love—Religious aspects—Christianity. I. Title.
BS2372.W44 1992
225.6—dc20   91-45828
                                                                  CIP

Printed in Mexico on acid-free paper.

Contents

Preface

In all of the New Testament there is only one single philosophical question. It is asked, not by a Christian or by a Jew, but by a pagan Roman.

A Jew named Jesus of Nazareth stood accused of religious and political sedition. Who was this Jesus of Nazareth? What did he claim to be? Was he innocent or guilty of the charges laid against him? Pontius Pilate, his Roman judge, was interrogating him.

Although the prisoner gave evasive answers about his pretensions to kingship, he did not impress Pilate as the kind of man who posed a danger to the Roman imperial order. Palestine produced both prophets, religious fanatics, and Zealots, nationalistic revolutionaries. From the mystical otherworldliness of Jesus' answers during the interrogation, Pilate was coming to the conclusion that Jesus was a prophet, not a Zealot. He was, therefore, harmless to Rome.

"All who are on the side of truth listen to my voice," Jesus said to Pilate.

Pilate retorted with the philosophical question, "Truth? . . . What is that?"[1]

It was order, not truth, that concerned the Roman imperial government. And so Pilate judged Jesus of Nazareth innocent.[2]

In recognizing Jesus as a prophet and not a Zealot, Pilate was correct. But in adjudging Jesus innocent Pilate was wrong. Jesus was guilty. What he was guilty of neither his accusers nor his judge fully understood.

"Truth? . . . What is that?" That question has been variously interpreted. Was Pilate musing, like a Greek philosopher, on the nature of Truth itself? Was he asking for the particular judicial truth about the prisoner before him? Or was he uttering just a weary sigh of Roman cynicism? In any case, the question went unanswered.

Whether we ask about Truth itself or only the particular truth about Jesus of Nazareth, Pilate's question remains unanswered still.

On another occasion Jesus had said, "As for me, I speak the truth."[3] His listeners might have passed their own judgments on that claim, but we cannot do so. As far as we know, Jesus never wrote down a single word of his truth. He left neither a psychological self-revelation nor an exposition of his ideas. For us, therefore, there is no truth from Jesus of Nazareth. However, we do possess some purported truth *about* Jesus of Nazareth recorded in four biographies, the so-called gospels. But those gospels are quite distant from the person and mind of Jesus of Nazareth.

First of all, the gospels date from thirty-five to seventy years after his death. The average lifespan of the time was short, so much of the information in the gospels is at secondhand or thirdhand remove from the eyewitnesses to the events described. The gospels are not contemporary reportage, but rather postmortem reconstructions.

Any story is embellished in the retelling, especially when there are few eyewitnesses available to correct it. The gospels are late retellings of a story that could no longer be corroborated or corrected by living eyewitnesses. Behind the gospels lies a long oral tradition about Jesus. How reliable that tradition is we have no way of determining.

In addition to that temporal distance, there is a cultural distance to contend with. Jesus, a Palestinian Jew, thought and spoke in Aramaic. But the gospels were all written in Koine Greek, the vernacular of the cosmopolitan Mediterranean world. The Jesus who speaks to us in the gospels does so in a language alien to him. Even if he knew Greek, which is possible, he must have thought and spoken in Aramaic. As the gospels translated his words, so did they inevitably distort his ideas.

Worse yet, the writers of the gospels, like the writers of all the other books in the New Testament, were anxious to *prove* something about the person of Jesus of Nazareth. In their attempt to prove something about him, they did not, and could not, take Jesus simply as he was. The gospels promote the person that Jesus' followers thought him to be. That, then, is the editorial bias of the gospels.

The gospels lack the authoritativeness of eyewitness accounts. They are late, secondhand, anonymous works. Authors' names were

attached in an attempt to secure for the gospels convincing authoritativeness. The *author* was the authority. Appeal was made either
to the authority of men who had been associates of Jesus himself,
like Matthew and John, two of Jesus' chosen apostles; or to men
who had played some role in the propagandizing efforts of the early
Church or had some association with the most prominent leaders
of the sect—like Mark, who reputedly derived his information from
Peter, the chief apostle; or Luke, who was an associate of Paul, the
master propagandist.

The Gospel of Matthew is first in order, as it was first in preference
in the early Church. It succeeds in establishing the affiliation of the
Church to Jesus and of Jesus to the heritage of Judaism. But at
the same time that it incorporates Judaism, it repudiates the Jews.
Matthew is retrospective, conservative, dogmatic. His gospel provides
a formal exposition of the ethical and moral teachings of Jesus, along
with promises of rewards for conformity to, and threats of vivid
punishments for violation of, the ethical and moral standards. The
Gospel of Matthew is law and judgment. As such, it served well
the emerging authoritarian tendency of the early Church.

Mark, the second gospel, begins and ends abruptly. Within its
brief text Jesus' deeds are recounted, but few of his words and not
very much about his person. Mark portrays Jesus and his apostles
as all-too-human. The Marcan abruptness, lack of ideology, and the
sometimes unflattering portrayals were not to the taste of the early
Church.

Like Matthew, and unlike Mark, Luke devotes a considerable
portion of his version of the biography of Jesus to the Master's
teachings. Luke complements Matthew. Matthew looked back to the
Jews' past; Luke looked around at the great cosmopolitan world of
his own time. We might say that Matthew's approach is temporal
and Luke's is spatial. And so, where Matthew is Jewish-sectarian
and conservative, Luke is cosmopolitan and liberal. Luke included
some parables of Jesus recorded nowhere else. That last fact alone
ensured that Luke's gospel would find a ready acceptance in the early
Church.

The Gospel of John is a problem, as every great work of art
is. Not just another version of the same story of Jesus, the Gospel
of John seems to be almost a different story about a different person
altogether. The Jesus of John speaks in a different manner about
different *truths* than those recorded in the other three gospels. John

is the least biographical, the most heavily expository, of the gospels. It is mystical, and therefore, to the Church, was necessarily suspect of heterodoxy. But in the Gospel of John there is a beautiful vision.

Of the four gospels Mark seems to be the stump in the grove. Because it claimed the least about the person of Jesus, it was, to the Church, the least satisfying gospel. However, modern textual analysis has determined that, far from being the stump, Mark is the root of the gospel story, the primary source. It is the earliest, the most primitive, the most artless, and because of all that, probably the most important of the written sources.

Modern scholars agree that both Matthew and Luke copied Mark. They took over Mark's basic outline of the life of Jesus, the incidents in that life, the general order of those incidents, and even the words of the storytelling. Almost all of Mark is in Matthew, and most of Mark is in Luke. Instead of three biographical traditions, therefore, there was only a single basic one, the one in Mark. Matthew and Luke are mostly Mark revised and edited. That is why those three gospels are called *synoptic:* they all share the same perspective of a single biographical tradition.

Matthew and Luke copied Mark. They also had access to a common source, so-called *Q,* containing the teachings attributed to Jesus, the very element of the story that Mark had lacked. To the deeds of Jesus from Mark, Matthew and Luke added the words of Jesus from *Q,* their common source. Each had further access to a source, or sources, that the other did not know about or did not use. Taking the deeds of Jesus from Mark, then, and sharing the words of Jesus with each other, Matthew and Luke each provided some other information uniquely his own.

Mark had begun his biography of Jesus abruptly, with the appearance of John the Baptist, forerunner of Jesus. He had ended it abruptly, with the dismay of the women at the discovery that Jesus' body had disappeared from its tomb. Matthew and Luke embellished Mark's story at both ends. They provided genealogies, as well as nativity, infancy, and childhood legends about Jesus, as a prelude to his public career; and the Resurrection, various miraculous appearances, and a missionary commission as a climactic conclusion. Matthew and Luke wrote more explicitly, and therefore more satisfyingly, than Mark on the subjects of the legitimacy and the person of Jesus of Nazareth.

The Gospel of John is very late and very elaborate. Whether

it has any dependence at all on Mark or Matthew or Luke is problematical. John is the font of a separate stream of tradition. Mark
was ambiguous; and Matthew and Luke, for all their assertions, still
proved inadequate. Beyond them John pronounced a vision that was
cosmic in its claims about the person of Jesus of Nazareth. John
is not so much a biography as a cosmology.

Just how reliable are the gospels as accurate biographies of Jesus
of Nazareth? When we compare them, we find both convergent and
divergent traditions. The oral tradition about Jesus was narrow, the
sources for his life few, and the possibilities for verification and cor-
rection limited. And because each gospelwriter's main purpose was
to prove something about Jesus, rather than to understand him, there
was considerable editorial distortion. The Jesus of John, the latest
gospel, bears little resemblance to the Jesus of Mark, the earliest.
Authentic memories came to be mingled with some quite fantastic
legendary fabrications. Trying to find the historical Jesus of Nazareth
in the texts of the four gospels seems to be the pursuit of a phantom.

Because Matthew and Luke derive from Mark, we cannot use
any one of those three gospels to check the truth of any other. John
stands alone; but if John contradicts the other three gospels, how
can we decide which is the more accurate? Are there any other sources,
outside the New Testament, against which we can check the accuracy
of the biography of Jesus contained in the gospels?

There are some passing references to Jesus of Nazareth or to
his followers in the Roman historians Tacitus and Suetonius and
in the Jewish historian Josephus. But those sources are as late or
later than the gospels, and they are even more culturally removed.
What we find in non-Christian sources seems based on mere hearsay. It adds nothing and corrects nothing. Further, it is unlikely that
other non-Christian sources will be discovered, because after the
Christians gained control of the Roman Empire, following the
conversion of the emperor Constantine, they were vigorous in the
censorship or destruction of any pagan sources that were critical of
their origins or doctrines. And so we are left with the gospels, and
almost nothing else.

If we want to apply a scientific or historical *test of truth* to
the contents of the gospels, we find that the task is an impossible
one. The test of truth cannot be applied. And isn't that precisely
what religious *faith* is: the security in knowing that the test of truth
can never be applied?

Pontius Pilate may have been the last human being capable of determining the truth about Jesus of Nazareth. Pilate failed, leaving us with his vexing question, "Truth? . . . What is that?" The truth about Jesus of Nazareth cannot and will never be determined. His truth died with him.

Because the writers of the New Testament were trying to prove something about Jesus, they concentrated their attention upon his person. However, Jesus of Nazareth was a prophet whose mission was something more than mere self-promotion. Jesus taught *values.* As well as a repository of conceptions about the person of Jesus, the New Testament is also a digest of the values that he taught.

It was very early in the postmortem reconstruction that the Christians shifted emphasis away from the values toward the person. Isn't it long past time to shift the emphasis back again, away from the person—whom we cannot know, anyway—to the values, which are fully laid out in the pages of the New Testament? Jesus' followers proclaimed *him,* but what Jesus proclaimed was *values.*

Values means what is good or bad, good or evil, wholesome or corrupt, life-enhancing or life-destroying. Jesus the prophet taught concepts of morality and ethics. He taught values.

As an administrator, Pontius Pilate was not concerned with truth. If we, as philosophers and psychologists, delve into the values of the New Testament, we, too, can dispense with the test of truth. Values are not true or false; they are better or worse.

Jesus of Nazareth passed judgment on the values of his society, reaffirming some, repudiating others, and teaching certain innovative values. That was his task and mission. It is also ours. We can, and we ought to, pass judgment on the values in the New Testament. We should try to determine which of those values are better, and which worse, than their antithetical ancient and modern values.

What was the essence of Jesus' teaching? What was his *prime value*? According to the interpretation of his followers, all that Jesus taught could be condensed and expressed in a single word—*love.* The prime value of Jesus of Nazareth was love. That is also the prime value in the New Testament.

We cannot know the truth about the person Jesus of Nazareth. But we can pass a modern judgment on his prime value and on all his subsidiary values, as they are laid out before us in the five hundred pages of the New Testament.

When we hear the word *truth* we stand back, baffled. But when we hear the word *love* we pounce. Isn't love our modern obsession, our modern expertise, our modern competence? We have now had a century of scientific psychology, and before that enough cultural explorations of sex, love, and romance to give us a rich heritage of experience. That is the very trait that makes us modern. We know what love is.

Whatever the truth about Jesus of Nazareth, his prime value and the prime value of the New Testament was love. Instead of the test of truth, therefore, we will apply a *test of love*.

Most New Testament scholarship falls into the categories of exegesis, exposition, or commentary. An exegesis is an explanation of the meaning of the text. Such explanation has been necessary, because of both the temporal and cultural distance separating us from first-century Palestine, and the obscurity of the archaic English in the old translations, such as the King James Version. Exposition and commentary are further explanations and interpretations of linguistic, ideological, or cultural matters; or they may be just an extended sermon on the text. Whatever criticism there is in exegesis, exposition, or commentary is usually restricted, because the followers of Jesus are still trying to prove something about him.

We are fortunate in having several excellent modern translations of the New Testament, such as *The Jerusalem Bible*. In those translations the meaning of the text is more directly accessible to us, so that we are not so dependent on the secondhand explanations of exegesis, exposition, and commentary. We can proceed to a higher, a more important, task. That task is a *revaluation* of the values in the New Testament. When we apply the test of love, we are making a revaluation of values.

A revaluation of the New Testament is a criticism of the values expressed by Jesus of Nazareth or by his adherents. It is difficult to distinguish which values belong to Jesus himself and which to his adherents, because what Jesus says in the New Testament is only what his adherents permitted him to say. In our revaluation, therefore, we may not be going into the mind of Jesus of Nazareth, so much as into the minds of his postmortem partisans, as they reveal themselves throughout the twenty-seven books of the New Testament.

Recognizing that the test of truth cannot be applied, we do not pretend that we say anything certain about the historical person Jesus of Nazareth. Such questions of fact are indeterminable, and so they must be secondary. If some of the assertions that the partisan promoters

of Jesus made about him seem anachronistic or legendary or mythological, we criticize those conceptions. But we do not make any new
assertions about the historical person. In this revaluation, the name
Jesus does not designate the historical person Jesus of Nazareth; still
less does it refer to any divinity. The Jesus of this revaluation is
only the literary character who is the protagonist of the gospels and
the type and model of the rest of the New Testament. This Jesus
is a fiction and an ideal.

A revaluation, then, is a kind of literary criticism. The historical
person Jesus of Nazareth may not be accurately portrayed in the
New Testament; but the values ever since attributed to that person
are there in clear modern English. To those values we apply the critical sense of literary analysis, of philosophical rationalism, of our
modern psychological insight, as well as our understanding of so-
ciology and politics.

A revaluation has nothing to do with anyone's faith or belief.
Revaluation is a questioning of all the most basic assumptions
that underly faith and belief, in this case the faith and belief associated with the New Testament. This revaluation is not a book
about the Book. It is a book about the values contained within
the Book.

If Jesus, the fictional protagonist of the New Testament, preached
a doctrine of love, his life, career, and values must be interpreted
in terms of the human emotionality of love. We who understand
what love is are competent to apply the test of love.

The time is overripe for such a revaluation of Christian values.
A century has passed since the publication of the pioneer effort in
that task, Nietzsche's *The Antichrist,* which was intended to be the
first book in a thorough revaluation of all values. Nietzsche never
accomplished his revaluation, nor have we adequately followed up
on his challenge to apply philosophy and psychology to the criticism of religion.

Perhaps Nietzsche's great contribution to the problem of the New
Testament was his distinction between the art of good reading and
bad reading, not only bad reading, but the *art* of bad reading. Bad
reading is an art that Christian readers have cultivated to an exquisite refinement. Their reading has been a self-hypnosis of rote and
repetition of chapter-and-verse. If they found a contradiction, they
tried to *harmonize.* Harmonize, a beautiful word for a disreputable
practice! Christian readers have been afraid that their scriptures would

somewhere fail the test of truth. And so they have read blindly, uncritically—harmoniously.

In applying the test of love to the values of the New Testament, we have to cure our addiction to the art of bad reading and try to cultivate the art of good reading instead. Good reading is a necessary discipline for a revaluation.

We are approaching the end of the second millennium of the Christian values. While those of an apocalyptic bent might look forward to the year 2000 with anxiety about the End, we see it instead as a time for a millennial revaluation of Christian values. The End may or may not be imminent; but the millennial revaluation should be. What do we, standing at the end of our millennium, have to say about the values with which and under which we have lived these past two thousand years?

Context

"A tribe enslaved to superstition."[1] That is how the great Roman historian Tacitus characterizes the Jews of the first century A.D.

Unlike the modern sophisticate, who tends to identify religion and superstition as one and the same, Tacitus recognized a distinction between the two. *Religion* meant a cultural consciousness and a community ritual; it was traditional, seemly, and socially useful. *Superstition,* on the other hand, meant belief in the extravagant and the fantastic. It was the gullibility and credulity of the ignorant and the cowardly. Religion was admirable, a social good; superstition was contemptible, a private or tribal mania. It was by means of those definitions that Tacitus could characterize the pagan Romans as a religious people and the Jews as "a tribe enslaved to superstition."

To us the word *superstition* denotes the nonrational and the irrational, the simpleminded and unscientific. It is a too-ready belief on too little evidence.

We would agree with Tacitus that ignorance and fear afflict the superstitious, and that education and science are the remedies for superstition. Scientific knowledge and understanding should supplant unfounded belief and give us the nerve to face our primitive fears. The modern mind wants to make the irrational rational. That was the very goal that modern psychology set for itself. And we moderns are all psychologists.

Tacitus characterizes the Jews as superstitious. Shortly before he renders that judgment, Tacitus himself seems to make his own descent into superstition.

At that time, Tacitus tells us, there was a feeling of expectancy throughout the Roman world. There was a certain prophecy, much repeated and widely known, that out of the land of Judaea would appear a great man destined to be a great ruler.[2] Such a prophecy actually did come to pass, in the first century A.D.

A great man, the story goes, came forth out of the land of Judaea. Walking along one day, he encountered a blind man. The blind man threw himself at his feet and begged to be healed. And the great man took the saliva from his own mouth and anointed the blind man's sightless eyes. At that touch they were opened and made clear, so that the poor wretch, known as a blind man by all the people, was given sight. The bystanders were awed by the miracle, and by the power shown by the great man who had come forth from Judaea.

And there came another wretch, this one disfigured by a withered hand. He, too, threw himself at the feet of the great man and begged to be healed. The great man condescended to heal him with a touch. The withered hand became whole. The awe of the people increased, and they spread the reputation of the great man, even though he himself was reluctant to make his powers known.

Tacitus reports those two magical and miraculous cures in his *Histories*. The man who performed them had come out of Judaea, just as the prophecy said, and he became the greatest of all rulers. He was king of kings and lord of lords. He was the Roman emperor, Vespasian.[3]

The setting for Vespasian's miracles was Alexandria in Egypt. The Egyptians, according to Tacitus, were ignorant and fear-ridden. They were all-too-ready to believe the fantastic. They craved miracles. Like the Jews, the Egyptians were, he says, a people "enslaved to superstition."[4]

As an educated and sophisticated aristocratic pagan, Tacitus recognized two antithetical ways of interpreting the world and its events. One way was logic and reason. It was the way of the Greeks and the Romans—the West. The other world view was illogical, irrational, and unreasonable. It was the way of the Egyptians and the Jews—the East.

The tales of Vespasian's two miraculous cures seem to have come out of a literature quite different from Roman history.[5] But Tacitus reports the miracles in the Roman way, which was rational and, therefore, skeptical. According to Tacitus, when the two beggars beseeched Vespasian to cure them, Vespasian laughed in their faces. The notion of dispelling blindness and infirmity with a mere touch was preposterous. Vespasian's laugh was Roman skepticism.

Vespasian had come to Alexandria from Judaea, it was true—

he was the commander of the legions sent to Judaea to quell a Jewish Zealot revolt; but Vespasian was an Italian from the hills near Rome. As a Roman, as a skeptic, Vespasian laughed. He refused to compromise his reputation by engaging in superstitious dabblings that would only earn him a behind-the-back mockery from his Roman contemporaries.

But then Vespasian had second thoughts. Contemptuous though he was regarding Egyptian superstitiousness, he had, as a Roman, the duty to be diplomatic. And so, after taking an opinion poll of the local doctors and being assured that his reputation would not be compromised, Vespasian indulged his subjects. He made a half-hearted attempt at a cure.

Against his own rational expectations, Vespasian succeeded. The two beggars were healed. At that prodigy Vespasian wavered in his Roman skepticism. He went to visit the temple of the local god to try to find out what powers resided there. Now the ruler of the world, he needed strength. And he wanted to know the future.

We might say that Vespasian nearly *converted* to the superstitions of Egypt. At the least he was of two minds, the one a rational, skeptical mind that laughed at superstition, the other an irrational mind that was all-too-susceptible to belief.

Vespasian was not unusual in being of the two minds. Nearly everyone in the cosmopolitan world of the Roman Empire wavered between reason and superstition. Tacitus himself could be of the two minds. In one passage he speculates that the prophecy and the tales of the miracles might have been created after Vespasian had come to power, in order to embellish his reputation and make him seem personally entitled to the exalted position he held in the world. That was the rational explanation. In another passage Tacitus writes that there were credible eyewitnesses to Vespasian's miracles, men who had nothing to gain from flattery. Perhaps the miracles had occurred after all.[6]

Tacitus included the story of Vespasian's two miracles in his *Histories*; but they were not of the essence of either the history of the period or the biography of Vespasian. Tacitus put the episode into his narrative as an anecdote. The miracles were not to be taken as any indication, much less proof, of some kind of supernatural power residing in the person of Vespasian. The greatness of Vespasian was proved in military and diplomatic, that is, in Roman, terms. The miracles and the superstitions of the East were a diversion for the Roman reader.

Tacitus' venture into the infernal regions of the superstitious mind was just a foray. The essence of his *Histories* was the political and social world of the Roman Empire. Vespasian may have been a savior of the world, but not in a sense to gratify the cravings of the superstitious. Vespasian had put an end to the civil war of A.D. 69, in which four emperors had met violent deaths in just over a year. Like Augustus before him, Vespasian restored world peace. For what he had achieved, some Romans recognized and appreciated Vespasian as a *savior.* The superstitious peoples of the East could imagine for themselves what supernatural force had given Vespasian the powers to attain his achievement.

At about the same time that Tacitus was writing his *Histories,* another book (or, more accurately, a series of books) appeared. That book, too, deals with a civil war or revolution of sorts, one not in the earthly Roman Empire but in the *Kingdom of Heaven.*[7] In that book the real and actual world of emperors and kings, of politics and society, is just a shadowy backdrop to a narrative of some remarkable events in the inner mind of the East. In that book there is little history, but there are many miracles. No one is skeptical of the miracles; no one laughs at them. On the contrary, miracles of healing, along with numerous portents and prodigies, are presented as proof of the unique greatness of a certain man who came forth from Judaea; of the goodness of his character and of the truth of his words. His miracles are not included in the narrative simply for their entertainment value. They are intended to secure the conviction of the hearer or reader. They are proof.

Had Tacitus read that book, he would have contemptuously dismissed it as Eastern superstition of the rankest sort. After all, it had been written by the Jews, that "tribe enslaved to superstition." The hero of the book is a healer, teacher, and reputed king named Jesus of Nazareth. The book is, as we now call it, the New Testament.

When we open the New Testament, we find ourselves, on the very first pages, in a world of dreams. There are no fewer than five dreams in the first two chapters of the first book of the New Testament, the Gospel according to Matthew.

A Jew named Joseph had discovered that his fiancée was pregnant, and he knew that it was not his doing. He decided to break off the engagement, but his intention was frustrated by a dream. Deep in the sleep of his troubled mind, Joseph was told by the dream that his fiancée had conceived in an uncanny way and that he should both marry her as he had promised and accept her child as his own.

After that child was born, some Magi appeared in search of the great ruler who was to arise in Judaea. The Magi had calculated the date and hour of the ruler's birth; but they made a mistake in judgment when they confided in Herod, the reigning king of Judaea. Recognizing the link between prophecy and politics and determined to hold his power against all upstart claimants. Herod feigned co-operation but plotted infanticide. He asked the Magi to report to him on the results of their search. In the second dream of the narrative, the Magi were warned of Herod's evil intentions and told to return home without informing Herod of the newborn king that they had, in fact, found.

In the third dream Joseph was directed to take his wife and uncanny child and flee to Egypt, far from Herod's malevolent power. After Herod's death, a fourth dream ordered Joseph to return to Israel, where, he was assured, his family would now be safe. The fifth dream came as a reconsideration. Herod had been succeeded by his son, and under the principle of *like father like son* the danger to Joseph and his family still remained. The fifth dream directed Joseph out of Judaea, the realm of the evil Herod and his son, and northward to Galilee. There Joseph finally stopped dreaming and settled down in the town of Nazareth.[8]

What strikes us about these dreams is how undreamlike they are. In none of the five dreams is there any symbolism or imagery or incoherence or kaleidoscopic visualism, those characteristics of every dream that has ever been dreamt by a human being. On the contrary, the five dreams in Matthew are as plain and simple as a direct order given in daylight and wakefulness; the meaning of each is clear and straightforward. Such dreams have never been, and could never be, dreamed. Five short, very undreamlike, dreams serve to dispense with the preliminaries. After those dreams the real story can begin, like the flash of dawn that startles the sleeper into wakefulness.

The New Testament conception of dreams is that they were not out of one's own individual experience, but rather, a communication from *somewhere else*. The dreamer was not a composer of the dream; he was the recipient. Some external cosmic force was communicating with him for some specific purpose. The dream issued instructions.

Cosmic forces, whatever they may be, are more powerful than

the individual; and so the dreamer was compelled to obey his dreams. Any resistance would foolishly pit his weak will against a superior force of cosmic will. The New Testament dreamers were not puzzled by their dreams or skeptical of them. Doubt or skepticism, even puzzlement, would mean resistance and impiety against a cosmic force. Therefore, the dreamers of the five dreams did what they were told, promptly and unhesitatingly.

In the world view of superstition, any willfulness of a human being is subject to the superior willfulness of the cosmic forces. The consequence of that belief is the passiveness of the actors. The five dreamers did not decide to marry the fiancée anyway, to frustrate Herod's evil designs, to flee to Egypt, to return to Israel, or to relocate to Galilee. It was the cosmic will that made those decisions. The dreamers could only do what they were told by their dreams. They were passive actors, boardpieces shuffled around to set a stage for a cosmic event.

Modern psychologists reject any kind of external agency in the explanation of dreams. From the perspective of scientific psychology, then, the dreams of the New Testament are superstitions superstitiously interpreted.

The New Testament begins in dreams, and a dreamy aura hangs over all the subsequent text. It is a world of dreams. Did Jesus of Nazareth ever dream, we wonder? What did he dream? And how did he interpret his dreams?

The aura of dreams is the aura of night. Under that aura the Magi rode their camels onward in search of the great ruler who was to come out of the land of Judaea.

Now, those Magi were neither wise men nor kings, as they have sometimes been called. They were astrologers. Their so-called wisdom was the mechanical determinism of astrology; whatever noble status they might have attained was derived from their influence over the minds of the susceptible and superstitious. The wisdom of those wise men would find its proper modern outlet in the horoscope columns of today's pulp press.

The Magi fit into the New Testament narrative as well as do the dreams. They create the aura of night to complement the aura of dreams. The Magi had consulted their astrological tables and done their calculations. And, in the dark of night, they had seen a star. The Magi were dreamers, too. They set off, by night, in search of that star, and when they slept—by day, necessarily—they dreamed dreams.

If Mary's pregnancy was uncanny, and if the birth of her child was due to a cosmic force, then there had to be a cosmic witness to that truth. The bright shining Star of Bethlehem was that witness. To the Magi, the astrologers, the meaning of the star was as plain and clear as the meanings of the five dreams, one of which they themselves had dreamed. The Star of Bethlehem, shining over the birthplace of the uncanny child, gave a cosmic significance both to the event of that birth and to the entire life of that child. That child, Jesus, was born under a good star. He was a favored son of the cosmic forces.

Like Vespasian, Jesus worked miracles. Like Vespasian, Jesus could be recognized as the fulfillment of the well-known prophecy. He was born under an auspicious star.

The educated modern mind has little use for the mechanical determinism of astrology. The Star of Bethlehem proves nothing to us. Like our dreams, so, too, our virtues and faults, our characters, are out of ourselves, not in our stars. And it is just because we take responsibility for ourselves that we are able to appreciate Jesus of Nazareth in a way that his propagandistic partisans could not. We can appreciate him for his character.

The problem with the astrological argument of mechanical determinism is that it deprives Jesus of his achievement. What did his character matter, if his *fate* was predetermined by the sign and seal of the Star of Bethlehem? Was he just another of the passive actors, shuffled around on the stage in accordance with the cosmic script? Under the glow of the Star of Bethlehem, Jesus could be and become no more nor less than what he was predestined to be. He was not the willful doer of his own acts.

The Magi, the charlatan-astrologers, lavished gold, frankincense, and myrrh upon the infant, but what they gave in wealth they took away in integrity. As they returned to their haunts and their hocus-pocus, they took with them the vulnerable humanity and the self-developed character of Jesus of Nazareth. The Magi were thieves in the night.[9]

The inclusion in the narrative of the Magi and their star works to undermine any modern belief in the historicity of the entire story told in the gospels. We become suspicious of fraud. To us the propaganda value of the Magi's witness is counterproductive.

Not so to the ancient Jews, who had suffered under the yoke of a succession of foreign powers, among them Persia and Babylonia.

The Magi had originated as a priestly class in Persia and had then spread to Babylonia. To the Jewish mind, then, the Magi were symbols of the religion of Persia and Babylonia, two powers that had oppressed the Jews.

A delegation of Magi came to Judaea in search of the great ruler. Finding a Jewish infant whom they recognized as the fulfillment of their calculations, they fell upon their knees before him and did him homage. That act was a historic turnabout. The oppressor powers, those who had crushed and exploited the Jews, now threw themselves prostrate before a Jewish infant and acknowledged him as a great ruler. The empires of Persia and Babylonia, and their religion with them, groveled, in the persons of the Magi, before the Jewish *Kingdom of Heaven.*

The homage of the Magi and their self-abasement gratified the chronic Jewish craving for retribution against their historic enemies.[10] In touching that sensitive nerve in the unconscious of the ancient Jew, the inclusion of the Magi in the gospel narrative of Matthew was a masterstroke of gratifying propaganda.[11]

Astrology was an Eastern superstition that infiltrated even the Roman mind. The poet Horace countered such superstition with the rational, skeptical voice of the West. In one of his odes, Horace advises his readers to resign themselves to whatever the future holds and to put no trust in the hocus-pocus and charlatanry of astrology.[12] The phrase used by Horace to describe the tables and calculations of the astrologers is *Babylonian numbers.* It was just such a number that the Magi had calculated to determine the appearance of the new Judaean king. Their Babylonian number was a date.[13] Besides the Babylonian numbers of the Magi, we find in the New Testament a homegrown Jewish numerology. Numbers were magical and mystical. The New Testament sometimes reads like a code book of a cult of mystic numbers.

Matthew begins his gospel by tracing the hereditary descent of Jesus from Abraham, the primal patriarch of the Jews. He divides his genealogy, his list of names, into three periods: the first from Abraham to David, the second from David to the deportation to Babylon, and the third from the deportation to Jesus of Nazareth. At the end of the list Matthew provides the key to its interpretation. The sum of generations in each of the three periods is exactly the same, namely, fourteen.[14]

That seeming coincidence, which might have been missed had

Matthew not pointed it out, is not coincidence at all, but calculation. The basic principle underlying the roll of many names is the recurrence of a single number. The number is not a comment upon the genealogy; rather, the genealogy is composed to conform to the number. That number, fourteen, is a recurring one. What determines its recurrence is the appearance of a significant person (Abraham, David) or event (the deportation to Babylon). It is just such a person or event, marking the end of one era and the beginning of the next, that necessitates a stop-counting, start-counting-again.

Abraham was the primal patriarch, the ancestor of all the Jews. He had performed the primal religious act, the covenant with Yahweh. David was the king under whom the Jews attained a briefly held, but long-remembered, political power. The deportation to Babylon was the tribal humiliation that had to be reversed in order to restore Jewish self-esteem. Abraham, David, and the deportation thus represent primacy in religion, greatness in politics, and the worst of religious and political humiliations.

After the fourteenth generation since the deportation, the time was ripe for another significant person and event. Matthew proceeds to name Jesus of Nazareth as that significant person. Jesus was not just a priest or prophet, but the *Messiah*, the *Christ*, the long-awaited superliberator himself. The significant event follows the genealogy straightaway. It is the birth of Jesus, the Messiah, the Christ.[15]

Such imposed order and pattern is characteristic of the Jewish view of history, which was teleological. Within the mind of Yahweh, their tribal god, there had been conceived for the Jews a systematic and orderly divine plan. That mind had determined that from Abraham (the promise) to the Messiah (the fulfillment) the plan of generations was to be in the sequence and recurrence of the number fourteen.

Such an artificial and deterministic view of history is rendered absurd in the continuation of its logic. Who was the significant person, what was the significant event, for example, in the fourteenth generation after Jesus? Well, if we take twenty years as the standard generation and add fourteen of those generations to the year of Jesus' death, we arrive at about the year A.D. 310. And, indeed, we do find at that time both a significant person and a significant event, namely, the emperor Constantine and the conversion of the entire Roman Empire to Christianity. Such is the peculiar logic and, at least in this case, the strange plausibility of the mysticism of numbers and the deterministic view of history.[16]

We may do an accounting (indicative, but by no means exhaustive) of some other mystical numbers in the New Testament; for example, the number three.

The gospels are narratives, and three is a very useful number for the purposes of narrative. Many anecdotes, jokes, or fairy tales contain three principal characters, the last of whom is somehow different from the other two, as in the Three Little Pigs. An application of this literary use of the number three in the New Testament is in Jesus' parable of the talents, in which the third man, the one who hoarded his master's money, is distinguished from, and contrasted with, the first two men, each of whom had invested his master's money.[17]

Three is also the usual number of the episodes in a short story. ("The wolf went to the first pig's house. . . . Then he went to the second pig's house. . . . And finally he went to the third pig's house. . . .") After the third episode the story ends. In Matthew's narrative of the temptation in the desert the devil first took Jesus to the wilderness and tempted him once, then he took Jesus to the parapet of the Temple and tempted him a second time, and finally, he took Jesus to a high mountain and tempted him a third time.[18]

This triad of characters and episodes is a kind of universal literary convention. Moreover, in the New Testament the numbers have a mnemonic, a propagandistic, and an occult significance: they help memory, they induce belief, and they arouse awe at the uncanny.

On the occult level, three is the number of speech as understood in specifically Jewish terms, that is, good-or-evil speech, prophetic speech, and loyal-or-disloyal speech. The devil tempted Jesus three times. Jesus predicted his own death three times. Peter denied Jesus three times. Before his death Jesus prayed three times in the Garden of Gethsemane. Pilate judged Jesus innocent three times. After his death Jesus asked Peter three times if he loved him, and Peter affirmed his love three times. Three is the mystical number of the spoken word—of temptation, prophecy, prayer, judgment, question, answer, affirmation, and denial.[19]

The number five is the bread-and-bodies number. In the First Miracle of the Loaves, Jesus fed five thousand bodies with five loaves of bread. Not coincidentally, the number of baskets of scraps left over was twelve, the number of Jesus' apostles, so that there was one basket for each of them. The basketload of bread could thus stand as a symbol of the nourishment provided to each of the apostles by their Master.[20]

Matthew and Mark report a Second Miracle of the Loaves, a parallel episode in which they jumble the numbers. Unconsciously adding the two fishes of the First Miracle to the five loaves, they write that Jesus began with *seven* loaves and a now unspecified number of fishes. In the Second Miracle the number of loaves is made to correspond to the number of baskets of scraps, also seven.[21]

In the New Testament seven is likewise the devil's number. Devils come in sevens. Seven is the number of devils that Jesus exorcised from Mary Magdalene. Jesus associated the Pharisees, his enemies, with the devil, when he attacked them in a sevenfold indictment. When Peter asked Jesus if a man should forgive his enemies as many as seven times, Jesus affirmed forgiveness but repudiated the devil by telling Peter to forgive seventy-seven times instead.[22]

In the Acts of the Apostles we find a variation on the theme of seven as the diabolical number. Some exorcists tried to appropriate the magical power of the name of Jesus without proper authorization. In that story the devil was only one in number. It was the quack exorcists, the devilish fakers, the human devils, who numbered seven.[23]

Twelve is the number of propagandistic affiliation. There were twelve patriarchs and twelve tribes, so Jesus chose twelve apostles. Each apostle was to be the new patriarch of a new tribe.

The early Christians tried to find in the Old Testament numbers that in some way prefigured what came to pass through Jesus. Any numbers in the Old Testament, just as any heroes or events or concepts, could be extracted and applied in some context in the New Testament. They could be used as *types*. The Christians wanted at the same time to supersede and to incorporate the Old Testament into their own literature. And so they developed the techniques of the propaganda of affiliation.

For example, Moses had spent forty days and forty nights in solitary communion with Yahweh on Mt. Sinai, fasting all the while. Like Moses, his *type*, Jesus endured his own forty days and forty nights of solitude and fasting. Jesus' forty days and forty nights in the desert further recall the forty years of the Israelites' wandering search for their Promised Land. Forty is the number of a suspenseful sojourn.[24]

After Jesus' Resurrection, he lingered among his disciples for yet another period of forty days.[25] Those last forty days provide the mission of Jesus with a chronological symmetry of number—the forty days in the desert before his mission and the forty days among his disciples after his Resurrection—and recall once again the *types* of Moses' forty days and nights on the mountain and the Israelites' forty years of wandering. The number forty rounds off the life of Jesus and associates Jesus, the teacher and lawgiver of the new covenant, with Moses, the teacher and lawgiver of the old (superseded) covenant. Forty, like twelve, is a statistic in the propaganda of affiliation.[26]

In any number in the New Testament we might detect literary convention, propagandistic Old Testament type, or occult symbolism. There might even be some accurately reported statistics. Which numbers are factual and which are occult may be disputed, but that there is a pattern of mystical numerology throughout the New Testament is evident. Like the words, the numbers carry their own special significance.

The early Christians were a secret society. In the New Testament, the lore of a secret society, there are esoteric allusions and codes. We may speculate about the meanings of those secrets, but that there were secrets we need not be cryptographers to discern. A number is a specific datum. Many of the numbers in the New Testament have a specific occult association and significance.

Besides the numbers, there are other *figures* in the New Testament narrative, figures not out of mystical math but out of surrealism. Angels and devils, phantasms flitting on and off stage, mingle with human characters. Many of the dreams of the New Testament are terrifying nightmares, full of surreal specters.

Emerging out of the underworld of the unconscious, the angels and devils haunt the narrative landscape of the New Testament. The angels and devils are personifications of the lesser cosmic forces. Those forces are interpreted dualistically, on the one hand beneficent, on the other maleficent.

The angels, the beneficent spirits, were primarily messengers whose task was to make known the divine will. They did so in dreams or in personal apparitions. In his dreams Joseph saw the figure of an angel, who told him what to do. In the case of Mary, an angel appeared to her directly as a daylight apparition. A single angel was enough to convey that very personal message, the news of pregnancy, to Mary; but for the cosmically significant event of the birth of the Messiah, a full complement, a veritable heavenload, of angels appeared over Bethlehem to announce the news to the world.[27]

The angels were Jewish messenger-spirits. Like all Jews, they practiced social separatism, and therefore did not appear to gentiles or pagans. In Matthew, Joseph's dreams had angels in them; but the Magi, being gentiles, had a dream devoid of any angel.[28]

The angels were not just the page-boys of heaven. They had powers of their own. It was an angel that liberated Peter from prison.[29] The power of angels was sometimes expressed in military terminology. Jesus warned those who had come to arrest him that he could call twelve legions of angels to his defense, not just twelve apostles, if he wanted to put up a resistance.[30] The moral cosmos was a battleground in the legionary warfare of good and evil, of angels and devils.

The devils, the maleficent spirits, were tempters and tormentors. Devils seem to have run rampant throughout Palestine in the first century A.D. One devil was bold enough to tempt Jesus the Messiah himself. In his threefold temptation, that devil tried to lure Jesus into worship of Cosmic Evil. He tempted by pandering to the human physiological weakness of hunger, to the human psychological drive of ambition for power, and to Jesus' own susceptibility to idolatry-of-self. Jesus rejected each temptation in turn. He refused to turn the stones into bread, he declined the rulership of earthly kingdoms, and he abstained from proving his invulnerability by taking up the challenge of the devil's dare. The temptations overcome, Jesus then drove off the devil and summoned the angels to minister to him.[31]

The episode of the temptation in the desert is, by the way, a curious revelation of the thinking of the Jews, who were a very literary people. After Jesus resisted the first temptation[32] and argued his resistance with a quote from the Old Testament, the devil turned the tables by accompanying his second temptation with a pertinent Old Testament quote of his own! Jesus countered with another quote as rebuttal, and, after the third temptation, with still another, that time a decisive one. Both the devil and Jesus adopted the same methodology, namely, searching through scripture for convincing arguments. Of course, as the saying goes, "the devil quotes scripture to his own purpose"; but then doesn't everyone?

The quote and counterquote of the episode of the temptation approaches whimsical philosophical jousting. If the quotes are all accurate, what was there to choose—on an authoritarian basis—between the justification for the resistance to temptation and the justification for succumbing to it? Jesus quoted scripture to the devil, and the devil quoted it back. In the New Testament even the devils are Jewish, that is, they are biblical scholars.

The gospelwriter had no such flippant conception of the episode of the temptation as whimsical literary wit; his intentions were serious and propagandistic. But it strikes the student of culture as an exquisite irony that both Jesus and the devil would appeal to the authority of a common source.

The relationship of Jesus to the angels and the devils is stated in terms of his personal power. On the one hand, he could summon legions of angels to his assistance, as a general would mobilize his forces. On the other hand, Jesus alone could singlehandedly subdue any devil, or devils, or even legions of devils. After overcoming the three temptations, Jesus drove off the devil with a curt word, as if dismissing a menial. ("He gives orders even to unclean spirits and they obey him."[33]) Jesus was the one who had power over the devils, no matter how numerous their forces or how various their guises.

The devils' guises were various indeed. "Devil" is the name given in the New Testament to a variety of human physiological, neurological, neurotic, and psychotic afflictions. The tempter was also a tormentor. Devils infested the bodies and minds of the Jews with scourges of all sorts.

There is pathology and insanity on nearly every page of the gospel narrative. The "possessed, epileptics, the paralyzed"[34] were everywhere. Children fell down foaming at the mouth, throwing themselves into fire and water; women wailed in wild neurotic hysteria; men dwelt among the corpses in the tombs, howling out their madness, flagellating themselves and threatening passersby. The devils swarm over the New Testament narrative landscape and into, through, and out of the bodies and minds of the tortured human beings who are the characters. The devils turn the Good News into a horror story.

The New Testament is the most revealing historical documentation we have of the longing for health in a medically ignorant society and of the variety of superstitious recourses resorted to by the desperate.

There was in Jerusalem a certain pool of magic water. Around the pool were five porticoes, under which huddled the chronically ill and infirm, hopeless cases all, except for the possibilities of the healing waters of the pool. For, at indeterminable times, an angel would descend from heaven and stir up the waters of the pool. The first person who plunged himself into the pool after it had been stirred up would be cured of his affliction. Only one person was cured at a time. The rest would have to await their chance at the next stirring. Crowds loitered in the porticoes on the brink of the pool, in watchful anticipation.

One day Jesus happened to walk past the pool, where he met a man who had been chronically ill for thirty-eight years. When asked by Jesus whether he truly wanted to be healed, the man responded that he did; but, because of his feebleness, there was always someone who plunged into the waters before him. Jesus told him to stand up and walk, and at that moment the man was immediately cured. The mere word of Jesus proved as effective as the healing waters.[35]

The magic waters of the pool were healing, but they could cure only at intervals and then only one person at a time. The ill and infirm had to cling to the edge of the pool and there await the pleasure of the visiting angel and the stirred waters. Like Lourdes, the pool was a place of a now-and-then, just-for-the-few, and only-those-present kind of healing. But Jesus' healing power was a fountain, more generous and free-flowing than the fickle waters of the pool.

Jesus was a healer. He could cure whenever he wanted to and as many as he wanted to. It seems that he wanted to cure all the time, and that he wanted to cure everybody indiscriminately. Jesus did not refuse those who had faith, nor did he insist that the ill come in pilgrimage and do homage to him. Instead, he wandered the towns and roadsides in search of those in physical or spiritual need, upon whom he generously poured out the power of his gift. And there was no affliction in the entire inventory of human suffering that he could not cure. "All kinds of diseases and sickness"[36] were dispelled by his will, his word, his touch.

Jesus cooled the bodily fire of fevers. He infused or restored the sensitivity of sense, in the blind or the deaf. He stopped the flow of gynecological hemorrhage. He cured dropsy and limbered the limbs of the crippled and the paralytic. Whether the infirmity was congenital or whether caused by disease or accident didn't matter. The health that had never been he infused, the health that was lost he restored. Jesus could restore the health and limbs of even those who suffered from that most dreaded of afflictions, leprosy, the necrosis of horrid disfigurement and living death.[37]

In the ancient mind leprosy was the most revolting of diseases. It offended the aesthetic sense. Epilepsy, that strange neurological disorder, was the most uncanny of diseases. It baffled analytical reason.

The victim of leprosy got horribly worse and worse, but the one who suffered from epilepsy was now inexplicably ill and in a few minutes inexplicably well again. The Jews attributed epileptic seizures to the *possession* of the body by devils. Jesus' healing mastery overcame both the symptoms of epilepsy and the forces of the indwelling devils. He was able to cure the *epileptic demoniacs.*[38]

Finally, in the most stunning of his healing miracles, Jesus could raise the dead,[39] and, in the ultimate of self-healing, he could raise himself (or be raised up) after his own death. Jesus was the Master Healer with power over diseases, devils, and even over death itself.

How was Jesus able to perform his healing miracles? According to Luke, "power came out of him that cured them all." "The Power of the Lord was behind his works of healing."[40] It was not Jesus himself who cured, so much as the Power that resided in him.

From anthropological terminology we may borrow the term *mana* to describe Jesus' healing power. Mana is a mysterious supernatural power in certain people or things. Supernatural in origin, it is also supernatural in its operation. Mana is the uncanny power that produces paranormal phenomena. There was mana in the pool of healing waters in Jerusalem; it was a weak mana that acted briefly and occasionally. And there was mana in Jesus. It was a powerful mana, so potent that it flowed almost continuously, so multidimensional that it produced a rich kaleidoscope of paranormal effects. Jesus was so suffused with mana that at times his body glowed with it. That is how we might interpret the episode of the so-called Transfiguration of his body.[41]

The level of mana in Jesus was not constant. At times it ebbed, and Jesus found himself unable to perform a healing miracle.[42] At other times it flowed out weakly, in which case Jesus had to repeat his attempt at a cure in order to achieve it.[43] Being charged with mana, Jesus could be inadvertently discharged of it by mere physical contact with another body. Once, while pressing his way through a crowd, Jesus felt that discharge. "Somebody touched me," he said, "I felt that power had gone out from me."[44] It was as if an electrical charge were grounded, and so, discharged. At such times when the mana ebbed in him, Jesus must have had to guard himself against indiscriminate contact with other bodies. Generally, however, his mana was so potent and brimming that he was even able to parcel some of it out to others. Jesus could lay his hands on his disciples, and infused with mana, they, too, could go forth to heal, drive out devils, and raise the dead, in short, perform the very same healing miracles as their Master.[45]

Each miracle of Jesus was an act of individual kindness. But Jesus had more of a mission than the haphazard healing of every sick and ailing individual that he happened to come across. Jesus' miracles were signs, or proof, that he represented a beneficent power and authority come to mankind. They were proof of Jesus' goodness and truthfulness, as well as of his legitimacy as the Messiah, the Christ.

No matter how many individuals he might cure, Jesus could not banish human sickness and infirmity forever. He cured some individuals in order to draw the attention of all the people to him and to what he had to say. There was a more pervasive, a more intractable, kind of pathology that Jesus wanted to heal. It was the religious pathology of the Jews. The mana of Jesus would effect the cure for that religious pathology, just as it had effected the cures for the physiological pathology of disease and death.

The Jews interpreted illness and disease in moral terms as divine punishment for sin. The sin might have been committed by the afflicted individual, by his father, or by an ancestor. For the Jews, the afflicted were the guilty ones, cursed by some sin. They harbored devils. Sin itself was "in the seed," that is, it was hereditary, in the family, or even more broadly, in the human race as a taint passed down the generations through the seed of Adam, the primal sinner.

The Jews thought that physical affliction was a symptom of some kind of inherent moral evil. Every ill person had a devil within. On one occasion when Jesus stopped to help a poor unfortunate, someone asked him whether it was the man himself who had sinned or whether it had been his father, that is, whether the guilt was personal or hereditary. Jesus answered that the man was afflicted only so that the power of God could be shown to men. Physical ailments bore no moral stigma.[46]

Jesus contradicted the traditional Jewish association of physical affliction with guiltiness. The afflicted were not guilty; they were just unfortunate. Jesus proceeded to deal with their misfortune therapeutically, not moralistically. However, there were certain other sick ones, who, even if outwardly well and well-to-do, were quite guilty in Jesus' eyes. It was not the symptom, the outward sign, that had any moral significance. It was the inner heart.

Jesus did cure the symptoms, the outward signs, of physical illness, but that was only to draw attention to his true healing ministry, which was to the inner heart, or soul. The pathology of the body was secondary and incidental. It was the pathology of the soul, of the collective tribal soul, of the Jews that most concerned Jesus the Master Healer. He was not a mere magician; he was the Messiah. As such, he wanted to exorcise the values of the devils and to restore the values of Yahweh, the tribal god.

The values of Yahweh had once been bestowed upon the Jews as a special gift, but now those values were corrupted. Jesus' mission was to restore the tribal values to pristine purity and the tribal soul to health.

Symptoms are signs of pathology in the human body. It was values, the now-corrupted values, of the Jewish people that were the symptoms and signs of the pathology in the Jewish soul. Jesus was a healer of values. That was his mission as he himself saw it. But values are not so amenable to cure as are symptoms. The Pharisees did not want to be cured of their values.

Jesus directed the full force of his mana upon the sickness in the collective tribal soul of the Jews. He concentrated his verbal mana, his healing words, in an attempt to restore values and heal the sick soul. The failure of his life was that his healings of the body so impressed the people that they distracted from, instead of attracted to, the more urgent task of the spiritual healing of the collective soul. Jesus cured many individual Jews of their bodily maladies; but his mana proved inadequate to heal the deep and chronic spiritual pathology of the Jewish people.

The feverish, blind, deaf, hemorrhagic, dropsical, paralytic, leprous, epileptic, insane, even the dead, eagerly responded to Jesus' offer to bestow his healing mana upon them. But the Pharisees, the Values Establishment, resisted their necessary cure. They even plotted murder against the healer. It was only after his own death that Jesus was to succeed in fully overcoming the Establishment, in a triumph that may have been, in the last analysis, more political than spiritual.

Jesus became a healer, so that he would be listened to as a teacher. The many acts of individual kindness were as nothing compared to the supreme act of kindness that Jesus wanted to bestow upon the Jewish people. "Salvation" or "redemption" are the terms used to describe that act of supreme kindness.

Jesus' contemporaries proved incapable of reacting to him on a spiritual level. Instead, they reacted in a superstitious manner. The people were thrown into consternation by the healing miracles. They never regained their composure enough to see beyond the magic to the meaning, beyond the gift of physical health to the greater gift of spiritual wholesomeness.

In the usual interpretation of the response to Jesus' miracles, both the blessed recipients and the bystanders reacted with joy and gratitude in an aura of happy exultation that such good could be worked among men. The actual psychological atmosphere was quite different. The people were frightened out of their wits by what Jesus could do. After Jesus exorcised some devils, the people "were afraid,"[47] so much so that "the whole town . . . implored him to leave the neighborhood."[48] When he cured a paralytic, "a feeling of awe came over the crowd."[49] That was not joy, gratitude, and happy exultation. It was fear, terror, awe. It was superstition.

The people reacted to the phenomena of the miracles and to the person of Jesus with a frantic ambivalence of attraction and repulsion. Ignorance and fear, the twin wellsprings of superstition, overcame them. Jesus inadvertently whipped up a mass hysteria. Frenzy and enthusiasm, superstitious dread, distracted from, rather than drew attention to, Jesus' higher mission.

When Jesus healed, the bystanders shrank back in fear, terror, and awe. The desperately ill had to embolden themselves to advance close to Jesus to seek a cure. One woman hoped to gain a cure but escape a direct confrontation with the terrible sorcerer by merely touching the fringe of his cloak. She would try to draw off his mana undetected.[50] Such superstition, which we recognize as idolatrous fetishism,[51] debased, rather than raised, the spiritual level on which Jesus conducted his mission.

Jesus cured by the outflow of mana, whether through a touch or even through a mere word. And so, his words, like his body, had magic power. That is why we find in the Greek texts of the gospels a few words in Aramaic, the language Jesus spoke. Those words are the very words of his magic curative power, as he actually spoke them: "Ephphatha," the magic word that healed deafness, and "Talitha, kum!," the magic words that raised the dead. Those Aramaic words were incantations, verbal mana, the magic words, abracadabra.[52]

Jesus poured forth his mana in ways other than medical miracles. In the two Miracles of the Loaves he distributed bread, and so life, to the multitude. There is no pathology in those miracles. Jesus satisfied healthy bodily hunger as a metaphor for the satisfaction of spiritual

hunger, which was his primary mission. He would nurture and nourish and satisfy all those, no matter how many, who came to him
with their human needs. The Miracles of the Loaves are the most
attractive of Jesus' many miracles. In them he gave bread, food, life
to the healthy, just as on other occasions he gave cure and restoration to the unhealthy. The Miracles of the Loaves were a wholesome
outpouring of mana.[53]

Less edifying are the miracles in which Jesus made a raw show
of his mystical powers, as in his calming of the storm and in his
walking on water. Those miracles, so suspect of coincidence and the
optical illusions that come in times of weariness and overexcitement,
seem like mere magician's stunts, devoid of any moral content and,
therefore, of any significance for values. There was no benevolence
or benefit. They were just intimidating exercises in power and an
attempt at a proof that Tacitus would have regarded as superstitious.
Jesus calmed the storm and walked on the water to demonstrate
that Nature was as subservient to his mana as were the devils and
death. But Nature cannot be taught morals or values. Those miracles
were mana dissipated.[54]

There was another miracle, a very minor one, of a seeming
innocence that is almost whimsical. One day the collector came
around for the Temple tax, a small levy, a mere half-shekel per
person, for the upkeep and embellishment of the Temple in Jerusalem. Jesus told Peter to go fishing for the tax. He said that if
Peter opened the mouth of the first fish he caught, he would find
inside a nice shiny shekel, which would pay the tax for both Peter
and himself![55]

That anecdote seems like a tall tale, an entertaining fish story.
The story of the money in the fish's belly is an old one. It is based
on the real tendency of fish to strike at, and sometimes to swallow,
any shiny objects they come across. But the stories in the New
Testament are not meant to be amusing, whimsical, or entertaining.
Each one has a specific propaganda intent.

In Jesus' opinion, the Temple tax should have been collected
from the dispersed Jews, the *foreigners,* not from Galileans, natives
like Peter and himself, who, presumably, supported the Temple enough
by their frequent presence there. However, since it was a penny-minor
issue, Jesus decided to deal with it in an evasive manner. Neither
he nor Peter should pay; that was the principle involved. But the
tax would be paid, so as not to offend the collectors, who, after

all, were discharging a charitable function. So, let the fish cough up the shekel.

Jesus was thus able to observe propriety without violating his convictions or sacrificing his principles. He confronted an ethical prob lem and resorted to an expedient solution. As we shall discover in our discussion of his values, Jesus was generally an uncompromising character to whom expedience was repugnant. The episode of the Temple tax is unique in portraying Jesus as a sensible moderate who could be expedient without scruple.[56]

Jesus performed a variety of miracles that asserted his power over pathology, the devils, death, and Nature. In addition to his personal miracles there are other portents and prodigies throughout the New Testament. Jesus was not personally responsible for their occurrence, but they happened only because of him. Matthew, particularly, felt the necessity of giving his narrative cosmic significance by introducing into it some cosmic upheavals.

In Matthew, it was the appearance of the new star in heaven that portended the birth of the Messiah. At the death of the Messiah on the cross, Matthew reports that there was an earthquake, one of such devastation and terror that it split the rocks of tombs and roused the dead to come forth and walk the earth as zombies.[57]

The Gospel of Mark recounts how the three women on their way to the tomb of Jesus on Sunday morning wondered how they would be able to roll back the stone door. When they arrived, they found that it had already been rolled back, presumably by someone else. According to Matthew, however, it was a *violent earthquake* that had rolled it back.[58] That second earthquake in three days must have been an aftershock of the one that occurred at the crucifixion. In any case, like the thunder in *Hamlet,* the two earthquakes give a cosmic significance to the action. The Gospel of Matthew begins with the cosmic witness of the new star above and ends with the terrestrial witness of a double earthquake below. Matthew makes a heavy clatter of the stage machinery.

Cosmic events occur throughout the gospels. And looming over the narrative is the Cosmic Presence, that of Yahweh, the tribal god of the Jews. Yahweh Himself intrudes into the story at certain significant moments. He is the Thunder-Voice that descends to announce and affirm what is too momentous to be entrusted to his menials, the messenger-angels. Yahweh watches, Yahweh speaks. And, in accordance with the Jewish teleological view of history, it is Yahweh who directs and determines the entire course of events.

Another cosmic presence haunting the gospels is Satan, creature of Yahweh, now become Yahweh's implacable adversary. As Yahweh is the patron of the Jews, and so Supreme Beneficence, Satan is their adversary, supreme malevolence. He commands legions of devils, whom he sends into the world against the Jews, trying to subvert the advocacy and the divine plan of Yahweh. Over the earthly scenes in the gospels we can hear the clash of warfare in the cosmic battleground. On the one side, Yahweh and his legions of angels; on the other side, Satan and his legions of devils. Satan, unlike Yahweh, makes no personal appearance in the gospels; but his presence is felt nonetheless. He is thought about, he is talked about, he is feared.

Jesus is the hero of the gospels because he stood in a unique relationship to both Yahweh and Satan. Jesus was the Messiah, or Christ, that is, the one anointed by Yahweh for a special mission of universal and eternal significance to the human race. That mission was salvific and redemptive in nature. Jesus, as the one who would effect the salvation and redemption was, therefore, the superior of all the angels ever sent on emissary missions.[59] Furthermore, Jesus was a man-in-the-flesh, not a phantasm of dreams and apparitions. In him there was what would later be interpreted as a twofold incarnation of both God and man. Jesus was a paradoxical composite of *Son of God* and *Son of Man.* Jesus was the person in whom some Jews were to assimilate themselves to their god.

Jesus was the most potent force that Yahweh ever sent against Satan and his minion devils. It was Jesus who tipped the balance in the cosmic moral war. His mana was superpotent, and it was adversarial to evil. Jesus was the Master Adversary against evil. Although Jesus grapples with many lesser devils, the one dramatic lack in the gospels is a direct confrontation between Jesus and Satan himself. Nonetheless, the impression made by the operation of Jesus' mana is clear: Jesus was a match for Satan.

The god Yahweh appears in much of the Old Testament as a tribal tyrant, cruel, jealous, and vindictive. The religious mind of Jesus was one of exquisite spiritual sensitivity. That mind transformed Yahweh from a patriarchal tyrant into a *heavenly Father* who wanted and deserved not fear, but love.

As Jesus *revalued* the Jewish association of disease with sin and guilt, so did he revalue the image of their tribal deity. He went on to revalue most of the values of the tribal religion of the Jews, although he himself claimed that he did not revalue, but merely wanted to restore the values as they had been in their pristine purity.

If Yahweh became a Father most fully through Jesus, then Jesus himself stood in a filial relationship to that Father. That would be the justification that Jesus would offer for his right to revalue the old Jewish tribal values.

For those who read the New Testament, there is a double problem. The first is the value of Jesus' revaluation of Judaic religious values; the second is the legitimacy of Jesus himself, his *right* to that revaluation. The New Testament preaches values. It also promotes a person.

Before trying to make an evaluation of the values in the New Testament, we must first recognize the psychological context in which those values are set forth. An accurate description for that context would be *superstition,* as Tacitus understood the word. The values in the New Testament are proclaimed, and, in a major part, *proved,* by dreams, astrology, mystical numbers, prefiguring *types,* phantasmal angels and devils, miracles and magic, portents and prodigies, predestination, and the dualistic cosmic personages Yahweh and Satan.

If that context, *superstition,* no longer stands for us as proof, then we will have to evaluate the values-in-themselves. We will have to try to do a *modern* revaluation of Jesus' values and interpret the religious in philosophical and psychological terms.

There are political considerations, too. The Jews of the ancient world had suffered a long series of subjugations and repressions by the great foreign powers of Egypt, Assyria, Babylonia, Persia, Greece, and, just a half-century before the gospel narratives open, Rome. Centuries of oppression had smothered the tribal aspirations of the Jews. They were suffocating as a people. They craved deliverance. They gasped for liberation.

A belief had arisen among the Jewish prophets that a liberator-revolutionary would come to effect a deliverance. In a people whose religion was political and whose politics were religious, the character of that liberator, called the *Messiah,* was variously interpreted. Some saw him as the Master Prophet, others as a generalissimo. Whether he would come as a religious or as a military-political leader, or both, the Messiah would be the one to end the chronic subjugation of the Jews and to exalt the tribe over all the other peoples of the earth. He would effect a great historic turnabout.

By the time of Jesus, the anticipation of the arrival of the Messiah had become both a religious and political time bomb. The Romans, conquerers of the entire civilized world of the Mediterranean, must have seemed to the Jews their most imposing and powerful subjugators. So apparently invincible, the Romans aroused the most intense frustration and the keenest craving for the deliverance and liberation that would come in the person of the Messiah. It was the Roman Caesar who was to call forth the Jewish Messiah, at last.

When the Magi told Herod that they thought that a new king of the Jews had been born, Herod was understandably apprehensive. After all, he felt a personal threat to his own power and to his own dynasty. The gospel affirms that it was not only Herod who was anxious and apprehensive. "So was the whole of Jerusalem."[60] Messianic expectancy had reached a fever pitch. Any portent or prodigy, such as the Star of Bethlehem, could signify the arrival of the longed-for Messiah. At any moment there could be a boilover of mass hysteria.

There was frustration and longing in the collective tribal soul of the Jews. Politics and religion were both about to go into convulsions. "A feeling of expectancy had grown among the people."[61] Something momentous was about to happen. The arrival of the Messiah, the liberator-revolutionary, was imminent. And that Messiah would come. He had to come, because Yahweh, through the voices of his prophets, had promised him and because the collective tribal soul needed him. The Jews were not sure what the Messiah would do when he came. Nor were they sure, despite certain specific prophecies, exactly from where, when, or how he would arrive. Who would be the Messiah? How could he be recognized? How could he prove that he, and only he, was the awaited one, the true Messiah, come at last?

Legitimacy

When there suddenly appears a genius and leader who takes hold of the mass psychology of a society, it seems to the masses that he must have somehow come from somewhere else. As deterministic as our attitudes may be about the common man, we are not so convinced that the uncommon man is in any way explained by his society. The uncommon man should have uncommon origins. Only an uncanny, even an otherworldly, origin could account for his sudden apparition, his potency, and his dominance. The ego of the common man cannot accept the idea that genius, like character, develops itself, out of its own discipline. And so the common man has attributed to the uncommon one some strange, uncanny, or even divine origin.

In the ancient world strange, uncanny, and divine origins were commonly attributed to great men. As a typical example we may take the myth of origin for Romulus, the founder of Rome. We recount a late version of that myth, as written by the historian Livy just a few decades before the birth of Jesus.

The Romans considered Romulus a historical person, but they traced his origins in a mythological manner. The god Mars raped a virgin named Rhea Silvia. Because of the scandal of illegitimacy, Rhea was punished. Her infant son Romulus, along with his twin Remus, was put in a basket, exposed, and set adrift in the Tiber, from where they were rescued by a she-wolf. That, then, was the origin of Romulus—as monster, bastard, and foundling.[1]

The Jews were monotheists. Their one and only god was an Ever-Other-Essence. Yahweh, their god, had created the man Adam, it is true; but He created him out of inanimate earth, rather than out of the seed of His own body. All that ever passed between the world of men and the realm of Yahweh were words—prayers from one side, orders and directives from the other. The Jew could only regard as disgusting and repellent the pagan myths about sexual promiscuity between gods or goddesses and mortals in the generation of such demigod bastard heroes as Romulus.

The ancient Jews had no taste for divine-human monsters or demigod bastards, but they did resort to the foundling myth to explain genius, as, for example, in the story of the infant Moses cast adrift in a basket and floating down the Nile to his destiny.[2] However, they interpreted the story in teleological terms. They posited a plan and a purpose. All history was a salvation-history, a playing out of a purposeful plan. The myth of the foundling sounded too much like chance to be fully congenial to the Jewish mind. Moses needed more than his uncanny origin as a foundling to be legitimized; he needed a divine commission.

Because the Jews proved chronically wayward, Yahweh found it necessary to send them not only Moses but a steady stream of prophets to exhort them to follow his instructions and return to the predetermined path he had laid out for them. Yahweh did not generate those prophets *ex nihilo* for their missions. Instead, he surveyed the population and picked out someone suitable for his purposes, appointed him, and set him to work. In the Jewish explanation for the origins of genius, Yahweh was a Great Contractor with an eye for talent; he recruited Moses and all the prophets to his service. Prophets, therefore, were made, not born.

To the question, "Where does the genius (prophet) come from?" the Jew would have answered, "He is chosen and appointed by God." Correspondingly, to those who asked of Jesus, "Where did the man get this wisdom and these miraculous powers?"[3] the traditional Jewish answer would have been, "He must have been chosen and appointed." The Jewish genius, or prophet, should be neither monster, nor bastard, nor foundling, but a human being specially chosen by Yahweh.

To the followers of Jesus he was not *a* prophet, but *the* prophet, the Master Prophet. In common with the earlier prophets, Jesus was, in some way, a chosen-appointed; above and beyond the earlier prophets, Jesus was unique in being the Anointed One, the Messiah, the Christ. How could that uniqueness be demonstrated? How was the Master Prophet different from all those who had come before, and all (if any) who would come after?

According to the New Testament, Jesus was not one of the chosen many, but the One to whom the chosen many led. All the other prophets were precursors of this Master Prophet, in whom, as the Messiah, the task of prophet was fully accomplished at last. After the Messiah, there would be no more prophets.

How could the legitimacy and preeminence of Jesus be proven? "This is the carpenter's son, surely?"[4] the people wondered. The most obvious objection to the legitimacy of Jesus was his lowly, or at least undistinguished, parentage. Could an uncommon man have a common father?

In the Jewish mind, which was thoroughly patriarchal, it was the concept of *father* that confers legitimacy. A common craftsman like Joseph seemed an unsatisfactory figure for the father of Jesus, the Master Prophet, the Messiah. Someone more imposing was needed. In the New Testament we find several different, and quite contradictory, answers given to the question of the origin and legitimacy of Jesus.

The Gospel of Matthew begins, "Abraham was the father of Isaac, Isaac the father of Jacob, Jacob the father of Judah . . . ,"[5] and on and on in the three fourteen-generation periods from Abraham to Jesus. The refrain of "father . . . father . . . father . . ." is the flowing sentence of the patriarchal mind. From the very first words of the first gospel we discover that the Jews were a patriarchal people.

In his genealogy Matthew lists forty male legitimizers of Jesus. (He includes four females, three named and one unnamed, but that inclusion is incidental and parenthetical.) According to Matthew, then, the legitimacy of Jesus was not to be found in one father alone, named Joseph, but in the flowing unbroken hereditary line of patriarchal descent from Abraham, the primal patriarch, who himself had been chosen and appointed by Yahweh. Jesus was the son, not of one common father, but of a long series of uncommon, illustrious fathers.

It is as if there were a cumulative effect to all that heredity: the patriarchal principle is repeated and reaffirmed until all legitimacy culminates and reaches its climax in the last name on the list, which is Jesus. Jesus himself had no sons; therefore, legitimacy climaxed and ended in him.

That the genealogy of Matthew is mainly an occult exercise in mystical numerology is evident from the fact that his male names fall so neatly into the three equal periods of fourteen names each. Matthew even double-counts one name, Jechoniah, in order to achieve his numerological scheme.[6]

Besides the genealogy in Matthew, there is another one in the
New Testament, that in Luke. Luke is not so patriarchal in perspective
as Matthew. He waits until his narrative is well underway before
he inserts his genealogy of Jesus. *Insert* is an accurate verb, because
the list in Luke interrupts the narrative awkwardly, instead of, as
in Matthew, preceding the narrative and entirely establishing its significance.

Matthew traces Jesus' patriarchal descent from Abraham to
Joseph. Luke goes about it the other way: he traces the line up,
from Joseph back to Abraham, and then beyond Abraham and the
origin of the Jews to Adam and the origin of the human race itself.
Luke describes Adam, in an unorthodox and inappropriate manner,
as the *son of God,* thereby drawing God directly into the role of
legitimizer.

That Luke had little real interest, or confidence, in his genealogy
is indicated by his retrograde direction as well as by the qualifier,
"Jesus . . . the son, as it was thought. . . ." "Son of . . . son of . . .
son of . . ." leads back to Adam and, ultimately, to God. And then
what? Luke resumes his interrupted narrative. In Luke the genealogy
only leads out of the narrative, unlike in Matthew, where it leads
into it.[7]

To determine the worth of the argument of legitimacy by patriarchal descent, we can compare the genealogies in Matthew and Luke.
For the generations between Abraham and David there is a fair correspondence of names, except that Luke lists one generation more
than Matthew. From David to the Babylonian Captivity the names
in the two genealogies do not match up at all. And from the Captivity
to Joseph and Jesus, only a few names correspond. Strangely, the
two genealogies do not agree on the name of Joseph's father, the
most recent and seemingly most easily identifiable ancestor.

Matthew lists forty-two names in three neat groups, from Abra-
ham to Jesus. Luke lists fifty-six for the same time span, excluding
Jesus. Did he add another neat fourteen-name section of his own?[8]
To pack his list Luke seems to have repeated names or like forms
of the same names, for example, Mattathias twice, Matthat twice,
Mattatha, and Maath.

The two genealogies are a veritable hocus-pocus of names and
numbers. In that context it is unlikely that they accurately document
family history.

In a patriarchal culture, a genealogy is a stereotypical formula for legitimacy. According to the prophecy, the expected Messiah was to be a *son of David*. If Jesus was to be that Messiah, then his lineage would have to be traced to David the king, and, by logical extension, to Abraham, the primal patriarch.[9] The genealogies serve that purpose. They are the stereotypical formulas so congenial to the patriarchal, retrospective Jewish mind. The genealogies are arguments; but they are not facts.

Biblical literalists since the famous Bishop Ussher have come to grief in their attempts to correlate the biblical genealogies to the billion-year spans posited by the fossil record and the theory of evolution. Further, unless we assume that dotards commonly generated first-born sons, Matthew's fourteen mystical generations for the known historical period of five hundred years from the Babylonian Captivity to Jesus are far too few. Worse, the genealogies in Matthew and Luke cannot stand against each other, much less against external scientific or historical referents. In the two New Testament genealogies of Jesus we have a stereotypical patriarchal formula; in short, a literary device, but no real family history at all. The proof of the legitimacy of Jesus as the Messiah remains to be demonstrated in a manner that would stand up to modern criticism.[10]

Matthew, the most thoroughly Jewish of the four gospels and therefore the most patriarchal and retrospective, sought the legitimacy of Jesus, first and foremost, in the flowing seed of patriarchal descent. Luke's inclusion of the genealogy of Jesus only as an insertion that interrupts and leads out of the narrative indicates a much different perspective at work in the Gospel of Luke. Such a perspective might find a different solution to the problem of legitimacy. That is, indeed, the case.

Luke begins his gospel with a charming folktale about a pious old couple named Zechariah and Elizabeth. They had just about given up hope of having children when an angel named Gabriel appeared to Zechariah and announced that Elizabeth was shortly to conceive. The doubtful Zechariah was stricken mute by the news; but in due time his wife conceived, just as the angel had promised.

The angel then proceeded on another fecundating mission, this time to a virgin named Mary. He predicted a pregnancy for her, too. "The Holy Spirit will come upon you . . . and the power of the Most High will cover you with its shadow,"[11] is the imagery that the angel used to describe the manner of Mary's impregnation. Although, like Zechariah, Mary had her doubts, she was compliant.[12]

There were two prodigies now: an old woman conceived and a virgin conceived. The personal link between the two prodigies was the messenger-angel Gabriel. A further link, an episodic one, is provided by Mary's visit to Elizabeth, in which the two women paid each other homage for their uncanny fertility.[13]

The child of Zechariah and Elizabeth was John, later to be called the Baptist. John was conceived in uncanny circumstances, to an unlikely mother and a problematical father, and named by an angel. John retreated into the desert, and then emerged to baptize, urge repentance, and preach in parables and metaphors. Because of his baiting of the Establishment, John ran afoul of the ruling powers, and was martyred at last. In these respects, the biography and career of John the Baptist, we notice, parallel the biography and career of Jesus.

The people's question about John the Baptist, namely, "What will this child turn out to be?"[14] sets up a dramatic suspense. That same question and that same suspense apply to Jesus. The basic message of John's preaching, "Repent, for the kingdom of heaven is close at hand,"[15] is also attributed to Jesus, and in identical words.

The uncanny conception of John the Baptist is a dramatic preparation for the uncanny conception of Jesus. Both are explained by the axiom that "nothing is impossible to God."[16] The biography and career of John the Baptist are a preview of, prelude to, and immediate *type* for, the biography and career of Jesus.

What we may have here is not biographical coincidence but dramatic invention. Prefiguring parallelism was a popular Christian literary device. In John the Baptist the early Christians found a close, even a contemporary, *type* for Jesus.

Besides serving as *type,* John the Baptist had an important dramatic role to play. A prophet gave testimony, or witness. A prophet himself, John would give testimony to the legitimacy of Jesus as the Master Prophet, the Messiah. A prophet is made so in the recognition by another prophet. Prophets, like royalty, legitimize one another.

Before we go on to consider the testimony of John the Baptist to Jesus, and some other peculiar testimonies as well, we pause to puzzle over the reconciliation of the two quite irreconcilable "proofs" of legitimacy, namely, the argument of the genealogy and the tale of the virginal conception. Matthew and Luke both contain both proofs. Matthew begins with the genealogy, then follows it, most paradoxically, with the tale of the virginal conception (but without

the parallel between Elizabeth and Mary and the mutual homage
in the incident of the Visitation). Luke begins with the two uncanny
conceptions and then inserts a genealogy, which, as we have seen,
does not match the one in Matthew. Two different, two incompatible
traditions, must have been at work. We need to make some sense
of, if not to harmonize, them.

Matthew lays down the genealogy of Jesus, an argument that
he renders irrelevant by the virginal conception. For if Joseph was
not the father of Jesus, then the entire patriarchal descent ends with
Joseph; it establishes Joseph's legitimacy, but not that of Jesus. Because
of the virginal conception, Abraham, Isaac, Jacob, Judah, and all
the others have no biological relation to Jesus. Use of the genealogy
for purposes of patriarchal legitimacy becomes absurd.

Commentators explain away the problem by forcing the distinction that Joseph, although not the biological father of Jesus, was
the *legal* father. Even so, a genealogy shows blood relatedness. Legal
relatedness is an implication from blood relatedness. A genealogy
is the flow of patriarchal seed; it is not a record of a series of adoptions,
although there may have been some adoptions along the line. *Father*
means father, not foster father. The argument of genealogy is one
of blood relatedness, of heredity, not just of inheritance rights, of
adoption. The virginal conception stops the continuous flow of patriarchal seed, the flow through the mystical numbers of generations,
just before the name and person of Jesus. By the genealogy Joseph
is legitimized.[17] By the virginal conception Jesus is rendered illegitimate, by blood, if not by law.

According to the tale of the virginal conception of Jesus, a mortal
woman was inseminated by a god. Although married later, she gave
birth to a son who was illegitimate, in the sense that the legal father
was not the biological father. In the discovery of that baby, by the
Magi in Matthew or by the shepherds in Luke, we find the symbolism,
as in the phrase, "wrapped in swaddling clothes and lying in a
manger,"[18] of the myth of the foundling. (Isn't the baby in the manger
the same symbol as the baby in the basket in the stories of Romulus
and Moses?) What, then, was the origin of Jesus, as set forth in
the tale of the virginal conception? Why, he was a monster, a bastard,
and a foundling. A very uncanny, a very pagan explanation!

What seems to have happened is that two different legitimacy
formulas, the Jewish one of patriarchal descent and the pagan one
of uncanny prodigy, both found acceptance and were combined into

a forced assimilation. Matthew begins with the Jewish formula, then adds the pagan one. Luke begins from the pagan perspective, then inserts the Jewish genealogy to conform to the other tradition. The myth of the origin of Jesus becomes at once Jewish and pagan. An awkward accommodation! In fact, Christianity was to become just such an awkward accommodation of the Jewish to the pagan.

The Jewish patriarchal question of legitimacy is, "Could the uncommon man have a common father?" The Jewish answer is the genealogy, a list of uncommon fathers. The pagan matriarchal question of legitimacy is, "Could the uncommon man have a common mother?" The pagan answer is the virgin mother, the most uncommon mother possible.

Myth is more beautiful all the more imaginative that it is. We do not put myth to the test of truth. But when myth is put into a dogmatic context and passed off as fact, as *proof,* rather than as poetry, then the test of truth must be applied. By that test, the genealogical lists of dead patriarchs float in an upper aether of irrelevance. The virginal conception merges into the muddle of cosmopolitan paganism. Alexander the Great, too, was the son of a divine father. Neither law nor biology nor critical common sense would recognize any legitimacy based upon those two defective and contradictory proofs.

Following up on his mythological tale of uncanny conception and birth, Luke presents Jesus as a child prodigy. When Jesus was only twelve years old, he awed the Temple savants with his knowledge of scripture.[19] However, in that some geniuses mature late, while some child prodigies come to nothing, Luke's tale of Jesus' youthful brilliance, the argument of precocity, proves nothing and is actually quite superfluous.

Now, what about the testimonies?

As precursor, John the Baptist had as his basic life's task the testimony and witness to Jesus. It would seem that he could have fulfilled his role quite easily by simply pointing to Jesus and saying, "He is the One we are all waiting for. He is the Messiah."

Because the gospels are compilations of variant, and sometimes contradictory, oral traditions, the witness of John to Jesus is presented in three incompatible versions. By one account John recognized Jesus even before either was born. By another account John gave confident witness upon meeting Jesus as an adult. By a third account John had his doubts about Jesus.

In accordance with his taste for pagan prodigies, Luke reports that the fetal Baptist leapt in Elizabeth's womb when Mary, newly pregnant, came on her Visitation. A premature, and most uncanny, witness, to be sure![20]

The Gospel of John, the latest, the most artistic, and the most explicit of the gospels, presents the Baptist as an adult giving plain overt testimony to Jesus: "This is the one I spoke of when I said: A man is coming after me who ranks before me. . . . Yes, I have seen and I am the witness that he is the Chosen One of God."[21]

According to Matthew and Luke, the Baptist sent some of his disciples to ask Jesus, "Are you the one who is to come, or have we got to wait for someone else?"[22] Not only was John unsure about Jesus, but he asked Jesus to bear witness to himself!

So, there were three traditions about the testimony of John the Baptist to Jesus: the premature witness, the confident adult witness, and the questioning doubt.

All four gospels do agree that John considered himself a precursor: "Someone is coming, someone who is more powerful than I am, and I am not fit to undo the strap of his sandals."[23] Did John recognize Jesus as that someone? The gospelwriters want to claim that he did. But the variations and inconsistencies of their accounts raise a tantalizing question: Might the early Christians have appropriated (kidnapped) the figure of John the Baptist for their own propagandistic purposes? Did they take the most prominent prophet contemporary to Jesus and put into his mouth the Christian message that no more prophets need be expected, because the Master Prophet and Messiah had come at last? By recounting John's testimony in such contradictory ways, the gospelwriters have made us wonder exactly what, if anything, John the Baptist thought about Jesus, anyway.

Jesus, on the other hand, had John the Baptist very much on his own mind. When he heard that John had been arrested, Jesus retreated in empathetic apprehension. Jesus identified the opposition to John with the opposition to himself. He praised John as the greatest man ever born, but then paradoxically put John in his place, declaring that he was inferior to the least of Jesus' own followers. And when he heard that John had been executed, Jesus withdrew once again, into a solitude of grief.[24]

Jesus and John the Baptist became so closely associated that there even arose a confusion of identities between the two. "Who do people say I am?" Jesus asked his disciples. "And they told him, 'John the Baptist,' they said. . . ."[25] Racked with superstitious guilt at having executed John, Herod thought that Jesus was only the Baptist's ghost come back to haunt him: "It is John whose head I cut off; he has risen from the dead."[26] The identities and characters of John and Jesus became muddled.

In the relationship of John the Baptist to Jesus, there is a parallelism of career, a possibility of appropriation of John by the early Christians, a confusion of identities, and, perhaps, a question of collusion. John and Jesus paid each other mutual compliments and gave each other some kind of mutual recognition, just as their mothers, Elizabeth and Mary, had done in their pregnancies. Such mutual recognition necessarily raises the question of collusion or conspiracy. "I did not know him myself,"[27] John said as a disclaimer of collusion with Jesus. However, because John and Jesus were blood relatives through their mothers, John must have known about, and known, Jesus.

Who, then, was Jesus? "He is a prophet, like the prophets we used to have,"[28] was all that most people would admit. If Jesus was thought to be just another prophet in a long line, then John the Baptist, the greatest of his contemporary prophets, failed to give convincing testimony to the supremacy and uniqueness of Jesus. John did not unequivocally recognize Jesus as the One, the Messiah.[29]

Was there any other prophetic testimony to Jesus, testimony from disinterested observers?

Luke tells how a prophet named Simeon recognized the baby Jesus as someone special. Like John the Baptist leaping in the womb in recognition, the premature testimony of Simeon sounds like a pagan prodigy. Luke provides an antiphon to Simeon's testimony in that of the prophetess Anna. Female prophecy was uncommon among the patriarchal Jews, but common among pagans. In Anna, then, a pagan sybil may have made her way into the Jewish scriptures.[30]

Against the oracular hysteria of pagan female sybils stands the old Semitic patriarchal authority. Therefore, Yahweh Himself, the highest authority in the patriarchal Jewish mind, would give the most convincing testimony to Jesus. It is Yahweh who appoints prophets. Couldn't Yahweh bear supreme witness to the one who would bear ultimate witness to Him? Matthew, Mark, and Luke each contain similar episodes of Yahweh's witness to Jesus.

After he was baptized by John, Jesus heard the Thunder-Voice from heaven. It told him (but not the bystanders), "You are my Son, the Beloved; my favor rests on you."[31] By calling Jesus *Son,* Yahweh Himself took on paternity, legitimizing Jesus.

To the patriarchal question, "Could the uncommon man have a common father?" Yahweh's assumption of paternity is an even better answer than the genealogy. Divine paternity is the ultimate Uncommon Father.[32]

As if one testimony from Yahweh were not enough, the Thunder-Voice returns in echo on another occasion, the so-called Transfiguration, in which Jesus made a glowing show of his mana. On that occasion Yahweh added as an afterthought, "Listen to him."[33] The eyes and ears of the three apostles present must have already been so overawed that the "Listen to him" was unnecessary. (In any case, Jesus had taken the three apostles to the mountain top to show them something, not to tell them something.)

If Yahweh testifies, what other testimony is needed? Strangely, the gospelwriters do not take Yahweh at his word. Instead, they follow a dualistic scheme: they recruit devils to the task of prophetic witness to Jesus. Some devils possessing the bodies of two madmen both resisted and recognized Jesus when they asked him, "What do you want with us, Son of God?"[34] Against Jesus' desire for secrecy other devils cried out upon meeting him, "You are the Son of God!"[35] And so the devils "knew who he was."[36]

Jesus received recognition as the *Son of God* by both Yahweh and the devils. That parallel and dualistic testimony established Jesus' legitimacy as both advocate of Cosmic Good and adversary of Cosmic Evil.

The twofold testimony from heaven above and hell below, although compelling in its dramatic effect, is logically defective as proof. After all, what is the value of the testimony of the Prince of Lies? And can god and devil achieve a harmony of perfect agreement? Either the devil spoke the truth once, or Yahweh lied once. (Wouldn't a single honest word redeem the devil forever? Wouldn't a single lie compromise God forever? Both would become all-too-human.)

Just as John the Baptist gave at best an equivocal testimony to Jesus, the devil, too, had his doubts. During the temptation in the wilderness, in which Jesus underwent the ordeal of his prophetic apprenticeship, the devil was openly skeptical. He twice prefaced his temptations with the taunt, "If you are the Son of God";[37] then he challenged Jesus to prove it. The devil's doubt on that occasion is inconsistent with the certainty of his testimony from within the bodies of the madmen, "You are the Son of God!"

Jesus had been in the desert for the sojourn of forty days and forty nights, fasting all the while. Knowing that, the devil first tempted him with hunger, an animal weakness. "If you are the Son of God, tell these stones to turn into loaves."[38] The devil wanted Jesus to prove that he was the Son of God by means of a miracle, a *sign*.

Although Jesus rebuffed him, the devil tried a second time, repeating the skeptical qualifier: "If you are the Son of God . . . throw yourself down [from the parapet of the Temple]."[39] The devil again asked for a sign, this time a stunt that would prove Jesus' invulnerability, immortality, and so, divinity. Again, Jesus rebuffed him.

By the third temptation the devil had decided that Jesus was an imposter. He dropped the qualifier, "If you are the Son of God," and offered the world and its kingdoms to Jesus if Jesus would bow down and worship him. Twice rebuffed but now convinced of his own superiority, the devil thought that he could get Jesus to succumb to a merely human political ambition, one that would induce Jesus to submit to the superiority of Cosmic Evil. Jesus dismissed the devil, and the devil departed, not at all convinced about Jesus, but rather, we conclude, fully unconvinced.[40]

The devils who "knew who he was" and the devil of the temptation who was skeptical may have been different members of a legion; that could account for the inconsistency of the recognition in the one instance and the disbelief in the other. Or, since the temptation came before the episode of the two madmen, the devil might have been a disbeliever at first, but then become a believer sometime later. If so, then the devil *was* all-too-human; he was able to learn.

The episode of the temptation in the wilderness is presented in a full account by Matthew and Luke, but it is only alluded to by Mark. Mark is the oldest, shortest, and insofar as succinctness indicates reliability, perhaps the most reliable of the four gospels.

The question of the origins and legitimacy of a great man tends to occur late, after the story of the great man's career has become well known.[41] Mark, the earliest gospel, is mostly concerned with Jesus' career, with bare biography. Mark constructs no genealogy, says nothing about the virginal conception, and presents John the Baptist and Jesus in sequence, but not in the explicit relatedness of the other gospels. Mark does include the two testimonies from the

Thunder-Voice and those of some devils. About the temptation Mark says only, "The Spirit drove him out into the wilderness and he remained there for forty days, and was tempted by Satan. He was with the wild beasts, and the angels looked after him."[47]

That succinct but suggestive mix of *the Spirit, wilderness, Satan, beasts,* and *angels* stirred the imagination of those who craved a rich, well-embellished story. In this, as in other instances, Matthew and Luke embellish the bare-bones tradition that we find in Mark. They script a dialogue for Jesus and the devil and construct a little scene, where Mark had only indicated an episode.

The legitimizing purpose of the episode of the temptation in the wilderness is to show that Jesus underwent his ordeal of preparation for messiahship, that he had acquired a mastery of self that proved equal to a confrontation with the devil. The devil administered a kind of graduation test to him, and Jesus passed.

The entire significance of temptation, the succumbing or resisting, is a human one. The temptation of a divine being is absurd, because, for a god, succumbing to temptation is impossible and resisting it is no accomplishment. From the later, much later, perspective of Christian theology, in which Jesus of Nazareth had become fully God, equal-to-God, the temptation is an absurd episode devoid of logic and meaning.

Why the temptation, then? Was it a mere empty formality? The answer depends upon whether we take the temptation as a test for future legitimacy or as a proof of a legitimacy already established. If we consider Jesus a human being aspiring to messiahship, then the episode of the temptation was a suspenseful trial and ordeal. The prophet achieved his coming-of-age. If we consider Jesus a Person of the Eternal God, however, then the temptation episode was a hypocritical gesture, futile alike for Jesus and the devil. That second consideration brings us to the Gospel of John.

We haven't yet turned the pages of the Gospel of John to search out his solution to the problem of Jesus' legitimacy. John is the latest, the most elaborate, the most sophisticated, of the four gospels. According to John, Jesus is God incarnate and so beyond temptation. Fully convinced of the divinity of Jesus, John dispenses with the temptation episode. In the Gospel of John divinizing mythology has become doctrine.

John is so different from the other three gospels that it is less a fourth version than a revaluation. Mark keeps Jesus in his place and time; Matthew refers him to the patriarchal past; Luke puts him in the context of cosmopolitan paganism. John dissociates the person of Jesus from his place and time, from his ancestors and contemporaries, and so from his historical humanity. In John, Jesus is already becoming the mystical fantasy-figure that theology would later make of him.[43]

John does not argue from any genealogy; that would make Jesus only one among many Jewish prophets. John gives no account of the virginal conception; that would make too much of the human mother. He includes the witness of the Baptist, in its most explicit form; the promotion of the person of Jesus must be unequivocal. John dispenses with the episode of the temptation, because the temptation of a divine being, even if a mere formality, would be absurd. Nor does he include the testimony of Yahweh the Thunder-Voice at Jesus' baptism and the Transfiguration. For the First Person to testify to the divinity of the Second Person is likewise absurd, in light of the presupposition of the divinity of Jesus.[44]

John's is a gospel of cosmic love and poetic mysticism. Instead of the mere temporal, chronological, or accurately historical there is the sublime vagueness of the eternal cosmic.

But what about the problem of legitimacy? "Where did this god come from?" is an even more challenging question than "Where did this uncommon man come from?"

To that more vexing problem of the origins of the god, John composes a mystical answer: "In the beginning was the Word; the Word was with God and the Word was God."[45] That myth of origin is sophisticated theology. *In the beginning:* preexistent eternality. *The Word:* the Force that created the cosmos with a mere phrase, "Let there be. . . ." *The Word was with God:* copresence with divinity. *The Word was God:* consubstantiality with divinity. Quite a load of theology in a single verse! And with that single verse the humanity and the historicity of Jesus are gone forever.

How to associate a Jew named Jesus of Nazareth with the supreme, preexistent, divine Cosmocreator was the very problem of legitimacy all over again. John makes the association in another dense nugget of theology: "The Word was made flesh."[46] That is a beautiful formula, alluringly mystical. Of course, metaphorical mysticism provides no proof that would satisfy a historian or biographer. Theology is not concerned with that sort of proof. Rather, it resolves any contradictions by mystical paradoxes. "The Word was made flesh"—that was to be the theological formula for the legitimacy of Jesus.

John pronounces the formula of Incarnation at the very beginning of his gospel. The Incarnation, John's prelude and prologue, stands as a counterpoise to the genealogy and the virginal conception in Matthew and Luke.[47]

Divinization solves the problem of legitimacy once and for all. Jesus the God, one with the One God, needs no testimonies. He himself is the most credible witness to himself. He himself is his own authority. His being is his legitimacy.

John puts into Jesus' mouth some formulations that were blasphemous to traditional Jewish piety: "The Father and I are one."[48] Again, "the Father is in me and I am in the Father."[49] Yet again, turned around, "I am in the Father and the Father is in me."[50] Even if such consubstantiality could be interpreted only mystically, rather than ontologically, the blasphemy is overt. It was that blasphemy that severed the Christians from the Jews, as if Jesus were a new beginning, and not a late continuation.

The Jewish prophet, hitherto witness to Yahweh the God, became in the person of Jesus, as Messiah and Christ, both one-with-God and God Himself. And so there would be, there could be, no more prophets, because the Messiah had come in the person of the One God. Any later prophets would be anticlimax.

The doctrine of the Word in the Gospel of John is a metaphorical mysticism. Although blasphemous, it is nonetheless a Jewish, not a pagan, conception. In the Jewish mind, a literary mind, there was a strong fetishism of the book and an idolatry of the word. Words were magic. The *Word* did indeed confer legitimacy. That is why, in all the gospels, Jesus referred the words of the Old Testament to himself; he arranged and interpreted events according to the prophetic words of the Old Testament. To Jesus and his partisan promoters, the old events, the old words, prefigured the New Events, the New Words.[51]

"The Word was made flesh"—that is not a fact but a poem, not proof of legitimacy but mysticism. According to John, the origin of Jesus was not in the seed of the patriarchs or in the body of a human female but in words, and beyond words, in the preexistent, creating, supreme *Word* itself.

During the temptation in the wilderness, when the devil asked Jesus to worship him, Jesus rebuffed him with the monotheistic answer, "You must worship the Lord your God, and serve him alone."[52] In John, Jesus has apostasized from Jewish monotheism and succumbed to the devil's temptation to idolatry of self: "The Father and I are one."[53]

The four gospelwriters could not just take Jesus at his own words and deeds. Instead, they resorted to all kinds of explanations for him, all sorts of theories to legitimize him. There were the two non-matching patriarchal genealogies, and against them the incongruous pagan tale of the virginal conception. There was the figure of the precursor, John the Baptist, who may or may not have recognized Jesus, and who in any case became confused with him in identity. There was the testimony of Yahweh the Thunder-Voice at the baptism of Jesus and at his Transfiguration. There were devils who knew Jesus and others who were skeptical. There was the theologically sophisticated doctrine of the Word and all those other words in the Old Testament that could, with sufficient ingenuity and unscrupulousness, be taken as testimony to Jesus. If all of that failed to convince, there was Jesus' own witness to himself, even his witness to his own divinity. To a basic question, barely considered by Mark, there was to be, just two generations later, in John, a most fantastic answer.

Besides the Baptist, Yahweh, and the devils, there were other lesser personal witnesses to Jesus, such as the Magi. In response to the miracles there was the eager worship and acclamation of the mob; but that no more proves Jesus' legitimacy than the worship and acclamation of the mob proves the worth of demagogues, dictators, or rock stars.

In such testimony as that of Jesus' first convert, the centurion whose servant Jesus cured, or of Jesus' last convert, the centurion at the crucifixion who exclaimed, "In truth this was a son of God,"[54] we detect once again the Jewish tribal craving for a turnabout or retribution against their historic enemies. The Roman witness of the centurions was like the Babylonian witness of the Magi. Rome would bow to Jerusalem—that was the point, the very political point, of the centurions' witness.

That Jesus was someone special is also demonstrated by his miracles, his *signs*. The miracles, including the culminating one of his Resurrection, are presented as proof of Jesus' legitimacy and authority. However, in the context of *superstition*, those miracles raise doubts instead of resolving them. Even Jesus himself had second thoughts about appealing to the evidence of his miracles as proof.[55]

Many answers are offered in the four gospels to the question, "Where did the man get this wisdom and these miraculous powers?" The farfetched otherworldliness of those answers tends to leave the modern mind as skeptical as Tacitus. And worse, the legitimizing theories would make of Jesus' life not a supreme human achievement, but rather a mere divine condescension.

A man's origins neither explain his achievements nor explain away the effort that genius must make to actualize itself. The question of the origins and legitimacy of Jesus is interesting but irrelevant, except to the dogmatic predestinarians and determinists who want to prove something they are already convinced of, whether it be the messiahship or the divinity of Jesus. To really understand Jesus and his genius, we need to examine his words, his deeds, and, by inference, his mind. We want to try to appreciate Jesus in a way that his idolatrous followers could not. We want to try to appreciate Jesus for his character.

Ego and Alienation

If a man who is ambitious has not been born into a high social position, if his legitimacy is not hereditary, he necessarily resorts to promoting himself. The question of Jesus' legitimacy must never have been resolved during his life, because we find him, again and again, throughout the gospels, promoting himself.

First of all, Jesus assumed a role in relation to all that had come before in the Jewish religion: "Do not imagine that I have come to abolish the Law or the Prophets. I have come not to abolish but to complete them."[1]

By that very self-assertive assertion Jesus disarmed those who feared that he was a destructive ideological revolutionary. There was disingenuousness in that assurance: Jesus may not have intended to *abolish* the Law and the Prophets, but he did reinterpret and, at times, even contradict them. One of the recurrent formulas in Jesus' speech was the refrain, "They have told you . . . but *I* tell you. . . ."[2]

In his prohibition of divorce, for example, Jesus directly contradicted the Mosaic Law. He also preached the notion, subversive to such a legalistic religion as Judaism, that a good heart and good acts were more important than observance of the Law. Further, Jesus felt free to dispense himself and his disciples from the Law, as in the case of the sabbath observance, which he held but lightly. "And he said to them, 'The Son of Man is master of the sabbath.' "[3]

Although he did not declare the Law abolished, Jesus did presume to reinterpret, to contradict, and to devalue the Law, insisting that his own words took precedence over the words of the Law.

Correspondingly, his person took precedence over the prophets, whose traditional role had been to bear witness to Yahweh. According to Jesus, however, the role of John the Baptist, the last and greatest of the prophets, was to bear witness to *him.* Jesus himself changed the prophetic role, which had been merely functionary, into something more self-seeking. As the Messiah, the Master Prophet, it was he, and he at last, who would *complete,* that is, fulfill, perfect, and finish off, both the Law and the Prophets. Instead of urging loyalty to Yahweh, as all the prophets had, Jesus urged loyalty to himself: "This is working for God: you must believe in the one he has sent."[4]

What Jesus wanted from his followers was not only faith in what he said, but faith in his own person. That is what makes Jesus a religious leader rather than a philosopher. A philosopher thinks out and teaches values, ethics, perhaps a world view. The best philosophers are those who send their disciples away from themselves. The prime value of the philosopher is integrity, not loyalty. The religious leader, by contrast, teaches doctrines that are indefensible rationally, doctrines that must be believed rather than understood. The disciple, then, must take both the teaching and the teacher on *faith.*

The religious leader, unlike the philosopher, demands allegiance to himself and to his *truth.* He draws disciples to himself and induces them to submit. Any disciple who leaves, far from having grown up or become independent, has committed an act of treachery, of betrayal. A philosopher may challenge the disciple with, "What do *you* think?" The religious leader orders his disciple, "Believe in *me.*" The inflated ego, a vice to a philosopher, is, in the religious or, more precisely, the cultic, leader, an accepted personality trait, even a proof of legitimacy.

From his followers Jesus demanded total subservience: "The disciple is not superior to his teacher, nor the slave to his master. It is enough for the disciple that he should grow to be like his teacher, and the slave like his master."[5] The *imitatio Christi,* the mere imitation of Christ, was the highest ambition permitted the disciple of Jesus.

And so Jesus became not the founder of a philosophical school, but rather, the central figure in the cult of himself: "Happy is the man who does not lose faith in *me.*"[6]

Every such cult of a Revered Person has a sinister obverse to the adoration and emulation of the Person. That sinister obverse is a fanaticism over the Person: "He who is not with me is against me."[7]

Jesus divided his contemporaries into two groups, those with him and those against him. He made an uncompromising demand of allegiance to his own person. Men were to be judged according to whether they accepted or rejected that allegiance. Such an absolute either-or, appalling to a philosopher, is an intolerant fanaticism distressing to find in an otherwise noble character.

It is the fanatic who forces upon others the either-or, the with-me or against-me. To the fanatic, neutrality is evil and doubt is damnation. "Take sides!" the fanatic insists.

Jesus blessed those who had faith in him. He was grateful for their faith, their loyalty, and their allegiance. That can be taken as an appreciation of wholesome fellowship. But the sinister obverse, "He who is not with me is against me," was a bullying of the uncommitted mind, an intolerant ultimatum that would set an ominous example for the disciples. The fanatic destruction of classical culture, the repressive conformity of the Dark Ages, the self-righteous militarism of the Crusades, the Holy Inquisition and burnings of heretics, the wars of religion—all those horrors of Western civilization were there in the seed germ of that single terrible sentence, "He who is not with me is against me."

At this point we must pause to consider the paradox in the character of Jesus. On the one hand, he could inculcate a fanatic and intolerant partisanship; on the other, he preached a gentle tolerance summed up in the idea, "Love everybody." How could the same person both incite to hatred and encourage to love, pushing his disciples to the extremes of each? Jesus of Nazareth is portrayed in the gospels as a fanatic oscillating in ambivalence.

We must keep in mind that the gospels are not so much biography, as they are propagandistic tracts. Like the patriarchs and prophets in the Old Testament, Jesus, too, was a personification of an ideology. Like Socrates, his philosophical counterpart as teacher, the Jesus we know is a dramatic fiction. We cannot hold the historical person Jesus of Nazareth accountable for *all* the words put into his mouth by the Christian propagandists.

Here are the words put into Jesus' mouth in a vision detached from any biographical context: "I know all about you: how you are neither cold nor hot. I wish you were one or the other, but since you are neither, but only lukewarm, I will spit you out of my mouth."[8] There we have it again: the either-or ultimatum, the condemnation of neutrality, the damnation of doubt. Some translations are more vivid, with the words *vomit* or *spew* instead of the less offensive *spit*. The intolerant fanaticism comes through in any version.

We recall the scene of Jesus and the children. What would Jesus

have done to one of those children on his lap, if while being preached
to, the child had said no to Jesus? The word no is, after all, one
of the very first in a child's vocabulary; it is, in fact, the very declara-
tion of independence by the developing individual. Would Jesus have
dashed the child's brains onto the rocks at that little no?

Would Jesus of Nazareth have so bullied the *little ones*—the
doubtful, the unsure, the uncommitted—with the violent imagery of
vomiting? It is unfortunate that such intolerant excesses were never
stricken from the texts of the New Testament. Such editorial censorship would have been constructive to the reputation of the Revered
Person. Instead, intolerant excesses, in a variety of formulations, were
put into the mouth of Jesus. The ultimatum on *hot* or *cold* and
the threat to *spit* were attributed to Jesus, the Prince of Love himself;
and the Book of Revelation was attributed to John, the beloved
disciple. It seems out of character for both. It seems, in fact, like
character assassination.

The gospels are propagandistic. They were written to proselytize.
We wonder whether the early Christians, who so unscrupulously appropriated the Old Testament for their own purposes, might not have
similarly transformed the character of Jesus. Did they remake Jesus
in their own image, and impart to his character the same bullying
of the mind that they themselves practiced upon the converts? In
the gospels the character of Jesus is a composite of collective memory
(whether accurate or inaccurate) on the one hand, and propagandistic characterization on the other. Literary art falsifies as much as
it records, making it difficult to distinguish recollection from propaganda.

We must be reserved in accepting all the words put into Jesus'
mouth as accurate expressions of his true teaching and sentiments.
In one instance we can detect how an intolerant either-or ultimatum
attributed to Jesus actually expressed the missionary fanaticism of
his followers. That instance is the either-or ultimatum near the end
of the Gospel of Mark: "He who believes and is baptized will be
saved; he who does not believe will be condemned."[9]

Now, any literary critic recognizes (and biblical scholars admit)
that verses nine to twenty of the sixteenth chapter of the Gospel
of Mark do not belong to it, but were, rather, tacked on as an addendum. In the New Testament such tampering with the text is not
rare.[10] In many places editorial interpretations, subsequent doctrine,
or an even more intransigent assertiveness have been forced onto

the primitive text. That was done not in the interests of biographical accuracy but to serve propagandistic purposes.

In the addendum to Mark, the following words are put into the mouth of the resurrected (that is, the ideological) Jesus: "Go out to the whole world; proclaim the Good News to all creation. He who believes and is baptized will be saved; he who does not believe will be condemned."[11] In that sequence of sentences we see clearly how an intolerant ultimatum is within a missionary context. Those are not the words of Jesus of Nazareth to his disciples but the exhortation of the missionaries to one another. In the phrase, "Go out to the whole world; proclaim the Good News to all creation," we hear the voice of Paul, rather than that of Jesus.[12]

We must wonder just how much the early Christians recast Jesus in their own image. Just how much of Christian intolerance is attributable to Jesus, how much to the traditional Jewish sectarianism, and how much to Paul and the other early Christian leaders, we may never be able to determine. That very indeterminability makes the character of Jesus an eternal enigma. We do not know what he was like; we only know what his followers wanted him to be.

Does that mean that we can neither praise nor blame Jesus for his own words, because we do not know if they were his? Well, if we cannot apply praise or blame to the historical Jesus, we can do so to the fictional character, who is, in any case, the only Jesus we have. And the character of that fictional Jesus is a disturbing one, swollen with ego and bitter with alienation.[13]

The attitude of ego is, "I am someone special." The attitude of alienation is, "I am different from, and better than, everyone else around me." Jesus promoted himself. He also devalued his society, especially its religious Establishment.

The Jews, as a patriarchal people, accorded respect to the well-born, the aged and experienced, and the learned. Jesus was of obscure birth, he was young, and he was, as far as we know, merely self-educated.[14] That triple impediment tended to disqualify him from a role of authority in his society. Jesus could overcome the social prejudices against his lowly birth, his youth, and his lack of education only by attacking the values on which the prejudices were based and the Establishment that maintained those values. Jesus' insecurity concerning the question of his legitimacy impelled him to attack the legitimacy and authority of the Jewish Establishment.

The religious Establishment of the Jews was the scribes and Pharisees.[15] Jesus shared with John the Baptist, his cousin and alter ego, an intense resentment of Establishment authority and an outspoken contempt for its members. Both Jesus and John insulted the venerable greybeards face-to-face in such vivid and shocking terms as "fools and blind!" "brood of vipers!" "whitewashed tombs!" and "hypocrites!"[16] They were so bold as to refer to the most respected members of their society, the actual keepers of Judaic values, in terms of abuse that must have been profoundly upsetting . . . and not only to the Pharisees.

The New Testament has so libeled and caricatured the Pharisees that we tend to think of the word *Pharisee* as synonymous with *hypocrite*. That hypocrisy abounded in the Jewish, as subsequently in the Christian, Establishment, we need not doubt. However, that wholesale condemnation of the Pharisees as a class which we find in the New Testament is purely propagandistic.

The Christian propagandists had to carry on the subversive, anti-Establishment posture of Jesus for the same reason that Jesus had initiated it, namely, to deal with the problem of legitimacy. The Pharisees had tradition and learning as the basis of their authority. What entitled Jesus or any of his followers to be religious leaders? They upset tradition and were not in any way learned. Therefore, they resorted to libeling the Establishment, in order to undermine its authority and usurp its status.

We should recognize the gospel portrayal of the Pharisees for what it is, a propagandistic caricature. We should dispense with the equation of the terms *Pharisee* and *hypocrite*. After all, when Paul proclaimed, "I am a Pharisee,"[17] he did not mean, "I am a hypocrite."

Jesus expressed his social alienation explicitly: "I tell you solemnly, no prophet is ever accepted in his own country."[18] Society was adversarial to ego. Jesus considered himself different from, and superior to, all those around him. By his words and acts, he sharpened those differences and asserted that self-proclaimed superiority, until between him and the Establishment there developed a crisis of confrontation.

The Establishment could not ignore Jesus, because his miracles had attracted to him a mass following. The enthusiasms of the masses are always a danger to any Establishment.

On what basis could the Jewish religious Establishment launch their counterattack against Jesus? Mutual personal animosity was not adequate justification. To the beneficent acts of the Master Healer little objection could be made, except criticism of Jesus' spontaneous generosity in healing even on the sabbath, which would convince only those in whose religiosity there was more scruple than compassion. And so it was the words of the Master Prophet that the Pharisees attempted to discredit. They tried to trap Jesus by clever dilemmas. Jesus responded in kind. There ensued, in an ideological power struggle waged by verbal sparring, a fascinating semantic repartee of trick questions and evasive answers.

When the Pharisees asked Jesus whether it was lawful to give tribute to Caesar, they knew that an affirmative answer would offend Jewish political Zealotry, whereas a negative answer would sound seditious to the Roman overlords. Either a yes or a no would discredit Jesus. Jesus sprung himself from the trap with an ambiguity: "Give back to Caesar what belongs to Caesar—and to God what belongs to God."[19] That response was no answer, but because the Pharisees were not logicians, they did not press Jesus further. Jesus won that round. In the thrust of question and counterthrust of response, defeat and loss-of-face resulted from dropping the sword, from being caught speechless. Jesus stymied the Pharisees with a cryptic ambiguity.

Jesus had repeatedly challenged the authority of the Pharisees. They countered by asking the upstart about the basis of his own authority. Adopting a tit-for-tat methodology, Jesus answered their query with a verbal trap of his own, namely, the question of whether John's baptism was from God or from men. If the Pharisees answered *from God,* then Jesus could have asked them why they had opposed John; if they answered *from men,* they would incur the hostility of the many people who venerated the Baptist. In that second skirmish of wits Jesus stymied the Pharisees again. They could not answer; they lost face; they were humiliated.[20]

The dilemma-questions of the tribute to Caesar and the authority of John the Baptist are presented by the gospelwriters to show that Jesus was more shrewd and clever than his Establishment opponents.[21] We might draw a different conclusion—that Jesus resorted to the same devious, insincere methods as his adversaries.[22]

Jesus and the Pharisees both had hidden motives in their dealings with each other. Jesus recognized the Pharisees' motives—hadn't he, after all, driven them to their opposition, repeatedly impugning their character by indicting their *hypocrisy*? But when the Pharisees retaliated on the question of character, as they had on the question of authority, they struck a most sensitive nerve. Jesus lashed back at his most vituperative.

On one occasion the Pharisees wondered aloud if Jesus could cast out devils only because he was one of them. Of course there was malice in that supposition; but Jesus was, after all, *on speaking terms* with the devils. They negotiated with him, and sometimes he acquiesced, as when the devils requested to be cast from the possessed man into swine.[23] So the Pharisees' supposition did have its logic. When they insinuated that Jesus was a familiar of Beelzebub and Satan, Jesus cursed them: " 'I tell you solemnly, all men's sins will be forgiven, and all their blasphemies; but let anyone blaspheme against the Holy Spirit and he will never have forgiveness: he is guilty of an eternal sin.' This was because they were saying, 'An unclean spirit is in him.' "[24]

The concept of an eternal, unforgivable sin is heterodox in Christianity. It is indicative of the severity of Jesus' alienation that he identified the eternal, unforgivable sin with opposition to his own person. An attack upon the ego aroused a curse upon the critic.[25]

Again, it is unfortunate that Jesus failed to show restraint, to maintain the distinction between principles and persons. In the valuation of good-or-evil, Pharisaic hypocrisy is a minor matter. In any case, the corrective to hypocrisy is honest thinking and good and simple conduct, not an ever-more-devious cleverness and squabbling in the streets.

Jesus claimed the right to condemn those guilty of the eternal, unforgivable sin of opposition to him, because he himself was in close association with Yahweh the Judge: "So if anyone declares himself for me in the presence of men, I will declare myself for him in the presence of my Father in heaven. But the one who disowns me in the presence of men, I will disown in the presence of my Father in heaven."[26] Jesus promised a cosmic reward for the allegiance of his adherents and threatened a cosmic punishment for the opposition of his adversaries. Once again it was a bullying of the uncommitted mind.

In that quotation, from the Gospel of Matthew, Jesus assumed the role of intercessor with Yahweh. In the Gospel of John, Jesus claimed consubstantiality with Yahweh. The two are as one, whether as objects of love . . . or as objects of hatred: "Anyone who hates me hates my Father."[27] Jesus equated opposition to his person with hatred of God. Jesus' identification of himself with Yahweh magnified the enormity of any opposition to him. Such opposition was now an impious blasphemy and hatred of God—the one truly unforgivable sin.

What unexpected terrible threats were implicit in John's doctrine of consubstantiality! What could be more attractive than a love divine, what more frighteningly awesome than a divine hatred, expressed as the threat of eternal damnation? It raised the stakes in the choice of allegiance to Jesus or opposition to him. The ultimatum, "Take sides! Choose, and choose well, or be damned," induced a panic of the will. Harassed and intimidated, pulled and pushed between hell and heaven, the uncommitted mind faced an overwhelming moral dilemma.

It was in the solitary withdrawal of his forty days and nights in the wilderness that Jesus must have nurtured his feelings of alienation. He came out of the wilderness to launch a premeditated campaign intended to subvert Establishment authority. Jesus, wanting to draw the religious impulse of the people to himself, was unrelenting in his attacks upon the Pharisees. That the Pharisees responded to Jesus' insults with hatred is just predictable human nature; that they formed a conspiracy to remove him is intelligible power-politics. Any Establishment does not endure insults to its dignity or challenges to its authority lightly. By incessantly baiting the Pharisees, Jesus fueled their self-defensive instinct and goaded them to thoughts of murderous reprisal. The sociological situation was that of the alienated revolutionary against the Establishment.[28]

Besides the vituperative insults, the accusations of hypocrisy, the devious verbal dilemmas, and the righteous curses in the manner of the Old Testament, Jesus also carried on his campaign in the more subtle manner of parables in which he cast the Pharisees in the role of villain. The parables played upon the common people's resentment against the privileged classes.

In the parable of the Pharisee and the publican, for example, Jesus characterized the Pharisee as self-righteous and contemptuous of the common people, whereas the publican was decorously reverent and self-effacing in the Temple of Yahweh. In that parable Jesus made the common man, of whom he was one, superior to a member of the elite. The parable of the Pharisee and the publican is a masterpiece of proletarian propaganda.[29]

If we can see Jesus in the publican and the publican in Jesus (that is, both alienated commoners), we might find autobiographical significance in Jesus' other parables. The famous parable of the prodigal son seems like a poignant confession of alienation and a longing for reconciliation. Jesus was not a spendthrift debauchee like the prodigal, of course; but in Jewish society sectarian faithlessness was equated with moral prodigality. The prodigal sought reconciliation with his father, just as Jesus, in self-doubt, must sometimes have longed for reconciliation with *his father,* that is, the patriarchal past of orthodox tradition and custom. The chronic tension between Jesus and the Establishment must have been as stressful to Jesus as it was to his opponents. In the parable of the prodigal son we might detect the strain and some weakening of Jesus' resolve. How wonderful would reconciliation be, reconciliation, the cure for alienation! [30]

In his teaching Jesus identified himself with the outcasts. In his choice of companions he did the same, gathering around himself a community of the alienated classes. "Tax collectors and sinners . . . there were many of them among his followers." [31] Tax collectors were despised because they represented the hated occupying power of Rome. [32] The "sinners" with whom Jesus consorted were not murderers, cutthroats, and brigands, but various categories of the ritually "unclean," that is, those who most offended the religious sensitivity of the Establishment.

Tax collectors, reformed prostitutes, and lower caste riffraff— Jesus was no respecter of person or privilege. Jesus may not have found such companionship very edifying, but his choice of companions was calculated as part of his campaign against the entrenched Establishment and its values: "Tax collectors and prostitutes are making their way into the kingdom of God before you," [33] Jesus taunted the Pharisees.

The tax collectors and sinners were the ostracized; their mere presence around Jesus was subversive. Because, however, they were tainted classes, Jesus could not induct them into the role of active propagandists. To fill that role Jesus chose a group of ordinary men, untainted and unobjectionable, with little social awareness and probably no special grudges against the Establishment. Those were Jesus' apostles, the Twelve. In order to secure their allegiance and services, however, Jesus had to teach them alienation, to mold them into a distinct community of the alienated.

A basic statement of Jesus' own alienation was, "He who is not with me is against me." He expanded the scope of that statement by identifying the apostles with himself. The formula in the gospel, "Anyone who is not against us is for us," [34] is a benign one; but because that formula, too, is an absolute either-or, it implies the opposite, "Anyone who is not for us is against us."

To the either-or ultimatum regarding himself, Jesus added a them-and-us separatism in regard to the apostolic brotherhood. He characterized his chosen ones as the alienated elect: "They [the apostles] do not belong to the world any more than I belong to the world."[35] In fact, the apostles had very much belonged to the workaday world of their society; but Jesus took them away from that society and drew them to himself and to his alienation. He wove the ties that bound them to him.

Jesus warned his apostles about the trials involved in their new belonging: "If the world hates you, remember that it hated me before you. If you belonged to the world, the world would love you as its own; but because you do not belong to the world, because my choice withdrew you from the world, therefore the world hates you."[36]

So, it was to be them-and-us in an intense love-hate relationship. How could Jesus recruit apostles with the promise that they would be hated? Who would respond to a call that included this fate?— "They will hand you over to be tortured and put to death; and you will be hated by all the nations on account of my name."[37]

It is possible that in such words we hear the plaintive voice of the early Christian missionaries, who, when encountering hostility and persecution, needed to bolster their morale by a suitable prophecy from the Master's own lips. The warnings of hatred and persecution put into the mouth of Jesus might actually belong to the decades after his death. On the other hand, those words are consistent with the character of Jesus as portrayed in the gospels. Jesus could have foreseen what the reaction to his subversive antivalues would be. Hadn't he himself, by his insults, accusations, humiliating dilemmas, curses, and villainizing parables, aroused the Pharisees to hatred? Wouldn't his disciples, acting in Jesus' name, preaching his doctrines, and adopting his methods, arouse a similar hatred? We needn't see any divine prescience in such predictions. A masterful psychologist like Jesus could anticipate the likely responses to such provocative words and acts.[38]

Alienation has its trials, and Jesus warned of them. But alienation has its rewards, too, and in his recruiting program Jesus promised: "Happy are you when people hate you, drive you out, abuse you, denounce your name as criminal, on account of the Son of Man. Rejoice when that day comes and dance for joy, for then your reward will be great in heaven. This was the way their ancestors treated the prophets."[39]

What a startling emotional mix there is in that rhapsody! There is happiness in hatred, joy in being driven out, abused, and denounced; there is rejoicing and dancing, and, most significantly, there are rewards in heaven, all for suffering on account of the Son of Man. By following Jesus, the apostles, those simple and hardy workaday men, would join the prestigious rolls of the prophets themselves, and they would receive an ultimate compensation in the afterlife. What promises Jesus made to his initiates! He presented alienation as a positive value.[40]

In such a welter of passion and ambivalence, wild promises were complemented by dire threats: "He who rejects me and refuses my words has his judge already; the word itself that I have spoken will be his judge on the last day."[41]

That threat is from the Gospel of John. Just as the sinister implication of divine hatred was implicit in John's doctrine of consubstantiality—if you hate the Son, you hate the Father, and they both will condemn you to hell—so do John's metaphors take on perverse meanings. In John, Jesus is the *Word*. But in the passage from John just quoted, it is the *word* that condemns the disbeliever to hell. The *Word* has become the *bad word*.

Ego and alienation, either-or and them-and-us, promises and threats, all in rhapsodies of apocalyptic rewards and retributions— that is how Jesus bound the apostolic brotherhood of the alienated elect to himself.

To his apostles, his new brotherhood of the alienated elect, Jesus promised the status of prophet and eternal rewards in heaven. Those promises were gratifying to ego and heartening to ambition. But what was the possibility, the likelihood, of the apostles' achieving the earthly mission that Jesus sent them on? The initiate needed more than an imaginary status and distant rewards to sustain his vocation; he needed the prospect of a well-lived, a worthwhile, and an effective and productive life. It is achievement and accomplishment that compensate for the loneliness and ostracism of alienation. And so Jesus promised his apostles earthly success in their religious and political mission on his behalf.

How could that success be achieved, especially against the determined opposition of the entrenched Establishment? Only a catastrophic social upheaval would enable the brotherhood of the alienated elect, the ill-born and uneducated, to prevail over the Establishment. Social cataclysm is exactly what Jesus did prophesy, in a variety of curious aphoristic nuggets that we may call *turnabout formulas.*

"Many who are first will be last, and the last, first."[42] That formula is the fervent hope and chronic ache of every alienated soul, anarchist, and revolutionary who has ever lived. Alienation craves justification, which can be achieved only by the overthrow and destruction of the Establishment. The most exquisite gratification for the isolated ego and alienated soul is the prospect of cataclysm, society topsy-turvy, values inverted, the powerful powerless, and the powerless powerful.

A second turnabout formula was another paradoxical them-and-us: "Everyone who exalts himself will be humbled, but the man who humbles himself will be exalted."[43] The exalted ones were *them,* the proud Pharisees, the Establishment; the humble ones were *us,* the publicans, prodigals, Jesus himself, and the apostolic brotherhood. Self-humiliation was to be the technique, the method, the strategy, by which the apostles would achieve their earthly ambitions. By subverting the value of pride, they would humiliate the proud.

Jesus promised his apostles an earthly success. The aphoristic turnabout formulas were that promise. The first would be last, the last first. The proud would be humiliated, the humble made proud. Those turnabout formulas were truly seditious to the society and its values.

In a third turnabout formula Jesus said, "I tell you, to everyone who has will be given more; but from the man who has not, even what he has will be taken away."[44] That prophecy sounds pro-Establishment, even capitalistic; it seems to contradict the promises to the "last" and the "humble" of the first two formulas. Perhaps the third formula has to do with a turnabout that had already occurred. The apostle was the one *who has,* and the Establishment member the one *who has not.* By that interpretation, the formula would apply more to ego than to alienation. The apostles, ostensibly have-nots, actually were the haves. They had the saving allegiance to their Master and all the promised rewards for that allegiance. The Pharisees, ostensibly the haves, actually had nobody and nothing.

Anyway, after distinguishing the first from the last and the exalted from the humble, Jesus told his apostles what would be required of them in order to effect the turnabout, the social cataclysm: "Anyone who wants to save his life will lose it; but anyone who loses his life for my sake, that man will save it."[45]

It was sacrifice of oneself for the cause of allegiance to Jesus that would enable the apostles to succeed, to *save* their lives, that is, to find their lives worthwhile. There would be a great turnabout, and the apostles were the very ones who would effect it. Absolute allegiance to Jesus, the egoist, and total self-effacement, even to the extreme of martyrdom, would be necessary to achieve the necessary social upheaval.

As Jesus promised his apostles a victory on earth, so did he predict the Establishment's downfall. From those who had been cast down, the victors would hear a pleasant music, the "weeping and grinding of teeth."[46]

Meanwhile, the apostles were not to be daunted by resistance or opposition to their mission. Jesus told them to shake off the dust of the towns that did not receive them. The rejected ones could reject in turn—alienation has its own righteousness.[47]

Jesus' campaign against the Jewish religious Establishment and its values was overtly anarchistic, seditious, and revolutionary. Yet, despite all his subversive propaganda, his calumnies, and even his outrageous blasphemies, the Jesus of the gospels claimed complete innocence of any wrongdoing: "They hated me for no reason."[48]

We can only gasp at that protestation of innocence, whether it be naive or disingenuous. All the apostles, disciples, and martyrs who imitated Jesus were to follow his precedent in proclaiming their utter innocence, all the while that they, too, were subverting the cherished traditional values of the ancient world, both Judaic and Greco-Roman.[49]

The fate of Jesus, of his apostles, and of the Christian martyrs has long posed a historical riddle. How could the Prince of Love and his community of lovers have aroused such intense and universal hatred? If the Christians were, in fact, hated *for no reason,* then the persecutions they encountered make no psychological or sociological sense.

Subsequent Christian generations have gullibly believed the self-exoneration of Jesus and his followers. But in setting about the overthrow of traditional values, the Christians were all-too-guilty. Their ideological destructiveness aroused the antagonism, hatred, and popular persecution of the societies in which they carried on their campaign. Innocent? No, they were guilty, in word and in deed. The cultural crime the Christians stood convicted of was nothing less than destruction of the cherished values and traditions of antiquity.[50]

In the supercharged atmosphere of religious and political ferment in the Palestine of Jesus' day, it should not surprise us that Jesus' aims and intentions were misinterpreted. Everyone recognized Jesus as a healer, a prophet, and a revolutionary of some sort; many misconstrued his person and his campaign as merely political. Jesus himself contributed to that misunderstanding by his cryptic pronouncements, but he had little inclination to political Zealotry.[51] As Jesus told Pilate, his kingdom was not of this world.[52] To Jesus, spiritual values transcended political values. Nonetheless, in an irony of fate, Jesus was to be convicted and executed as a political revolutionary, a would-be *King of the Jews*. Herod's fears seemed justified in Pilate's verdict. And Jesus suffered death for the wrong reason.

According to the account given in the gospels, the Establishment of scribes and Pharisees manipulated Roman fears of revolution in order to rid themselves of a man who, they knew perfectly well, was a religious, rather than a political, revolutionary. However, if we ponder the sociological situation at the time, we perceive that the *values revolution* of Jesus was just as much a threat to the political, as it was to the religious, Establishment.

Jesus felt a deep repugnance toward the idea of domination, whether it was the religious domination of the young by old men implicit in patriarchal Judaism[53] or the political domination of Palestine explicit in the Roman military occupation.[54] Of a deeply spiritual temperament, Jesus directed his opposition to the religious, rather than to the political, Establishment. He evaded the question about tribute to Caesar. Jesus saw himself as the Messiah, not as a Zealot. However, because both the religion and politics of his day were imbued with the domination that he thought evil, Jesus was, necessarily, both a religious and a political revolutionary. He himself attacked the religious Establishment. It was left to his followers to take on Rome.

The scribes and Pharisees had history and tradition on their side, but, according to Jesus, they had forfeited their right to authority because of their hypocrisy. Jesus told the people that they had to listen to and obey the Pharisees, but they were not to emulate them.[55] Jesus himself would teach his contemporaries how to behave, how to live spiritual lives. His prescription was antithesis to domination, both religious and political. His prescription was pacifism and loving-kindness.

"So always treat others as you would like them to treat you,"[56]

Jesus directed his followers. That was a principle of reciprocity, the reciprocity of benevolence. There had been a principle of reciprocity in Judaism, too, a reciprocity of punishment. It was the *lex talionis,* the "eye for an eye, tooth for a tooth" of Old Testament vengeance. To Jesus the punishment of one man by another was the worst of that domination that his sensitivity rebelled against. Charity should replace punishment. If everyone were charitable, there would be no sins or crimes to be punished. In any case, only Yahweh had the right to punish. And Yahweh, no longer tribal tyrant as He was portrayed in much of the Old Testament, had now become the loving Father.

The Jewish Establishment, with its Sanhedrin Court, was very much in the punishment business. Punishment is the way in which patriarchal authority asserts power over subjects. Jesus' pacifism was an antivalue to power.

Punishment is derived from law. In the Old Testament there is a compendium of laws of all kinds, laws by which patriarchal power could be maintained. According to Jesus, the Pharisees had turned the Law into a thousand daily acts of compulsive petty scrupulosity. Their legalism punished in each and every moment. Jesus was as much outraged by those laws as he was by the notion of punishment. He followed up his command to charity, "always treat others as you would like them to treat you," with the comment, "that is the meaning of the Law and the Prophets."[57]

Of course it is no such thing. The Old Testament taken altogether does not add up to the law of Christian charity. All the while denying that he wanted to abolish the Law and the Prophets, Jesus presumed to sum them up. What he was really doing was sweeping away the entire complex structure of Jewish history, law, and authority and starting again from a fresh principle, that of reciprocal loving-kindness and charity. That was nothing less than a revolution in values.

Jesus knew that his doctrine would arouse the opposition of the Establishment. Simplicity is exactly what any Establishment does not want. What would learning avail, if religion were simple? By devaluing law, punishment, authority, and learning, Jesus attempted to make the Establishment irrelevant and superfluous. He tried to sweep it away by simplicity.[58]

Simple love was a subversive antivalue and, as such, would arouse the most intense hatred—not because the idea of love itself is hateful, but because the seditious simplicity and democracy of love threatened the Establishment prerogatives and undermined the traditional elitist values. "Men will betray one another and hate one another,"[59] Jesus predicted correctly.

The Pharisees and the Romans had power behind their hate; Jesus and his disciples were powerless behind their love. Jesus did not want his followers to pervert themselves by the Zealotry and violence that he so opposed. ("All who draw the sword will die by the sword."[60]) He taught his disciples how they were to respond to the hatred they were inevitably to encounter: "Love your enemies, do good to those who hate you, bless those who curse you, pray for those who treat you badly. To the man who slaps you on one cheek, present the other cheek, too."[61]

That directive had to be, and still is, one of the most startling prescriptions for behavior ever made by a religious teacher—the prescription of absolute pacifism. Jesus ordered his followers to *love, do good to, bless,* and *pray for* the *enemies, those who hate you, those who treat you badly.* The idea is stunning. Its realization is impossible.

Jesus' concept of justice through pacifism has been taken as a social prescription, comparable to the theories of the Greek philosophers or the code of law of the Romans. As a social prescription, pacifism is absurd. With the good turning the other cheek, the criminals would run amok.

The Greek philosophers were concerned with justice in the abstract; the Romans worked over the real problems of law and government. Jesus' mind, by contrast, was religious, rather than philosophical or political. What Jesus was talking about was not the social order of the world but the inner soul of his followers. His pacifism was not meant as a social prescription.

"Offer the wicked man no resistance,"[62] Jesus ordered his disciples; but he should have added, "for the good of your soul." Jesus himself set the example for the self-discipline by his behavior during his arrest, trial, and execution. The Establishment was violent, and therefore evil; the good man must not pervert himself by retaliatory violence. All aggression, all terror must be renounced. For the sake of his soul—never mind society—the good man must *offer the wicked man no resistance.*

Some early Christians must have recognized that Jesus' pacifism (which is a passivism, too) was a spiritual, not a social, prescription. In the Epistle of James there is already the idea of the *sin of omission:*

"Everyone who knows what is the right thing to do and doesn't do it commits a sin."[63] Passivism, inactivity, noninvolvement could be a sinful dereliction of spiritual duty.

Turning the other cheek does not check evil; it gives evil its opportunity. Pacifism permits evil to be inflicted upon the pacifist, the passive one. Not a social prescription, then, Jesus' pacifism was a spiritual discipline, a self-discipline. The self-discipline that Jesus commanded was so severe and so stressful that it could become an emotional complex. At its worst, pacifism is a self-righteous, but thoroughly masochistic, response to sadistic aggression.[64]

Jesus reacted against the powers of his society by going to the ideological antithesis to power, which is pacifism, passivism, powerlessness. His willful suffering without resistance, his passion and death, showed his own commitment to his antithesis and antivalue.

Unfortunately, because Jesus demanded an *imitatio Christi,* he also set the stage for the martyr complex, that self-righteous masochism and enthusiastic suicidalism we find among the early Christians. Jesus, the strong one, was a pacifist. Some early Christian martyrs were masochists. In any case, it was no historical accident that there were martyrs. It was an inevitable consequence of Jesus' antivalue and example of pacifism and passivity. Martyrdom was the ultimate necessity, for reasons that we will have to explore further.

Jesus and his disciples were the powerless alienated, the unarmed revolutionaries. Jesus recognized the futility and immorality of violence. Besides, his kingdom, the kingdom of values, was *not of this world.* The revolution in values was to be conducted in human souls. It was the disciplined mind and the self-controlled emotions that would effect the triumph of the values revolution.

The discipline of pacifism was the psychological technique, or method, by which the followers of Jesus, the helpless, the unarmed, could overcome their adversaries. Pacifism was a strategy. Jesus said explicitly: "Remember, I am sending you out like sheep among wolves; so be cunning as serpents and yet as harmless as doves."[65] The apostles were to be shrewd sheep, calculating doves.

Cunning and harmless—that was the strategy. It was psychological jiu-jitsu against the Establishment.[66] That it could succeed was demonstrated by Jesus himself on the cross. His composed self-discipline converted the Roman centurion who had power over him, in whose custody Jesus had been helpless. The strategy could work, and it would work. But there would be some neurotic consequences, as we find in the martyrs.

"Let anyone who despises me, hurt me. I yield totally." That was antithesis, antivalue, and strategy all in one, a subversive assault that would undermine Jewish patriarchal power and eventually precipitate the collapse of Roman imperial power. In retrospect, we can grasp just how brilliant that strategy was. But what a physiological and psychological toll it took on its adherents; how much new, how much different, suffering it has caused! Revolutions oscillate to the opposite extremes of the Establishment they attack. It is an open historical question whether the casualties of surrender have been fewer or more than those of aggression.

Jesus was one of those rare geniuses of ego and alienation who succeed in setting the values of their society topsy-turvy. His values program was a spiritual campaign against domination and power, to be conducted with a cunning mind and a self-discipl ned mastery over the passions. Jesus' teaching and example went hand-in-hand to demonstrate an anti-Establishment strategy. The essence of that strategy was pacifism.

The genius of Jesus of Nazareth was as a *values revolutionary*. His strategy, his values, his revolution succeeded.

In Judaism the past has always been a drag upon the refining of values. Religion does not evolve by the repetitive quoting of old texts. That is why Jesus swept away that part of the Jewish past that was a drag upon true spirituality. "They have told you . . . But I tell you . . ." was a common refrain in his teaching.

The Establishment challenged Jesus' legitimacy, his right to overturn the past. "You are testifying on your own behalf; your testimony is not valid,"[67] they objected.

To the impediment of his obscure birth, Jesus claimed to be a (or the) Son of God. To the impediment of his youth, he asserted, "before Abraham ever was, I am."[68] To the impediment of his lack of learning in the Law, Jesus devalued learning and the Law itself. Against learning and Law he taught a simple notion of reciprocal lovingkindness: "Always treat others as you would like them to treat you. That is the meaning of the Law and the Prophets."

With his ego struggling against the problem of his legitimacy and his sensitive alienation ever probing and criticizing the values of his society, Jesus undertook a revolution in values. As the disciplinary strategy for that revolution he adopted pacifism, which was antithesis and antivalue to the cruel domination and power permeating his society. That Jesus himself and all his followers were to suffer in the living out of their values and their self-discipline was a necessity, a requirement for personal salvation, the spiritual victory. Every war, even that on behalf of the Kingdom of Heaven, has its casualties.

Antifamilialism

Jesus revealed his alienation from his society when he told the people, "A prophet is only despised in his own country." Then, in a confession that was more personal and heartfelt, he added, "among his own relations and in his own house."[1]

Jesus drew three concentric circles of alienation around himself, the most distant one that of his country, a closer one that of his relations, and the closest that of his own house. By drawing those three walled circles around himself, Jesus makes us wonder: Was the son as much estranged from his family as the prophet was alienated from his society? Jesus took on the Establishment of scribes and Pharisees in a direct confrontation. Is it conceivable that he had a similar confrontation with his own mother and father?

The theological mind would not even consider such a question. The divinely chosen parents, Mary the compliant virgin and Joseph the noble protector, would never have had any doubts about, nor would they in any way have opposed, the mission that was their son's divinely ordained destiny.

In the Gospel of Matthew, after Joseph had discovered that his fiancée was pregnant, an angel told him that Mary's son was to be "the one who is to save his people from their sins."[2] Similarly, in the Gospel of Luke, the angelic messenger told Mary that she would conceive and that her son "will be great and will be called Son of the Most High."[3] Both Jesus' father and his mother were explicitly informed about the predestined mission of their son even before he was born. The support for his mission would seem to have been secured by the angels' prophecies.

That is why it is surprising to read in the Gospel of Mark that "his [Jesus'] relatives . . . set out to take charge of him, convinced he was out of his mind."[4]

By that version, Jesus' family,[5] far from believing in his predestined mission, thought that he was insane in so setting himself against his society. Instead of supporting Jesus in his task, his family wanted to *take charge of him,* which would have meant preventing him from doing what he was born to do.

Mark is the earliest, the most primitive, gospel. That incidental comment in Mark represents early, primitive, biographical candor. It suggests a situation of familial strife that is very human in its plausibility. Jesus set himself against his society with such fanatic zeal that his family feared for his sanity and safety. Out of familial love they wanted to *take charge of him,* to remove him from the stimuli to his mania, to keep him home for a quiet convalescence. They were worried about him. They thought he needed help.

As a healer, Jesus went about curing the physical and mental afflictions of the people. As a prophet and teacher, he diagnosed the spiritual sickness of his society. But his family was concerned about his own health. Wasn't Jesus himself heading for some kind of breakdown? Didn't he need to be rescued from his delusions? His family became *convinced he was out of his mind.*

This is another instance of how incompatible traditions were woven into the multicolored fabric of the four gospels. One interpretation of Jesus' family relationships, a theological one, is represented in Matthew and Luke, where the angels informed Joseph and Mary of their son's special mission and destiny.[6] Another interpretation, a candid biographical one, is represented by Mark, who reveals that Jesus' family not only doubted his mission, but even his basic mental health. Those two traditions are contradictory and incompatible. In accordance with other patterns of editorial bias that we have detected in the gospels, we conclude that Matthew and Luke introduced late mythological embellishments into the story, whereas Mark, earlier and simpler, was, more likely, closer to the actual biography of Jesus.

The gospels reveal, as they conceal, that Jesus suffered from an estrangement from his own family. He himself regretted this estrangement when he confessed, "A prophet is only despised in his own country, among his own relations, and in his own house." Jesus was not just repeating a proverb; he was making a personal confession.

It was probably estrangement from his family that drove Jesus out of his own house in Nazareth to Capernaum, where he took up independent adult residence. In Capernaum, Jesus stepped from the close circle of familial estrangement into the more distant circle of alienation from society. Out of bitter frustration Jesus was to climax his series of community condemnations by laying the curse of Sodom upon the insignificant village he had chosen as home: "And as for you, Capernaum, did you want to be exalted as high as heaven? You shall be thrown down to hell."[7]

Retracing Jesus' steps from Capernaum back to Nazareth, and setting aside the theological perspective, we can reconstruct the course of Jesus' familial estrangement in a sequence that is all-too-human.

Luke tells of Jesus' precocity. Because genius is generally precocious, we can accept the likelihood of an adolescent, or even a pre-adolescent, self-assertiveness on Jesus' part.

This is the tale that Luke tells of the precocity of the genius: When Jesus was twelve years old, he gave his parents the slip in Jerusalem, in order to join the doctors of the Law in the Temple for religious discussions. Joseph and Mary had to track him down; it took three days for them to find him. With human parental concern Mary scolded him, "My child, why have you done this to us? See how worried your father and I have been, looking for you."[8] Jesus answered his mother in a rude and rebellious manner: "Why were you looking for me? Did you not know that I must be busy with my Father's affairs?"[9]

We would think that Jesus' rhetorical question would have jogged Joseph's and Mary's memories to recall the angels' messages to them; but Luke relates that "they did not understand what he meant."[10] We must conclude either that Joseph and Mary were obtuse, or else that they had no inkling of the predestinarian conviction we would expect them to have. After all, the appearance of an angel is an experience one is not likely to forget.

The episode of the boy Jesus among the doctors may be merely mythological.[11] Even so, we may infer some sort of adolescent rebellion by Jesus, a rebellion that was directed into religious channels very early, whether or not there were discussions with the Temple savants.

The seeking of one's identity and the search for a vocation are characteristic psychological events of human adolescence. But adolescence is a time of self-doubt, as much as of self-assertion. In the first phase, the adolescent phase, of his estrangement, Jesus could rebuke his parents for their interference, but he was not yet ready to separate himself from them. After the episode with the doctors in the Temple, Jesus returned home with his parents "and lived under their authority."[12]

As every young man must do, Jesus did eventually assert his full independence. He left childhood and family behind, and embarked upon the mission of his maturity. In that, the second phase of Jesus' relationship to his family, his estrangement intensified. "Not even his brothers, in fact, had faith in him."[13]

When his mother and family "were anxious to have a word with him"[14]—again, perhaps, over his welfare, since they were anxious about him—Jesus asked another rude rhetorical question: " 'Who is my mother? Who are my brothers?' And stretching out his hand toward his disciples he said, 'Here are my mother and my brothers.' "[15] In that rebuff Jesus explicitly repudiated his natural family and claimed instead a familial relationship with his apostles, the brotherhood of the alienated elect. That is surely evidence of severe estrangement.

The episode of Jesus' rebuff to his family is reported in all three of the synoptic gospels. In Mark, the earliest, it occurs within an obvious context of alienation: Jesus announced his estrangement from his family right after they had questioned his sanity and after the Pharisees had accused him of being a devil. ("Insane" and "possessed by a devil" may be taken as equivalent indictments of Jesus' alienation and equivalent skepticism about his mission.) Jesus was saying that he needed emotional support from his family as little as he needed vocational approval from the Establishment.[16]

Familial estrangement and social alienation are complementary. Keeping both family and society at a distance, and asserting one's ego against both—that is the characteristic stance of the alienated revolutionary. As a values revolutionary, Jesus was to assert new and different familial and social values against the conventional ones.

The values revolution that Jesus undertook brought emotional grief to himself as well as to his family. In the third phase of his relationship to his family, after his mission was accomplished, Jesus reconciled himself to his family. The estranged, alienated stance had become irrelevant. Just before his death on the cross, Jesus looked down upon his mother and upon John, his beloved disciple. "Jesus said to his mother, 'Woman, this is your son.' Then to the disciple he said, 'This is your mother.' And from that moment the disciple made a place for her in his home."[17]

As his last act before dying, Jesus healed his estrangement from his own family. He joined his natural mother to his chosen brother, John, in a new family relatedness. During his career, Jesus had been forced to assert his kinship of ideology against his kinship of blood. At his death, the accomplishment and completion of his values revolution, Jesus could drop the stance of estrangement and alienation, reconciling himself with all those who had cared for him. He urged a harmonious fusion of his natural family and his ideological family.[18]

Those, then, were the three phases of Jesus' estrangement from his family, reconstructed in their likely course. As an adolescent Jesus first asserted his independence from family and his ambition for a religious mission. Then, as a mature prophet of ego, he repudiated his family relatedness and chose instead a new family, his apostles, the brotherhood of the alienated elect. At last, when he felt that his mission had been accomplished, he reconciled himself to his family and his natural and chosen families to each other.

That sequence, although repugnant to theology, is intelligible and plausible from the psychological and biographical standpoint. It is, in fact, all-too-human. The same sequence can be traced in the lives of many great creators, geniuses, and revolutionaries.

It is only in the Gospel of John that we have evidence of the third phase of the sequence, the reconciliation. The strongest impression of Jesus' attitude toward family left in the gospels is that of the second phase, namely, Jesus' estrangement from family and its values. Unfortunately, because of his prophetic ego and his social alienation, Jesus exaggerated his estranged stance to such an extent that his personal family problems could be translated into a doctrine of antifamilialism.

There are psychological components in every ideology. Jesus' struggle against the lack of support, even the opposition, from his family impelled him to an extreme adversarial stance against family in general, just as his revolutionary ambitions impelled him to an extreme adversarial stance against the Establishment.

Jesus the revolutionary, having erected walled circles against family and society, needed companions in his isolation: "He appointed twelve; they were to be his companions."[19]

The apostles were family men, with years of emotional commitment to their wives and children. Jesus wanted to take them along with him, in every detail of ideology and every aspect of self-discipline. To do that, he had to detach their loyalty from their natural families and transfer it to their new ideological family. As Jesus taught his apostles alienation from the Establishment and its values, so did he teach them estrangement from their own families and from family values.

How Jesus went about that difficult task has set the precedent for the general approach of Christian teaching ever since. Jesus induced an *apocalyptic anxiety* in his followers: "For in those days before the Flood people were eating, drinking, taking wives, taking husbands, right up to the day Noah went into the ark, and they suspected nothing till the Flood came and swept all away."[20]

Prophesying a new cosmic disaster, Jesus warned that those who were living the normal life of eating and drinking, marriage and family, were the foolhardy unwary who would be swept away. He variously predicted the apocalypse as the destruction of Jerusalem, the end of the world, the coming of the Day of Judgment, or the arrival of the Kingdom of God. In any case, the End was imminent. Everyone should forsake his social relatedness and save his own soul.

In the Gospel of Matthew, Jesus evoked the cosmic catastrophe of the Great Flood. In the Gospel of Luke he added Sodom and Gomorrah. Now, the Great Flood and Sodom and Gomorrah haunted the ancient Jewish mind with the same symbolism of universal doom that Hiroshima and Nagasaki hold for the modern mind.

From the religious perspective, it can be argued that Jesus recalled the Great Flood and Sodom and Gomorrah on the one hand, and predicted the destruction of Jerusalem and the end of the world on the other, only in order to concentrate attention on matters of spiritual significance. From the psychological perspective, however, such rhetoric of past destruction and imminent doom serves to panic the listeners, to sever them from the real, here-and-now, social world and to induce in them the religious neurosis that I call the apocalyptic anxiety.[21]

The human mind realizes how small and precarious is our daily contentment, our eating and drinking, our marriages, families, and children. Sickness, war, or natural disaster could sweep away at any moment everything we treasure. The seeds of anxiety are warm and wet, ready to sprout. The strategy of religious teachers has always been to pour water upon those seeds and to cultivate that anxiety. The power of religion over the mind is based upon human insecurity, one aspect of which is proneness to the apocalyptic anxiety.

"Save your soul! Save yourself!" was the implicit message in all the apocalyptic rhetoric of Jesus. The Establishment seemed secure, he taught, but it would be swept away in a great turnabout. The daily family life of men seemed the norm, but in the coming cataclysm it would be swept away like so much flotsam in the Great Flood, like so many smoldering cinders over Sodom and Gomorrah.

Having induced the apocalyptic anxiety, Jesus then proceeded to teach overt antifamilial doctrine: "Do you suppose that I am here to bring peace on earth? No, I tell you, but rather division. For from now on a household of five will be divided: three against two and two against three; the father divided against the son, son against father, mother against daughter, daughter against mother, mother-in-law against daughter-in-law, daughter-in-law against mother-in-law."[22]

Jesus took a thorough inventory of family relatedness and re-interpreted it as family estrangement. The import was this: "Do not cling to the family for support. The family is nothing but a pack of adversaries. Save your own soul! Save yourself!"

The psychological roots of that antifamilial stance were in Jesus' estrangement from his own family. During his mission that estrangement was at its most acute. His relatives were trying to *take charge of him*. Jesus retaliated by an extreme statement of antifamilialism.

Jesus had to teach estrangement to his disciples, in order to sever their allegiance from their families and draw total loyalty to himself. Of course antifamilial doctrine is socially subversive, too, subversive to values. Jesus was a values revolutionary. His mission was to subvert values.

The main characteristic of family loyalty is that it is an organic loyalty that tolerates dogmatic differences. Family relatedness lasts a lifetime, through all those changing circumstances of other allegiances or involvements. Children must rebel against their parents, it is true, but they later realize that their rebellion was a merely episodic necessity in their adolescent assertion of independence. Through all internal tension or external pressure, the family members are always trying to come back to one another, to stay together in the only enduring relatedness that human beings have. Any dogmatic differences are subversive to family. Ideology is the enemy of blood. The total abandonment of family merely in the name of an ideology —that is nothing less than revolutionary fanaticism.

In normal times such ideological hostility to family would have repelled listeners; but in a climate of messianic expectations, imminent cataclysm, and apocalyptic anxiety, the disintegration of the family would be a merely expected symptom of the End-time. The apocalypse would necessarily be preceded by the familial strife of "a man against his father, a daughter against her mother, a daughter-in-law against her mother-in-law."[23]

It was because he could tolerate no divided loyalties that Jesus set the family against itself. Recognizing that the gospel Jesus frequently presented either-or ultimatums to his followers, we may conclude that the uncompromising antifamilialism attributed to Jesus is compatible with his character and his methods.

Even so, we pause once again to ask whether the familial strife of the early Christians might not have been retrojected to the time of Jesus and his first Twelve. As the beatnik nonconformists, the counterculture, of their day, the early Christians must have suffered lack of understanding and support from their families. There must have been many instances of son-against-father, daughter-against-mother, and so on, in the families of the early Christians. Putting prophecies of family strife into the mouth of Jesus would have been an emotional anaesthetic to his followers, who themselves suffered from family estrangement. Many an early Christian must have had parents who wanted to *take charge of him.* He would have been reassured if he believed that his "insane" estrangement had been imposed by the Master himself.

The problems of textual tampering and retrojection of later experience run throughout the gospels. In our study of values we have no choice but to take the text as it is, keeping in mind that it is the fictional Jesus that we are describing, not the historical Jesus. According to the gospel texts, the idyllic trio of the Holy Family is a fantasy. Jesus was deeply estranged from his family, and he taught his followers to be estranged from theirs.

In assessing the familial relationship of the devils, Jesus observed that "no household divided against itself can stand."[24] Despite recognizing that truism, Jesus proclaimed that he had come to divide many a household against itself. In other words, his intentions were explicitly antifamilial.

That Jesus' own personal experience was at the root of his doctrine can be demonstrated by the patterns of consistency that run throughout his teaching. We find in his antifamilialism, for example, the very same characteristics that we detected in his alienation. Those characteristics are the either-or ultimatum, the them-and-us stance, the carrot-and-stick of promises and threats, and the link between ego and alienation.

"If any man comes to me without hating his father, mother, wife, children, brothers, sisters, yes and his own life too, he cannot be my disciple."[25] There we have the either-or ultimatum: the disciple had to choose between his family or Jesus, one or the other, because Jesus tolerated no divided loyalties. ("He who is not with me is against me.")

"A man's enemies will be those of his own household."[26] There, in plain words, is the them-and-us stance once again. Jesus joined the family to the Pharisees in the category of *them,* the enemies; and he joined the apostles, now estranged from their families, to himself as the *us.* The household, that circle concentric with the Establishment, but closer to the person, was an even greater obstacle to the values revolution, because its emotional hold upon the individual was stronger. As it was to overthrow the Establishment, so the brotherhood of the alienated elect was to supplant the family. Meanwhile, the family stood with the Pharisees, on the other side of the lines of demarcation, in a them-and-us confrontation.

By insisting upon the either-or ultimatum and inculcating the them-and-us stance, Jesus induced his disciples to desert their wives and abandon their families, in order to join the new brotherhood of the alienated elect. What magnetism Jesus must have had, to get normal men to take such a step!

The apostles themselves must have been nagged by guilty second thoughts at such abandonment of their wives and children. "What about us?" Peter asked Jesus. "We have left everything and followed you. What are we to have, then?"[27]

It was not enough for Jesus to separate his apostles from their families. He also had to keep them with him, to reassure them that what they had done, which, by conventional social standards, was an irresponsible act, was fully justified by the importance of the mission they had been called to. In order to keep the apostles bound to him, Jesus resorted to the carrot-and-stick of promises and threats.

Jesus answered Peter's question like this: "Everyone who has left houses, brothers, sisters, father, mother, children or land for the sake of my name will be repaid a hundred times over, and also inherit eternal life."[28] For those who had abandoned their families to follow him there was to be a sublime compensation. Nothing less than *eternal life* would be their reward.

That was the inducement, the promise. To complement it, Jesus issued a caution, a threat: "You will be betrayed even by parents and brothers, relations and friends; and some of you will be put to death."[29] So, just as loyalty to Jesus would be rewarded with eternal life, any relapsed loyalty to family would be punished by treacherous betrayal and death.

It seems incomprehensible to us how normal men could be led into the antisocial act of abandonment of family by such a line of explanation and justification. We keep waiting for the apostles to come to their senses and go home, to give up the fishing for men and return to the fishing for food for their families.

We moderns are less enthusiastic, more analytical, in our judgments and choices. The Palestine of Jesus' time was a seething ideological cauldron. Under subjection to the Romans, frustrated in all their political and religious pretensions, the Jews were prone to outbreaks of the mass hysteria of Zealotry and messianism. They were very susceptible to the social neurosis of apocalyptic anxiety. It is in the worst of times that religion runs roughshod over the mind. In the most desperate circumstances men commit the most desperate acts. And doesn't the salvation of one's soul justify any act, no matter how repugnant to conventional values?

The ego of Jesus demanded everything of his apostles' loyalty to him, including their abandonment of all other loyalties: "Anyone who prefers father or mother to me is not worthy of me. Anyone who prefers son or daughter to me is not worthy of me."[30] The ego cannot stand competitors for love and loyalty. In order to be *worthy* of Jesus, the apostles had to forsake any other love and loyalty.

Ego does not take into account the needs and feelings of others. The ego is unfeeling in its demands. "Another man, one of his disciples, said to him, 'Sir, let me go and bury my father first.' But Jesus replied, 'Follow me, and leave the dead to bury their dead.' "[31] We might regard this as a cruel, selfish retort to the willing, but griefstricken, disciple; but the point Jesus was making was that the family are the *dead.* The true disciple was the one who closed his mind to any family loyalty, to any family responsibility, both immediately and forever.

"Brother will betray brother to death, and the father his child; children will rise against their parents and have them put to death. You will be hated by all men on account of my name."[32] In the sequence of those two appalling sentences the circle of estrangement from family ripples out to the wider circle of alienation from society. Estrangement precedes alienation and is its prerequisite. Betrayal and hatred are the tests of fire of the soul's commitment to the salvation of itself. The End-time is imminent. Saving one's soul is the only preoccupation, the righteous monomania, against which any other concerns or involvements must be renounced and rejected.

In Jesus' various pronouncements on family, just as in his pronouncements on society, we detect those consistent patterns of psychological motifs: the either-or ultimatum, the them-and-us stance, the coupled promises and threats, the ego, and the profound alienation against all the concentric circles around oneself.

Such extreme antitheses, such stark confrontations, are shocking to our more moderate, our more philosophical, temperaments. Religion is, by its very nature, immoderate, extreme in both its demands and its claims. In that Jesus was a religious leader and not a philosopher, he preached the extremes against any moderation.

Jesus was a values revolutionary. Such men always show a shocking ruthlessness and a disregard for the human consequences of their teachings and disciplines. Just as a political revolution is generally followed by reprisals, a purge, even mass murder of adversaries, so a values revolution involves a kind of slaughter and massacre of conventional values. Jesus warned that he had come not to bring peace, but a sword.[33] So we should not be surprised at his ruthlessness in hacking his way through the treasured values of his society. He was not squeamish about any human consequences or casualties.

Traditional commentators have shown a remarkable blindness to the ruthlessness of Jesus' directives and disciplines. The stereotypical image of Jesus as the meek and humble preacher who was made to suffer and die for no real reason is at variance with the texts. If we but read the gospels without preconceptions, if we experience the effects of Jesus' ideas and actions upon his society, we perceive what a truly dangerous subversive Jesus of Nazareth must have been. His fate was not an inexplicable tragedy. It was a premeditated inevitability. Jesus was not a harmless lover. He was the most dangerous threat that any society can face, namely, the values revolutionary.

Once he had secured the transfer of his apostles' loyalties from their natural families to their new ideological family, the brotherhood of the alienated elect, Jesus had to face the same problems that any family faces. One of those problems was the economic one. How could the ideological family support itself?

The basic premise of Jesus' doctrine on economics was that "you cannot be the slave both of God and of money."[34] Very typical of Jesus' thinking, that premise was another either-or. Had Jesus taught in Athens, one of his listeners would certainly have responded with, "Why a slave of either? Why a slave at all?" The discussion would have then gone forward on lines of reasoned moderation. But Jesus taught in Palestine, to the Jews, whose minds were inclined to religious fanaticism, not to philosophical moderation. The religious mind may question authority and legitimacy, but it very rarely challenges reasoning. That is why a series of unchallenged either-or alternatives can lead on to ideological positions of extremism.

Jesus forced upon his apostles the choice between God and money. Then he ordered them to "provide yourselves with no gold or silver, nor even with a few coppers for your purses . . . for the workman deserves his keep."[35] Jesus told the members of his ideological family that they must acquire nothing. Like all workmen, they would somehow earn their keep; but they must subject themselves to the discipline of moneyless poverty.

The communal economic discipline that Jesus imposed upon his apostles was less severe than the self-discipline of John the Baptist, whose food was locusts and wild honey, whose clothing was a camel-hair shirt, whose shelter was the open desert.[36] When you socialize the prophetic vocation, you must necessarily settle for a less stringent discipline. Simple poverty would be enough to detach the apostles from both movable and fixed property, so that they could take up the peripatetic life without any ties to things, places, or people.

Jesus insisted upon the discipline of poverty with another typical ultimatum: "None of you can be my disciple unless he gives up all his possessions."[37] He put the apostles' love of their possessions against love of himself and forced them to choose. One disciple, who was rich, chose his possessions, but the Twelve saw that as the lesser choice and so chose Jesus.[38]

Jesus very plainly demanded poverty as a necessary discipline for his followers. The wealthy Christian Establishment today—whether it is the artistic splendor of the Vatican, the multimillion-dollar affluence of the TV evangelists, the Sunday-suit complacency of a suburban congregation, or the brick Baptist church among the wood shacks of Kentucky—today's Christian Establishment stands wholly outside Christian discipline. There are plenty of moneychangers for Jesus to drive from the Temple today.[39]

Back in the beginning, Jesus made an unqualified command of poverty. Acquire nothing, is what Jesus insisted. Acquire nothing, and keep nothing, too: "Give to anyone who asks."[40]

Christian charity complemented Christian poverty. The hand should not grab, nor should it even grasp. By accumulating no more wealth and by unburdening themselves of all that they had, the apostles would live openhanded lives. Each would endure the same privation, and the community as a whole would be held together by the democratic equality that comes from being reduced to nothing.

"Give to anyone who asks" was a kind of economic pacifism. The apostles were to yield to anybody both their possessions and themselves. There is a consistency and correspondence in the disciplines of poverty, charity, and pacifism: "Give up, give, and give in."

Jesus and his apostles lived a life of egalitarian communism. The embarrassed Church Establishment has since tried to deny that.[41] Against the Church the gospels clearly describe the communistic communal life of Jesus and his apostles.

That the apostles recognized the personal disciplines of poverty and charity and the communal discipline of communism as permanently necessary is evident from their continuation of those disciplines after the death of Jesus. The practices of the early Christians, as we know them in the Acts of the Apostles, were not organizational innovations. They were merely obedient executions of the Master's directives. Acts reports that "the faithful all lived together and owned everything in common; they sold their goods and possessions and shared out the proceeds among themselves according to what each one needed."[42]

"From each according to his ability, to each according to his need" is a modern socialist slogan very much in harmony with the thinking and practices of Jesus, his disciples, and the early Christian community.

For us in the late twentieth century communism is as much a contemporary, as it is an antiquarian, subject. Because we have experienced the great communist movements of our own century, we are in a better historical position to judge the rationale for communism among the followers of Jesus.

Marxist theory sets up an irreconcilable conflict between the oppressed proletariat and the oppressing capitalists. Through a historical process of inevitable certainty the proletariat will overthrow the capitalists and establish a utopian community of equality, brotherhood, and social harmony.

Jesus was led to communism by the similar conceptions of his own thought. He, too, set up a class conflict, in his case between the "little ones" (the alienated elect) and the "scribes and Pharisees" (the Establishment), counterparts in religious terms to the "proletariat" and "capitalists" of Marx. We have seen from his apocalyptic rhetoric that Jesus himself believed in an inevitable historical process, in which there would be a great turnabout, analogous to the Marxist proletarian revolution. Jesus carried historical inevitability into the realm of metaphysics by references to the coming Kingdom of God, the Day of Judgment, and cosmic apocalypse. Despite the difference in the terms they used, the general line of Jesus' and Marx's thinking on communism are similar.

Marx presented communism in economic terms, Jesus in religious terms. Marxism, as has often been recognized, has its religiosity. So, too, religion has its economics.

Both Marxist Communism and Christian communism are rooted in alienation against society and its status quo. In both ideologies we detect the envy of, and the grudge against, the Establishment. Both set the alienated class into subversive activity against the Establishment. Both are ideologies of longed-for cataclysm.

Marx and Jesus each thought in Jewish apocalyptic categories. In the Jewish world view the alienated oppressed—whether "chosen people," the "elect," or the "proletariat"—are forever struggling to overthrow a corrupt Establishment of overlords—be they the Romans, scribes and Pharisees, or capitalists—and effect a cataclysmic turnabout, whether the messianic Kingdom of God, the Day of Judgment, or the victory of the proletarian revolution.

Marx proceeded from an economic, Jesus from a religious, grudge. But how is it that communism in both cases serves alienation and leads to the longed-for turnabout of historical inevitability?

Jesus set up the false antithesis of God-or-money; but it would be a poor god indeed who was threatened by money. As much as moralists of all kinds have attacked money as the currency of greed, in practice most men try to accumulate property not only for themselves and for their lifetimes, but for the well-being of their families, both during and after their lifetimes. Most property has been not personal but familial. An attack upon property, then, is an attack upon the family.[43]

As we have seen during this century, and especially recently, modern Communism is an economic failure. Its most profound effects have been social, which, in most intimate terms, means familial. That communism is inherently subversive to the family and its values is evident from the history of China since 1939. Chinese Communism swept away several millennia of traditional family values in a terrible social cataclysm.

In modern Communism, the family exists merely to serve the economy, rather than the other way around. To Jesus the family was the source of supply for recruits to the values revolution. Family would serve that revolution, not the revolution serve the family. Apostolic communism detached the recruits from their families. Jesus' communism was the economics of antifamilialism.

The family has always been the bulwark of society. If you disrupt the family, you can subvert the society. Jesus took the apostles away from their families for the same reason that the Chinese Communists took children away from their parents, namely, to secure a total, a totalitarian, loyalty to ideology.

The family is inherently conservative. The success of any revolution depends upon overcoming the conservative resistance of family values. It is only by separating the individual, heart-and-soul, from family loyalty that the revolution can be accomplished.

When Jesus inducted the apostles into his revolutionary army, he imposed the threefold economic discipline of poverty, charity, and communism. What they had to give up was clear to the apostles, but what would they gain? " 'What about us?' he said to him. 'We have left everything and followed you. What are we to have, then?' "[44] Although those words were Peter's, each apostle must have asked that question.

Whenever Jesus took something away from his disciples, he promised them something in compensation. As for renunciation of family, so, too, for renunciation of property, Jesus laid up hundredfold credits against the debits. He promised a future, but a more spiritual, wealth to compensate for the immediate, material wealth that the apostles had to give up: "Sell all that you own and distribute the money to the poor, and you will have treasure in heaven; then come, follow me."[45]

Jewish society valued wealth as a sign of divine favor. As part of his subversive program, Jesus repudiated that valuation. It was to the *poor,* not to the well-to-do, that the Kingdom of Heaven belonged.[46] It would be as difficult for the rich man to get into heaven as for the camel to get through the eye of a needle.[47] Although Jesus backed off a bit by admitting that God could thread the needle with a camel, that is, admit the rich to heaven, the vivid simile made its impression upon the apostles and impelled them to their choice.

To his revolutionary brotherhood of the alienated elect, Jesus gave a psychological strategy against the Establishment. That was the discipline of pacifism. He gave the brotherhood its economics. That was the discipline of communism. For the renunciation and sacrifice in each of those disciplines Jesus promised compensatory rewards.

Both the psychology and economics of alienation were fully accepted by the apostles. They became pacifists and communists. But there was yet another problem that Jesus had to face, one that would require an even more severe self-discipline, one that would want even greater rewards. That problem was the very physiology of alienation.

The Eunuch Ideal

W e have tried to understand Jesus in terms of his social relatedness, first to the Establishment, then to his family. We
will pursue that theme in a study of Jesus' relatedness to women,
and to his apostles. As a seeming exception to the general pattern
of Jesus' relatedness, which was adversary-ally, either-or, there was
one group, namely, the children in his life. To them Jesus felt a
sympathetic relatedness: "Let the little children come to me, and do
not stop them; for it is to such as these that the kingdom of God
belongs."[1]

It is an attractive trait in Jesus' character that he showed such
compassion toward children. However, we have let our natural sentimentality toward children and our stereotypical image of Jesus as
the harmless lover blind us to the recognition that, even when Jesus
seemed to be merely relaxing with children, he was, in fact, waging
his propaganda campaign against the Establishment. "I bless you,
Father, Lord of heaven and of earth, for hiding these things from
the learned and the clever and revealing them to mere children."[2]

Against *the learned and the clever,* that is, the scribes and Pharisees, Jesus put forward the model of the child as a moral ideal. It
was to children that the Kingdom of Heaven belonged. Jesus told
his apostles to imitate children: "Unless you change and become like
little children you will never enter the Kingdom of Heaven."[3]

A patriarchal society values age and experience. Jesus subverted
that valuation by holding up the model of youth and naiveté. The
Jews valued learning and wisdom. Jesus put forward the ideal of
ignorance and simplicity. Mere children stood higher in the Kingdom
of Heaven than did the learned sages of the Establishment.

What Jesus taught might be termed *infantilism as a moral ideal.*

As an antithesis to the prevailing Jewish ideal, that of age and learning in the Law, Jesus' model and ideal had an obviously subversive intent.

Viewed from the psychological perspective, such infantilism is an inversion of the traditional values structure, for it is the task of childhood to learn values, not to model them. Infantilism as a moral ideal is an antidevelopmental notion. In defense of Jesus' model and ideal the distinction has been made between the *childish* and the *childlike.* That semantic nicety does not answer the objection. Jesus urged his disciples to regress from their maturity, their adulthood, back to infantilism. Viewed again in psychological terms, the concept is one of regression.

We may surmise that the stress of his battles with the Establishment, in those very adult realms of religion and politics, must have induced Jesus to look back upon childhood, including his own, as an innocence left behind. If only everyone were simple and honest and pure of heart, if everyone were like children, there would be no need for a cataclysmic values revolution. Ignorance would be bliss, compared to the wrongheaded learning, the hypocrisy, the presumptuousness, the arrogance of the scribes and Pharisees.

As every parent knows, children are neither simple nor honest nor pure of heart. By setting up children as models, Jesus succumbed to sentimentality, to nostalgia, to romanticism.[4]

Jesus' notion of infantilism as a moral ideal was a sigh out of his heart; it was not sound thinking from his mind. However much we love and cherish children, whatever their behavior, we cannot in common sense nor in healthy maturity look to them to guide us on moral and ethical issues, to set the standard for adult behavior. Neither *childish* nor *childlike* is an appropriate ideal for an adult. Our psychological task is to grow up and to continue to grow. Unless we, too, want to succumb to the uncritical swoon of sentimentality, nostalgia, and romanticism, we must recognize that infantilism in thought or behavior is nothing but relapse and regression.

Infantilism as a moral ideal makes no more religious sense than it does psychological sense. Children must develop their moral sensitivity, just as they must develop all their other human faculties. That children often startle adults with their candor only indicates their social inexperience, not their moral superiority. Children are not inherently honest; they lie for their own purposes just as any adult does. The romantic stereotype of the child as an innocent does not stand up to criticism.

Morality is not an inherent trait that erodes as we grow up. Morality is a germ of sensitivity and discipline that we must cultivate over many years of effort. The Jewish ideal of the rabbi-sage is superior, both psychologically and religiously, to Jesus' romantic model of the child.

In the gospels no one objected to Jesus' valuation of infantilism as a moral ideal. The listeners might have been surprised at it, but they ventured no rebuttals. Perhaps they took it as just tender sentiment on Jesus' part. Once again we observe that the intellectual atmosphere in the gospels is religious and authoritarian; it is not philosophical and rational. When the Master had just put the child on his own lap, what disciple would dare to put the child in his place?

Romantic sentimentality about children, one that goes to the extreme of asserting the child as a moral model, presupposes the complete innocence of the child. Now, the distinction between the *innocence* of childhood and the *corruption* of adulthood is based on a judgment about that major difference distinguishing the child from the adult—sexual awareness.

The romantic, unlike the modern psychologist, has seen the child as nonsexual. The romantic ideal of childhood, we must recognize, is based upon the assumption of the sexlessness of the child. Of course children are either of one sex or the other, but in the romantic image, children's minds and behavior are supposed to be utterly ignorant and innocent of their own sexuality.

Jesus' standard of infantilism as a moral ideal was multifaceted in its subversiveness. Politically, the child was set up as antitype to the Establishment model of the elder-sage. Religiously, the ideal of infantilism was antithesis to the Old Testament ideal of wisdom. Psychologically, the infantilism ideal meant regression from normal healthy maturity. Furthermore, in teaching infantilism as a moral ideal, Jesus was promoting another, although only implicit, ideal. That was the ideal of sexlessness.

The gospels lack that interplay of assertion and counterargument which makes the Greek philosophical dialogues so stimulating. Jesus taught men what to believe; he did not challenge them to think for themselves. Unlike Socrates, who drew out the values of his listeners, Jesus imposed his own values upon his listeners. However, there are in the gospels a few fascinating exchanges between Jesus and his critics, usually members of the Establishment. There are revelations in those situations where Jesus responded to challenges, rather than just delivering his monologues of parables and pronouncements. The episodes of verbal sparring with the members of the Establishment are valuable, precious instances of a disputation that is almost Greek and philosophical. Jesus' innermost thinking came out in spontaneous response to challenges to him.

There was an archconservative Jewish party called the Sadducees. The Sadducees did not subscribe to doctrines that had developed late in the history of their religion. They did not accept the notion of the resurrection of the dead, for example. When Jesus taught that heterodox doctrine, the Sadducees put their heads together and challenged him.

Like the Pharisees, the Sadducees concocted a dilemma-question to trap Jesus. Their question was this: If a woman married and was widowed, again and again, so that she had seven husbands during her lifetime, to which one would she be married at the time of the so-called resurrection of the dead?

We might have expected Jesus to answer that, since all the marriages were valid, she remained married (spiritually, at least) to all seven of her husbands. What God had joined together, no matter how many times, death could not put asunder. That answer, a defense of the inviolability of the marriage covenant, would have satisfied the legalistic Jewish mind. Instead of such a solution to the dilemma-question, however, Jesus explained away marriage itself! "At the resurrection men and women do not marry; no, they are like the angels in heaven."[5] In other words, marriage is not eternal. In heaven we cease being husbands and wives and become *angels* instead.

Matthew and Mark give that brief answer, but Luke expands upon it: "The children of this world take wives and husbands, but those who are judged worthy of a place in the other world and in the resurrection from the dead do not marry because they can no longer die, for they are the same as the angels, and being children of the resurrection they are sons of God."[6]

People commonly marry, Jesus said, but "those who are judged worthy of a place in the other world . . . do not marry." Jesus identified spirituality with celibacy. The *worthy* do not marry, he said, "because they can no longer die." So Jesus counterposed spirituality and celibacy on the one hand and marriage and death on the other. He characterized the worthy as *angels* and *children,* that is, the nonphysical and the sexless.

In his answer to the Sadducees' dilemma-question, Jesus asserted these principles. Better no marriage than any marriage, better angels and children than husbands and wives. That must have bewildered the Sadducees. Their question, after all, was about the resurrection of the dead, not about marriage. How much more than they had asked for came out so unexpectedly in Jesus' answer. And what a revelation of values there was in his off-the-point response![7]

If adult sexuality is presumed to be a taint upon childhood sexual innocence, then marriage, which is an institution of adult sexuality, must be some kind of tainted relatedness that we acquire during life, but which we must shed in order to return to the purity of angels and children, that pristine innocence that enables us to be worthy of admission into the Kingdom of Heaven.

Jesus had a pronounced tendency to deal with human problems by wiping them away with religious jargon. As a self-disciplined ascetic, he showed little sympathy for human need. According to him, sexuality would not be a problem if we all just became sexless children once again. Marriage would not be a problem, because, from the eternal perspective, marriage was merely a temporary earthly expedient that would be sloughed off. And what about divorce? Jesus forbade it completely. When his apostles thought that too severe a prohibition, Jesus agreed with them that it would be better not to be married at all. He then added a statement that must have stunned his disciples:

"There are eunuchs born that way from their mother's womb, there are eunuchs made so by men, and there are eunuchs who have made themselves that way for the sake of the kingdom of heaven. Let anyone accept this who can."[8]

That is an overt statement of the most extreme antisexualism. The answer to the human problems of sex, marriage, and divorce was castration of oneself. Make yourselves into eunuchs for the sake of the Kingdom of Heaven, is what Jesus told his followers. Immediately after that pronouncement, Jesus embraced the children and promised the Kingdom of Heaven to them. Metaphor and model thus combined to get Jesus' message across. He intertwined the infantilism ideal with the eunuch ideal. He set both against sexuality and marriage.[9]

What Jesus said about the problem of divorce is that self-castration, that is, celibacy, was preferable to the risks of marriage. Because marriage itself was a temporary earthly expedient that meant little in the spiritual realm, it would be better to forgo it completely. Heaven would go to the angels, the children, and the eunuchs.

The previous texts are the scriptural origins of the Christian cult of celibacy and virginity, which was to become an essential aspect of Christian self-discipline and *worthiness*. According to the gospels, Jesus' answer to the human problem of sexuality was the *eunuch ideal*.

Nietzsche recognized the element of cruelty toward self in any high religiosity, and there could be no more cruel discipline for the highly religious than adherence to, and practice of, the eunuch ideal. Jesus himself realized the severe difficulty of that discipline: "Let anyone accept this who can," he said. On the other hand, Jesus promised spiritual compensation, the Kingdom of Heaven, for bodily self-denial. If one wanted to be worthy, it was necessary to destroy the sexual for the sake of the spiritual.

Modern psychologists understand how dangerous and unhealthy it is to suppress an instinct. Jesus, however, was not a counselor but a values revolutionary. He promoted a hypertrophied religious consciousness, in comparison to which all other human concerns would atrophy in consequence. The metaphor he used in his answer to the problem of sex was castration. His ideal, a highly religious, and so a cruel, ideal was the very eradication of the sexual instinct. Although Jesus reacted against the cruel domination of one man by another, he apparently felt no such repugnance toward the throttling of oneself.

Jesus' antinatural and antisexual bias expressed the typical ascetic prejudice of the mind against the body. The eunuch ideal also served the particular values revolution that Jesus was trying to put into effect. Sexual attraction divides loyalties. As we have discovered, Jesus could not tolerate divided loyalties. He had required his apostles to desert their wives and abandon their families. He had impelled them to that drastic renunciation by inducing the apocalyptic anxiety. To bind his apostles even closer to himself, Jesus now told them that abstinence, like absence, was for the good of their souls.

Antisexual and antimarital pronouncements were part of the alienation and antifamilialism in Jesus' values program.

Every added discipline would give the brotherhood of the alienated elect a more exalted sense of its status. Pacifism, poverty, and now celibacy—that threefold discipline would be the strength of the apostolic brotherhood, as it later proved to be the strength of the early Christian community.

Despite Jesus' qualifier, "Let anyone accept this who can,"[10] the Church has since taught the celibacy discipline as a comprehensive moral ideal, that is, "Everyone should accept this." What Jesus imposed as narrow discipline the Church proclaimed as universal doctrine. As it was to the meek and to the poor, so it was to the eunuch that the Kingdom of Heaven belonged.

A literary religion like Christianity demands full adherence to its texts. According to those texts, any person who does not accept and live in accordance with the threefold discipline of pacifism, poverty, and celibacy cannot claim to be a fully committed disciple of Jesus. There was to be a slacking off, even a hypocrisy, of course. The Catholic Church actually became warlike, rich, and profligate. In the sixteenth century, when a few purists returned to the texts, they recognized the Church's hypocrisy and reacted against it. That return to the texts was the Reformation. And so there came into being some reincarnations of the early Christians, like the Quakers (the pacifists) and the Puritans (the eunuchs).[11]

Some philosophical and religious doctrines are traceable to the physical and psychological peculiarities of the teachers and preachers. Socrates poked his finger into the eye of Greek aesthetic culture, but then Socrates himself was notoriously ugly. Epictetus saw little value in Greek athletics, but then Epictetus was a cripple. The Buddha had a hypersensitivity to suffering, and so he taught a doctrine of compassion. Much of what is presented as objectively valid morality or ethics reflects the quirks of the advocate. Paul, a sexual neurotic, taught phobic antisexualism. Was Jesus' own antisexualism similarly linked to his personal emotional makeup, as much as to his social program as a values revolutionary?

Extremes of doctrine reflect a disproportion in the preacher's own makeup. The undersexed, setting themselves up as model, teach a doctrine of sexlessness. Conversely, the oversexed suffering from bad conscience, like Saint Augustine, take up an antisexual stance in reaction to their earlier sexual extremes. Was Jesus himself undersexed or oversexed?

Because of his teachings on pacifism, passivism, and indiscriminate desexualized love, there arose a stereotypical image of the person of Jesus as an aetherial presence among gross mortals. The artists, particularly, have portrayed Jesus as a sexless wraith of hermaphroditic beauty and feeble physicality, as if he were one of those eunuchs "born that way from their mother's womb."

If we examine the gospel texts, however, we discover that Jesus was not the androgynous wimp that we see in the pious holy pictures. He was no wimp. Even with twelve henchmen behind him, it must have been a scene of sheer physical strength and intimidating power when Jesus took up the whip and slashed his way through the money changers in the Temple. Moreover, Jesus very much enjoyed the company and indulgence of women.

Luke tells the story of Jesus' visit to two sisters named Martha and Mary. Martha set about preparing the meal for her guest, but Mary sat at Jesus' feet and engaged him in intimate conversation. When Martha complained that her sister should help her with the work, Jesus told Martha that Mary had chosen *the better part.* That is a revealing scene of ego and intimacy. Jesus enjoyed contact with women—and not with women in a merely domestic role. He basked in the adulation and indulgence they showed toward him.[12]

An even more revealing episode is the so-called anointing at Bethany. A version of that incident is in all four of the gospels, but there are significant differences in detail.

According to Matthew and Mark, who give similar accounts, while Jesus was in the house of Simon the leper, a woman came in and poured a very expensive aromatic perfume, or ointment, upon his head. The apostles objected, on the grounds that the perfume, a costly commodity, could have been sold and the money distributed to the poor. Jesus answered, in egoistic fashion, that they always had the poor with them and could take care of them at any time, but that he himself would not always be with them. Jesus gave the anointing a funereal significance, namely, that the woman was preparing his body for its burial! Jesus then commended the woman and said that her act had earned an immortality in the remembrance of his followers. Why that should be so is not at all clear.

In Luke, the Simon who hosted Jesus is identified as a Pharisee, rather than as a leper. That puts the episode in a political, rather than a therapeutic, context. About the woman Luke says that she "had a bad name in the town."[13] Luke describes the anointing like this: "She waited behind him at his feet, weeping, and her tears fell on his feet, and she wiped them away with her hair; then she covered his feet with kisses and anointed them with the ointment."[14]

That version of the incident is highly charged with emotionalism and sensuality. Luke characterizes the woman as a slut, but he backs her away from the person of Jesus, as it were. Instead of her massaging Jesus' hair with her hands, as in Matthew and Mark, she wiped Jesus' feet with her hair. She kissed, caressed, and anointed his feet. Mark had identified the ointment as nard, a musky perfume. So the incident was clearly one of sensual indulgence, no matter what other interpretations, such as the funereal one, might be attached to it.

In Luke's version the apostles do not seem to be present. Instead, it was the Pharisee who objected to the anointing, not on behalf of the poor, but on grounds of moral propriety. It was not seemly for a prophet to permit a woman of ill repute to touch and caress him. Once again Jesus justified the woman, but not with the funereal interpretation. Jesus told the Pharisee: "you poured no water over my feet; but she has poured out her tears over my feet and wiped them away with her hair. You gave me no kiss, but she has been covering my feet with kisses ever since I came in. You did not anoint my head with oil, but she has anointed my feet with ointment."[15]

That last sentence indicates that Luke displaced the anointing from Jesus' hair, as in Matthew and Mark, to his feet, a safer distance from Jesus' person. Because he characterizes the woman as having *a bad name,* Luke censors the scene, but at the same time he gives it an even more voluptuous description. It was on the basis of his own need for sensual indulgence that Jesus justified the woman. He concluded his justification by telling Simon that the woman's sins must have been and must be forgiven, because she had shown *great love.* Jesus then forgave the woman's sins.

John provides further information by identifying the woman as Mary, the sister of Martha, the same Mary who liked to dote upon Jesus and sit at his feet in intimate conversation. Aside from that specific, John follows the version of Matthew and Mark in the objection on behalf of the poor and in the funereal interpretation, but he follows Luke in the anointing of the feet, rather than the head.[16]

Whatever the variations in the four versions, the episode of the anointing has that exquisite sensuality of harem indulgence that we find in the Arabian Nights. Jesus clearly enjoyed contact with women and their adoring indulgence. Unlike Paul, Jesus had no sexual phobia. And unlike Augustine, he had no bad conscience. Jesus was accused of consorting with prostitutes, but his retort was that he had come to minister to sinners, who needed him, not to the upright and unobjectionable, who did not.

The Establishment could attack Jesus on his legitimacy, his hetero-doxies, and his lax observance of the sabbath; but Jesus' enemies did not attack him on the basis of his personal morality,[17] which was irreproachable. To Simon the Pharisee's objection to Jesus' allowing an immoral woman to touch him, Jesus could maintain that her sensual homage to him was a way of penance that came naturally to her. Only a strong character could permit others to do penance in such a tempting manner. That Jesus was such a character is indicated by the fact that in none of the four versions of the anointing is there even a hint that the woman's adoring indulgence was a temptation to Jesus.

There is no indication of any sexual neurosis in Jesus' makeup. As an ascetic, a master of self-control, Jesus could relish the exquisite sensuality of fasting in the desert on the one hand, and the sensual indulgence of the anointing on the other, at the same time maintaining a detachment from both. Jesus' antisexualism was not a complex; it was a discipline. Jesus demanded much of his followers, but even more of himself. As well as a severe social discipline, he imposed a severe self-discipline.

Suppression of the sexual instinct seemed strategically necessary in Jesus' values program of alienation, antifamilialism, turnabout, and apocalyptic expectation. If you wanted to save your soul, you had to give up everything: job, property, family, marriage, even emotional gratification. All those features of ordinary life were just so much distraction from what really mattered, namely, the salvation of the soul before the imminent apocalypse.

Disciplinary celibacy is a chronic stress upon the human being. A suppressed instinct erupts in a kaleidoscope of disguised expressions. In Jesus' teaching and acts there are some indications of the personal stress caused by the celibacy discipline.

Many of Jesus' parables dealt with seed imagery. There was the seed that fell on good and bad ground, the seed that sprang up and grew spontaneously, and the weeds among the wheat. There were the parables of the mustard seed and of the grain of wheat that had to die in order to spring up and yield its harvest.[18]

In an agrarian, pastoral culture, we would expect similes and metaphors drawn from agricultural economy. However, the imagery of insemination, of spent seeds, of sprouting and growth, or of withering and sterility also comes to bear upon the practice of celibate self-denial. "The sower of good seed is the Son of Man,"[19] said Jesus in a self-identification. Jesus was a sower. The seeds were his values. And so there is a poignance in those parables. Jesus must have wondered whether his potency as a religious teacher would compensate for the self imposed impotence of his celibacy.

The seed imagery in Jesus' teaching reveals something of the stress of celibacy. So does one of his impulsive acts, one that has hitherto remained inexplicable and out of character. That impulsive act was Jesus' cursing of the fig tree.

As he was walking down the road one day, Jesus felt the pangs of hunger. He went up to a fig tree looking for some fruit, but found the tree without any. In anger and frustration he cursed the tree and it withered away.

Jesus' curse of the fig tree seems perverse and inexplicable. The sequel to it provides no illumination. The apostles noticed the withered tree and brought it to Jesus' attention. Jesus told them that his curse showed the power of faith. Faith could move mountains, and if the apostles had faith in their prayers, they would be able to do such a thing as Jesus had done to the fig tree.[20]

Jesus' explanation to the apostles is a non sequitur. There are other such instances in the gospels where the act described and the pronouncement attached to it bear no logical relation to each other. That is evidence of editing and compilation. In the patchwork of the gospels there are many out-of-sequence episodes and illogical juxtapositions.

Mark specifically mentions that "it was not the season for figs."[21] That makes Jesus' curse all the more irrational. His explanation about faith moving mountains was either a coverup of his true feelings at the moment or else a feeble editorial attempt at interpretation.

If we reconstruct the episode, we can imagine what a shock the curse of the fig tree must have been to the apostles. Jesus, who in his healing practiced a benevolent *white magic,* was now performing a *black magic* of a frightening kind. Jesus could kill as well as heal. His black magic in this, the sole recorded instance, was impulsive and irrational; it must have thrown the apostles into a state of superstitious awe. They realized that they had a curse to fear, as well as a blessing to enjoy.

That Jesus' curse of the fig tree was impulsive and irrational is the key to its explanation. Like the seed imagery in his parables, the barren fig tree forced to Jesus' attention the antithesis between fecundity and sterility in nature, and so between fulfillment and self-denial in the human body. Jesus' curse was an outbreak of the feeling of frustration with his *hunger,* that is, with the discipline of celibate self-suppression. A curse upon sterility of all kinds, said the human need in Jesus.

The curse of the fig tree is devoid of religious content. The interpretation about faith moving mountains is a non sequitur, probably an editorial insertion out of some other context.[22] The curse of the fig tree may have a biographical significance. It shows that Jesus suffered from the stress of celibacy.

Jesus made another cry from the heart, one that showed once again a personal frustration with his sexual discipline. While on his way to his death on Calvary, that is, at the time of the most severe physical and emotional stress of his life, Jesus cried out in despair, "Happy are those who are barren, the wombs that have never borne, the breasts that have never suckled!"[23]

The context of that outburst was within his apocalyptic rhetoric on the destruction of Jerusalem and just before his own apocalyptic death on the cross. Jesus had been pronouncing and prophesying doom and destruction throughout his career. Now, in his last hours, he delivered a parting shot out of his own frustration. Those were his last words to the women who had adored and indulged him. The happiest women, he said, were those of ever-empty wombs and ever-dry breasts.[24]

It was out of frustration and despair that Jesus exclaimed, "Happy are those who are barren, the wombs that have never borne, the breasts that have never suckled!" That outburst has since been engraved into the corpus of Christian values as a veritable sterility ideal, the antisexual mate to the eunuch ideal.

The female, just as much as the male, should suppress, even eradicate, her sexual nature. There would be nuns as well as priests. Instead of love and sex, the mutual fulfillment of man and woman, there was to be celibacy and virginity, the mutual estrangement between them.

And so the embalmed mummy of antisexualism was installed in the Christian Church and has remained in residence there ever since. No religion has been more notoriously antisexual than Christianity.

Now, in any cult of the Revered Person, such as Christianity, values have their justification inasmuch as they can be traced to the life, as well as to the teachings, of that Person. In order to justify

Christian antisexual values, to present them as spiritual ideals, the person of Jesus himself had to be thoroughly desexualized. A mythology of sexlessness had to be developed. In the three later gospels, Matthew, Luke, and John, we discover just such a mythologizing of Jesus' origins. His father, Joseph, was neutered; his mother, Mary, conceived while still a virgin. And "born not out of human stock or urge of the flesh,"[25] Jesus was the *Word* become flesh.

We know from the texts of those gospels that even before the end of the first century of the Christian era Jesus' origins had been removed from any association with sexuality. That process of desexualization has continued throughout the subsequent history of the Church, with explanations of, and elaborations upon, the virginal conception and birth. It was held that Mary suffered no labor pains, that she did not lose her virginity during the birth process,[26] and that she steadfastly remained a virgin throughout her remaining life. In order to defend that last claim, the *brothers* and *sisters* of Jesus mentioned in the gospels were demoted to mere cousins.

To the body of Joseph, his father, Jesus had no blood relatedness at all; but he necessarily had a relatedness to the body of his mother. The desexualizing mythology, then, had to be extended even further back, to Mary's own origins. It was only in 1854 that that problem was definitively solved, by the doctrine of the Immaculate Conception.

When the Christians took the Old Testament away from the Jews, they took with it the concept of original sin. Because of Adam's primal sin, his seed was tainted ever after. Original sin was the hereditary taint passed down through all the generations of humankind. That taint threatened the mythological purity of Mary.

According to the doctrine of the Immaculate Conception, Mary was conceived and born free of original sin, the only mortal ever to have been excepted from the taint. And so the last logical link between Jesus and sexuality (the taint) was thus severed by the quite late elaboration of the doctrine of the Immaculate Conception.

As a myth of origin, the Immaculate Conception of Mary was a logical corollary to the virginal conception of Jesus. But from the standpoint of values the notion of a uniquely *pure* conception means that all others have been *impure.* Looking back upon the promulgation of the doctrine, Nietzsche made the appropriate wisecrack that the Immaculate Conception *maculated* (filthied) conception itself. The doctrine was a slander of sexuality.

Jesus was not normally conceived, nor was he normally born.

Instead, he was *incarnated.* Desexualized in his origins, he also had to be desexualized in his life. Although the theologians condescend to point out that Jesus felt human emotions—he wept, for example—and that he could indulge in human playfulness, such as his pun in the naming of Peter as the "rock" on which he would build his Church, they do not admit that he ever had any sexual feelings at all.

Despite the gospel reports that Jesus habitually consorted with prostitutes and that he was besieged by adoring female fans, he was supposedly immune from the vocational wiles of the former and the self-offering of the latter. As we have observed in the episode with Martha and Mary and in the anointing at Bethany, Jesus was actually sensual by nature, but with that refined sensuality of the self-disciplined ascetic. The theologians have preferred the image of the androgynous wimp to the dangers posed by the acceptance of Jesus as a vigorous, normal, male human being.

Firmly grounded in the desexualizing mythology of Jesus' own origins and person, antisexualism could be taught as a comprehensive system of values, as a *morality.*

We have accepted too uncritically the stereotype of ancient pagan society as riddled with sexual immorality of all kinds. If that were true, then Christian sexual morality would have been a wave of human decency that swept over the corruption of the ancient world. It would have been one of the most noble moral advances in the history of the human race.

The stereotype of pagan decadence, however, is based on Christian antipagan propaganda,[27] as well as on the satiric and moralistic writings of the pagan Romans themselves, in short, on highly tendentious, and therefore suspect, sources.

Although pagan culture was imbued with an enthusiastic eroticism, the Romans had a highly developed moral sense of family and responsibility. If we go to the evidence of archeology, to funeral inscriptions, for example, we find evidence of a wholesome normality and familial tenderness that exposes the stereotype of the Roman orgy as a wild caricature. The sexual excesses of certain emperors, as reported by Suetonius, are no more representative of pagan Roman society than the sexual excesses of the early Renaissance popes are representative of Christian society. Our image of ancient pagan society as sexually degenerate is a caricature.

The Christians did not invent responsibility and decency in sexual behavior. Their innovation was that such responsibility and decency were to be achieved by the suppression of the sexual instinct itself. Their sexual morality, rooted in the purported origins, teachings, and person of their Master, was the eunuch ideal and the sterility ideal. That represents a moral advance only if we believe that natural instinct is inherently evil.

With any denial of sex there must be a corresponding denial of death. Mary, by her Immaculate Conception, was free of original sin and the taint of sexuality. So, too, should she be free of death. Mary did not die. Instead, she was assumed into heaven, so that her incorrupt body would not be corrupted by the process of "dust to dust." Leaving earth behind, her body rose up into the spiritual aether. As Mary's Immaculate Conception was analogous to Jesus' virginal conception, so her Assumption was analogous to his Resurrection and Ascension. Both Jesus and his mother were fully dissociated from sex and death.[28]

Paradoxically, with the denial of sex, there is a morbid attraction to death. It is death and only death that provides liberation from all sexual feeling and temptation. Christian antisexualism led straight into a necrophilic ideal. The Christians shunned the allure of a naked Venus, only to become fixated upon the idol of the god in his death throes on the cross. The Christians succumbed very early to catacomb sensuality, an unwholesome necrophilic longing.[29] That longing expressed itself in the ascetic ideal.

Asceticism is the living out of the discipline of antisexualism. From the deserts of Egypt and Palestine, the ascetic movement spread throughout the Mediterranean basin during the first centuries of Christianity. It was to become a characteristic feature of Christian society during the medieval millennium, first in its individual expression in the anchorite and hermit, and later in its institutional setting in the monastery and convent.

Christian antisexualism acquired its mythology, its morality, and its private and social discipline. It also acquired its elite. Because Jesus had taken on celibacy for himself and imposed it upon his apostles, it followed that those who imitated that example would live higher Christian lives than those who were not able or willing to do so. In the hierarchy of antisexualism the celibate are the elite class, the married a kind of spiritual middle class, and the lay single the plebeians.

The social reorganization of ancient society according to the values of antisexualism effected a cataclysmic revolution. The family, the bulwark of Roman society, was relegated to an inferior status. The most important community in Christian society was not to be the family, the kinship of blood, the organic group of the sexually related; it was to be the Church, the kinship of ideology, led by an elite of the sexually self-suppressed. Antifamilialism and antisexualism are different words for the same system of values.

The discipline of ascetic celibacy bound together first the apostolic brotherhood, then the elite class of the Church. In the Church the values of antisexualism were to be fully institutionalized. Antisexual doctrine would be promoted and perpetuated by those with a strong stake in it, namely the celibate clergy. The elite taught their own values, which were those of the eunuch ideal. Celibacy, which Jesus had taken on as a necessary strategic discipline for himself and his cadre of revolutionary shock troops, was extended by the Church, the dominant social organization, into an all-encompassing human ideal. The discipline for the few was enshrined as the ideal for the many.

Full support for that valuation could be found in the inspired texts of the gospels. Christian antisexualism was from the Master himself. As long as the Church maintained its dominant social position, the values of antisexualism permeated society; and as long as the gospel texts are held as divinely inspired absolute truth, those values will continue to permeate society.[30]

We moderns, we psychologists, tend to see celibacy according to the French witticism, that is, as the strangest of the sexual perversions. The modern rejection of the values of celibacy has crippled the Catholic Church. If a religious vocation requires celibacy, the modern person will not embrace it. What we crave is normality. We want to be healthy. We want love and marriage.

The eunuch ideal has become a cultural anachronism. The Catholic Church still asserts the values of celibacy and virginity, but there are fewer and fewer people who accept them. It is not that we are less capable of high spirituality. It is only that we are better psychologists. In trying to cure ourselves of self-abuse, we recognize willful celibacy as just another, an even more devious, category of self-abuse.

In exposing and criticizing the eunuch ideal, we might just be beating a dead horse. Celibacy seems to have become a quaint antiquarian subject. We have cured ourselves of it. If only we could cure ourselves of the rest of Christian antisexualism! As long as we associate sexuality with *taint* and *sin* and *guilt,* according to the Christian valuation, we are not cured yet.

Jesus of Nazareth was a values revolutionary. In all the various aspects of his teaching and disciplines we detect a fully interrelated subversive values program. His pacifism was subversive to both the patriarchal domination of the Jews and the martial spirit of the Romans. His communism was subversive to the family, the bulwark of Roman society. His antisexualism was subversive to the erotic Greek culture of the Mediterranean.

The Jews, Romans, and Greeks were all to fall under the assault of Christian values. The civilization of the West was forced to take its vows of poverty, chastity, and pacifism.[31] Christianity was a cultural cataclysm. One of the antivalues precipitating that cataclysm was the eunuch ideal.

Dissonant Themes, Consonant Relations

For the eunuchs "born that way from their mother's womb" and for the eunuchs "made so by men," sexuality is not much of a problem. A privation due to nature in the first case, and a deprivation by means of the knife in the second, have cut off the flow of male sexual drive.

For the eunuchs "who have made themselves that way for the sake of the kingdom of heaven," however, sexuality persists as a problem. Psychical castration does not have the irrevocable permanence of physical castration. The resolve to celibacy is always subject to doubt, to reconsideration, or, in religious terms, to *temptation.*

The discipline of celibacy is not just abstinence from sexual intercourse but, even more, an abstinent frame of mind. Accordingly, there must be abstinence from thoughts as well as from deeds. "Lead us not into temptation" is the fervent prayer of those who practice the celibate self-denial of body and mind.

In those who are committed to the eunuch ideal, any sexual thoughts, no matter how random, present the extreme danger of a relapse to healthy normality. So the celibate must always be on the defensive. Succumbing to the allure of a woman could topple the entire elaborate structure of his ascetic religiosity.

Jesus warned his apostles against doubt, against reconsideration, against temptation. He did so in another severe disciplinary statement: "If a man looks at a woman lustfully, he has already committed adultery with her in his heart."[1]

What is significant about Jesus' warning is the moral equivalence of the thought and the deed. Jesus claimed that lust in the mind was tantamount to adultery in the flesh.[2]

The allure of the body of woman is a counterargument to the

ascetic discipline of celibacy. Women were subversive agents in Jesus'
values revolution. But women could become subversive to the revolution, too, because their allure undermined the discipline of celibacy
and refuted the ideal of the eunuch. So, for Jesus, women were
temptation still.

As we discovered in the episode of the anointing, Jesus himself
could maintain a detachment from that allure; but he must have
had his doubts about his followers. He warned them against woman
in one of his typical extreme formulations. Lust was the wanderlust
that distracted from the celibate resolve; lust led to loss. Therefore,
lustful thought could cause damnation.

"If a man looks at a woman lustfully, he has already committed
adultery with her in his heart." The Christians took that equivaluation
as an oracular principle of sexual morality. What it really was, was
a vocational necessity for the celibates.

Lustful thoughts were second thoughts. Sexual desire was a reconsideration. In order to adhere faithfully to the resolve to celibacy,
the disciple had to permit himself no lustful thoughts, no sexual de-
sires at all. He had to castrate his mind, if not his body, for the
sake of his soul. Refrain, abstain, in every thought, in every moment
—that was the discipline necessary for the maintenance of the eunuch
ideal.

What if the disciple should lapse into a momentary, an impulsive, sexual thought or feeling? What if he did look at a woman
lustfully? "If your right eye should cause you to sin, tear it out and
throw it away,"[3] Jesus ordered in an excess upon an extreme.

Tearing out the eye, or *plucking* it out, as in other translations,
is a patent castration-image. Beneath psychical castration there lurks
the longing for a complete, a physical, castration. If the eye were
plucked out, if the male were fully castrated, then there would be
no more temptation to lust, no more susceptibility to woman.

A dim view through dark glasses is preferable to the blindness
of empty eye sockets. We have no recorded instance of a disciple
blinding himself in obedience to Jesus' order;[4] but that the followers
of Jesus have all taken a dim view of human sexuality, we have
abundant evidence in the New Testament and in subsequent texts
of Christian values.

It is vocationally appropriate for the celibate to cringe at the
sight of woman, to be self-defensive and phobic about *lust,* and to
threaten himself with blindness as a punishment for his second thoughts

about the eunuch ideal. However, what is appropriate for the celibate is not applicable to the rest of us.

In our modern legal thinking, we have abandoned the Jewish equivaluation of the thought and the deed. "There is no such thing as a crime of thought," Clarence Darrow insisted. In our morality, too, we know better. We no longer indulge in that wearying self-flagellation over every random, spontaneous, capricious, thought, image, or impulse that flits through our minds. We understand that *lust* is normal, even if problematic.

Jesus identified lust with adultery, the spontaneous thought with the deliberate deed. He urged a castration of the senses as the method of self-defense against sin. If we apply the test of love, we detect in Christian antisexualism some illogical and unwholesome aspects.

First of all, although we admit that "the thought is father to the deed," we recognize that not every thought is paternal. Our thoughts are random, spontaneous, and capricious. To charge all of them with a heavy load of moral responsibility is absurd. Our fantasies are many; the acting out of them is rare. During adolescence, especially, we are almost constantly preoccupied with sexuality. We attribute that preoccupation to hormones, not to spiritual depravity.

Neither in our legal system nor in our sensible morality do we accept the notion of a *crime of thought.* Deliberate plotting may indeed be criminal in intent, but there is no crime until a deed has been committed. We are culpable for our deeds, but not for our dreams.

Another problem with the Jewish equivaluation of the moral gravity of the bad thought and the evil deed is that of proportion. If random lust is as evil as a specific adultery, then adultery is that much less an evil. Our moral valuations should make distinctions; they should not muddle. By broadly overemphasizing the moral gravity of the lustful thought—which he did to assert a narrow vocational discipline—Jesus inadvertently deemphasized the moral gravity of the sexual misdeed. (And didn't he forgive the convicted adulteress without ado?[5]) If adultery is only as evil as any random lustful thought, then adultery itself is not that bad. Such muddled valuation has been common in Christian morality, as it must be in any system that makes the interior thought the moral equal of the overt deed.

Jesus' prohibition of sexual desire tends to induce unwholesome psychological states. Any thought, any momentary lapse, could lead to damnation; therefore, any moment could be the moment of doom.

The moral mind quavers in a chronic state of apprehension, scrupulosity, and self-induced guilt. The moral sense becomes narcissistic: one's own thoughts, one's own interiority, become more important than others' welfare and the social sphere, which is where ethics and morality properly belong.

Jesus himself, the Master of mastery, could be sensual in his self-denial; but his followers, from Paul on, succumbed to a sexual phobia of the most neurotic kind. It was the psychologization of morality, as in Jesus' prohibition of lust, that set Christian morality on its course of phobic antisexualism. We ourselves do not see in such phobia any high moral value. The sick have made themselves harmless, but that does not mean that we aspire to be sick.

Worst of all, Jesus' warning against lust set up an estrangement, a mutual suspicion, between men and women. The sexes posed spiritual dangers to each other. For too many centuries we have taken the celibate vocational bias, that peculiar antisexualism, as a generally applicable sexual morality. Haven't we finally recognized our mistake? Haven't we had our own second thoughts, our own reconsideration? Don't we realize that the eunuch ideal, far from expressing any high spirituality, is nothing but a vocational bias, a necessary self-discipline, but for the celibates only?

Our inner good sense tells us that man and woman can and should be nurturing partners to each other. The sexes should fulfill one another, in a true human fulfillment; and sexuality, far from being an evil, is actually a blessing. As male and female nurture and nourish each other, so sexuality should nourish us all. This is the paradox of sexuality—it is our most difficult human problem, but it is also our fulfillment.

These, then, are the philosophical and psychological objections to Jesus' prohibition of *lust:* First, we do not hold ourselves culpable for random, spontaneous thoughts. Second, the overvaluation of the bad thought, the sin, necessarily undervalues the evil deed, the crime, to the detriment of our true social responsibilities. Third, the self-surveillance of mind-control induces a variety of unwholesome psychological states. Far from being high spirituality, it is a sickness, a neurosis. Finally, the prohibition of *lust* causes a mutual suspicion and estrangement between man and woman, who, instead of being adversarial to each other, should be mutual fulfillment.[6]

The lustful thought, in Jesus' disciplinary terms, meant an adultery (apostasy) against the celibate resolve and the eunuch ideal. Jesus associated another kind of faithlessness with adultery, namely, divorce.

There are four versions of Jesus' prohibition of divorce in the gospels. Each is different from the other, not only in nuance, but even in essential content. Comparing the four versions of the prohibition of divorce, in their variations and in their contexts, is illuminating. It shows how difficult it is to determine Jesus' actual teaching, when the only record we have is the heavily edited, reworked, and biased compilations of memories and myths, the four gospels.

We accept Mark as the oldest, simplest, shortest, and perhaps the most reliable, of the gospels. So we begin with Mark's version of the prohibition of divorce. Jesus said, "The man who divorces his wife and marries another is guilty of adultery against her. And if a woman divorces her husband and marries another, she is guilty of adultery, too."[7]

According to Mark, it was not the divorce itself, but the remarriage, whether by man or woman, that constituted the adultery. Jesus issued the prohibition in response to a question from the Pharisees; in his answer Jesus directly contradicted the Mosaic Law, which did allow divorce. He justified himself by saying that Moses had permitted divorce only because "you [he meant the Pharisees] were so unteachable."[8]

In Mark, the prohibition of divorce occurs in a context of sexual discipline. It follows the passage about plucking out the eye to prevent sin[9] and precedes the scene with the children, in which Jesus proclaimed infantilism as a moral ideal. So there was a progression of thought: Lust is a danger, marriage is a danger, both presented the danger of adultery; therefore, be like the sexless children.[10]

There are two versions of the divorce prohibition in Matthew. The first is in this formulation: "Everyone who divorces his wife, except for the case of fornication, makes her an adulteress; and anyone who marries a divorced woman commits adultery."[11]

According to that version, it was the mere divorce, not the remarriage, that constituted adultery. An exception, fornication, is introduced.[12] In an interesting lapse of logic, when a man divorces his wife, he does not become an adulterer; instead, he "makes *her* an adulteress"! There, in that little phrase, is evidence of the Jewish patriarchal grudge against woman. Only in the second half of the prohibition does the man commit adultery, by marrying a divorced woman—in other words, by being seduced to it by an *adulteress.*

The first version of the prohibition of divorce in Matthew follows Jesus' disclaimer that he had not come to abolish, but to complete the Law and the Prophets. In a series of revaluations and contradictions of the Law, Jesus repeated the refrain, "They have told you . . . but I tell you. . . ." What he told them was, first, that lustful thoughts were adultery; second, that the eye should be plucked out if it is lustful; and third, that divorce, whether with or without remarriage, was an adultery.[13]

The second version in Matthew is this: "The man who divorces his wife—I am not speaking of fornication—and marries another, is guilty of adultery."[14] Here it is remarriage that constituted the adultery. The context is, as in Mark, Jesus' response to a test question by the Pharisees.[15]

That version must have been included in order to bring the meaning in accord with that of Mark, namely, that it is the remarriage, rather than the mere divorce, that constituted the adultery. The phrase "and marries another" has been added, but the exception of fornication is left in. It seems as if side by side with the attempt to accord with Mark there remained the stubborn heterodoxy of the exception.

The second version of the prohibition of divorce in Matthew directly precedes the proclamation of the eunuch ideal and the scene with the children, the infantilism as a moral ideal. The association of ideas is similar to that in Mark: Marriage is a danger, lust is a danger; therefore, be like the children.[16]

In the Gospel of Luke the prohibition reads: "Everyone who divorces his wife and marries another is guilty of adultery, and the man who marries a woman divorced by her husband commits adultery."[17]

As in the version in Mark and the second one in Matthew, but unlike the first in Matthew, it was the remarriage, not the mere legal act of divorce, that constituted the adultery. No exception for fornication is made in Luke.[18]

The context of the prohibition of divorce in Luke is no context at all. It directly follows this sentence: "It is easier for heaven and earth to disappear than for one little stroke to drop out of the Law."[19] By prohibiting divorce, Jesus was himself knocking more than a "little stroke" out of the Law; he was directly contradicting the Law of Moses. There is no logical sequence of ideas in Luke's version. The prohibition of divorce occurs in a heavily edited passage in which parables and sayings on diverse subjects are strung together.[20]

From the standpoint of moral doctrine, the four variants of Jesus' prohibition of divorce in the gospels present problems of interpretation. Did Jesus forbid the legal act of divorce, or only remarriage after divorce? Did he allow fornication as grounds? The exception occurs only in Matthew, it is true, but that it was no mere textual error is indicated by the fact that it was repeated, insisted upon, in the second version, the one introduced to bring it into accord with Mark.

Now, the Pharisees and all the Jews drew a clear distinction between divorce and adultery. The former was permitted, acceptable, and regulated according to the Mosaic Law, whereas the latter was a sin. What justification did Jesus offer for the revaluation, or, more precisely, the *equivaluation,* that he made?

We might have expected Jesus to advance the argument from compassion, that is, that divorce is harmful to children and their welfare; or the argument from the social good, that divorce is destructive to the family, the basic unit of society. We have discovered that, contrary to the popular stereotype, Jesus in his values revolution showed an *un*compassionate ruthlessness, and even taught explicit antifamilialism. Instead of a humane or social argument, Jesus quoted authoritative scripture: "God made them male and female. This is why a man must leave father and mother, and the two become one body. They are no longer two, therefore, but one body."[21]

On the human problem of divorce Jesus took an authoritarian stance and insisted upon an irrevocable absolute: "What God has united, man must not divide."[22]

The Catholic Church has maintained that it was Jesus himself who instituted the sacrament of matrimony at the wedding feast of Cana. (Quite a feat for a guest, to institute that to which he had been invited!) Jesus was indeed the institutor of the Christian discipline of celibacy; but he named God as the creator of human marriage. It was God who united, and man could not undo what God had done. According to Jesus, marriage was not just a contract of partnership between two human beings; it was a sacrosanct part of the creative act of the deity. The human ring of the marriage bed was raised into the cosmic realm. Worse than a sexual infidelity against the spouse, divorce was covenantal faithlessness against God. Divorce was adultery and apostasy.

Jesus' absolute prohibition of divorce is a severe doctrine, one that takes no account of the human problems in marriage. But moralists have not been concerned with acquiring human understanding; nor did Jesus take into account the human consequences of his doctrines. He assumed the extreme position and insisted upon the most severe discipline. He forced choice with either-or alternatives. He issued ultimatums. And he induced an apocalyptic anxiety with his rhetoric on the imminence of salvation or damnation.

Even his own apostles were shocked at Jesus' dogmatic intransigence on the subject of marriage. They asked him how anyone could put on such a stringent straitjacket. Jesus answered them with the even more stringent straitjacket of the eunuch ideal.[23]

The effect of Jesus' prohibition of divorce was to make marriage a once-and-for-all irrevocable decision, just like the resolve to celibacy. As lust was faithlessness to celibacy, so divorce was faithlessness to marriage. Both lust and divorce were, therefore, *adultery*.

If the celibates, those committed to the eunuch ideal, must suffer the straitjacket of their irrevocable decision, so, too, should the married be outfitted with their own straitjacket, in order to make marriage fearsome, in order to lessen its attractiveness to half-hearted celibates. The prohibition of lust poisons a man's mind against woman. The prohibition of divorce poisons his mind against marriage. But the poisoned mind is not the one best qualified to determine good and evil. Poisoning the mind is a phobic disciplinary self-defense. The absolute prohibitions of lust and divorce express the vocational bias, and provide the vocational justification, of the celibates.

In pursuing our revaluation of the love cult, we now proceed from the dissonant themes—lust, castration of the senses, adultery, and divorce—to some surprisingly consonant relations, namely, those of the gospel Jesus to the women in his life.

After Adam and Eve committed the original sin, for which Adam bore the responsibility and Eve the blame, they covered their nakedness, their shame, with clothing. That their nakedness proved shameful indicates that the Jews associated sexuality with sin from the very first days of their religious mythology. The allure of Eve was the danger to every man. Clothing, the antivisual bias against *idolatry* (a clothing for the eyes), and the celibate ideal of phobic abstinence were defenses against the allure of Eve. Woman is a problem for man. But isn't man also a problem for woman? Jesus certainly was.

Whatever residue of the Jewish patriarchal bias there might have been in his thinking, Jesus had no personal grudge against women; he accepted them on a human basis. He himself might have thought of his relationship to women in terms of its subversiveness to the patriarchal Establishment. However, by redeeming women from the emotional, social, and spiritual strictures of patriarchal society, Jesus aroused gratitude, devotion, love, and even passion from the women in his life.

In our stereotypical image of Jesus we have very much underestimated his profound emotional impact upon those around him. We have tended to envision Jesus standing upon a grassy knoll, with the crowds sitting quietly around him, perhaps taking notes to write gospels from. Contrary to that idyll, everything about Jesus was supercharged with intense passions, whether furious hatred and murderous scheming by the Establishment or idolization by the women.

It was a doctrine of *love* that Jesus supposedly preached. That a cult of love should appeal to the emotionalism of women is not surprising. And that Jesus the liberating lover should draw love to himself is only human nature.

While recognizing Jesus as the Master Healer and Master Prophet, or, better, as a values revolutionary, we can also recognize him as a charismatic charmer. Just how Jesus could cast a spell of charm over women is shown in the intimate episode of the Samaritan woman at the well. That story is told in the Gospel of John.

Now and then Jesus would withdraw from his confrontations with the Establishment, in order to release himself from the tensions and marshal his strength for his next move. On one such occasion of strategic retreat, Jesus happened to pass through Samaria on his way to Galilee. Tired and thirsty under the high-noon sun, he sat down by himself at a well.

When a Samaritan woman came by to draw out some water, Jesus asked her for a drink. The woman was surprised that Jesus, a Jew, would ask a Samaritan, one of a pariah race, for a drink of water. Jesus promised her, somewhat playfully, that he would repay her by giving her *living water* in return.

Misunderstanding the metaphorical allusion, the woman asked Jesus to give her some of that living water that would relieve her once and for all from both thirst and the daily duty of drawing and hauling common water.

At that point in the conversation Jesus must have become conscious of the impropriety of his speaking to a strange woman in such an intimate and informal manner. He told the woman to bring her husband back to the well, so that the teaching on the subject of the living water could continue with due regard for social propriety. When the woman answered, flirtatiously, that she was single, Jesus in turn responded—with the omniscience characteristic of him in the Gospel of John—that even though she had had five husbands, the latest was no husband, but, perhaps, an illicit paramour.

Far from being offended by the implied moral censure of her conduct by Jesus, the woman continued the conversation, but along defensive Samaritan sectarian lines. Jesus retorted that "salvation comes from the Jews,"[24] not the Samaritans; but then he backed off by saying that God wanted "worship in spirit and truth,"[25] irrespective of sectarian differences.

Picking up on Jesus' theme of reconciliation and harmony, the woman then appealed to a common ground between the Samaritans and the Jews—namely, that they both looked forward to the Messiah. Jesus stunned her by telling her that he himself was the Messiah.

The disciples interrupted the intimate tête-à-tête by returning from town. They "were surprised to find him speaking to a woman."[26] The disciples sensed the double impropriety of Jesus' association with a Samaritan and his unchaperoned rendezvous with a strange woman. They offered their Master something to eat (he never did get his drink of water!), but Jesus responded with some metaphors on food, to complement the living water that he had offered to the woman.

Jesus' friendliness, playfulness, charm, and unexpected tolerance had so discomposed the woman that she was swept away by her enthusiasm for the stranger at the well. Embarrassed in her enthusiasm, she abandoned her water jar and ran back to town. The woman so convinced the townspeople that there was a prophet, perhaps even the Messiah himself, in their midst, that they invited Jesus to accept their hospitality for a few days. They, too, then became convinced about Jesus. Woman's enthusiasm was a prelude to religious conversion.

The episode of the Samaritan woman at the well is manifold in its psychological significance. First, it shows Jesus as the fully liberated and liberating values revolutionary. If the Jews and men wouldn't accept his message, Jesus would go to the Samaritans and to women, snubbing both sectarian animosity and social convention. At the same time, he remained the staunch partisan, insisting that salvation came from the Jews. There was that paradoxical combination of alienation and authoritarianism in Jesus' character. Further, Jesus revealed himself as an egoist. He told the woman that he himself was the Messiah. He told her in the simple self-assertiveness of the words, "I am he."[27]

Jesus deliberately bewildered people, whether with parables, as in the synoptic gospels, or, as in John, with mystical metaphors, such as those on living water and food. And Jesus possessed such self-assurance and charm that he could walk into a situation where nothing was to be expected but hostility, and arouse an acceptance and enthusiasm that was highly emotional, even amorous.

Even more than the episode of Martha and Mary or the anointing at Bethany, the intimate encounter of Jesus and the Samaritan woman at the well fully reveals the overwhelming personal charm that Jesus could exert upon the women who came into contact with him.[28]

Just after Luke reports the female homage given Jesus in the anointing episode, he indicates that women were a part of Jesus' regular entourage: "With him went the Twelve, as well as certain women who had been cured of evil spirits and ailments."[29] The women who followed Jesus had been cured by him; their devotion of accompaniment was a loving gratitude for his healing. It is interesting to observe that Jesus generally sent away the men he had cured; he did not permit them to tag along with him.[30] But Jesus apparently enjoyed the company of women and their idolization of him.

In a patriarchal society a good woman is submissive, subservient, and inconspicuous. Among the Jews women did not participate in a prophet's mission. Jesus created a scandal by permitting women to intrude into religion, hitherto an exclusive power base of men. Jesus must have relished the scandalized discomfiture of the Pharisees at the subversive liberties he permitted to women.

The women who went with Jesus "had been cured of evil spirits and ailments." Jesus the Master Healer ministered to them in a psychiatric capacity. He also permitted reformed prostitutes, like the famous stereotype, Mary Magdalene, to become part of his circl .[31] That was an even more outrageous antagonization of the Pharisees and of their sense of social and moral propriety. As we read in Luke's version of the anointing, Simon the Pharisee was appalled at Jesus' allowing one of his women to caress him.

More than just fans of Jesus' person, the women were patrons of his values revolution. They contributed to the apostolic brotherhood "out of their own resources."[32] It was women who provided the first material support of the sect.

Nor were the women mere extras in the cast of the gospel story. They played a prominent role in the climax of that story, in the very events of redemption, and in what was to be the ultimate accomplishment of the values revolution.

As Jesus, convicted and condemned, made his way to Calvary for his execution, Luke writes, "Large numbers of people followed him, and of women too, who mourned and lamented for him."[33] Luke includes in his crucifixion scene a parallel passage: "All his friends stood at a distance; so also did the women who had accompanied him from Galilee, and they saw all this happen."[34]

By the deliberate, repeated inclusion of women in the scenes of Jesus' suffering and death, Luke gives approval to woman's grief: They "mourned and lamented him." He also gives credibility to woman's testimony: "They saw all this happen."

As in the scene of the crucifixion, so, too, in the incident of the empty tomb does Luke interpret the events in terms of woman's grief, of woman's testimony: "When the women returned from the tomb they told all this to the Eleven and to all the others. The women were Mary of Magdala, Joanna, and Mary the mother of James. The other women with them also told the apostles, but this story of theirs seemed pure nonsense, and they [the men] did not believe them."[35]

Like his version of the anointing, so Luke's report on the empty tomb is highly charged with female emotionalism, as if woman's worship had become woman's hysteria. Those who loved Jesus with a woman's passion could not endure the reality of his death and the finality of separation from the man to whom they felt gratitude for their emotional, social, and spiritual redemption—the man who had become the all in their lives.

Luke takes the women as credible witnesses. According to Luke, the men felt slighted that the miracle had been first revealed to the women and not to themselves. The male disciples, perhaps out of jealousy, were skeptical, despite the fact that Jesus had predicted his resurrection from the dead. "Some women from our group have astounded us: they went to the tomb in the early morning, and when they did not find the body, they came back to tell us they had seen a vision of angels who declared he was alive. Some of our friends went to the tomb and found everything exactly as the women had reported, but of him [Jesus] they saw nothing."[36]

With an irony to mock men, Luke makes the disciple say those words to the resurrected Jesus himself! The disciples, the men, did not recognize Jesus even when they spoke to him; their skepticism was a kind of blindness. But the women knew. The women were right. There was more truth in the love and longing of women than in the doubt and skepticism of men.

Peter, the chief apostle himself, went to the tomb, discovered the binding cloths of Jesus' body, but nothing else, then left bewildered.[37] Even he could not draw the conclusion that came so readily to the excited minds of the women.

Had Luke finished his gospel with just the testimony of the women and without the authority of the men's concurrence, the story would have lacked cogency. So Jesus finally appeared to the apostles; he told them to touch him, then he ate some fish to prove that he was no ghost, no mere figment of the women's excited imagination.[38]

In all four gospels it is the women who took the initiative in the report and rumor that Jesus had risen from the dead; they played a primary and active role in the Resurrection event. The women could not endure the death of their beloved Master. What their grief led them to do is left to the reader's speculation.

We wouldn't expect the patriarchal Jews to give much credence to the testimony of women. Much of the religion and culture of the Jews was directed to keeping women in their place. But the world was wider than the patriarchal prejudices of the Jews. Luke was directing himself to that wider world, to the pagan cosmopolitan world. As the pagan gospel, Luke is also the gospel of women.

Throughout his gospel Luke gives prominence to women. He prevents the story of Jesus from becoming a runaway patriarchal tale by introducing female characters to balance the male ones. In the birth of John the Baptist, Elizabeth is as important as Zechariah. In the birth of Jesus, Mary is more important than Joseph. Mary's soliloquy, the Magnificat, is antiphon to Zechariah's prophecy, the Benedictus. The prophetess Anna is allowed her say on the destiny of Jesus after Simeon had made his prophecy. To the male disciples Luke counterpoises an assortment of women: Mary Magdalene, Joanna, Susanna, Martha and her sister Mary, and the unnamed female members of Jesus' regular entourage. Luke is the gospel of women. As such, it proved to be an opening to a historical opportunity.

Unlike the Jews, the Italians and other Mediterranean peoples worshipped female goddesses. Those peoples would not have had a favorable reaction to the cult of Jesus if presented only as in Matthew, the narrowly Jewish, the patriarchal, gospel. Luke bestowed a blessing upon the female principle.[39] It was the Gospel of Luke that made Christianity congenial to the pagan cosmopolitan Mediterranean world.

We wonder whether there could have been any *Roman* Catholic Church without the Gospel of Luke. The veneration of Mary as a virtual mother-goddess and the sentimentalization of infancy in Luke's nativity and childhood stories struck responsive chords in the racial unconscious of the pagan Italians. Luke, the pagan gospel, the gospel of women, proved to be, also, the gospel of Christianity's cultural and political success. When the Romans embraced Christianity, the sect was well on its way to world dominance.

It is to the Gospel of Luke that Christianity owes the balance of its appeal, to both sexes, and to any culture.[40] It is generally believed that Luke wrote under the influence of Paul, the very man who laid out the strategy for taking Jesus away from the Jews and transporting him into the pagan cosmopolitan world. In any case, Luke opened up the Christian sect to acceptance by the pagan cosmopolitan world. Luke made a major contribution to the historical destiny of Christianity.

It was a woman, Mary Magdalene, who was the first person to see Jesus after he had risen from the dead.[41] As she approached him in her ecstatic joy, Jesus warned her, "Do not cling to me."[42]

Jesus may have wanted others' love for him to be spiritual, not emotional, physical, or amorous. But as we understand love, we recognize that much of the love for Jesus was (and is) precisely emotional, physical, even amorous.

Jesus warned Mary Magdalene not to cling to him only because he fully expected her to, she very much wanted to, cling to him. The person of Jesus aroused just such a longing. There are several instances in the gospels of that kind of erotic idolatry in which women wanted to be touched by him, to touch him, to *cling to him.*[43]

As much as the women, so, too, the apostles wanted, in their own way, to cling to him. The paradoxes of the apostles' love for Jesus are the same paradoxes that we observe in the very ideology and in the practice of Christian love:—

Love and Eroticism

Jesus' spiritual sensitivity reacted against the patriarchal domination in his society. One of the patriarchal values that Jesus overturned was the reciprocity of punishment, the "eye for an eye" of Old Testament law. Jesus claimed that he himself had not come to judge but to redeem. He taught that society could be redeemed if men abandoned punishment for a new reciprocity, the reciprocity of charity: "Always treat others as you would like them to treat you."[1]

That directive has been taken as the Golden Rule of Christian behavior and ethics. Such a formula of universal benevolence was not original with Jesus. It was, in fact, a philosophical commonplace; we can find similar formulations in Confucius, Plato, and Seneca. What is significant about the Golden Rule is that it is not an objective ethical standard detached from personal interest. It is, rather, a psychological rationale for ethical behavior, a rationale based precisely upon personal interest.

"Always treat others as you would like them to treat *you*." In other words, try to put yourself in the other person's place and him in yours. Then see if you would like what you are about to do to him. The Golden Rule is an invitation to empathy, to human understanding. It is thoroughly psychological, personal, even egoistic, in its approach to ethics.

It is the paradox of the Golden Rule that ego and self-interest are appealed to as the rationale for disinterested and altruistic behavior. The rights of the ego itself are the determinant of the rights of all other, even conflicting, egos. The Golden Rule is analogous to the idea of the "invisible hand" in economics; that is, the selfish activities of individuals somehow balance one another out, resulting in the common good of all. We know, both from our knowledge of psychology and from experience, that neither the Golden Rule of Christianity nor the invisible hand of capitalism work so well as their proponents have claimed.

Not everyone needs or wants the same thing from everyone else. With so many different needs and wants, there can be no true reciprocity; after all, some people just want to be left alone. Because every ego has a different self-interest, an ethics based upon the sensitivity of a particular ego just cannot magically result in the well-being of a society of diverse egos. What I want is not what everybody else wants or deserves.

The Golden Rule, in its positive formulation, is too simplistic to serve as a rationale for ethical behavior. Moralists, including Christian ones, have preferred a negative formulation of the Golden Rule, as a kind of comprehensive commandment: "Don't do to others what you don't want done to you."

The negative version of the Golden Rule appeals to an empathy of feeling, rather than to an empathy of egos. Instead of identifying with the other person's needs and wants, we should try to feel the other person's hurt. In a world where hurt is everywhere, we should not inflict any more hurt ourselves, lest someone inflict it on us.

The negative version of the Golden Rule is operative when we tell a small child who has just struck another child, "How would you like it if someone did that to *you?* How would *you* feel?"

The negative version of the Golden Rule induces anxiety and apprehension. It controls behavior by threatening punishment. The punishment will not be immediate and intelligible. It will be far off, unexpected, uncanny, and for that very reason, all the more frightening. By now we should know better than to try to teach children morality and ethics by such terror tactics of threats and punishments.

The Golden Rule, whether in its positive or negative formulation, appeals to the ego, to its self-interest or its anxiety over possibly being hurt. If we can truly feel the other's hurt, then we can acquire some empathy and human understanding. But because the Golden Rule was turned into the commandment "Don't do to others what you don't want done to you," it became yet another "Thou shalt not." Besides, it is too tainted with egoism and a potentially morbid sensitivity. The Golden Rule is inadequate as a standard for human behavior. Something more specific, more active, was needed.

Jesus went beyond the empathy of the Golden Rule. He taught

a *sympathy,* an active compassion, as the standard of human behavior. That directive has become known as the law of *Christian
charity.*

Beyond sentimental benevolence and restraint from evil, Christian charity is a philanthropy of good deeds. This was Jesus' conception of charity: "I was hungry and you gave me food; I was thirsty
and you gave me drink; I was a stranger and you made me welcome;
naked and you clothed me; sick and you visited me; in prison and
you came to see me."[2]

Though God-fearing and law-abiding, the Pharisee was smug
and self-satisfied too, standing in self-righteous detachment in front
of the Temple. The Pharisee claimed to adhere to the Law. Jesus
looked beyond the words of the Law to the pristine spirit of law
itself. To be truly righteous, a man must give of himself and his
possessions: he must feed the hungry, quench the parch of the thirsty,
clothe the naked, be hospitable to the stranger and comforting to
the ill and unfortunate.

It was not enough to refrain from inflicting hurt, Jesus taught;
one must also *do* good to *be* good. In urging his disciples to dedicate
themselves to the bodily and spiritual needs of their fellows, Jesus
approached a sublime ethics of human compassion. However, the
values revolutionary inserted an egoistic qualifier into what should
have been an objective and disinterested standard of ethics.

What Jesus said was, "I was hungry and you gave *me* food;
I was thirsty and you gave *me* drink; I was a stranger and you made
me welcome; naked and you clothed *me;* sick and you visited *me;*
in prison and you came to see *me.*"[3] Jesus made the satisfaction
of his own egoistic need for acceptance and allegiance the test of
the rightness of all behavior. He equated universal human compassion
with a very particular allegiance to himself. The motivation for
impersonal charity was to be the very personal love for Jesus. The
hungry, thirsty, stranger, naked, sick, and imprisoned were shadow
images of Jesus himself. Jesus taught his disciples that human suffering was their opportunity to show their love for him.

Jesus said, "In so far as you did this to one of the least of these
brothers of mine, you did it to *me;*"[4] and correspondingly, "in so
far as you neglected to do this to one of the least of these, you
neglected to do it to *me.*"[5]

Jesus made philanthropy a kind of loyalty test for his followers.
And for that test there would be a passing grade (eternal life) and

a failing grade (eternal punishment). Jesus, who claimed that he had not come to judge, nonetheless put the loyalty test of philanthropy into the context of the Last Judgment. To those who did not practice philanthropy in his name, Jesus would say, "Go away from me, with your curse upon you, to the eternal fire prepared for the devil and his angels."[6]

That was a reversion to the severe Old Testament judgmentalism that Jesus elsewhere repudiated. We discover once again the very same pattern of thought that we detected in the ego and alienation of Jesus as a values revolutionary: all human behavior was to be interpreted in terms of acceptance or rejection of the person of Jesus. There were bribes to acceptance of that person and threats of punishment for rejection of that person.

That method of behavior control—the "do it for me," the candy in the one hand and the threat of a spanking in the other—is one that we disapprove of in our child rearing. That method of inculcating ethics is devious, corrupting, and intimidating all at once. It is, however, characteristic of religious morality.

In religious morality a metaphysical order looms over the individual with cosmic vengeance for misdeeds and unimaginably gratifying rewards for good deeds. Religious morality is antithetical to philosophical morality, in which the disinterested is cultivated against the egoistic, goodness is for its own sake, not for future rewards, and the right is sought because it is itself the right, not because it is an edict from a Divine Despot.

The basis of the Golden Rule, in its positive formulation, was the ego. "Always treat others as you would like them to treat *you.*" The basis of the Golden Rule, in its negative formulation, was the fear of punishment. "Don't do to others what you don't want done to *you.*" In his law of charity, Jesus combined ego and fear. The ego used as basis was not that of the individual, but that of Jesus himself. The feared punishment was not an unexpected and uncanny one on earth, but the inevitable and cosmic one in hell. In Christian charity, instead of the empathetic relationship between the philanthropist and the beneficiary, there was to be a new empathetic relationship, the one between the disciple-philanthropist and his Master Jesus. The recipient of the charity was only the means for the disciple to get to Jesus.

To Jesus, the love of mankind was to be merely the test of his followers' love for him. But Jesus had taught the eunuch ideal and its desexualization of love. What was to become of all that suppressed erotic feeling when love was directed to the needy suffering, to fellow believers, or to Jesus himself? Just what, psychologically speaking, was the feeling of the person whose total emotionality was directed toward love of Jesus, who, like Mary Magdalene, wanted so much to *cling to* him? That question brings us to the problem of Christian love. It also brings us to the Gospel of John.

The Gospel of Mark is simple, nearly artless, biography. In Matthew and Luke there are the first editorial slants, the former Jewish, authoritarian, and retrospective; the latter pagan and cosmopolitan. Although we can detect differences in treatment and perspective among the three synoptic gospels, they are, nonetheless, similar versions of the same story. The Gospel of John is qualitatively different. It is a reinterpretation, even a revaluation, of the person of Jesus, of the content of his teaching, and of the very meaning of his mission.

According to John, what Jesus taught was not benevolence, philanthropy or charity, but *love:* "What I command you is to love one another."[7] Again, "This is my commandment: love one another as I have loved you."[8] In scores of such formulations John develops his theme, namely that Jesus was the Supreme Lover whose single message, in all its repetitions and variations was, "As the Father has loved me, so I have loved you. Remain in my love."[9] The Gospel of John is a gospel of love.

Who was John, and by what right was he entitled to make a revaluation of the person and message of Jesus? He identifies himself as "the disciple Jesus loved." He invariably uses only that form of self-identification in every episode where he appears in his own gospel.[10] Despite that mysterious, willful anonymity, tradition identifies him as one of the twelve apostles—John, brother of James and son of Zebedee.

In his own mind John was "the disciple Jesus loved." In other words, he claimed a personal emotional relationship to Jesus himself. Peter's authority was based upon an act of appointment by Jesus, such as that reported in Matthew, the authoritarian gospel. In his own gospel John does not report Peter's investiture, but he does imply that he and Peter were peers. John's own legitimacy and authority were not from any words Jesus said to him; instead, they were grounded in feelings that John had for Jesus, the same feelings that he felt Jesus had for him. John was the one beloved of the Supreme Lover.

Tradition states that the apostle John lived until the end of the first century. During the period of his association with Jesus, therefore, he must have been quite young, even a teenager. Artists have generally portrayed John as a pretty boy, a kind of mascot or pet of the apostolic brotherhood. Influenced by the erotic languor of the line "The disciple Jesus loved was reclining next to Jesus . . . leaning back on Jesus' breast,"[11] they have even represented John as the Ganymede of the Last Supper. Perhaps, under the influence of Greek philosophy, the person of John took on the character of a Platonic paramour of Jesus. Of all the apostles, John was the one whom Jesus most loved, and who, presumably, loved Jesus most, perhaps with the adolescent passion of simple hero worship.

In the scene of Jesus' arrest, as told by Mark, there is a curious incident, the significance of which remains hidden. Mark reports, "A young man who followed him [Jesus] had nothing on but a linen cloth. They [the soldiers] caught hold of him, but he left the cloth in their hands and ran away naked."[12] So, a certain young man or boy among Jesus' disciples, having found himself caught up in the frightening adult world of force and violence, panicked at the appearance of the soldiers, fled, and was allowed to escape. Was that boy "the disciple Jesus loved"? He had to be someone special, in order for Mark to include that seemingly trivial episode in his narrative of the arrest.

Anyway, John claimed a personal emotional relationship to Jesus. That relationship was *love*. John also claimed that Jesus drew him to himself in the unique relatedness of an adopted brother. As Jesus was dying on the cross, he gave his mother and John to one another, so that John might be joined to Jesus as a brother, flesh of his flesh, fellow son of the same mother.[13]

The mystical significance of that scene, which only John himself reports,[14] is that the love between John and Jesus climaxed in a kind of assimilation, a becoming-one, a union that approached the natural intimacy of blood relatedness. Jesus chose John as his brother, bestowing upon him the authority of a special loving relatedness, just as in Matthew Jesus chose Peter, conferring on him the authority of a chief executive.

Some early Christians believed that Jesus' special love for John was so intense that Jesus would not permit him to die, but would keep John alive until he himself returned in the Second Coming. When John did die, there must have been a disillusionment, both with John and with the imminence of the Second Coming. An appendix to the Gospel of John deals with the crisis of faith caused by the deaths of Jesus' two great intimates, Peter and John. It contradicts the superstition that John would never die but leaves open the imminence of the Second Coming.[15]

So John was the disciple Jesus loved, adopted brother, and mystical link both to Jesus as he was and Jesus as he would return. That there arose a mythology and superstition about John indicates that he was recognized and accepted as one of Jesus' closest intimates.

John's interpretation of the character of Jesus is the most peculiarly personal of all the gospels. His own sense of himself as the lover beloved of the Supreme Lover permeates his gospel with an aura of mystic love. John himself was a lover, a poet, and a mystic. He saw Jesus, his soul mate, in just those same terms.

John portrays Jesus as a man of profound emotionalism. In the episode of the raising of Lazarus, for example, Jesus reacted to the tears of Mary, the bereaved sister of Lazarus, with emotional paroxysms of his own: "Jesus said in great distress, with a sigh that came straight from the heart . . . Jesus wept . . . Still sighing, Jesus reached the tomb."[16]

Jesus reacted like a character out of melodrama, despite the fact that he had calmly told his disciples that Lazarus was not dead, but *resting,* and that his illness was merely an opportunity for Jesus to show his power. Jesus had even dawdled for two days before going to the aid of Lazarus. So his emotional paroxysms when he arrived strike us as illogical and histrionic.

Lazarus' sisters referred to their brother as "the man you [Jesus] love."[17] That characterization must have touched sensitive nerves in John, another disciple Jesus loved. John attributed to Jesus the extreme emotionalism that he himself would have felt—indeed did feel—at the death of his own beloved, Jesus himself. The similarity of the death and raising of Lazarus to that of Jesus must have formed another unconscious link in John's mind.

This is not to argue either that Jesus was or was not given to emotional outbursts. However, the strangeness of his emotions in the Lazarus episode indicates that John projected his own tumultuous emotionalism onto Jesus.

Intense love is monomaniacal. The Jesus of John had a monomania, an obsession with the subject of love. Excepting the many passages in which Jesus asserted his legitimacy by his relationship to the Father, most of the pronouncements of Jesus in the Gospel of John consist of monologues on love, the theme and variations. Those monologues are repetitious, monotonous, mystical. Instead of the didactic parables of the synoptic gospels, lessons on a variety of religious themes, John gives us poetry on a single theme, albeit a kaleidoscopic one—the theme of love. John's Jesus is not the Master Healer of Mark or the Master Prophet of Matthew and Luke. John's Jesus is a mystic. He is the Supreme Lover.

The poetic imagery in the Gospel of John is simple but powerful in its appeal to the longings of the human soul. The metaphors in the episode of the Samaritan woman at the well—*living water* and *food*—are typical of Johannine poetic imagery. In John the symbolism of Jesus' teaching is the elemental one of nourishment, satisfaction, oneness, and an assimilation that approaches incorporation or consubstantiality.

The first miracle that John reports is Jesus' transformation of water into wine in a marriage setting at Cana.[18] With a wonderful inventiveness of variation, John proceeds to develop the imagery of food (bread, fish, body) and drink (water, wine, blood). "I am the bread of life," Jesus said, "He who comes to me will never be hungry; he who believes in me will never thirst."[19] Jesus and his love provided the food and drink for those whose souls were hungry and thirsty with love-longing. To John, Jesus was the satisfaction of all human need.

Of course such a personal and peculiar revaluation of the person and message of Jesus must be highly distorted. There is no detachment or objectivity anywhere in John; the critical sense is entirely absent. John is lover, poet, and mystic. His twin ideals are love and truth; but the "truth" in John is poetic and mystical, not biographical and historical. That is why he could effect a thorough revaluation of the person of Jesus and of the content of his message, while at the same time keeping an honest conscience. John was Christianity's first mystic, as well as its first poet.

Working with poetic license, but under the authority of his personal relatedness to Jesus, John transfigured the historical Jesus of Nazareth into a mythical, mystical symbol. Again and again Jesus proclaimed himself in the formula "I am . . . ," followed by a metaphor.[20] He described himself as "the bread of life"; "the living bread"; "the light of the world"; "the good shepherd"; "the resurrection"; "the Way, the Truth, and the Life"; "the true vine"; "the gate"; and so on. In the Gospel of John, Jesus has become a composite of metaphors.

What Jesus is in John's gospel is not what Jesus was but what Jesus was to John. The Gospel of John is a brilliant flight of poetic and mystical imagination. It is a vision.

In the Gospel of John, Jesus is the Supreme Lover who preached a love more intense, more profound, than the simple benevolence or philanthropy or charity that he taught in the three synoptic gospels. What did John mean by *love*?

In beginning his narrative of the Last Supper, the first in the series of events that constituted the redemptive mission of Jesus' life, John says that, "He had always loved those who were his in the world, but now he showed how perfect his love was."[21] That was meant as an explanation of the self-sacrifice of Jesus on the cross, but it is immediately followed by an act of *perfect love* of a different kind, the love shown by Jesus in washing the feet of his apostles.

Shortly before, Jesus himself had had his own feet anointed by Mary of Bethany.[22] Now he performed a similar act of loving servitude upon his apostles. He stripped himself down to the single garment of the slave, took a basin of water, then washed and dried the feet of all his twelve apostles in turn.

In nomadic culture washing the feet of the guest is a courtesy performed by a servant or by the wife of the host. In washing his apostles' feet, Jesus set an example of humble self-effacement. Such servitude and feminine lovingkindness showed *perfect love*.

In the Gospel of Matthew there are turnabout formulas in which the first would be last and the last first. Those turnabout formulas are in the context of Jesus' alienation against the privileged position of the Establishment elite. John rarely stoops to the rancor and petty politics of Jesus' confrontations with the Pharisees. Instead, he prefers to show Jesus himself performing a loving turnabout in which the first willingly puts himself last and permits the last to be first.

After washing his apostles' feet, Jesus told them that he was, and rightly so, their Lord and Master.[23] He himself was the first of them, but the first should put himself in loving servitude to the last. Jesus directed his apostles to imitate his example, to wash each other's feet in a sacramental ritual. Each should be the servant of the other. Each should minister to the other.[24]

By washing his apostles' feet, Jesus showed that perfect love was willing servitude. That incident was the symbolic prelude to the supreme act of perfect love. It was on the cross that Jesus, the suffering servant, truly showed "how perfect his love was."

Jesus did not die quickly or abruptly. He was subjected to a prolonged period of physical and emotional abuse, of agony in the body and stress in the spirit. In none of the synoptic gospels is the story of Jesus' passion told with such poignance and pathos as in the Gospel of John.

During his trial Jesus suffered abuse at the hands of the guards of the high priest and the Roman soldiers of Pilate. Matthew reports that the guards "spat in his face and hit him with their fists"; and that the soldiers scourged him, then "spat on him and took the reed and struck him on the head with it."[25] Mark says that the guards "started spitting at him, and, blindfolding him, began hitting him with their fists and shouting, 'Play the prophet!' And the attendants rained blows on him." The soldiers "struck his head with a reed and spat on him."[26] In Luke, the guards "were mocking and beating him."[27]

In the synoptic gospels, Jesus suffered contempt (the spitting and mocking), as well as ridicule of both his religious pretensions as a prophet and supposed political pretensions as the King of the Jews (the reed scepter, the crown of thorns, and the purple cloak). He suffered the mindless brutality against a helpless person (the hitting, striking, scourging, beating, raining blows).

John reports the abuse inflicted upon Jesus as follows: The soldiers "slapped [Jesus] in the face."[28] John deemphasizes the mindless brutality of the soldiers in favor of the calculatedly cruel personal insult. What poignance and pathos there is in the comparative economy of John's reportage!

Two other incidents unique to the Gospel of John further intensify the pathos in his narrative.

After Jesus had expired on the cross, "one of the soldiers pierced his side with a lance; and immediately there came out blood and water."[29] Not only was that a needless desecration of the beloved body, an unnecessary cruelty, but the image of the flowing blood and water is a vivid symbol, rich in meaning. Jesus' love and life flowed out in blood and water. Blood and water were the poignant, pathetic last drops of his perfect love.

As a variant on the symbolism of the lance that pierced Jesus' side, John tells the story of doubting Thomas, the apostle who refused to believe that Jesus had risen from the dead unless he could touch the wounded body of his Master. Jesus appeared and told him, "Put your finger here. . . . Give me your hand; put it into my side."[30] Thomas' finger of doubt, in its own way, was as wounding as the cruel lance of the soldier. There was the same pathetic imagery in both. Such pathos is exquisite.

By including the incident of the lance, John has made a significant contribution to the Christian iconography of the crucifixion. The image of the beloved body exposed in its suffering—the pathos of blood and water—was to have a powerful effect upon the imagination of the Christians. The life and liveliness of the living Jesus, his healthy love, the values of his revolution, even the triumph of his Resurrection—all that was to become secondary to the supreme Christian symbol, the blood-stained crucifix.

To Jesus himself, his death must have meant only the means of accomplishing his values revolution. His followers, however, valued the means over the end as the symbol of Jesus' love. They became enchanted by the spell of love-as-pathos, so vividly real in the fixation-idolatry of the crucifix. Much of that spell of love-as-pathos is from the Gospel of John.

Not only did perfect love mean self-effacement unto death; it was also the rationale for ethical and moral behavior: "If you love me you will keep my commandments."[31]

We consider parents ill-advised to appeal to a child's love for them in order to control the child's behavior. But to the mystic, if one is filled with the spirit of love, it follows that all one's actions are done in the spirit of love. The true lover cannot, and does not, sin. His law is the *law of love,* which is as much the law of his own organic being as it is of his behavior. Once again John goes beyond the synoptics.

To John, God is not the fearsome law enforcer we find in Matthew. He is the loving Father. The words *sin* and *judgment* are in John's vocabulary, it is true; but the lover is not motivated to moral behavior by fear of punishment. The lover is motivated by the law of love. The aura, the being-and-becoming, of love sweep away all temptations and moral problems with a great wave of spiritually erotic good feeling.

It is in the Jesus of John—or was it in John himself?—that the primitive patriarchalism of Old Testament threats and punishment was supplanted by a new moral principle: "Just love. Love is the answer." That is the summation of the moral teaching in the Gospel of John. Despite the later multiplication of commandments

and the heaping up of ecclesiastical regulations, the elemental simplicity of John's mystic message has persisted throughout the history
of Christianity. Stripped to its essentials, the message of Jesus was,
"Just love!"

John was a mystic, and to the mystic, love is oneness. Perfect
love was, ultimately, a becoming-one with Jesus and, through him,
with the loving Father. Jesus said, "May they all be one. Father,
may they be one in us, as you are in me and I am in you . . . that
they may be one as we are one. With me in them and you in me,
may they be so completely one . . . so that the love with which you
loved me may be in them, and so that I may be in them."³² That
is the singsong of mystic oneness. As Jesus was one with the Father,
so the believer could become one with both, merging into a cosmic
oneness. That becoming-one with Jesus and with the Father was both
the expression and the reward of perfect love.

By now it should be clear that John was a genius who totally
transfigured the character of the historical Jesus and wholly revalued
his teaching, at least as we can compare John's version with that
of the three synoptics. John's gospel was the first masterwork in the
literary process by which Jesus of Nazareth was taken out of his
place and time and elevated into the upper aether of cosmic concepts
and metaphysical symbols.

The Gospel of John is a panerotic rhapsody. And it is a kind
of love letter in memoriam, written in the spirit of poetry and mysticism, out of nostalgia and longing for the departed beloved. It is
a great romance, full of feeling, passion, and pathos. Whether any
of it is *true* in the historical sense is beside the point. As poetry,
as mysticism, the gospel is true, even if that truth is a distortion,
even if it is a *revaluation,* of the values actually taught by the historical
values revolutionary named Jesus of Nazareth.

The New Testament includes three epistles attributed to John.
In themes and phraseology, they seem to be echoes and afterthoughts
of the great gospel.

The first epistle, like the gospel, begins with "the Word." It revives the metaphor of "the light," expresses the twin ideals of love
and truth, and harks back to John's crucifixion scene with the pathos
of water and blood. The mystical climax of John's first epistle is
the perfect love that rises to cosmic oneness: "God is love and anyone
who lives in love lives in God, and God lives in him."³³

The other two epistles are single-page spurts, tantalizing as all brief writings are. The second epistle treats the ideal of "our life of truth and love" and urges believers, "let us love one another."[34] It is love and truth once again in the third epistle, with the emphasis this time on the latter: "Our testimony is true."[35]

The Apocalypse, or Book of Revelation, has also been attributed to John. Revelation is an appalling diatribe, full of rabid hatred, sadistic fantasies, and the lust for revenge. It seems inconceivable that *the disciple Jesus loved,* the mystic lover, could have had anything to do with it, although the Revelation figure of the *Antichrist,* that dualistic nemesis in Christian thinking, does appear in John's epistles.[36] In any case, the Book of Revelation does neither the early Christians nor the person of John the mystic lover any credit at all.

In the Gospel of John disinterested benevolence has become charged with mystic erotic feeling. General philanthropy or charity has become a specific love for the person of Jesus. That love was to be the prime value for Christian being and behavior. It was a love ostensibly desexualized, nonegoistic, and indiscriminate.

For a mystic such as John, a fusion of religious sensitivity and erotic feeling presented no moral problem. But for the nonmystic, the common believer in Jesus, could love be fully desexualized, freed from egoistic self-interest, and indiscriminate? Was such a love humanly possible?

The eroticization of philanthropy in the Gospel of John, that mystical muddle of sex and religion, necessarily posed an extreme danger to sexual morality. The pagan Greeks, too, were lovers. Pagan Greek eroticism expressed itself in the carnal aesthetics of nudity, as in human athletes and divine idols. Such an idolatry of the human body could lead to such excesses as promiscuity, perversion, and sexual irresponsibility.

Would the indiscriminate erotic enthusiasm of the Christians, would it, too, be liable to such corruption? Would indiscriminate love become promiscuity?

There are indications in the epistles of Paul that some early Christians did indeed interpret Christian love as sexual freedom and irresponsibility. Nonetheless, Christian sexual morality was responsible and exemplary. How did the Christians avoid the fate of the Greeks? How did those lovers avoid becoming victims of their own erotic enthusiasms?

The answer to the control of erotic feeling among the Christians is in an antithesis formulated in the Gospel of John: "It is the spirit that gives life, the flesh has nothing to offer."[37]

Christian love, emanating from a spiritual source, repudiated carnal sexuality. The result was one of the strangest emotional complexes in the history of human behavior, a thoroughly desexualized erotic enthusiasm, indiscriminate but not promiscuous.

John's opposition between spirit and flesh—a very Jewish opposition—would set the boundaries to Christian love. The Christian would live wholly in the spirit and renounce the flesh. Such an attitude could become phobic antisexualism, as in Paul and Augustine; but in John the mystic, the emphasis is wholesome and positive, firmly on the side of the spirit.

We can find no trace in John's gospel of the eunuch ideal, that craving for self-castration. Nor does John bother at all with such dissonant sexual themes as the morbid scrupulosity about lust or the problem of divorce. As for adultery, John has Jesus forgive the woman taken in adultery, without a sermon or penitence or any ado.[38]

To the mystic, love is the answer to the problem of sexuality. Instead of being an adversary within, sexual drive is a wholesome source of mystic religious feeling. In a healthy mystic, sexuality is a spiritual energetic. It, too, can flow naturally into that mystic oneness that is the goal of love.

As we discovered in the passages about the eunuch ideal, lust, divorce, and adultery in the synoptic gospels, the early Christians did not prove capable of that wholesome emotional and religious fusion that came so spontaneously to John the mystic lover. For the average person there had to be warnings, commandments, and prohibitions—in short, a return to Old Testament judgmentalism, with its threats of hell for sexual sins.

The mystic fusion of sex and spirit in John proved to be an unintelligible rhapsody. It was Paul who laid the foundations of Christian sexual morality, not with the spirit but with the whip. Standing in righteous opposition to the eroticism of Mediterranean culture, the eunuch ideal was propagated and cultivated with a vengeance.

Although sexuality was not to be a problem for the Christians, their *love* was. By adopting the eunuch ideal, they may have conquered lust, but they could still love. And more than anything they wanted to love, everybody and anybody, everywhere and all the time, with every other human being the image of Jesus, who was the common love of them all.

Theirs was a love wholly distinct from the discriminate choice of the mating bond and from the specific organic relatedness of family blood. It was a love antisexual and antifamilial. The Christian *brothers* and *sisters* were all spiritual mates to one another. It was love and only love all the time. And, as for their enemies, well, even Christian pacifism was made amorous.

The wellspring of the general love for all men was to be the particular love for one man, Jesus of Nazareth. Moreover, love for the *person* of Jesus, in turn, became love for the body of that person. Christian love, ostensibly spiritual and antiphysical, became an attraction to, and an idolatry of, the carnal body of Jesus. Despite the Johannine opposition of the spirit and the flesh, what happened was this: *The spirit became flesh.* Christianity turned idolatrous.

In the Transfiguration episode, those apostles most intimate with Jesus saw his body transformed before their eyes. On the top of a high mountain, where the physical and the spiritual intermingled, the body of Jesus shone with a supernatural brightness. The Transfiguration was an apotheosis, a becoming-divine, of the body of Jesus. When the light dispersed, the body of Jesus became human once again.[39] Later, after his death, the body of Jesus underwent a second, and that time a permanent, apotheosis in the Resurrection.

The complementary events of the Transfiguration and the Resurrection are the scriptural sources of the idealization of the body of Jesus. When Christianity entered the milieu of Mediterranean culture, the body of Jesus was recast according to the Greek aesthetic. As we discover in the iconography of early Christian Rome, Jesus was even to become assimilated to Apollo, as an idolatrous image of the ideal male body of divine beauty. The Jewish prophet was given the face of a Greek god.

Because of the tragic fate that befell the body of the historical Jesus, Christian erotic idolatry also took on an aspect of pathos. The symbol, or, more accurately, the idol, of the crucifix exposed the suffering body of the beloved to worship by his believers.

The crucifix had no part in the cult of the very first Christians, who were awaiting the imminent return of Jesus in his Second Coming. On that occasion he would appear in the glorified bodily form he had shown at the Transfiguration and the Resurrection. Later, when the hopes for that Second Coming proved illusory, Christian longing for the body of Jesus lapsed into grief and disappointment. And so the crucifix, the exposed suffering body of the beloved, became the great idol of the Middle Ages, that millennium when Christianity went into its doldrums.[40]

It was the *spirit* that was supposed to give life. The *flesh* had nothing to offer. By prohibiting any *graven images* of flesh, the Jews had safeguarded themselves against any idolatry. The Christians unwisely succumbed to an iconographic idolatry, despite the fact that they so fulminated against the pagan idols around them.

To Paul the erotic idolatry of the statues of Artemis of Ephesus was scandalous blasphemy. To later Christians the erotic idolatry of the body of Jesus, whether in the idealism of the Transfiguration and the Resurrection on the one hand, or in the pathos of the Crucifixion on the other—that erotic idolatry became a very focus of the cult.

The *spirit* persisted in the gospel words of Jesus and in the other literature of the New Testament. But the *flesh* appeared, too, in mosaics and paintings and sculptures and crucifixes, all overtly idolatrous expositions of "the sanctuary that was his body."[41] Christianity developed its own carnal aesthetic. What began as a literary cult became an artistic one as well.

The Christians succumbed to the same kind of corporal idolatry that they had found so scandalous in the pagans. Henceforward, there would be a visual, an artistic, a pagan Christianity alongside the verbal, literary, Jewish Christianity of the New Testament. A full history of Christian iconography, of Christianity as a cult for the eyes, has yet to be written. But Christianity became more amorous, more voluptuous, more symbolically explicit, than the merely literary cult we find in the New Testament.

The ultimate goal of passionate idolatrous love is the same as the goal of the mystical longing in the Gospel of John, namely, *oneness*. The Christian longing for the body of Jesus needed for its wish-fulfillment both a becoming-one and a being-one with that body. The Christians developed a sacramental rite of becoming-one with the body of Jesus, and they elaborated a doctrine of being-one with that body. The becoming-one was the Eucharist. The being-one was the *mystical body*.

During the Last Supper, at the impending hour of his destiny, Jesus took bread, broke it, passed it around to his apostles and said, "Take it and eat . . . this is my body."[42] Completing the imagery of the grim ritual, Jesus then took a cup of wine, saying, "this is my blood,"[43] and passed it, too, around to his apostles. According to Luke only, Jesus instructed his apostles to repeat his ritual: "do this as a memorial of me."[44]

What Jesus did at the Last Supper was a symbolic dramatization of his destiny. As he broke the bread, he said, "this is my body;" that is, his own body would be broken and torn apart, just like the bread in his own hands. He carried the analogy further by calling the wine his *blood,* which was about to be "poured out for many for the forgiveness of sins."[45]

In Jewish thinking, life was believed to reside in the blood; that accounts for the Old Testament taboos on bloody meat. So the breaking of the bread-body and the pouring out of the wine-blood was a vivid Jewish symbolism of Jesus' imminent loss of life. When he told the apostles, "do this as a memorial of me," he must have had in mind a funereal commemoration.

Surprisingly, John does not report the incident of the institution of the Eucharist, despite the fact that throughout his gospel he expresses a mystical obsession with the metaphors and imagery of food and drink, body and blood, hunger and nourishment. The Last Supper farewell ritual that John reports is the washing of the feet of the apostles. After that ritual Jesus told his apostles, "I have given you an example so that you may copy what I have done to you."[46]

Instead of taking the washing of the feet, that act of humility and self-effacement, as their sacrament, the Christians took the Eucharist. Far from demonstrating humility and self-effacement, the Eucharist revealed the most presumptuous human ambition possible, the ambition of becoming-one with a god.

John does not report the institution of the Eucharist, but he does rhapsodize on the bread-and-wine, body-and-blood metaphors of the Eucharistic ritual: "My flesh is real food and my body is real drink," Jesus said. "He who eats my flesh and drinks my blood lives in me and I live in him."[47] In John there is no sacramental practice associated with Jesus' mystical metaphors, but, even so, the imagery proved offensive to Jewish sensitivity. "This is intolerable language," some of Jesus' disciples said in revulsion. "How could anyone accept it?"[48] To the Jews the idea of eating bloody meat was an outrageous violation of one of their most ancient taboos.

The accounts of the Last Supper in the three synoptic gospels leave us with the strong impression that Jesus meant the meal as a dumb-show by which his apostles would participate, symbolically at least, in Jesus' death. The meaning of the ritual seems wholly

funereal.[49] The Eucharist, as a Christian sacrament, has since lost
its funereal associations. Instead, it is taken as a mystery-rite by which
the believer becomes one with the body of Jesus. How did such a
thorough revaluation of the symbolism and meaning take place?

A metaphor may be anything you want it to be, and a ritual
can be reinterpreted according to the needs of the participants. The
Christians, taking the incident of Jesus' last meal and some mystical
metaphors of love-longing, such as those in John, combined them
in a new relatedness. It was only in a mystical discourse, unrelated
to any biographical act, that Jesus had said, "If you do not eat the
flesh of the Son of Man and drink his blood, you will not have
life in you. Anyone who does eat my flesh and drink my blood has
eternal life, and I shall raise him up on the last day."[50] That text
has since been taken as the key to the essential meaning of the Last
Supper meal, never mind that it occurs in a completely different
context.

At the Last Supper Jesus had broken the bread and poured
out the wine as if to say, "This is what I am about to go through
for your sake, my body broken and my blood spilled." The Christians reinterpreted that symbolism. They took Jesus' meaning as, "Eat
my body and drink my blood, and you will become one with me,
you will live forever like me."

It is characteristic of Christian censorship that the anointing at
Bethany, which was such an overtly erotic homage, was given a funereal interpretation. Conversely, the Last Supper meal, overtly a funereal ritual, was interpreted in terms of love-longing. The words
of Jesus, "do this as a memorial of me," were taken as an invitation
to frequent, repeated acts of becoming-one with the body and blood
of a divine being, and so with divinity itself. What was metaphor
and gloom became reality and ecstasy. The reinterpretation of the
Eucharist was the wish-fulfillment of the Christians for oneness with
the body of Jesus.

In the Eucharist the believer becomes body-in-body with the divine
body of Jesus. Because Jesus declared, "The Father and I are one,"[51]
the Eucharist also enables the believer to become one with God. Such
a notion, of course, was blasphemous and repugnant to Jewish sensitivity and its humble recognition of God as an Ever-Other-Essence.
Judaism was a religion of propriety. Christianity was a cult of *love,*
immoderate both in its expression and in its ambitions. Christian
immoderation proceeded to "blasphemous," but immensely gratifying,

extremes. Not only did the Christians elevate their Master, Jesus of Nazareth, as another god next to the God, but they also insinuated themselves into the godhead through the common magic ritual of their becoming-one with God in the Eucharist.

Christian love and longing, so supercharged as it was with eroticism, necessarily presented that danger to sexual morality that we recognized before. It was precisely in the context of Jesus' mystical discourse about his body as bread and his blood as wine that John injects the caution, "It is the spirit that gives life, the flesh has nothing to offer." In other words, carnal rhetoric should not become carnal practice. Jesus continued, "The words I have spoken to you are spirit and they are life."[52]

The Eucharist meant an incorporation into the body of Jesus, a consubstantiality with that body and with its divinity. However, the Eucharistic ritual is necessarily an episodic and short-lasting becoming-one. Love, longing, and ambition craved more. Could there be a lasting being-one with the beloved body?

It was Paul who provided for that lack: "All of us, in union with Christ, form one body, and as parts of it we belong to each other."[53] That metaphorical doctrine, called the *mystical body,* was a permanent being-one with the beloved body of Jesus, a state beyond the episodic becoming-one of Eucharistic ritual.

Such carnal-erotic rhetoric, once again, is dangerous to morality. Just as John had to warn against a crude interpretation of his mystical metaphors of body and blood, (which he did by his opposition between "spirit" and "flesh"), so Paul found himself forced to insist upon an exclusively spiritual interpretation of his metaphor of the mystical body: "You know, surely, that your bodies are members making up the body of Christ; do you think I can take parts of Christ's body and join them to the body of a prostitute? Never!"[54]

The Christians took their philanthropy in an erotic spirit. The pagans rumored it about that the Christian cultists were orgiasts who delighted in incest between brothers and sisters, in a love as promiscuous as it was indiscriminate. Some unscrupulous initiates probably did take advantage of female sexual and religious hysteria among the Christians for their own sexual purposes. Real incidents, as well as misunderstandings, must have fueled the pagan rumors.

When the Christians gave philanthropy and benevolence an erotic charge, they introduced the potential mischief that the opposition between "spirit" and "flesh" and the warning against the prostitution of the mystical body attempted to avert. Human nature being what it is, the libido did not simply evaporate at the proclamation of the eunuch ideal.

Jesus had made the practice of general philanthropy a test of his disciples' allegiance to him. According to the Gospel of John, Jesus was the Supreme Lover who both loved and demanded love. And so, among the followers of Jesus, philanthropy became charged with eroticism and with an erotic association with the person, even the body, of Jesus. Benevolence and philanthropy were transmuted into erotic love, although the eroticism was desexualized to accord with the eunuch ideal. What had begun in the empathy of the Golden Rule developed into the sublimated passion of Christian love. Christianity was one of the most stunning demonstrations of the psychological possibilities of human feeling.

As we observed in the relations of Jesus to the women in his life, Jesus' emotional effects upon those around him were profound. After an encounter with the resurrected Jesus, some disciples wondered to themselves: "Did not our hearts burn within us as he talked to us on the road and explained the scriptures to us?"[55]

The same charismatic spell that the historical Jesus of Nazareth exerted upon his contemporaries the mythological Jesus was to exert upon all later generations. Christian love was not to be the simple philosophical ethic of doing what is right for right's own sake; it was to be an intense passion of hearts burning with love for the person and body of Jesus, the Supreme Lover.

Jesus was a world-historical values revolutionary, both in Palestine during his lifetime and in the Mediterranean world as a cult figure after his death. In his teachings Jesus presented antitheses to, and in his person he himself was antitype to, the values and types prevailing in the cultures of the ancient world. Against the judgment and punishment of patriarchal Judaism, Jesus was the Master Prophet who taught love as the new law. Against the carnal eroticism of the Greeks, Jesus became the Supreme Lover who took eroticism away from the *flesh* and installed it in the *spirit*. Against the aggression and terror of Roman militarism Jesus taught pacifism and submission. Both what Jesus really was and what he was later interpreted as being (no matter how different) constituted antitypes. Both what Jesus really taught and what his teaching was later interpreted as being (no matter how different) constituted antitheses.

Jesus was a values revolutionary who upset the status quo of human relationships, just as he upset the religious Establishment of Palestine and the social structure of the Roman Empire. It was because Jesus was the values revolutionary, the antitype who taught antitheses, that he was prosecuted and executed by the Jewish and Roman Establishments. And it was because his followers, who were organized as values revolutionaries, imitated Jesus as antitype and propagated Jesus' teachings as antitheses, that they were persecuted by the peoples of the Mediterranean.

Jesus chose and trained a cadre of revolutionaries to help him in his campaign and to carry it on even after his death. He issued a corporate charter,[56] and he specified just how it was that his adherents were to be distinguished from those around them: "I give you a new commandment: love one another; just as I have loved you, you also must love one another. By this love you have for one another, everyone will know that you are my disciples."[57]

The Brotherhood of the Love Cult

Every values revolution is a starting-all-over-again. In some values revolutions that means starting back at the very beginning, at the time when values were simple and pure and the keepers of the values honest and deserving of respect. That kind of values revolution is archconservative, even reactionary. When Jesus said that he had come to fulfill, rather than to destroy, the Law and the Prophets, he meant that he saw himself as the restorer of pure Judaic religious values. Jesus' revolutionary strategy was to present his subversive antivalues as nothing but the pure, original values reasserted against later corruptions.

According to Jesus, means and ends had become confused, the spirit had been lost for the sake of the letter, complexity had overrun simplicity, and hypocrisy lorded it over honesty. Jesus stood in the same relationship to Judaism as the sixteenth-century reformers stood to Christianity. True religion, having lost itself in complexity and hypocrisy, needed to be rediscovered. It had to be restored to its pristine purity.[1]

Such a restoration is beyond the capacity of a single reformer. The values revolutionary, therefore, has to recruit a corps of ideological shock troops to join him in the assault upon the Establishment.

Jesus wanted to organize his revolutionaries within a framework intelligible to the people, one that would symbolize restoration of pristine values. The corporate consciousness of the Jews was in the twelve tribes of Yahweh's "chosen people." The twelve tribes of Israel had failed in their duty to true religion. Jesus replaced them by his twelve apostles, each apostle to be a patriarch of a new tribe, the apostolic group itself the *chosen persons* to succeed the *chosen people*.[2]

"He appointed twelve; they were to be his companions and to

be sent out to preach, with power to cast out devils."[3] The Twelve had a twofold mission. On the one hand, they stayed with, and supported, Jesus as his companions. On the other hand, they were sent out by Jesus as preachers and healers.

Any organization provides company, so Jesus may have derived considerable emotional support from the Twelve. "The disciple Jesus loved" must have soothed some of the intense loneliness felt by the alienated values revolutionary. But Jesus was a strong character, sure of himself and his mission. He knew that he would have to overcome his doubts and fears by himself. The emotional support of the Twelve probably meant less to Jesus than another, a more practical, kind of support they could provide.

Jesus' awesome miracles and his eloquent preaching drew to him crowds that could easily become mobs. The religious enthusiasm of the people, their messianic expectation and apocalyptic anxiety, could change into a frenzy that would pose a danger to Jesus' safety. It is in the context of the mass assemblies Jesus attracted that the apostles had their usefulness. The twelve burly aides could function as a squad for crowd control, both protecting their Master with a ring of defense and organizing and restraining the people, so that the mass would not become the mob.

The Twelve were Jesus' secret service, and his stage managers, too: they organized the people in a way conducive to effective healing and preaching.[4] They helped Jesus to control the social situation. Without the apostles Jesus' words might have been drowned out in the din of acclaim, his person swept along or even trampled over by the milling bodies of the masses.

The Twelve served as Jesus' bodyguards. Despite their acceptance of the discipline of nonresistance and pacifism, they were ready to resort to force and violence to protect the person of their Master. In order to carry out that task, they must have received a dispensation from the discipline.

The apostles went about armed and ready to defend their Master, despite the pacifist ideal of turning the other cheek. Jesus acquiesced, because he needed that strength around him so that he could control events until the time he was willing to give himself up.

The apostles were not only armed, they were quick to resort to arms. As the high priest's men approached to arrest Jesus in Gethsemane, the apostles asked, "Lord, shall we use our swords?"[5]

Without waiting for an answer, one apostle whipped out his sword and hacked off an ear of a servant in the arresting party.

By that time Jesus was ready to give himself up. The token resistance of a few swords among the Twelve and that single act of violence against the high priest's servant would be enough to impel the authorities to their prosecution. Jesus ordered his apostles to cease their resistance and to permit to happen what Jesus wanted to happen.[6]

The apostles, or some of them, went about armed, in order to protect Jesus against assassination. That might have been a practical necessity; but it did lay Jesus open to the very charge he was to be convicted of, namely, political sedition.

Zealotry was in the air, and to the Romans any leader who had armed followers was not a prophet but a Zealot with revolution on his mind. One of Jesus' apostles, Simon, was even called "the Zealot."[7] Despite Jesus' discipline of pacifism and his repeated emphasis upon the exclusively religious nature of his "kingdom," the Romans must have interpreted the violence of the arrest scene as sedition. That might have been the very misinterpretation that Jesus wanted, in order to impel the authorities to their prosecution and carry him along to his destiny.

As a mystic, Jesus needed to withdraw into solitude from time to time, to meditate, to pray, and to bolster his determination and his courage. It was at such times, especially, that he would send his apostles away from him. Paired up as his delegates and emissaries, the apostles "set out and went from village to village proclaiming the Good News and healing everywhere."[8]

The content of that Good News was the arrival of the kingdom through the person Jesus of Nazareth. The apostles spread the reputation of their Master, they disseminated his values, and they chronicled the proofs provided by his miracles. There are no specimens of apostolic preaching in the gospels—the focus of the gospels, after all, is on the person of Jesus, and the apostles are merely supporting players— but we can read samples of apostolic preaching in the Acts of the Apostles.

Besides promoting their Master's reputation and repeating his teaching, Jesus wanted his apostles to replicate his miracles, to perform the same kinds of healing that he himself did, that is, "cure the sick, raise the dead, cleanse the lepers, cast out devils."[9]

Again, it is to the Acts of the Apostles that we go to read about the miracles performed by the apostles. In the gospels we discover that it was not so easy to replicate the Master's miracles as it was to repeat his teachings. The apostles suffered the tentativeness, even the incompetence, of all apprentices.

There was a man whose son was an epileptic demoniac. Subject to convulsions, the boy would throw himself into fire or water, foam at the mouth, or lie rigid in a catatonic state. When the father appealed to the apostles, they tried to cure the boy but failed. After the symptoms returned, the father then appealed in desperation to Jesus, who drove the devil out and effected the cure at last.

Jesus expressed an exasperated impatience both at the lack of faith of the father and at the ineptitude of his apprentice healers. The apostles for their part were mortified at their failure. When they asked their Master why they had been unable to cure the boy, Jesus answered, in Mark's version, that the particular devil in question was an especially powerful one who could be driven out only by a certain exorcistic prayer. In Matthew's version, Jesus said that the problem was the apostles' lack of self-assurance, their too little faith.[10]

According to Luke, Jesus gave his apostles "power and authority over all devils";[11] but it is evident from the episode of the epileptic demoniac that some devils were less amenable to the apostolic power and authority than others.

The skills of mystical healing were not acquired fully developed and all at once. We know from Mark that Jesus himself had to develop and perfect his own healing skills. When the people brought a blind man, Jesus took him aside, put spit on his eyes, and laid his hands on him. Then Jesus asked, with apparent self-doubt, "Can you see anything?"[12] The blind man replied that he thought he could see people around him, but that they were blurry images, indistinguishable from trees. Jesus then laid his hands on the man again, in a repeat treatment. The second try effected the miracle and brought everything into focus. Even for Jesus the Master Healer the cure was not always immediately forthcoming. That should have made him more indulgent of his apprentices' inadequacies.[13]

Besides stumbling in occasional incompetence, the apostles were also prone to abuse their miraculous powers. On the way to Jerusalem, Jesus and his apostles sought food and lodging in a Samaritan village. In the spirit of Palestinian sectarianism the villagers would not give them any hospitality. Two apostles, James and John, responded with retaliatory animosity by asking Jesus whether they should call down fire and brimstone to destroy the village and its inhabitants. As happens in the "Sorcerer's Apprentice," power had gone to their heads. Jesus rebuked James and John for their mean-spirited vindictiveness, and the group went on to seek hospitality where they could find it.[14]

Luke reports that incident just after that of the epileptic demoniac. It seems that the apostles' ambitions were nothing daunted by their failures.

The sectarian animosity in that incident brings us to the problem of the Samaritans, which is also the problem of the scope of the apostles' labors. The Samaritans were a sect of heterodox and racially mixed Jews. We may take the very word *Samaritan* as signifying Jewish petty sectarianism.

Did the apostles have any mission to the Samaritans? In other words, did they transcend the petty sectarianism of their place and time? The evidence of the four gospels is contradictory.

The Gospel of Matthew is the most Jewish and, correspondingly, the most sectarian of the gospels. In Matthew, Jesus tells his apostles, "Do not turn your steps to pagan territory, and do not enter any Samaritan town; go rather to the lost sheep of the House of Israel."[15] Those instructions put the apostles' mission within sectarian boundaries. In Matthew, Jesus sees his own mission as circumbounded by sectarianism: "I was sent only to the lost sheep of the House of Israel."[16] Only at the end of Matthew, in a tagged-on appendix like that in Mark, is there a proclamation of a universal mission: "Go, therefore, make disciples of all the nations. . . ."[17]

Those are the words of the resurrected, not of the historical, Jesus. The words of the resurrected Jesus may be taken as Church policy. The missionary directives in Matthew, both sectarian and universalist, seem more like Church policy for the Christian proselytizers than Jesus' instructions to his twelve apostles. We detect in the contrast between the sectarianism of the early part of Matthew's gospel and the universalism of its last words the political conflict in the early Church between the Judaizers and the paganizers, between the Jerusalem Christian Establishment and Paul.

In the Gospel of Luke, the pagan gospel, the scope of the apostles' mission is cosmopolitan from the very beginning. Holding the infant Jesus in his arms, the prophet Simeon called him "a light to enlighten the pagans."[18] That phrase applies as well to the Gospel of Luke.

The rebuke that Jesus directed to James and John for their spiteful vindictiveness against the Samaritan village may be taken as Luke's own rebuke to petty sectarianism, like that in the early part of Matthew's gospel. In Luke's story of Jesus' mass healing of ten lepers, the only one to show gratitude was a Samaritan. In his parable of the Good Samaritan, Luke even transforms the Samaritan from a despised pariah to a model of morality.[19]

According to Luke only, Jesus appointed, besides the twelve apostles, seventy-two other disciples. Now, Jesus' public career was so short that it is unlikely that he had time to recruit, indoctrinate, and train such a large number of disciples. The Seventy-two might belong more to Luke's cosmopolitanism than to the biography of Jesus.

In his story of the Seventy-two (six times the Twelve), Luke chooses a symbolic large number, a cosmopolitan number, to set against the narrow sectarian number of the twelve apostles for the twelve tribes. That Jesus' instructions to the Seventy-two repeat those to the Twelve indicates that what we have here is symbolic parallelism, a literary device. In Luke the stifling sectarian straitjacket of the Jews is sloughed off. The cosmopolitan expansiveness of the Seventy-two opens historical opportunities beyond the twelve men for the twelve tribes.[20]

If Luke is cosmopolitan, John is cosmic. The mystic lover who dwells in the cosmic aura of love and oneness does not stoop to petty sectarianism. In the Gospel of John, Jesus even sits down by the well for a casual conversation with a Samaritan woman. Any sectarianism is repugnant to John's universal and cosmic love.

John makes it clear that Jesus was more than a Jew for the Jews: "Jesus was to die for the nation—and not for the nation only, but to gather together in unity the scattered children of God."[21] By the time of the Gospel of John, the Romans had destroyed Jerusalem and dispersed the Jews after a devastating war. The Christians realized that the only future for their sect had to be a cosmopolitan, a universal, one.

It is difficult to distinguish which parts of the gospels accurately portray the apostolic situation and which the organizational situation of the early Christian Church. Church policy may have been put into the mouth of the historical Jesus as easily as into the mouth of the resurrected Jesus. Both the sectarian Judaizers in the Church and the Pauline cosmopolites must have been strongly tempted to derive their authority from the Master himself. The struggle between factions accounts for the contradictory scopes in the gospel story, in some places narrowly sectarian, like the Jewish past, elsewhere widely cosmopolitan, because Paul had his way, and in the end universal and cosmic, in accordance with the mysticism of John.

We have already examined the severe discipline that the twelve apostles subjected themselves to at the insistence of Jesus, and how that vocational discipline was to become, in the Church, an ideology of universally applicable moral values. The apostles had to imitate their Master's alienation and practice nonresistance and pacifism, the strategy of the alienated helpless. They had to abandon their natural families for the sake of their new ideological family and accept the values of religious antifamilialism. They had to live in absolute poverty, give away all they possessed, and share of themselves. They had to practice celibacy of body and mind according to the eunuch ideal. And they were to live and act in the spirit of love, love for their Master and for one another.

The ascetic discipline of the apostles' lives was severe, but where Jesus required, he characteristically rewarded. In compensation for their self-denial, their self-effacement, and their self-sacrifice, the apostles were to enjoy unique status and authority.

Jesus impressed upon his apostles that they were the lucky special ones, born in the right place and at the right time. They would witness, and, better, participate in, the fulfillment of all the historic hopes of their people. They would experience what the prophets had longed for, namely, the arrival of the Kingdom of God upon earth.

If it is a natural human wish to live in interesting times, the apostles, of all men who had ever lived and of all who were to live, themselves lived in the most interesting time in the history of the human race. Beyond that, they were specially selected for an executive participation in the climax and culmination of human history. The Twelve were the lucky, special, of all men most fortunate, ones. Against that status and privilege any discipline, no matter how severe, must have seemed a light yoke.[22]

Jesus heightened the apostles' sense of status and privilege by characterizing them as what we would call the "in-group." It was to the apostles, and to them only, that the hidden depths of meaning in Jesus' teachings were to be revealed: "The mysteries of the kingdom of God are revealed to you," their Master told them. "For the rest there are only parables."[23]

In characterizing the apostles as the in-group, Jesus was presenting yet another variation on the alienated stance—the them-and-us, the select few versus the rejected many, the chosen persons versus the chosen people. Once again Jesus presented alienation as a positive value.

As the in-group, privy to the mysteries, the arcane and hidden meanings, the apostles were to constitute a secret society. We must remember that the gospels, which contained the interpretations of Jesus' parables, the arcane, hidden meanings, were themselves the lore of a secret sect. The early Christians zealously guarded their secret writings, and only after tests and initiation (Baptism) were the mysteries made available to the neophytes. Some bishops chose martyrdom rather than reveal the hiding places of the secret writings; those Christians who gave them up to the authorities for examination were reviled and damned, much as a modern Mason would be for betraying the innermost secrets of his lodge.

Jesus conferred status upon his apostles, both as the lucky special ones and as the exclusive in-group. He also conferred authority upon them. It was an authority derived from his person, and through him from the Father Himself. Jesus told his apostles, "Anyone who listens to you listens to me; anyone who rejects you rejects me, and those who reject me reject the one who sent me."[24] It was the Son of God, and above and beyond him, God the Father, who empowered the apostles for their mission and conferred upon them an authority that was nothing less than divine.

The apostles, then, enjoyed unprecedented status in human history and an unprecedented authority among men. They also had a personal, a very intimate, relationship to Jesus. Jesus described the relationship of the apostles to himself with a peculiar metaphor. He called them "the bridegroom's attendants."[25]

Jesus was asked why his apostles, unlike the disciples of John the Baptist and the Pharisees, did not fast as part of their religious discipline. Jesus replied that as long as "the bridegroom" (he himself) was with them, it was not appropriate for them to fast. But when the bridegroom would be taken from them, then they would fast and go into deep mourning.

It is a strange metaphor to describe the personal relationship between Jesus and his apostles, that of "the bridegroom" and "the bridegroom's attendants." In such a metaphor we would expect a bride. The bride would be the one to fast and mourn and grieve at the death of the beloved bridegroom. Here there is bridegroom and attendants, but no bride. Such a peculiar metaphor is a challenge to interpretation; perhaps it expresses nothing more than the old patriarchal bias that women just don't count for much, even if that means that the strong emotional attachment at a wedding is between the bridegroom and his attendants, rather than between the bridegroom and his bride.[26]

Anyway, the apostles had their discipline, their status, their authority, and their intimacy with their Master. They were also to have rewards for their loyalty and service. For each disciplinary renunciation there would be a hundredfold compensation. For the totality of their devotion there would be the supreme reward. Jesus described their supreme reward in varying terms, such as "heaven," "eternal life," or a "kingdom."

"You are the men who have stood by me faithfully in my trials; and now I confer a kingdom on you," Jesus told his apostles near the end of his life. What Jesus meant by "kingdom" or what the apostles interpreted the word to mean we can only surmise.[27]

The supreme reward in store for the apostles was elsewhere expressed by Jesus in terminology with which we have become familiar in other aspects of New Testament thinking. Jesus promised a supreme reward in Jewish terms, in pagan terms, and in mystical terms.

In Jewish terms Jesus told his apostles, "you will yourselves sit on twelve thrones to judge the twelve tribes of Israel."[28] In pagan, or should we say, superstitious, terms, Jesus told his apostles, "I have given you power to tread underfoot serpents and scorpions and the whole strength of the enemy; nothing shall ever hurt you."[29] And in the singsong jargon of mysticism in John, Jesus told them, "I am in my Father and you in me and I in you."[30]

Whether it was royal judgeship over the twelve tribes of the Jews, or magical power over the serpents and scorpions of primitive fears, or the mystical intercommunion with the Son of God and with God Himself—that was all heady stuff for a dozen Palestinian manual laborers. We wonder how the apostles could avoid falling into an ecstatic swoon of megalomania and a delirium of overweening arrogance.

With each apostle promised so much, there should have been no competition, rivalry, or discord among them. Nonetheless, competition, rivalry, and discord did infect the apostolic relationship. Before we explore the problems in interpersonal relationships among the apostles, we should first study the process of Jesus' selection of them and the smaller groups, or cliques, that developed within the Twelve.

The three synoptic gospels report Jesus' selection and recruitment process in a similar sequence, but with a few differences in detail. John describes the selection and recruitment in a way that differs from the synoptics both as to facts and to editorial intentions. Here is how Jesus chose his twelve apostles, with the variations among the four gospels:

According to Matthew, Mark, and Luke, Jesus first recruited two pairs of brothers, Peter and Andrew, James and John, all of whom were Galilean fishermen. These were the Four.[31]

Jesus then called a tax collector, whose name is Levi in Mark and Luke, but Matthew in the Gospel of Matthew. Tax collectors were private contractors who collected taxes for Rome and made a sometimes extortionate profit for themselves. In selecting a tax collector to be one of his apostles, Jesus delivered a deliberate affront to the political and religious sensitivity of the Establishment regarding the Roman (pagan) overlordship of Palestine. Jesus chose Matthew-Levi not only for his person, but also as a subversive values statement.[32]

After reporting Jesus' selection of the Four and the tax collector, the three synoptic gospelwriters then list the names of the Twelve. The lists are the same, except for the name of a single apostle, given as Thaddaeus by Matthew and Mark, Judas, son (or brother) of James (not to be confused with Judas Iscariot), by Luke.[33]

The apostle Peter is given prominence, or preeminence, in all three synoptic gospels. In Matthew, the preeminence of Peter is put in authoritarian terms when, in an investiture ceremony, Jesus said to him, "You are Peter and on this rock I will build my Church . . . I will give you the keys of the kingdom of heaven."[34]

Peter is given many speaking parts throughout the gospels. He is portrayed as an intensely loyal, assertive, sometimes impulsive, disciple. In Mark, the earliest gospel, Peter is not quite so prominent as he is in Matthew. In Matthew, Jesus and Peter both walk upon the water, but in Mark, Jesus walks alone. In Mark, Peter is rebuked for his concern about Jesus' welfare, but he is not invested with executive authority, as in Matthew. In the Gospel of Luke, Peter is linked with John, when the two make preparations for the passover supper.[35]

For the purposes of security and crowd control the Twelve formed a suitable corps. There were times, however, when Jesus wanted to make some special display of his mana, to impart an intimate self-revelation, or to share the stress of certain crises. On such occasions he wanted as company only Peter, James, and John, the Inner Three of the Twelve.[36]

Jesus took only the Inner Three with him when he raised the daughter of Jairus from the dead, when he transfigured his body, and when he suffered the agony of his last few hours in the garden of Gethsemane. Jesus' relationship with the Inner Three was more intimate and personal than his relationship with the other apostles. It was the most special of special occasions, the most intimate of intimate self-revelations, the most trying of all trials, that Jesus shared with the Inner Three.[37]

In the Gospel of John the story and the emphases are totally different from the synoptics. According to John, Jesus began his recruitment by drawing away two of John the Baptist's disciples.[38] One of those was Andrew, who went in turn to his brother Simon (Peter) and recruited him on Jesus' behalf. In other words, Jesus himself never recruited Peter directly. Peter came secondhand through his brother Andrew.

According to John, Jesus then called Philip, who, in turn, recruited Nathanael. Nathanael was at first reluctant and skeptical, but when Jesus told him about a vision he had had, Nathanael was swept away by enthusiasm. He burst out that Jesus was the "Son of God."[39]

It is remarkable how unplanned, how haphazard, the process of selection of the apostles appears in the Gospel of John. Of the first four two were chosen by Jesus, but the other two were recruited only secondhand. Peter and Andrew are members of the Four, just as they are in the synoptics, but, in John, Philip and Nathanael replace the James and John of the synoptic versions.

In an egalitarian spirit John gives speaking parts to those apostles mostly neglected by the synoptic writers, namely, Philip, Nathanael, Andrew, Judas (not Iscariot), and Thomas. And John is sometimes vague in his apostolic identifications, as when he writes about "the disciple Jesus loved," or "another disciple . . . who was known to the high priest," or "two more of his disciples."[40] That vagueness was not simply the result of carelessness, ignorance, or indifference on John's part.

To John, love is egalitarian, not authoritarian. John doesn't list the Twelve at all, perhaps because explicit inclusion means implicit exclusion. To John, any lover of Jesus becomes an apostle. Beyond the tribal Twelve of the synoptics, beyond the cosmopolitan Seventy-two of Luke, the brotherhood of the love cult may count itself in the millions. All who love Jesus are his apostles.[41]

In John, there are neither the Four nor the Inner Three. There is, however, the special relationship of "the disciple Jesus loved" to Jesus; but that relationship is an emotional one of love, rather than an authoritarian one of rank or inclusion.

Surprisingly, John is the only gospelwriter to report defections from Jesus' following. After Jesus' extreme mystical rhetoric about eating his body and drinking his blood, "many of his disciples" reacted with repugnance and abandoned him.[42] That was psychologically understandable; John recognized that Jesus aroused strong feelings, revulsion as well as love. Nonetheless, the editorial emphasis in John is generally upon the ultimate goal of mystical oneness, with Jesus and through him with the divine.

In John, Peter is linked to "the disciple Jesus loved" as peers whose relationship to each other was one of amicable intimacy. More ominously, Peter is linked to Judas, as opposites in their loyalty to their Master. It was just after Peter made his profession of faith that Jesus damned Judas, the one who was to betray him.[43]

Peter and John, in their loyalty and love, stood together on one side of Jesus. On the other side, alone, stood Judas, plotting betrayal in counterpoint to Peter's loyalty, feeling hatred in counterpoint to John's love. And with Judas, the fully isolated apostle, we head straight into the competition, rivalry, and discord among the twelve apostles.

If Jesus had indeed appointed Peter as his chief executive in such an investiture ceremony as we find in Matthew, then any personnel problems would have found their resolution in a simple principle, the primacy of Peter. But the apostles carried on as if Peter were just one of them, as if Jesus had never made it clear who his chief executive was. On the one hand, that relatedness was democratic. On the other, it was competitive and disputatious.

The apostles argued among themselves on the question, "Who is the greatest among them?"[44] Jesus intervened and told them that the one who wanted to be first must put himself last and be the servant of all. He should take "the least," the children, as model.[45]

Jesus himself must have been responsible for some of the competition and jealousy among his apostles. A teacher should never play favorites, but in his bestowal of privileged intimacies upon the Inner Three or "the disciple Jesus loved," Jesus was playing favorites, What every apostle craved was the utmost nearness to the Master, to the salvation he promised, to the supreme reward. Yet Jesus distinguished and discriminated among his apostles in the nearness that he granted to each. The consequence could only have been rivalry and discord.

The brothers James and John even pushed their fraternal blood relationship against the apostolic ideological relationship. They requested for themselves and each other the right-hand and left-hand positions next to Jesus' own glorious throne in the "kingdom." Jesus told them that they would share in his trials, but that it was not in his power to award exalted thrones. When the other apostles heard about the brothers' request for special privileges, they erupted in self-righteous anger. Jesus relieved the tensions of rivalry by repeating what he had said in the dispute about "Who is the greatest?"—namely, that each was to be the servant of all.[46]

The apostles do not seem to have accepted the primacy of Peter, at least during Jesus' lifetime. They were scheming and shoving one another aside in rivalrous attempts to secure greater nearness to their Master.

Peter may not have been recognized by the other apostles as the chief executive; but in the gospels he is, at least, the dominant apostolic personality. Of all the apostles we know Peter best; he is a clearly delineated character, strong and vigorous, loyal in a child-like way, aggressive and impulsive, but prone to waver under pressure. If "the disciple Jesus loved" is to be identified with John the apostle, then in John's gospel we have a full self-revelation of an apostle. Of the other members of the Four and the Inner Three, namely, James and Andrew, there is very little from which to form a judgment of character.

In the gospels the apostles sometimes serve a function like that of the characters in the Socratic dialogues, that is, they ask questions or introduce topics on which Jesus then expounds his teachings. The apostolic characters have such speaking parts, but they do not *do* much that has any crucial importance in the career and destiny of their Master. There were, however, two such acts that we do know about. Those were the denial of Jesus by Peter, which, although significant, was to have no actual influence on events, and the betrayal by Judas, which was significant, necessary, and a prime determinant of events.

If we follow Matthew, the two incidents that must have determined Peter's relationship to Jesus were the investiture and the rebuke. Peter was the man whom Jesus called first. He was the "rock" of the Church, the one to whom Jesus entrusted the "keys to the kingdom." To prevent Peter's status as first in order and first in rank from going to his head, Jesus gave him a shockingly severe rebuke, and in a stunningly abrupt manner.

When Jesus made the first prophecy of his own destiny, Peter objected, with understandable concern, "Heaven preserve you, Lord . . . this must not happen to you." Jesus responded to Peter's blessing and compassionate concern with an inexplicably cruel rebuke: "Get behind me, Satan! You are an obstacle in my path."[47] Following hard upon Peter's profession of faith in his Master and then the investiture, the Master's terrible rebuke must have left the loyal Peter in a state of chastened bewilderment.

By that time Jesus was determined to die. In his well-meaning blessing Peter was inadvertently opposing his Master's wish and will, he was inadvertently setting himself up as an obstacle to Jesus' longed-for destiny. Peter had stumbled headlong against Jesus' determination, and that is why Jesus reacted so severely. By appointing Peter chief executive on the one hand, then reviling him as "Satan" on the other, Jesus was exerting a kind of mind-control that kept Peter subject to the Master's will. The ambivalence of a loved one exerts an irresistible spell upon the one who loves.[48]

Peter's principal participation in the fulfillment of his Master's destiny was the threefold denial. Peter's denial of Jesus would cause his Master no real harm, but it was to become in Peter's own mind the worst moral failing of his life.

There is about Peter's denial a strange determinism. As in the episode of Jesus' first prediction of his own death, so, too, when Jesus predicted the denial, Peter resisted. To his Master's death Peter said, "Not you!" To his own denial Peter said, "Not me!" Once again, Peter was pitting his own force of will against that of his Master. But Jesus told Peter that he *must* deny him three times. That was not a prophecy, so much as an order, something that had to be done so that Jesus could accomplish what he wanted to accomplish.

If, as Jesus had insisted, the disciple should be to his Master no more than a slave was to his master, then a disciple must never be permitted to say no against his Master's yes. Jesus would brook no contradiction. And so Peter had to be put in his place. Peter had to be punished. The denial was to be that punishment

Peter was faced with a moral dilemma. To him, any denial would be a violation of his prime value, which was loyalty to his Master. Why was it that Jesus predicted, wanted, and required of Peter such a terrible sin against a disciple's loyalty? Jesus was subverting Peter's values, just as he was subverting the values of society. And Jesus could exert such force of will over Peter that he knew that somehow Peter would understand what had to be done, and that he would do it.

The weakness in Peter's character—his "tragic flaw"—was a tendency to lose courage at the critical moment. Peter would leap out of the boat to walk over the water to his Master, but the moment that the weight of his body began sinking into the deep he would panic. If Peter followed Jesus through the judicial proceedings, Jesus knew that people were bound to recognize Peter by his appearance, his behavior, or his accent, and that they would challenge him. Feeling the water about to well up around him, Peter would panic, falter, and ultimately do what was expected of him. He would undergo his punishment.

In order for Jesus to get Peter to commit a sin against his prime value of loyalty, he had to convince Peter that what had to be done was not treacherous or sinful, because the Master himself approved of it. Jesus got his message across in an ingenious exercise of mind-control, telling Peter, "I have prayed for you, Simon, that your faith may not fail, and once you have recovered, you in your turn must strengthen your brothers."[49]

The sequence of ideas in that sentence is remarkable. Jesus first said that he had prayed for Peter, that is, he blessed him and gave his approval. Then he called him *Simon,* rather than Peter, a subtle put-down reminding the apostle who and what he had been before his Master came to make the big difference in his life. Then, although Jesus had prayed that Peter's faith would not fail, he knew that it would, because he indicated that Peter would need *recovery.* Jesus appealed to Peter's sense of responsibility by asking him to "strengthen your brothers." So Jesus made it clear to Peter that he would fail the test of faith, but that he would recover and become the bulwark of the apostolic brotherhood.

By such subtle tactics Jesus maneuvered Peter into committing

the breach of faith and loyalty, the threefold denial of the Master.
When Peter did as the Master wanted him to do, "the Lord turned
and looked straight at Peter." Peter "went outside and wept bitterly."[50] The look that Jesus gave Peter was not so much a reproach
for failed loyalty or a pitiful glance of the wronged friend; it was,
rather, a *hard look,* an "I told you so," and, even more, a "Get
on with it."

Even if it was what his Master had wanted, what he had done
threw Peter into an emotional collapse. Denying his Master, he had
betrayed his own prime value of loyalty. What good could possibly
come of that? And so Peter "went outside and wept bitterly."[51]

Peter's denial must have appeared to the followers of Jesus as
similar to, if not as grave as, the betrayal by Judas. Jesus had promised
Peter recovery, it is true; but the threefold denial compromised Peter's
authority and impugned his reputation. He needed absolution; he
needed exoneration. And it is John the mystic lover who would absolve
and exonerate Peter.

John presents a scene in which the resurrected Jesus (that is,
the Christian community) rehabilitated Peter. Jesus asked Peter,
"Simon, son of John, do you love me more than these others do?"[52]
Although Peter answered that he did, Jesus repeated the question
twice more. Peter avowed his love, each time more vehemently. Jesus
accepted his avowals and restored his authority: "Feed my lambs
. . . Look after my sheep . . . Feed my sheep."[53]

The threefold avowal of love compensated for the threefold denial.
Peter was absolved, exonerated, and fully restored to his authority.
Then Jesus gave his final approval to Peter by renewing his call to
the Master's service. Just as he had said to Peter at the lakeside
very early in his mission, so did Jesus, now resurrected and triumphant,
say to Peter, "Follow me."[54] What Peter had done, what seemed
at first so terrible and treacherous, had not offended or harmed the
Master at all. Peter was saved.

The ordeal that Peter went through was similar to that undergone
by Judas. The sin of Judas was somewhat worse, and the fate he
suffered was far more terrible.

Jesus exerted the same force of will and mind-control upon Judas
as he had upon Peter, telling Judas that he must betray his Master.
Jesus predicted, or ordered, the betrayal, as he had ordered the denial.[55] The bewilderment that Judas felt must have corresponded to

Peter's, although what Judas may have thought or felt is not reported in the gospels.

Neither in Matthew, Mark, nor Luke are there any clues to the motivation of Judas for his betrayal of his Master. The worst they say about him is that "Satan entered into Judas."[56] That is little more than a trite Judaic formula. In the Gospel of John, however, Judas is subjected to everything from petty insult to character assassination to eternal damnation. Luke says that the devil entered into Judas; but John has Jesus say in judgment, "One of you *is* a devil."[57] The synoptic writers do not tell us why Judas did what he did. John tells us that Judas did what he did because of what he was.

The first thing that Judas was, according to John, was a petty thief. At the anointing at Bethany, objection was raised to the squandering of a precious commodity, on the grounds that the perfume could have been sold to buy bread for the poor. According to Matthew, it was "the disciples" who objected; according to Mark, "some who were there." John specifically names Judas as the objector; he objected, John says, not out of any concern for the poor, but because he was losing an opportunity to pilfer from the apostolic fund, of which he was the treasurer.[58]

In the synoptics the word *traitor* may be taken as simply a description of what Judas was to do and did. There are few other pejorative descriptions of Judas himself. John, however, characterizes Judas as a thief, a devil, and a son of perdition.[59]

In his Last Supper scene, John makes a perverse play on the Eucharistic theme of "This is my body." He reports that Jesus dipped a piece of bread (his "body") and handed the sopping bread (his "bloody body") to Judas, at the same time announcing that Judas was the one who would betray him. In symbolic pantomime and in explicit words, Jesus put his bloody body, his destiny, in the hands of Judas.[60]

Contradicting his earlier statement that Satan had already put the betrayal into Judas' mind, John now says that it was only when Jesus handed the symbol of his bloody body to Judas that "Satan entered him."[61] That strange association brought the wills of Jesus and Satan into concert.

John also includes in his scene of the conversation between Jesus and Pilate Jesus' gratuitous absolution of Pilate for his part in the execution of an "innocent" man. John couples the absolution of Pilate with a damnation of Judas. "The one who handed me over to you has the greater guilt,"[62] Jesus told Pilate.

To John, Judas had fallen out of love with the Supreme Lover. "The disciple Jesus loved" was himself so much in love with Jesus that he himself just could not forgive what Judas did. That is why we find in John the insult, character assassination, and damnation of Judas to an extent far beyond any of the synoptics.

Peter had lost courage. "The disciple Jesus loved" could forgive that; he could absolve and exonerate Peter, even restoring him to his full authority. But Judas had fallen out of love. To John the mystic lover, Judas was guilty of the one truly unforgivable sin.

In Jesus' Last Supper ritual of the washing of the feet, John puts into Jesus' mouth these words to Peter: "No one who has taken a bath needs washing, he is clean all over. You [Peter] too are clean, though not all of you are."[63] The "not all of you are" was a clear allusion to Judas. However similar their actions seemed, Peter and Judas were, according to John, opposites in character. Peter was "clean"; Judas was filthy.

In the synoptic gospels there is no such calculated campaign of character assassination against Judas, as there is in John. There is, however, Jesus' force of will against Judas: "Yes, the Son of Man is going to his fate, as the scriptures say he will, but alas for that man by whom the Son of Man is betrayed! Better for that man if he had never been born!"[64]

What a terrible thing for a lover and Master to say! For his denial Jesus offered Peter a prayer, forgiveness in advance, and the promise of recovery. For his betrayal Jesus punished Judas with a lament, forgiveness withheld, and a curse. As with the denial, Jesus himself wanted and willed the betrayal, but, nonetheless, "that man"— notice the anonymity, the contempt of the term—the very agent who effected the fulfillment of Jesus' destiny, would be damned, indeed was damned from the day of his birth. In his graphic pantomime Jesus put his *bloody body,* his destiny, in Judas' hands. Then he said to Judas, "What you are going to do, do quickly."[65]

After Judas realized what he had done and felt the full force of Jesus' curse upon him, he "was filled with remorse."[66] He fell into a state of emotional collapse, as Peter had done after his denial. Unlike Peter, Judas was not to come out of it. For him there was no promise of recovery, there was only the curse of predestined damnation. And so in rejection, isolation, loneliness, and grief, Judas took his own life. His death, his suicide, accompanied the death of his Master.[67]

If not the first martyr of the values revolution, Judas was, at least, its first victim.

The act by which Judas betrayed Jesus was a gesture of intimacy at once fraternal, familial, and erotic, namely, the kiss. The famous question, "Judas, are you betraying the Son of Man with a kiss?"[68] has generally been read with the accent on the word "kiss." It is correctly read with the accent on the word "betraying."

In his first epistle Peter tells the faithful, "Greet one another with a kiss of love."[69] Peter was not urging a memorial to the act of betrayal by Judas! He was telling the early Christians to continue the practice of the seal of relatedness that he himself had practiced with Jesus and the original apostolic group. The kiss was the common greeting and seal of relatedness of the brotherhood of the love cult.

After Jesus' death, the apostles endeavored to remember as much of his teachings as possible and to continue as faithfully as they could in the practices and disciplines that Jesus had imposed upon them. So, although the kiss of Judas is the only one recorded in the gospels, the kiss as seal of relatedness must belong to Jesus' lifetime and to the apostolic brotherhood, as well as to the early Church.

The scandal was not in Judas' kiss itself but in the treacherous motive behind it. That motive perverted the sign and seal of love. For Judas, the rejected and isolated one, the kiss had become a *kiss of death,* as in the Mafia. It was the act by which loyalty and fidelity made their last expression before they were transformed into their opposites. The kiss of Judas was such a kiss of death. It was a goodbye kiss, too. Jesus and Judas were parting, each man to his separate, but strangely similar, fate.

That Judas betrayed Jesus with the kiss, that he perverted the very seal of loving relatedness into a means of hateful betrayal, that must have horrified "the disciple Jesus loved." John is the only one of the gospelwriters who does not report the kiss of betrayal.[70] Although he devotes more attention to Judas' character and motives than the synoptic writers do, "the disciple Jesus loved" couldn't bring himself to report that kiss. The kiss of Judas was the most painful moment in the entire story of the relatedness of the brotherhood. At the very thought of that kiss "the disciple Jesus loved" shuddered and turned away.

As for Jesus himself, he took the kiss as merely a necessary prelude to the terrible ordeal that he was about to undergo. His attitude toward Judas was probably as we have it in his simple instructions, "What you are going to do, do quickly."

Jesus had more important things on his mind than a grudge against Judas. The values revolution he had set in motion was about to be accomplished. The kiss, the betrayal, was the necessary means to the self-sacrifice, the accomplishment. How Jesus longed for that kiss, how he longed for that self-sacrifice!

Martyrdom as Climax and Consequence

In the Palestine of Jesus' day the expectation of, and the longing for, the Messiah was a seething cauldron ever welling up to the brink of mass hysteria. Their scriptures had fueled the tribal self-estimate of the Jews. The Romans had smothered their nationalistic aspirations. Ideologically goaded and politically repressed, the Jews craved at the same time their fulfillment and their liberation.

In the confusion of longing and frustration the Jews saw their fulfillment and liberation sometimes in religious terms, as did John the Baptist; sometimes in military terms, as did the Zealots. They were suffering the frantic impatience of their messianism and apocalyptic anxiety. When would the Messiah come? It was only the Messiah and the social, even cosmic, cataclysm that he brought with him, that would at last fulfill the Jews, liberate them, and relieve them from their chronic anxiety.

In his parables and prophecies Jesus intensified the apocalyptic anxiety of his apostles. By the disciplines that he imposed upon them, he forced them to renounce all that was ordinary, normal, and merely human, so that they would be left spiritually naked, without attachments, and ready for the Apocalypse to come.

John the Baptist had made similar prophecies and exacted a similar discipline, at least of himself. Unlike John the Baptist, who thought of himself merely in the role of prophet, that is, as one who concentrated the people's attentions on repentance before the imminent arrival of the Messiah, Jesus came to believe that he himself was that Messiah now arrived, the divinely sent agent of his people's redemption.

An act of self-sacrifice would give paradoxical proof of Jesus' messianic legitimacy. It was the kiss of Judas that set into motion the process of the self-sacrifice. Before he made his self-sacrifice, however, Jesus had to fully inculcate his revolutionary values and exact his severe discipline. He had to hold himself to a predetermined messianic sequence. First would come the values revolution, then the self-sacrifice, and, at last, the Apocalypse.

Jesus himself was the one who would precipitate the Apocalypse. So infused with apocalyptic anxiety, he was barely able to hold to the messianic sequence. More than his contemporaries, he stood at the brink. Jesus wanted to get it over with; he longed for his climactic self-sacrifice and, beyond that, for the Apocalypse, with an eagerness that was almost frantic: "I have come to bring fire to the earth, and how I wish it were blazing already!" Jesus exclaimed. "There is a baptism I must still receive, and how great is my distress till it is over!"[1]

In that revealing outburst Jesus confessed the intensity of his own apocalyptic anxiety. How he longed for the cosmic *fire* of the Apocalypse, how he longed for the *baptism* of blood in his self-sacrifice! Apocalypse was Jesus' fervent *wish;* the necessary delay before his self-sacrifice was his impatience, his *distress.*

Jesus had an apocalyptic vision of the earth all afire and he himself burning in the holocaust. He longed for fire, like the one that had destroyed Sodom and Gomorrah, and for a baptism or flood, like that which destroyed all mankind save Noah and his kin. In the imagery of fire and water, of cosmic catastrophe, Jesus was expressing his own apocalyptic anxiety. He felt a strong impulse to get it all over with.

However, in his plans for himself, Jesus had to adhere to the messianic sequence. The teachings and the disciplines of the values revolution came first. So Jesus, the master of self-control, checked his compulsion to self-sacrifice. That self-sacrifice would be meaningless if the values had not been fully proclaimed and inculcated first. Jesus felt the necessity of restraint and timing. He reminded himself that, "the right time for me has not come yet . . . for me the time is not ripe yet."[2]

The clash of compulsion and restraint produces a chronic tension, and tension induces weariness. The weariness that Jesus felt was a world-weariness, a disgust with the people among whom he had to linger, to teach and heal: "Faithless and perverse generation!" Jesus complained to his contemporaries. "How much longer must I be with you? How much longer must I put up with you?"[3] At times Jesus succumbed to exhaustion, to disgust, to world-weariness.

The problem of Jesus' legitimacy as Messiah had not been resolved, despite the various and contradictory postmortem proofs and witnesses that we find in the New Testament. In the final analysis men would have to judge Jesus' claim to messiahship by his own words, his acts and powers, and his accomplishment. Jesus himself would be his own best witness—witness, a word which, in Greek, is *martyr*.

The designation *martyr,* meaning a person who willingly sacrifices his life in order to witness to, or prove, the truth of his beliefs, was later to be applied to some early Christians. In that he willingly sacrificed himself to prove his legitimacy and the truth of his teachings, so Jesus, too, was a martyr. He was, in fact, the first martyr of his own values revolution.

Jesus in death has more commonly been characterized as the "innocent victim." That characterization is not accurate, because he was neither innocent—he was, as we saw, quite guilty as a subversive values revolutionary—nor was he a victim, that is, a helpless one upon whom some punishment is unjustly inflicted.

Suffused with the supernatural powers of his mana, Jesus was by no means helpless. The bystanders at the cross wondered why he who had saved so many others could not save himself. But Jesus did not want to save himself. He wanted to make a deliberate self-sacrifice. And so the familiar Christian characterization of Jesus as the "innocent victim" would deny Jesus the very accomplishment that he strove for.

"I lay down my life in order to take it up again," Jesus said in one of his typical paradoxes. "No one takes it from me," he affirmed. "I lay it down of my own free will."[4]

If Jesus were a mere "innocent victim," a helpless one who had an undeserved punishment inflicted upon him, then the entire meaning of his life would have been compromised by an unforeseen fate, a stroke of bad luck, an accident. If innocent victim, then Jesus becomes a tragic figure, the good man who comes to a bad end through no real fault of his own. The gospels, however, are not tragedies. They are triumphs. Neither victim nor tragic figure, Jesus was the Messiah, the epic hero of such tremendous potency that he could effect a historical values revolution and even precipitate the cosmic Apocalypse.

Jesus' suffering and death were not inadvertent; they were intentional, wanted, *willed*. What happened to Jesus was only what he permitted to happen. He was a martyr, the witness who tries to prove the worth of his life and the truth of his beliefs by a gesture of total commitment, namely, willful self-sacrifice.[5] "I lay down my life . . . No one takes it from me; I lay it down of my own free will."

Some values revolutionaries do wind up as casualties of their own revolution. That is what happened to the Zealots of Palestine; they were all hunted down and exterminated by the Roman Imperial Establishment. They had their ambitions, they made their attempt, but then poor judgment, insufficient power, or bad luck brought them to an ignominious end. The Zealots were inadequate and they failed. Their deaths meant that something had gone wrong in their values revolution.

That Jesus of Nazareth, like many of the Zealots, came to an ignominious end on a cross did not mean that, like the Zealots, he had poor judgment, insufficient power, or bad luck. Jesus' death did not mean that something had gone wrong. On the contrary. His death was a paradoxical proof of his success and of the success of his values revolution.

Every values revolution has its casualties. In some values revolutions the leaders lose control, the situation becomes chaotic, and there is a bloodbath among the revolutionaries themselves, as happened in the French and Russian revolutions. Nonetheless, the revolutionary undertakes his campaign with the hope of succeeding in, and surviving, his values revolution. There may come a time, a critical time, when the revolutionary realizes that he himself might become a casualty of the forces he has set in motion. If that happens, then history judges him incompetent, impotent, or unlucky. He had failed to anticipate, to control, and to dominate; both he and his revolution were failures.

In the values revolution that Jesus set in motion the situation was different. He did not one day realize, too late, that the hostility he had aroused in the Establishment was about to snuff out his life. The inevitability of his death was no such belated realization. It was a predetermined act of will, one based upon Jesus' self-estimate. Jesus was not a victim. He was a martyr. His death was a triumph.

Out of his early sense of alienation, Jesus observed that a prophet is not accepted in his own country. Beyond mere rejection, Jesus felt that the fate of the prophet in Jewish society was death: "Jeru-

salem, Jerusalem, you that kill the prophets and stone those who
are sent to you!"[6]

Jesus considered himself the last and greatest of "those who are
sent." Death, the fate of the prophets, would be the fate of the Master
Prophet, the Messiah, too. Jesus expected and anticipated his own
death. He changed inexorable fate into willed destiny.

What Jesus expected to happen to him and how he saw himself
in relation to the prophets of the Old Testament is fully dramatized
in his allegorical parable of the wicked tenants. The parable and an
interpretation of its meaning follow:

There was a landowner (Yahweh) who planted a vineyard (Israel), complete with winepress (means to subsistence) and a tower
(Jerusalem and its Temple). The landowner leased the vineyard to
tenants (the Jews, or, more narrowly, the Jewish religious Establishment) and departed (left the Jews on their own). At the vintage
time (the Day of Reckoning) the landowner sent some servants
(prophets) to collect the landowner's share of the produce (fealty).
The tenants seized, thrashed, beat, even killed, every servant, one
after the other (the fate of the prophets). At last the landowner decided
to send his "beloved son" (Jesus) to collect what was due. The tenants
formed a conspiracy to take away the vineyard (to rise against Yahweh)
by killing the heir (Jesus). They did seize him and kill him.

At that point in the telling of the parable, Jesus asked his listeners
what they thought the landowner would do to the tenants. The obvious
answer was that the landowner would deprive the tenants of the
vineyard and cast them out; they would be punished.[7] Jesus elsewhere
made that punishment more specific: "Jerusalem will be trampled
down by the pagans."[8]

In the parable of the wicked tenants Jesus set forth what had
happened to the prophets and what he expected to happen to himself.
He also prophesied what would happen to Jerusalem in punishment
for its murders of the prophets and of the "beloved son," the Messiah.
Apocalyptic catastrophe was to be the punishment.[9]

We find in the synoptic gospels further evidence that Jesus' death
was a willing, willful self-sacrifice, a true martyrdom, rooted in Jesus'
self-awareness and self-estimate. Three times, in a triple affirmation,
Jesus prophesied his passion, death, resurrection, and the ensuing
Apocalypse. He did so in simple, specific terms, more patent than
the allegorical parable of the wicked tenants.

In his first prophecy Jesus revealed to his apostles that it was his destiny to go to Jerusalem, to suffer at the hands of the Establishment, to be put to death, and then to be resurrected. When Peter inadvertently opposed Jesus' will by praying that such things would not happen, Jesus lashed out a rebuke, calling Peter "Satan" and an "obstacle." Then Jesus told his disciples that they all would have to "take up a cross," and that the Apocalypse (the coming of the "Kingdom of God" or the Second Coming of the glorified Jesus as the "Son of Man") was imminent.[10]

The second prophecy was a reaffirmation of the destined suffering, death, and Resurrection. It occurs in the texts shortly after the first prophecy, as a repetition and reminder to the apostles. Their reaction to the second prophecy is variously reported: Matthew says that the apostles were saddened by it, but Mark and Luke report that the apostles did not understand what Jesus was talking about—despite the fact that what Jesus said seemed plain enough—and were afraid to press him on the subject.[11]

Jesus made his third prophecy in a disciplinary context. It directly follows his prohibition of divorce, the proclamation of the eunuch ideal, the notion of infantilism as a moral ideal, the imposition of the discipline of poverty and the promise of compensation, and a parable of the expected turnabout.

Jesus was telling his disciples that beyond all the disciplines he had imposed upon them—alienation, estrangement from family, poverty, and abstinence—there remained yet another, even more severe, discipline they had to commit to, namely, the willingness to sacrifice their lives. Their Master himself would set the example, just as he had in all other aspects of the discipline of the brotherhood.[12]

The triple affirmation of the three prophecies in the synoptic gospels is a typical New Testament numerological literary device. Like Peter's third denial and his third avowal of love, Jesus' third prophecy was the one *beyond second thoughts*. It made Jesus' willed destiny unequivocal and absolute.

The triple affirmation asserts that Jesus anticipated and wanted his destiny, that he recognized self-sacrifice as the highest discipline, the messianic necessity, and the prelude to the Apocalypse.

In the Gospel of John the narrative of Jesus' life is telescoped toward the end of that life. John has no interest in a mythology of Jesus' birth, his childhood precocity, or his formative years. What mattered to John was the climax of Jesus' life, the "perfect love" that he showed in his sacrificial death. That is why, after the mystical hymn of his prologue, John quickly dispenses with the Baptist, the selection of the apostles, and a token miracle, and then proceeds to the theme of the self-sacrifice of "the sanctuary that was his body."[13] John devotes a considerable part of his gospel to the meaning of Jesus' self-sacrifice.

In his gospel John dispenses with the three prophecies and provides instead a more psychological, a more human, description of Jesus' thinking about his destiny.

That Jesus recognized his death as a certainty and an inevitability John indicates by Jesus' self-restraining remark about the right time and the ripe time, and by his insistence that his death would not be an unforeseen fate, bad luck, or an accident, but rather a self-surrender made of his own free will.[14]

In place of parable and prophecy, John poses some mystical riddles, as when Jesus said, "I shall remain with you for only a short time now; then I shall go back to the one who sent me. You will look for me and will not find me: where I am you cannot come."[15] Again, "In a short time you will no longer see me, and then a short time later you will see me again."[16]

That mystical vagueness lacks the specificity of the three prophecies in the synoptic gospels. John compensates in two ways. First he reports some exchanges between Jesus and the crowds on the subject of Jesus' destiny. Then he gives us some of Jesus' inner reflections. Such episodes are psychological revelations, understandable and human beyond the literary artificiality of the three prophecies.

In one episode Jesus pleaded with the crowd, "Why do you want to kill me?" The crowd responded, "You are mad! Who wants to kill you?"[17] Just as Peter tried to bless away Jesus' first prophecy, so, too, the crowd disclaimed any desire for, or complicity with, Jesus' longed-for death.

John tells us that some thought that Jesus suffered from what we would call in modern terms, paranoia. The parable of the wicked tenants and the three prophecies, too, are liable to such a diagnostic judgment.

John must have sensed the implications of his reported exchange between Jesus and the crowd. If it were all just in Jesus' head, that would make him psychologically suspect. "You are mad!" was the verdict of the crowd. John contradicts that verdict by having someone in the crowd ask, "Isn't this the man they want to kill?"[18] So, someone did want to kill Jesus, after all. Ironically, the crowd's admission follows shortly after Jesus' self-restraining remark that the time was not yet ripe for his self-sacrifice.

In an interpretation of one of Jesus' mystical riddles about his "going away," "the Jews said to one another, 'Will he kill himself?' "[19] There the judging crowd wondered whether Jesus had suicidal tendencies. How much more plausible are these exchanges in John than the artificiality of the three prophecies in the synoptics. John makes Jesus' determination to martyrdom more psychological and more human.

More psychological, more human, and more stressful too. In contrast to the heroic self-assurance of the three prophecies of the synoptics, John portrays Jesus as racked by a very human self-doubt. He felt anguish, even reluctance, toward his destiny.

On one occasion of self-examination Jesus said, "Now my soul is troubled. What shall I say: Father, save me from this hour?" He stoked his resolve: "But it was for this very reason that I have come to this hour." He then appealed for help: "Father, glorify your name!" Support immediately arrived as the Thunder-Voice from heaven: "I have glorified it, and I will glorify it again."[20]

In that sequence of sentences is a self-revelation. Far from being sure of his destiny, as we would conclude from the triple affirmation of the oracular prophecies, Jesus was troubled about it; he even craved escape and deliverance from his destiny. He was able to muster his resolve by appealing to his messianic self-estimate: "It was for this very reason that I have come to this hour." He cried out a prayer of desperation and was vindicated in his purpose by divine approval.

Despite the fact that Jesus told the bystanders that the Thunder-Voice from heaven "was not for my sake . . . but for yours,"[21] the psychological reality was quite the contrary. Jesus had his doubts about himself and his messianic mission, some very human doubts. After the stress of that scene, "Jesus left them and kept himself hidden."[22]

According to John, the people suspected Jesus of paranoia and suicidal tendencies. And Jesus suffered some stressful soul-searching on the subject of his destiny. Now, the suicide of a solitary man is a private tragedy to which spectators can react with detached pity. But Jesus' death was not a mere suicide; it was a martyrdom. As the climax of his values revolution, his martyrdom had to be given a social, not merely a personal, significance. Jesus did that by inviting his disciples into participation in that martyrdom: "If anyone wants to be a follower of mine, let him renounce himself and take up his cross and follow me."[23]

By specifying the *cross,* Jesus predicted his own martyrdom by crucifixion, the most ignominious and demoralizing of all deaths. He asked his followers to take up their crosses, too, and follow him on the death march to the execution site. Life would become a death march for them all. The private destiny of one man would become a values statement by all those who believed in him.

Such an invitation to death was a challenge to the unsure, the uncommitted, and the cowardly among Jesus' followers. It was characteristic of Jesus to winnow the chaff by issuing an ultimatum, by confronting the reluctant with an either-or choice. First would come the proclamation of the discipline, then the ultimatum; both would be linked to personal loyalty to Jesus himself.

Every aspect of the discipline that Jesus imposed upon his followers was stated in egoistic terms of loyalty to himself: Only those who abandoned their families and renounced all their possessions, only those who became *children,* only those who embraced the eunuch ideal, and now only those who were willing to die were worthy of Jesus. "Anyone who does not take his cross and follow in my footsteps is not worthy of me."[24]

To those who would commit themselves to martyrdom, Jesus promised, just as he had for every other aspect of the discipline he imposed, a suitable compensation: "For anyone who wants to save his life will lose it; but anyone who loses his life for my sake will find it."[25]

Just as the Master himself, by *putting down* his life would *take it up again,* so his disciples, by *losing* their lives, would *save* them. There, in paradox and turnabout, was Jesus' promise of the compensation that would come to those who adopted the most severe aspect of his discipline, the willingness to martyrdom.

It was immediately after the first prophecy of his own passion that Jesus socialized the significance of his destiny by imposing the willingness to martyrdom upon his followers. The destiny of the Messiah was martyrdom. His disciples, those who followed him in everything, had to *take up their cross* and follow him to his destiny, too. Martyrdom for the Master and for all the disciples would be the climax of the values revolution. There would be the supreme self-sacrifice, rippling out into waves of martyrdoms and massacres, flooding into the cosmic bloodbath of the Apocalypse.

Jesus insisted that the willingness and readiness to martyrdom was a disciplinary necessity for those who wanted "to be a follower of mine," or who wanted to be "worthy of me." In the Gospel of John, the test of worthiness is always *love*. And so, it is in terms of love that John gives his version of Jesus' imposition of martyrdom as a necessary discipline: "This is my commandment: love one another, as I have loved you. A man can have no greater love than to lay down his life for his friends. You are my friends. . . ."[26] The logic of the argument would continue, "And so I lay down my life for you, and you must lay down your lives for one another."

To John the mystic lover, laying down one's life in a martyrdom was proof of *perfect love;* it was obedience to the commandment of love. Just as John had placed the rationale for all morality upon the personal love of Jesus—"If you love me, you will keep my commandments"—so did he make willingness to martyrdom the test of perfect love for, and fidelity to, Jesus. John fused love and death into a mystical amalgam.

John gives the same compensation as that stated in the synoptics, but with a characteristic change of verb: "Anyone who *loves* his life loses it; anyone who *hates* his life in this world will keep it for the eternal life."[27] Those who loved their lives more than they loved Jesus would lose their lives; but those who hated their lives for the sake of the love of Jesus would save their lives, would keep their lives, would be eternally alive. There would be a compensation, expressed once again in a paradoxical promise.

For John it was love that was the rationale for martyrdom, just as it was for all morality and for every aspect of the discipline that Jesus imposed upon his disciples. "If you love me . . ." Conversely, those who would not take up their cross for the sake of Jesus did not love him enough. Their unworthiness was not only doubt, or lack of commitment, or cowardice. It was a failure to love.

In the parable of the wicked tenants, in the three prophecies, and in the mystical riddles and exchanges with the crowd in John, Jesus anticipated martyrdom as the climax of his career. Who he thought he was, and everything that he said and did, especially his provocations of the Establishment, impelled him toward that very climax.

Jesus whipped up the enthusiasm of apocalyptic anxiety. But enthusiasm cannot be sustained for long; a personal climax and a cosmic catastrophe had to come soon and follow one another in swift order. It is inconceivable to picture Jesus living on to a long life, as a venerable sage, with the Jews carrying on in an atmosphere of restored calm and reformed religion. Neither Jesus nor his society was capable of moderate correctives. The apocalyptic anxiety was so intense in each and all that the only relief could be climax and catastrophe.

As much as martyrdom was the predetermined climax of Jesus' career, so, too, was it the logical consequence of all the values that Jesus had taught and the inevitable fate for all those who embraced such values.

Jesus had taught alienation. What is the eagerness for martyrdom but the utmost of alienation? He had imposed pacifism, which, when the discipline becomes a complex, is masochism. There is a descending continuum from pacifism to masochism to self-righteous suicide. Jesus had demanded that his disciples abandon their families and forsake all their possessions. The sense of family responsibility is a powerful check against the reckless foolhardiness of suicidal heroism. Jesus' disciples had no such check on their compulsion to martyrdom. Antifamilialism severs and isolates; it makes martyrdom that much easier. Similarly, worldly possessions and worldly ties attach one to life. Christian poverty and communism severed those material ties. Materialists do not martyr themselves; it is only the spiritual, the propertyless, who have nothing, no things, to live for. Finally, the eunuch ideal, celibacy, virginity, and self-denial cut the very instinctual roots of the love of life, namely, sexual passion and attachments. Antisexualism is a smothering of the life-force.

All the values that Jesus taught and the disciplines that he imposed served to detach the individual—intellectually, emotionally, economically, socially, even erotically—from relatedness. The apostles truly had nothing to live for. But they did have a lot to die for. What they had to die for was the love of their Master and the *truths* of the values revolution.

The brotherhood of the love cult had given up all ties and relatedness for the sake of the tie and relatedness to their Master. Every aspect of their discipline sharpened social estrangement and made even more intimate their tie and their relatedness to Jesus. When their Master demanded death and martyrdom, the disciples were left without any psychological checks to such an extreme. When Jesus beckoned them to martyrdom, they followed, because they loved him above, beyond, and instead of, any merely human, normal, or ordinary attachments. For them, too, martyrdom was a climax and consequence.

The disciples would prove willing and able to move toward that climax and accept that consequence. They were the true believers. Their goal and ideal was the *imitatio Christi,* the imitation of the Christ, their Master.

The Roman Empire was the most tolerant society in the history of the world to that time. In light of that fact, the persecutions of the Christians seem to be a historical paradox. Neither the Romans, nor the Jews, in fact, were to blame for the deaths of Jesus and his followers. Jesus himself was responsible. The gospels, those manifestoes of his values, are the proof.

The martyrdoms of the Christians, like the martyrdom of their Master, were not a historical anomaly but necessary and inevitable. Martyrdom was the consequence of the entire values system of the brotherhood. It was *the* Value, the life-and-death Value, to which all the other values led.

The narrative of the martyrdom of the Master is the climax of all four gospels. That death is a literary climax, as well as a biographical and ideological one. Matthew and Mark are very similar in their reportage of Jesus' death. In his version, Luke varies in interpretation and introduces scenes not in Matthew or Mark. John, as we would expect, reports the death of Jesus in his peculiarly personal way, reinterpreting and even contradicting the testimony of the synoptic gospels.

After Jesus was arrested, tried, and convicted as a political revolutionary, he took up his cross and began his death march to the site of the execution. According to Matthew and Mark, there was a passerby named Simon of Cyrene who was pressed by the soldiers to carry Jesus' cross for him. Ironically, a stranger, and an unwilling one at that, was the first man to heed Jesus' call to *take up the cross.*[28]

Jesus was crucified at a place called Golgatha, or Calvary. All four gospelwriters report that two criminals were crucified with him, one on either side in a symmetrical arrangement and framing. Flanked by the criminals as foils, Jesus was the centerpiece and focus of the scene. His essential goodness stood out in contrast to the evil of the flanking criminals and of the surrounding society.[29]

The bystanders mocked Jesus on the subject of his alleged statement that he could destroy the Temple and rebuild it in three days.

Their judgment was that Jesus' values revolution had failed. While the would-be Messiah was languishing into death, the Temple still stood strong.[30]

According to Matthew and Mark, Jesus' last words before his death were the opening line of psalm 22, "My God, my God, why have you deserted me?"[31] The bystanders misheard and misunderstood the slurred moans of the dying man. They reacted superstitiously. Some wanted to try to revive Jesus, but the others restrained them, waiting to see whether some kind of uncanny, miraculous deliverance was about to take place.

There was to be no deliverance. Jesus died. Matthew and Mark report that the world then fell into darkness. The inner veil of the Temple was torn in two, a symbolic fiction meant to convey the success of the values revolution, despite the verdict of the bystanders.[32]

The splitting of the Temple veil exposed its inner sanctum to the world. The hidden secrets, the meaning, the mystery, of Judaism were rendered worthless by that exposure. Another opening-up—the removal of the huge boulder that sealed Jesus' body in the sepulcher—would be the new mystery, as well as the ultimate proof of the triumph of Jesus' values revolution.

For Matthew the rending of the Temple veil seemed inadequate to convey the full importance of the upheaval of values. To that bit of minor theatrics, he adds some cosmic upheavals at the moment of Jesus' death. Matthew produces an earthquake, a splitting of the earth's bedrock, and a terrifying liberation of zombies.[33]

As a final assessment of the person of Jesus, both Matthew and Mark recruit a Roman centurion to give the testimony, "In truth this man was a son of God."[34]

Luke accords with Matthew and Mark in reporting that the passerby Simon of Cyrene was pressed to carry Jesus' cross for him. In Luke, as in Matthew and Mark, the bystanders mocked and taunted Jesus, challenging him to save himself if he could; but Luke does not include the narrow sectarian mockery on the subject of tearing down the Temple and rebuilding it in three days.

Jesus' sigh from the heart, "My God, my God, why have you deserted me?" as reported by Matthew and Mark, could be interpreted as despair by those not acquainted with its literary context in psalm 22. Luke avoids that danger of misinterpretation by putting into Jesus' mouth a line from psalm 31 instead: "Father, into your hands I commit my spirit."[35] According to Luke, Jesus did not yield to despair at the last moment. He surrendered himself in perfect resignation to his destiny.

Luke agrees with Matthew and Mark that at the death of Jesus the world fell into darkness.[36] Luke, too, splits the Temple veil as a dramatic symbol of the triumph of the values revolution against the Establishment.

The testimony of Luke's centurion is a more restrained judgment. Instead of "In truth this man was a son of God," the centurion commented, "This was a great and good man."[37] The phrase "son of God" is implausible and unintelligible coming from the mind of a pagan Roman in judgment upon an executed criminal. "A great and good man" is, however, what a soldier might say after having witnessed the courage and forbearance Jesus had shown in his suffering and death. A death well accepted impresses and converts more effectively than a life well lived.

Luke includes three incidents not in Matthew or Mark. First, he reports that Jesus paused on his death march to give a last lesson in apocalyptic anxiety, this time to the women who followed him. Jesus told them, "Happy are those who are barren, the wombs that have never borne, the breasts that have never suckled."[38] In the imminence of the dread Apocalypse, children and the future were curses. As there was the eunuch ideal for men, so should there be the sterility ideal for women. There was no future, so there should be no sex.

Luke somewhat counters the implicit anti-Semitism in the rending of the Temple veil by putting words of forgiveness and exoneration in the mouth of the dying Jesus. "Father, forgive them; they do not know what they are doing."[39] If only the Christians had taken that cue of cosmopolitan tolerance from Luke!

Finally, Luke records some conversational exchanges between the crucified Jesus and the two criminals who flanked him. After one of them admitted his guilt, repented of it, and also recognized the goodness of Jesus, Jesus responded to that change of heart and testimony by promising the criminal that he would join Jesus in *paradise* on that very same day. In a surprising irony, an outsider, not a member of the brotherhood, becomes the only person in the New Testament to receive a specific, personal promise of heaven.[40]

During his passion Jesus received no help or support from his own apostles and disciples. Instead, it was a stranger, Simon of Cyrene, who served Jesus by carrying his cross. It was an outcast, a criminal, who heeded Jesus' call to repentance. It was a pagan, the Roman centurion, who gave a last testimony to Jesus' legitimacy.

The exquisite irony of the stranger, the criminal, and the pagan, with all its implications on worthiness, is not to the taste of John. In his gospel, John eliminates Simon of Cyrene from the story. If anyone had to help Jesus carry his cross, then Jesus was inadequate to the task of the self-sacrifice. So John specifically contradicts the synoptics. "Jesus . . . carrying his own cross,"[41] is how John reports the scene of the death march.

Instead of the exchange between Jesus and the criminal, in which Jesus promised paradise, John records a more personal conversation, in which Jesus gave "the disciple he loved" and his own mother to each other in a new relatedness, now that their respective ideological and family relatedness were about to be severed by the death of Jesus.

As for the testimony from a centurion, John considers that superfluous, so he dispenses with it. It was the self-sacrifice, the martyrdom, that was the witness and proof and testimony to who Jesus was. Opinions of bystanders, whether favorable or hostile, do not count for much; so John edits out both the centurion's testimony and the petty mockery of the bystanders.

For John, neither stranger nor criminal nor pagan is of interest in the relatedness that Jesus showed during the last moments of his life. He excludes them, in favor of his own personal role as "the disciple Jesus loved." John's version of Jesus' martyrdom is peculiarly personal in all its aspects and details.

John had not found anything congenial in Matthew's eunuch ideal. Nor does he incorporate Luke's sterility ideal, proclaimed by Jesus to the women who accompanied him on the death march. That would have been a discordant clank in the hymn of *perfect love* that was the very meaning of the self-sacrifice.

To John, Jesus was the "light of the world," so John does not report any darkness at the moment of the death of Jesus. Because Jerusalem and its Temple had been destroyed by the Romans a generation before John wrote his gospel, he deletes the rending of the Temple veil. John's propaganda campaign was against the synagogue, not the Temple. For the spectacular histrionics of the earthquake, rock-splitting, and a mass raising of the dead, John substitutes the simple symbolism of pathos, the piercing of Jesus' side, from which *perfect love* flowed out in blood and water. In John's gospel, the death of Jesus is interpreted in terms of personal loss and personal grief.

Just before the flow of blood and water from the body of Jesus, John says that Jesus cried out, "I am thirsty."[42] For "the disciple Jesus loved," love was a pouring-out of everything from one who was himself parched.

The "I am thirsty" recalls psalm 22. Matthew and Mark had quoted the first line of that psalm, a cry of despair: "My God, my God, why have you deserted me?" Luke changed despair into resignation in his version of Jesus' last words: "Father, into your hands I commit my spirit." For John, resignation was still inadequate. He recognizes Jesus' death as his triumph and the triumph of the values revolution. And so, according to John, Jesus died with an exultant cry of triumph: "It is accomplished."[43]

In those words John makes Jesus' triumph unequivocal and explicit. The impression left by an ignominious death on a cross was, nonetheless, despair and resignation. An aura of shame hung over crucifixion, which was the capital punishment reserved for the dregs of ancient society. That there could have been any *accomplishment* in a crucifixion must have struck a citizen of the Roman Empire as an absurd and fantastic paradox. Crucifixion was a shame and a demoralization. How could anything be accomplished by such a death?

Jesus had submitted to his destiny. Because submission may be confused with helplessness and destined martyrdom with failure, the triumph of Jesus and his values revolution could not be considered as accomplished at the moment of his death. The misapprehensions of helplessness, failure, and shame had to be dispelled, if the full meaning of Jesus' martyrdom were to be grasped fully. What dispelled those misapprehensions, those misinterpretations, was the Resurrection. Like any truly successful revolutionary, Jesus would ultimately survive his own values revolution.[44]

Jesus' submission to his destiny was in accord with his conception of his messianic mission. At the moment of his death on the cross that historical mission was completed. But the values revolution had to go on until the cataclysm of the Apocalypse. There could be no letdown at the departure of the Master. That is why he returned. The Resurrection, the overcoming of death, was an act of awesome divine will that erased the mistaken notion of Jesus' human helplessness. The return to life, almost as if to spite the efforts of the

Establishment executioners, was the dramatic triumph that dispelled any notion of failure because of the ignominious death on the cross. What was thought to be the scandal and shame of crucifixion was transmuted into the glory of the Resurrection.

On Easter morning Jesus made himself Master of Life and the Afterlife, as on Good Friday he had made himself Master of Death and the Underworld. He became omnipotent; he became a god. When he rose from the dead and stepped forth from the sepulcher, then he truly could have exclaimed, "It is accomplished!"

That apotheosis made his every remembered word and act while alive the words and acts of a god among men. The Resurrection was the ultimate miracle-as-proof. It was the Resurrection that made the values Jesus taught and lived nothing less than divinely authoritative. Men might wonder and puzzle at the mysteries; but they could no longer question or criticize the values.

To make up for the inadequacies of all the prophets, Yahweh had come Himself in the person of his "beloved son." God had dwelt among us and told us how we must live. After that momentous occurrence human history had to be approaching its end. Anything afterward would be anticlimactic. The self-sacrifice and the Resurrection were preludes to the Apocalypse, the End. As for the values revolution, it had been fully accomplished, first in the paradoxical triumph on the cross, then in the miraculous triumph of the Resurrection.

At the start of his mission, Jesus had prepared himself by spending forty days alone in the wilderness. Now after the completion of the mission, he lingered the same amount of time, forty days, among his apostles. His resurrected presence dispelled their doubts and marshaled their resolve to carry on the values revolution until the day of the Apocalypse. Then Jesus ascended into heaven.[45]

Just as his death on the cross was only an illusory departure, so was his Ascension. The Resurrection, too, had been only an illusory return. The final return was to be the Second Coming, in which Jesus, as the glorified Son of Man, would himself personally usher in the Apocalypse.

Jesus had come and gone, then returned and left, but he would return once again. And so, while the other Jews continued to await the coming of their Messiah, the disciples of Jesus awaited the return of theirs. It was the apocalyptic anxiety all over again, the only difference being that it was now concentrated upon the known person of Jesus, the Son of Man, who had proven himself, by his self-sacrifice and Resurrection, the true Messiah, and beyond that, the *beloved son* of Yahweh Himself.

While Jesus was alive, his disciples had been reluctant to plunge into participation in his martyrdom. It was an unwilling stranger, Simon of Cyrene, who was the first to heed Jesus' call to "take up the cross." The apostles had spoken with bravado, as when Peter insisted that he would follow his Master to the death; but Peter succumbed to the cowardice of his triple denial of any relatedness to Jesus. Similarly, "Thomas—known as the Twin—said to the other disciples, 'Let us go too, and die with him.' "[46] Neither Peter nor Thomas nor any of the brotherhood died with Jesus. Jesus' destiny was his own very private, very solitary, one.

After their Master's death and Resurrection, his triumph and accomplishment, however, his disciples, too, began to crave their own personal triumphs and accomplishments. Their ideal was the *imitatio Christi,* the imitation of their Master. Martyrdom was the ultimate value of that ideal, the climax to which the love for their Master led. And so, the disciples wanted to die after him, to die like him, to die because of him.

From Apocalyptic Sect
to Cosmopolitan Church

The brotherhood of the alienated elect was now bereft of its Master. The Valuesgiver was gone; and all that the apostles had of him was in their memories. At his death they fell into a morbid mood, succumbing to a panic of grief and fear. It was out of their memories, out of their mood, and out of their panic that the apocalyptic anxiety arose as a desperate rallying enthusiasm. In the apocalyptic prophecies of Jesus the apostles found solace, hope, and a promise of ultimate triumph.

The apocalyptic perspective was not original with Jesus. He shared it with John the Baptist, who, in turn, was echoing the prophets who had gone before. Apocalypticism was an ideology of retribution and turnabout, of vengeance and vindictiveness. The tribal religion and the political frustration of the Jews fused into the fiery apocalyptic amalgam. As bad as what had already been, there were to come worse disasters and catastrophes, until Yahweh Himself intervened to effect an ultimate triumph of the Jews over all their historic enemies. Apocalypticism was an ideology of frustrated tribal ambition.

The disciples of Jesus had lived all their lives in that ideological atmosphere. Jesus himself thought and spoke in Jewish apocalyptic terms; moreover, he uttered his own prophecies about the course of apocalyptic fulfillment. After Jesus' death his disciples tried to remember and reconstruct his prophecies. In the three synoptic gospels we find those memories and reconstructions.

According to the gospels, there were to be four sequential events in the apocalyptic scenario. First, the city of Jerusalem would be leveled. Next, there would be a cosmic catastrophe that would destroy the earth itself. Then Jesus, in the guise of the Son of Man, would return in triumphant glory. And last, the Son of Man would preside over the Universal Judgment, in which his chosen elect would be vindicated and his enemies damned.

Jesus' alienation from his society had expressed itself in his confrontations with the religious Establishment. The symbols of the power of that Establishment were the Holy City, Jerusalem, and its Holy Place, the Temple. The triumph of Jesus' values revolution required the utter destruction of that city, the very one that had stoned and killed all the prophets, and of its religious bastion, that pretentious but hollow house on whose steps the money changers transacted their impious business. Jerusalem and its Temple had to be destroyed.

The prophecies of the destruction of Jerusalem are in all three synoptic gospels. A *disastrous abomination* would be set up in the Holy Place. At that utmost blasphemy a disaster would fall upon Jerusalem and Judaea, "such as, until now, since the world began, there never has been, nor ever will be again."[1] The once-and-for-all destruction of Jerusalem would be the final cataclysm in a series of disasters that the city had suffered throughout its long history.

As for the great Temple, Jesus responded to his apostles' admiration of its architecture and embellishments by prophesying, "I tell you solemnly, not a single stone here will be left on another: everything will be destroyed."[2]

It was to be only four decades after Jesus' prophecies of the destruction of Jerusalem and its Temple that it all came true. A Zealot guerrilla army had succeeded in routing the Roman legion sent to deal with it. The future emperors Vespasian and his son Titus retaliated by laying waste to Judaea in a systematic campaign to wipe out Jewish Zealotry forever. In A.D. 70, Titus laid siege to Jerusalem. In the course and consequence of that siege the Temple was burned down and the city itself was leveled, so that not one stone was left upon another, just as Jesus had prophesied.

In the Gospel of Luke we find, in the literal exactness of the apocalyptic prophecies regarding Jerusalem, evidence of eyewitness reportage of the siege of A.D. 70. Luke recounts the raising of fortifications surrounding the city, the massacre of the inhabitants, the leveling of the buildings, and the enslavement and dispersal of the survivors, all of which accords with the actual events of the siege as reported by the historian Josephus in his *Jewish War*. In the military detail and the literal exactness of Luke's version there seems to be after-the-fact reportage retrojected into the prophecy of Jesus. It is characteristic of apocalyptic prophecy to be vague. That Luke is specific is an indication of an anachronistic mix of past history and prophetic prediction.[3]

In the mentality of tribal megalomania, it was inconceivable that the world should survive the utter destruction of the tribal Holy City and the tribal Holy Place. The destruction of Jerusalem and its Temple was to be but a prelude to the cosmic catastrophe of universal doomsday: "Immediately after the distress of those days the sun will be darkened, the moon will lose its brightness, the stars will fall from the sky and the powers of heaven will be shaken."[4]

The destruction of Jerusalem and its Temple was a proof of the ultimate triumph of Jesus' values revolution against the Jewish Establishment. The destruction of the earth was just the old longing for the triumph of the power of the "Kingdom of God" (Jewish religious tribal power) over that of "the world" (Roman political imperial power).

The catastrophe in the Holy City and in the cosmos itself was to be a grandiose setting for the most climactic triumph of all— the Second Coming of the Son of Man, now returned in glory, victorious at last over Jerusalem, Rome, and the entire world.

That Second Coming of Jesus would be a glorious theophany, in comparison to which the Transfiguration was but a pale glimmer.[5] The triumph of the values revolution of Jesus of Nazareth would be not merely religious or political or temporal. It would be cosmic and eternal.

The Son of Man would return with a task in hand: the execution of final retribution. Jesus would preside over the Universal Judgment: "For the Son of Man is going to come in the glory of his Father with his angels, and, when he does, he will reward each one according to his behavior."[6]

As an overture to the symphonic apocalypse of the destruction of Jerusalem and its Temple, the cosmic catastrophe, the Second Coming of Jesus, and the Universal Judgment, there was to be a series of subsidiary events heralding the End Time. False prophets and pseudo-Christs would appear to bewilder the elect. There would be a welter of lesser, preliminary disasters, such as revolutions, wars, earthquakes, plagues, and famines. And the chosen elect would be persecuted in a last brief assault by their enemies just before the final retribution. Paradoxically, amidst and despite all those disasters, catastrophes, and cataclysms, the elect would have just enough time to proclaim the Good News to the world.[7]

When Jesus revealed that mind-boggling apocalyptic vision to his apostles, they were infused with combined dread and anticipation. They pressed him to find out just when all the Ultimate Events were to take place. But vagueness is characteristic of apocalyptic prophecy. And so Jesus told them that no one, not even he, knew exactly when everything would come about. The apostles were to stay alert, keep awake, and interpret the signs of the approaching End.[8]

By refusing to specify the time of the fulfillment of his apocalyptic prophecies, Jesus induced a free-floating anxiety in his disciples. He further intensified that anxiety by telling them that the Ultimate Events were imminent—closer than imminent, of an immediacy that would touch some of those who heard the prophecies from Jesus' own mouth.

Jesus expressed the imminence of the Ultimate Events in two formulations, both reported by all three of the synoptic gospelwriters. Jesus said to his apostles, "I tell you solemnly, there are some of these standing here who will not taste death before they see the Son of Man coming with his kingdom."[9] He also said, "I tell you solemnly, before this generation has passed away all these things will have taken place. Heaven and earth will pass away. . . ."[10]

So Jesus was at least specific enough to tell his apostles that they themselves, who had been born fortunate to witness the arrival of the Messiah, would also witness in their eventful lifetimes the fulfillment of his apocalyptic prophecies. How fired and fevered must have been the imaginations of the apostles as they accompanied their Master! And then they suffered the shock of recognition when the Master's death came in literal fulfillment of his own triply affirmed prophecies.

The apostles were, many of them, we presume, already in middle age. The End, therefore, had to be very near. The moment of the next breath could be the onset of the inevitable, inexorable process of the End. The apocalyptic anxiety of the apostles must have been almost unbearable.

In following Jesus' directive to be alert, to stay awake, and to look for the premonitory signs, didn't the disciples detect those signs of the End almost as soon as Jesus expired on the cross? The gospels indicate that they did so. After all, what was the significance of the tearing of the Temple veil, if not as the first crack in the bastion of the Holy Place and of the Holy City, in other words, the beginning of the First Ultimate Event? And what did the midday darkness and the earthquakes that accompanied the crucifixion mean, if not the onset of cosmic catastrophe, the Second Ultimate Event? Wasn't the Resurrection itself "the Son of Man coming with his kingdom," the Third Ultimate Event? The Temple falling, heaven and earth in upheaval, the Master returned from the dead . . . It must have seemed to the excited imaginations of the terrified disciples that the apocalyptic expectations of Jesus' prophecies were to be fulfilled, not in millennia, centuries, or even years, but in the matter of a few days or hours.

If that was their expectation, the disciples were to be disappointed. The Temple withstood the tearing of its veil, the sun shone again, and the earthquakes, if any, subsided, leaving Jerusalem standing and the globe intact. The Master, even though resurrected, was to linger only forty days and then abandon his disciples once more at his Ascension. The disciples had been deceived in their expectations. Something had gone wrong . . . or else they misunderstood.

Out of disappointment comes the self-accusation of misunderstanding. By the time the gospels were written, in the second half of the first century, many of those who stood with Jesus, and so were supposed to themselves witness the Ultimate Events, had died. Their generation, the generation of the Messiah, was dying with them. Doubts began to arise.

Because the apocalyptic prophecies of Jesus were, in fact, not to be fulfilled, they had to be reinterpreted. The Master could not be in error. All that he prophesied would happen yet, if only his followers, their anxiety now reduced, would learn a new discipline, the discipline of patience.[11]

The Christians gradually modified their expectations, resorting to an apocalyptic revisionism. The opportunity for that revision of the Master's prophecies came with the siege of Jerusalem by Titus in A.D. 70. At the conclusion of the Roman campaign the Temple was razed and the city leveled. The First Ultimate Event, at least, had happened in accordance with the Master's prophecy. The destruction of Jerusalem and its Temple was now historical fact.

But now, when would the other three Ultimate Events take place? That question has been a chronic Christian problem. By a reading not so much bad as ingenious, New Testament commentators have managed to extract the prophecy of the destruction of Jerusalem from its context with the other three prophecies. The First Ultimate Event had come to pass, they recognized with satisfaction. The others were to be postponed until some future, possibly some very distant, time. Even today they are still to come, even today, after a wait of two millennia.

Such a reading was ingenious, but not honest. The apocalyptic expectations of the early Christians, as stated in the gospel prophecies attributed to Jesus, were a unified vision, a sequential, nearly simultaneous, process. Matthew says that *immediately after* the destruction of Jerusalem the cosmic catastrophe would ensue.[12] The gospels clearly affirm that Jesus would return on the tide of that cosmic catastrophe and execute the Universal Judgment at once. The military event at Jerusalem in A.D. 70 could not be taken as the fulfillment of the apocalyptic vision, unless it was followed directly by the cosmic catastrophe, the Second Coming, and the Universal Judgment. It would all happen, and it would all happen together, in a necessarily interrelated sequence.

It was only by compartmentalizing every sentence of the gospel text that the Roman siege of Jerusalem could be interpreted as a fulfillment of the apocalyptic vision. Even if it is so interpreted, the Master was only one-quarter right and three-quarters wrong. Two millennia later the planet persists, the Second Coming is more or less awaited, and the wicked shirk off the Universal Judgment.

"These standing here" and "this generation" both passed away with their apocalyptic expectations unfulfilled. By the time of the siege of Jerusalem, Peter and most of the other apostles were dead. With the death of the last man of the Twelve—who was, according to tradition, John, "the disciple Jesus loved"—the Christian apocalyptic vision necessarily became a dead letter.[13]

If we now leave the four gospels behind and explore the other New Testament writings, we find the apocalyptic vision throughout, even if that vision became more and more blurry. On the one hand, the imminence of the Apocalypse received dogged reaffirmations; on the other, doubts and disappointment, an apocalyptic revisionism, introduced qualifiers and modifications. The Christians became "yes-and-sometime" about the Apocalypse, just as they are still today.

In the Acts of the Apostles, the second volume of Luke's gospel, we have a curious chronicle of the early days of the Christian sect. One of its first episodes is the Ascension, a departure that, Luke tells us, was only illusory. As Jesus was ascending to heaven, two angels promised the apostles that Jesus would return in the same way he was leaving, that is, by a heavenly apparition.[14] That promise, like Jesus' apocalyptic prophecies, evoked the Christian hope for the Second Coming. Some sense of the imminence of Jesus' return permeates the entire story of the early days of the Christian sect, as we read it in Acts, in the epistles, and in Revelation.

Again and again we encounter the apocalyptic refrain: "These are the last days," "Everything will soon come to an end," "The Lord's coming will be soon," and the strangely comforting "The time is close."[15]

After the brotherhood recovered from the shock of their Master's death, after they got over their grief, fear, and disappointment, they were able to transform their apocalyptic anxiety into a spiritual confidence. Instead of cringing at the imminence of the dread Ultimate Events, they could look forward to them with yearning and longing. Chronic tension and hysterical anxiety resolved themselves over time into a calm and confident expectation. A healing process was taking place in the minds of the brotherhood.

The members of the brotherhood considered themselves the chosen elect. That is why, once the Resurrection had enabled them to regain their composure after the death of the Master, they looked forward to the Ultimate Events with equanimity and confidence. What was anxiety about the future became a nostalgia for the past that had given their lives meaning, that past in which the Master had been present to them. Their fears and apprehensions were overcome by a love-longing for the departed Master. "Lord, come!"[16] was the fervent prayer and wish of every member of the brotherhood.

Love cannot endure absence; it craves the return of the beloved. Everything that the disciples of Jesus thought and said and did was pervaded by the spirit of longing for the return, the Second Coming, of their Master.

According to the Acts of the Apostles, the very first corporate act of the brotherhood after the Ascension of Jesus was a reclosing of the mystic circle of the Twelve, which had been broken by the defection and death of Judas.

It was Peter, as we would expect, who took the initiative. He recounted the treachery of Judas, and, with a pair of loosely appro-priate Old Testament quotations, convinced the brotherhood that they should choose someone to take Judas' place. Peter directed that the candidates be from among those who were with them from the time of John the Baptist, that is, eyewitnesses with an experience of the Master equal to their own.

As we would expect Peter to take the initiative, so would we expect him to make the appointment. It would have been an executive decision, in accordance with the investiture scene in Matthew, in which the Master had made Peter his chief executive. The relationship of the brotherhood was more egalitarian, less authoritarian, than the investiture scene in Matthew would lead us to believe. Instead of making a decision, Peter resorted to a throw of the dice.

The episode of the selection of the new twelfth apostle is more egalitarian than authoritarian. It also seems more superstitious than rational. Peter resorted to mere chance, as if the worthiness of the new apostle did not mean so much as the fact that the mystic circle of the Twelve would be healed and closed up again.

The choice of the new twelfth apostle occurred in an aura of compulsion, and, once again, of Jewish mystical numerology. When Peter stood up, he spoke, not coincidentally, to an audience of 120 (a tenfold of the Twelve). The brotherhood membership was a multiple of the mystic number; but the apostles themselves had deviated from it. Peter wanted a restoration of the mystic apostolic number that had been chosen by the Master himself. And so he resorted to chance and luck (*divine selection*) in order to heal the circle.

What Peter evidently wanted was not an administrator to join the organization, but a mere twelfth body to fill out the circle. After all, the Master had picked his Twelve apparently at random. It would have seemed impertinent for the apostles to violate that precedent by arrogantly making judgments on the worth of apostolic candidates.

The election of Matthias, the new twelfth apostle, has been in-terpreted as a first act of "Church" organization. What it really shows is how lightly the apostles considered their organization. (Is it con-ceivable that a pope would trust divine selection, chance, instead of his own managerial judgment, in choosing bishops?) In the expec-tation of the imminent return of the Master, the most important thing was to be ready. The restoration of the mystic circle of the Twelve was just such an act of readiness. As Jesus had chosen twelve, so should he find twelve when he returned.[17]

Infused with the hope of apocalyptic expectation, the apostles did not think in terms of founding or establishing any kind of ecclesiastical institution. Nor did they even consider themselves *Christians.* The texts make it clear that they were Jews still. Although, after the Master ascended to heaven, his apostles "worshiped him," they nonetheless "were continually in the Temple praising God,"[18] as we read in the very last words of the Gospel of Luke.

The apostles carried on their Jewish observances in the Temple. They were, of course, well aware that they were distinguished from other Jews by their relationship to Jesus as the Messiah. Like Jesus, they were Jews; but having been chosen by Jesus the Messiah, they were very special Jews, the chosen persons of the chosen people. And so, the apostles subscribed to both their general tribal tradition and their particular fraternal, or should we now say, sectarian, practices. Luke continues that theme in Acts: "They went as a body to the Temple every day but met in their houses for the breaking of bread."[19]

The apostles did not feel severed from Jewish religion; rather, they felt that they had witnessed, and participated in, the fulfillment of all the prophecies and longings of that religion. Any institutionalization of a Jewish brotherhood into a World Church lay beyond the lifetimes of the twelve apostles. However, every one of their acts would set some kind of precedent for the Church to come. What the apostles did as temporary expedients was to become a model for permanent Church organization.

In preaching the Good News of the Messiah, the apostles expanded the rolls of their brotherhood, until the sheer number of recruits made any kind of informal personal relatedness, such as that of the Twelve, impractical. As we saw, the election of Matthias had a significance more apocalyptic than organizational. But the proselytizing success of the apostles would necessarily present them with organizational problems.

An incident of that is in Acts. Some of the new disciples made a complaint about an injustice in the distribution of the communal resources. That was the first instance of a management problem that the apostles could not handle personally. They responded by freeing themselves of the responsibility. They would confine their own activities to prayer and propagandizing. The duties of distributing charity and managing the dole they would hand over to a new group, the Seven. The apostles delegated a responsibility. A hierarchy was emerging.

In the expectancy of the Master's imminent return, the distribution of food for the body was an insignificant task compared to the giving out of food for the soul, the Good News of the Messiah. The apostles had more important things on their minds than the mundane chore of operating the communal welfare program. Nonetheless, what was done as a temporary expedient would set a precedent for Church organization.

When they created the Seven, the apostles inadvertently institutionalized charity into a self-perpetuating organizational apparatus. The creation of the Seven meant a division of labor and a specialization of function, two characteristics of any organization that is on its way to self-justifying permanence and the drive for social power.

As Peter had let the luck of the dice have its way in the election of the new twelfth apostle, so in the selection of the Seven did he let the broader luck of democratic vote make the choice. It was not the Twelve who chose the Seven, but the whole assembly of disciples, which, we read, then numbered five thousand,[20] an even more unwieldy group than the 120 who were the membership on the earlier occasion of the election of Matthias. The apostles merely ratified the choice of the whole assembly. They laid their hands in rubber-stamp approval on the Seven, so lightly did they hold their own authority and power over organizational matters.[21]

The inadvertent institutionalization of the sect proceeded gradually. Expedient after expedient, taken by men with short-range views, were to have long-range consequences. It is only in the propaganda of self-justification that the modern Christian Church can interpret the haphazard organizational acts of the apostles as a premeditated program to found and establish an eternal World Church.

The idea of establishing an institutional Church was foreign to the apostolic mentality. To the apostles the future meant the Second Coming of their Master, a return so imminent that any long-range planning was pointless. Temporary expedients were all that were needed to keep the brotherhood and the disciples together. It was by their *love* and their *spirit* that they defined their relatedness, not by any offices, dignities, or rank in a hierarchy.

The attitude of the apostles toward the future was apocalyptic. Their attitude toward the past was nostalgic. What they awaited and what they most remembered were the same, namely, the figure of the Master who had given their lives meaning. For the little time that was left of their lives, the apostles tried to live just as their Master had lived, that is, in a mission of healing, preaching, and confrontation with the religious Establishment.

After the Master's Ascension, the apostles did not make a break and try to begin their lives all over again. Instead, they carried on and persisted in the Way that the Master had taught them. The pattern of his life, the *imitatio Christi,* was their ideal. In the imitation of their Master, the apostles healed, and preached, and assaulted the Establishment.

That is why we find in the Acts of the Apostles so many biographical parallels between the apostles and their departed Master. Peter and John may be taken as typical.

Jesus had been the Master Healer, a doctor of body and soul. So, too, were his apostles. When Peter and John encountered a cripple begging at the gate of the Temple, they healed him, in a setting and scene reminiscent of Jesus' miracles in the gospels. Peter later cured a paralytic, again reminiscent of the therapeutic versatility of the Master. Finally, to prove that their power extended into the underworld, Peter raised a woman from the dead, as the Master had raised the daughter of Jairus. All the healing miracles were done in the name of, in the memory of, and in the imitation of, Jesus the Messiah.[22]

The Master had used physical healing as a means to moral healing. The apostles did the same. Peter followed up his cure of the cripple at the Temple gate with a sermon proclaiming the arrival of the Messiah and the urgent necessity of faith and repentance.[23]

Healing and preaching had been characteristic of Jesus' messianic career. The question of his legitimacy, his right to heal and preach, had brought him into conflict with the religious Establishment. That same question of legitimacy, and the same presumptuousness and subversive intent, also brought the apostles into confrontation with the Establishment. Peter and John and, later, all the apostles were called before the Sanhedrin to justify themselves.[24]

As in the case of Jesus, the rulers, elders, and scribes objected to the impudence of the ill-educated and, therefore, illegitimate. As in the case of Jesus, they were stymied by the fact of the healing, that "white magic" that could only be interpreted as beneficent. As in the case of Jesus, they formed a conspiracy to eliminate the impudent upstarts; and, once more as in the case of Jesus, their behavior is interpreted as jealousy against those who were morally and spiritually superior to them.[25]

The apostles were not organizational entrepreneurs boldly embarking upon any such venture of religious capitalism and marketing as a Universal Church. They were unimaginative, nostalgic, conservative men. Their only ambition was the *imitatio Christi,* the simple continuation of the pattern of their Master's life, the healing, preaching, and anti-Establishment propaganda of the values revolution. The apostles were doing no more than just carrying on until the Master's return.

The brotherhood, by the addition of second-generation recruits, was now becoming a sect. The new recruits, those of the second generation, had not known Jesus or been selected by him. On the contrary, they themselves had chosen to join and belong.

What kind of people became converts to a cult of a Master they had never met? ("You did not see him, yet you love him."[26]) What kind of people could be convinced by secondhand testimony, hearsay evidence, paraphrased teaching, and wild apocalyptic prophecies and promises? They would be alienated ones, certainly, because Jesus' subversive values would appeal to the alienated. But would they be righteous and worthy, as were the original Twelve?

Jesus had chosen those whom he wanted, and subjected them to a severe discipline and tests of loyalty. The recruits of the second generation joined, instead of being chosen; their discipline, motivation, and loyalty were untested.

In their zeal to recruit as many as possible, the apostles were not disposed to reject many. The Good News was for everyone. Everyone, and anyone, should have access to the brotherhood. A consequence of the indiscriminate zeal of the apostles was a drastic decline in the quality of the members of the sectarian brotherhood.

The apostles themselves were humble before Jesus. In their social relations they were willing to practice the discipline of tactical humility, as their Master directed them, so that the values revolution, the turnabout, would succeed. Nonetheless, their self-estimate was high, based as it was on personal selection by, and intimacy with, the Messiah himself.

The Master had taught them to practice humility, to value humility. And so, the apostles recruited and attracted the already humble. The worthy alienated drew to themselves the like-minded, but, we discover, the unworthy, alienated.

How did the recruits of the second generation see themselves? What was their self-estimate? We read in the epistles that they thought of themselves as the "foolish," the "weak," the "common and contemptible," the "nothing at all," who, by their membership in a subversive anti-Establishment organization, had an opportunity to shame the "wise," the "strong," and "those who are everything."[27]

That is what became of the Master's discipline of childlike simplicity, self-restraining pacifism, and tactical humility! The recruits of the second generation were fools who gloried in their weakness, their commonness, their contemptibility, and their nothingness. The worthless considered themselves the worthy by virtue of their worthlessness. Now, that was a turnabout in itself, and a subversion, too, a subversion of the disciplinary severity of Jesus of Nazareth.

The Master had been a severe taskmaster to his apostles. He had imposed a superstringent discipline. He had brought out of his apostles what they could become. The apostles, in their turn as taskmasters, slacked off from that discipline. As we read in the epistles, they complained, or coaxed, or cajoled, or flattered, or pleaded, with the recruits. They wanted them to please try to be impossibly better than they were.

The new recruits had not known Jesus personally, had not come under the influence of his compelling personality. They knew the *imitatio Christi* only secondhand. They were less motivated and less committed than the disciples of the first generation. In Acts, we find evidence of reluctance in their motivation, of half-heartedness in their commitment, and of the consequent slacking-off from the pristine discipline of the brotherhood.

Poverty, the absolute detachment from material things, was a key part of the discipline that the Master had required of his apostles. The apostles recognized that. As we read in Acts, they set up a communal pool of property and endeavored to carry on the discipline. Some recruits, like a certain Barnabas, fully complied with the letter and the spirit of the discipline.[28] Luke follows up that model of disciplinary success with a case study of disciplinary failure.

There were two second-generation recruits, a husband and wife named Ananias and Sapphira, who sold their land in order to turn the proceeds over to Peter for the communal pool. Having second thoughts, perhaps for their old age, or for their family responsibilities, they held back some of the money from Peter. Peter figured out, or was tipped off about, their half-heartedness and deceit. He first interrogated Ananias, then Sapphira separately. Confronted with the truth, both died at Peter's feet, murdered, according to one ancient pagan literary critic. In any case, the episode "made a profound impression on the whole Church";[29] that is, it terrorized everybody.

The cautionary tale of Ananias and Sapphira is significant in several ways. First, it shows the half-heartedness and lack of commitment of the recruits of the second generation. We notice, too, that family loyalty put up a tenacious resistance to the antifamilialism in the doctrine of Jesus. In the sudden deaths of Ananias and Sapphira, whether by murder or divine wrath, we detect a propagandistic insistence upon, in response to the erosion of, the severe discipline. Worst of all, Peter's terror-tactics introduced coercion into the discipline, a submit-or-die. The story of Ananias and Sapphira is a confession of the loss of disciplinary innocence.

The Master had been tough with his apostles, but he had not intimidated them. He had let the rich man return to his riches, only making the comment about the camel and the eye of the needle after the man had gone.[30] The apostles, in their turn as taskmasters, found it necessary to intimidate and threaten the recruits of the second generation, those unworthy alienated ones. Both the imposition of, and the assent to, the discipline became corrupted.

The recruits of the second generation were happy in their self-estimate as weak, common, contemptible, lower-caste nothings. Their lack of character came out in such scheming as that of Ananias and Sapphira. If they could not sacrifice their wealth in the right spirit, how much less capable would they be of sacrificing their lives in the right spirit. The willingness to martyrdom was the highest and most difficult aspect of the Master's discipline. That discipline, too, could only be corrupted by the proletarian riffraff who now flocked to membership in the sect.

The Master himself had been the first martyr of his own values revolution. In his self-control during his ordeal, he set the example for the discipline. Some recruits were able to rise to that example, to reproduce the pattern, and to die in the manner of the Master. One of those was Stephen, the protomartyr, whose story is in Acts.

Stephen was one of the Seven. "Filled with grace and power,"[31] he was a formidable debater and a zealous true believer. Summoned before the Sanhedrin on charges of religious sedition, Stephen launched into a presumptuous and impudent speech recounting Jewish history from the time of Abraham. He made his harangue authoritative by including in it a liberal sprinkling of quotations from the Old Testament scriptures. He capped his salvation-history in a way reminiscent of, but not as subtle as, Jesus' parable of the wicked tenants. Stephen accused his listeners, the Establishment, of murdering all the prophets, and of adding to that enormity by murdering Jesus, the Just One, the Messiah.

That enraged the Sanhedrin. Stephen sealed his own doom by announcing a blasphemous vision of the Son of Man standing at the right hand of Yahweh. The Establishment had him hustled out of Jerusalem and stoned to death. (Stoning was the capital punishment for blasphemy.)

All that Stephen had proclaimed—Yahweh's plan for human salvation, the Jews' obligations to Yahweh and His plan, the roles of the prophets and the Messiah, and the culpability of the Establishment for the murders of the prophets and of the Messiah—all of that was fully in the spirit of the Master's example. Stephen followed that example to the utmost by willfully submitting to the martyrdom and by uttering words of forgiveness to his executioners. Stephen achieved a sublime triumph in his personal *imitatio Christi*.[32]

Stephen's courageous confrontation with the Establishment on behalf of the values revolution, his willingness to martyrdom, and his dying words of forgiveness, were in full conformity to the example and the discipline of the Master. Stephen was able to attain a martyr's justification.

Other, less worthy, recruits of the second generation were able, out of their alienation, to muster the courage to take on either the Jewish religious or Roman political Establishment. They may have shown a willingness to martyrdom, too, even if, as the cynical Romans interpreted it, their zeal was nothing but world-weariness and a suicidal compulsion. It was the self-disciplined detachment capable of forgiveness that they were not capable of; they lacked the character for it. Instead of accepting martyrdom as the necessary climax and consequence of their values revolution, the Christians were to become infected with resistance, resentment, and finally, vindictiveness and the lust for revenge.

Acts provides just such evidence of the corruption of the martyrdom discipline. Herod Agrippa had thrown Peter into prison, from which Peter escaped. The escape is followed immediately by a gloating, gleeful account of the death of Herod the persecutor: "He was eaten away with worms and died."[33] That Christian gloating and glee, righteously expressed in terms of *divine wrath,* was to reach its literary peak in the Christian apologist Lactantius' *On the Deaths of the*

Persecutors. Lactantius wrote in the fourth century; but as we see in Acts, the corruption had made its way into the discipline quite early.

It was the lust for revenge, not forgiveness, that was to characterize the Christians' attitude toward the necessary discipline of martyrdom. The Book of Revelation is an orgy of vindictiveness and revenge, all whitewashed once again as divine wrath. The persecutions of Nero and Domitian had put the discipline to the test of fire. The Christians failed that test. By the end of the first century, the voices of the dead martyrs were crying out, "Holy, faithful Master, how much longer will you wait before you pass sentence and take vengeance for our death on the inhabitants of the earth?"[34]

Blatant hatred was projected and expressed in the righteous terms of divine wrath. The necessary spilling of the martyrs' blood induced a bloodlust among the survivors. The Christians succumbed to vindictiveness, rabid in intensity, and opposite to the example and discipline of their Master. Jesus could forgive, Stephen could forgive, but the recruits of the second, and of later, generations were not capable of it.

Reluctance and half-heartedness corrupted the poverty discipline. The lust for revenge corrupted the martyrdom discipline.

The apostles, those who had come under the compelling influence of the Master himself, had been fully committed to the discipline of the brotherhood. Even Judas, by his suicide, proved that loyalty to the Master and inclusion in the brotherhood were a matter of life and death. The Master had screened and disciplined his adherents with that "hard stare" of his.[35] The apostles, in their turn as taskmasters, were not so discriminating or severe. Consequently, there was a rapid deterioration in the quality of the membership. Jesus winnowed the chaff. The apostles harvested it.

A positive valuation was put upon the "foolish," the "weak," the "common and contemptible," the "nothing at all." No such positive valuation could be put upon the other disreputable types that soon infiltrated the sect. The cast of Christian characters in the epistles includes "so-called brothers," "counterfeit apostles," "dishonest workmen disguised as apostles of Christ," "troublemakers," "slanderers," "imposters," "liars," and even "hypocrites," that class that had so aroused the Master himself.[36] The full circle from Pharisaic to Christian hypocrisy was traveled in a much shorter time than has been supposed.

The traditional image of the early Christian community has been as a pure and perfect elect, single-minded and harmonious, the keepers of goodness and truth in the midst of a world mired in evil and error. But that image, that idyl, of pristine purity is a romantic myth.

It is a principle in the sociological interpretation of law that no law is passed until it has been violated. A law is intended, not to prevent something from happening, but to deter the recurrence of behavior that the community has found insufferable. The Ten Commandments forbade idolatry, not to warn the Jews against it, but to call them back from it. As with law, whether civil or religious, so too with preaching and exhortation, should we read the content as against what has been, rather than what might be. Read that way, the disciplinary exhortations in the epistles dispel the romantic myth about the early Christian community as single-minded, righteous bearers of truth and the exclusive practitioners of goodness.

We read that shiftless parasites flocked to the commune where the needs of all would be provided, whether or not anyone was disposed to work.[37] Freeloaders bellied up to the table to gorge themselves at a meal that was supposed to have spiritual, even sacramental, significance.[38] As in any secret society, charlatans and hucksters—the "unprincipled people"—tried to pass themselves off as bearers of esoteric mysteries and secrets more special than the communally shared ones.[39]

Along with that deterioration in the quality of the membership went a contamination of the content of the Good News and a perversion of the very spirit of the brotherhood.

The content of the Good News among the early Christians did not remain as pure and simple as the Sermon on the Mount or Jesus' reduction of the Law and the Prophets to the Golden Rule; it became a promiscuous and adulterated mix of the Master's teachings with "all sorts of strange doctrines," "futile and silly speculations," "godless myths and old wives' tales," "wrangling about words," "antagonistic beliefs," "a travesty of the truth," and even "doctrines that come from the devils."[40] The perpetrator of Revelation had the unscrupulous audacity to put his own words of hatred, violence, and revenge into the mouth of the Master of Love and Peace himself.

"The whole group of believers was united, heart and soul,"[41] it says in Acts. That sentence, which has been taken as an accurate characterization of the early Christian sect is, however, unique in the New Testament. It is everywhere contradicted in the epistles, in Revelation, and in the rest of Acts itself.

The model of Jesus as a person and the integrity of the values program that he taught were quickly subverted by unscrupulous opportunists with conflicting and divisive ideologies. Far from being "united, heart and soul," the early Christian community was a people and an idea at odds with itself.

We read in the epistles that the *spirit* of the second-generation recruits was "wrangling, jealousy, and tempers roused, intrigues and backbiting and gossip, obstinacies and disorder," or, more succinctly, "wars and battles."[42] Those descriptions and all their variants hardly justify the sappy sentimentality about the happy commune of peace and love.

The spirit of the early Christians was not that of peace and love. It was the spirit of faction. Their confrontational stance against society was complemented by an equally acrimonious confrontational stance against one another. As fanatics, the early Christians were as zealous in their fraternal divisions as in their social subversiveness; they were divided, heart and soul. There are allusions to the spirit of faction on almost every page of the epistles.[43]

The three epistles of John are rhapsodies on the themes of love and truth. But they also expose the spirit of discord and faction among the early Christians. The first epistle reveals schism, the second heresy, and the third an ecclesiastical power struggle. Where was the place for the ideal of love and truth amidst the ideological welter of schism, heresy, and power struggle?[44]

Such unholy traits were mere years, not centuries, in the making. The reformers of the sixteenth century embellished the myth of pristine purity, in order to justify their own schism and heresy and power struggle against the Catholic Church. The reformers claimed that their mission was to restore the pristine purity of the early Christian community. But if we read the New Testament, if we read it with the art of good reading, we perceive that there never was any pristine purity to be restored. The corruptions were not a late development in an organization that had gone lax after a millennium and a half of power. It took only a single generation—that generation that had not known Jesus of Nazareth personally—for the cancer, the corruption, of both the model and the values, to thoroughly metastasize throughout the mystical body of the membership.

The sixteenth-century reformers envied the power and wealth

of the Catholic Church. And so they indicted the Church for its abuse of power and its love of wealth. In any values organization, power and wealth are absolutely corrupting influences. In the case of Christianity, too, they corrupted absolutely. And they corrupted early.

It was only in the fourth century, with the conversion of the emperor Constantine, that the Church acquired political power. Before that, its power had been merely spiritual. However, in the superstitious mind, spiritual power is the supreme power. We know that that power was, among the Christians, sometimes for sale. The story of Simon the Magician in the book of Acts is such an acknowledgment of the abuse of spiritual power.

Simon was a sorcerer and charlatan. In the cosmopolitan Roman Empire such characters flocked to places like Palestine, where the people were the most spiritual, or, as Tacitus would say, superstitious. Detecting in Christianity a magical power superior to his own, Simon joined the sect to see if he could turn its secrets to his own advantage.

When he saw Peter and John, two headmen of the sect, demonstrating their magic, Simon offered to purchase the secrets from them. Peter was appalled at the notion of buying and selling spiritual power, *simony,* as it has since been called (as if Simon the Magician were to blame for it). Peter rebuked Simon and threatened him with damnation, in an exhortation that seems directed more generally to the membership than to one particular charlatan. Simon, cringing in dread at an imminent retribution for his violation of a taboo, repented immediately.[45]

The episode of Simon the Magician is another cautionary tale of disciplinary, rather than just anecdotal, significance. It was not only Simon who tempted, or Peter and John who were tempted. The inclusion of the story in Acts and Peter's exemplary indignation acknowledge a problem that had been and was, rather than might possibly be.

The Christian sect claimed power over death. What, or how much, would that power be worth? The episode of Simon the Magician shows that such power tempted, if it could not corrupt, even the chief apostle himself. Peter had known the Master personally and had drunk deep of the values. Mere money was probably no temptation to him at all. It is too bad that the successors of Peter were not able to learn from, and to imitate, his moral example.[46]

Money could corrupt power. Money itself was also a corruption

of the discipline of poverty. At first the apostles attempted to maintain
a communal sharing of wealth. But as the members, out of their
poverty pooled their wealth, they raised the temptation from venial
to mortal. Ananias and Sapphira had only withheld from the pool.
Some less scrupulous and more enterprising recruits were dipping
into that pool for themselves in acts of outright theft and pilfering.

There were money scandals, to which we find about a half-dozen
vague allusions in the epistles. Like our modern TV evangelists, some
early Christian preachers were using their ministry as "a cover for
trying to get money."[47] Even some venerable elders and deacons were
guilty of a greed for money.[48] In the worst perversion of the poverty
discipline, the brothers were picking one another's pockets. The new
"house of prayer" was becoming a "den of thieves."

In dispelling the myth of the "group of believers . . . united, heart
and soul," we nonetheless recognize that there were among the early
Christians people of personal integrity, people who were fully capable
of commitment to, and practice of, the simple life of pacifism and
lovingkindness, in a context of spiritual renewal and apocalyptic
expectancy. There were, as there are today, *true Christians.* However,
if we weigh the evidence as presented in the New Testament, we
must characterize the reality of the early Christian sect as quite opposite
to the idyl and romantic myth.

The disciplinary laxity of the leadership, the mongrelization of
the membership, the corruption of the discipline, the syncretistic contamination of doctrine, the embitterment of the spirit, as well as abuses
of organizational power and wealth—all those, as we discover in the
New Testament itself, were characteristic and typical of the Christian
sect from its earliest days.

An accurate characterization of the early Christian sect might
seem to be of only historical interest. Neither the "imposters" and
"liars" nor the "godless myths and old wives' tales" bother us. Other
traits of the early Christian sect, however, set ominous precedents
for the way in which we ourselves think and the values we ourselves
hold. Particularly ominous was the dogmatism and intolerance of
the sect.

The Christians demanded that each recruit "accept and submit
to the word" "without reservation."[49] To them doubt was not the
healthy skepticism in the search for truth. Doubt was a moral evil.[50]

From the very beginning the Christians were dogmatists. They
subverted the value of tolerance, a humane value that had been so

well cultivated by the philosophers of the cosmopolitan Greco-Roman world. It was the Christians who set Western civilization on a course of dogmatism, that intellectual vice from which we "enlightened" moderns have still not fully freed ourselves.

The sinister obverse of dogmatism is the fanaticism of intolerance. The Good News was a "truth" that would claim millions of martyrs and victims in persecutions and wars throughout the Christian centuries. The will to Christian truth was a will to death, to martyrs and victims.

The early Christians did not turn the other cheek to those who thought differently from them. They struck back. During their politically powerless period, they resorted to the self-righteous ostracism of *shunning*. Shunning meant the exclusion of a member from access to Christian salvation. Such cruelty was perpetrated on ideological, just as well as on moral, grounds.[51]

When the Christians eventually acquired political power, they vented their intolerance in political ways, such as censorship, heresy trials, executions, holy wars, and Crusades. The dogmatism and the intolerance had come from the Jews, and, it must be recognized, through the Master himself. But the use of force was a lesson learned from Caesar.

Christian intolerance was of the essence, and expressed itself early. "If anyone does not love the Lord, a curse on him!"[52] That was to be Christianity's last word on the issue of ideological tolerance. Love, the Prime Value, became an ultimatum, with an explicit curse upon those who made any different choice.

And so the mean spirit of sectarian intolerance pitted itself against the tolerant pagan cosmopolitan society of the ancient world.

As the Christians worked out and elaborated their peculiar values, they felt a stronger and stronger sense of identity and a distinction from the peoples among which, and the societies in which, they lived. There were two peoples, particularly, from which the Christians had to distinguish themselves, namely, the Jews and the Romans.

It was from the religious traditions of the Jews that the Christians themselves had emerged. It was under the political dominion of Rome that the Christians lived. The Christians had to determine their relatedness to the Jews and to the Romans. The Christians had to develop a "foreign policy."

The apostles thought of themselves as no other than the Jews they were. To them the arrival of the Messiah in the person of Jesus meant not a break and new beginning, but a fulfillment of Jewish religious longing. Jesus had specifically told them that he had come not to destroy, but to perfect, complete, and fulfill the Law and the Prophets. After his death, the apostles, as we saw, carried on their Jewish observances side by side with their own sectarian practices.

Such easygoing two-mindedness could not continue long. After all, in the Christian view, it was the Jews who had agitated to have their beloved Master subjected to the ignominious death on the cross. To the Christians, the Jews had "murdered" the very Messiah who had come for their sake, for their salvation, and for their liberation. Hadn't the Jews, then, as far as the Christians were concerned, committed the most heinous of possible crimes? Didn't they now bear the curse of their terrible guilt?

The Christians became ambivalent in their attitude toward the Jews. That ambivalence is manifest in a sermon by Peter, delivered just after he had cured the cripple at the gate of the Temple in Jerusalem.

"You . . . accused the Holy One, the Just One . . . you killed the prince of life,"[53] Peter said to the crowd on the very steps of the Holy Place. It was a bitter indictment. Then, remembering the necessity of the Messiah's martyrdom, Peter went on to exonerate the Jews of their "crime." He did so by excusing their ignorance of the gravity of their deed: "Now I know, brothers, that neither you nor your leaders had any idea what you were really doing."[54]

In those words, put into the mouth of Peter by Luke in Acts, we hear an echo of some other words of forgiveness on the grounds of ignorance, those put into the mouth of the dying Jesus by Luke in his gospel.[55] The Christian policy toward the Jews, then, was forgiveness; but forgiveness means that there is a crime to be forgiven, and of that crime the Jews were guilty, even racially guilty.[56]

In fact, the Pharisees *did* know what they were doing in their plot against Jesus. They recognized him as an anti-Establishment subversive, a threat to their prestige and power. The Pharisees, therefore, proceeded against Jesus with full knowledge and clear intent. Peter's words of forgiveness, like those of his Master on the cross, were irrelevant because inaccurate. The Establishment did not act out of ignorance.

Luke's gesture of toleration in the words of forgiveness that he put into the mouths of both the Master and his chief apostle could not check the increasing bitterness felt by the Christians toward the Jews. Jews themselves, but estranged from the Jews and so from themselves, the early Christians vented their bitterness in an ever more strident rancor against the Jews as Christ-killers, the Messiah-murderers.[57] The seeds of all later Christian anti-Semitism were sown throughout the books of the New Testament.

Whatever the role of the Jewish mob in securing the death of Jesus, it was not the Jews, but the Romans who had actually killed the Messiah. Masters of the legal order, the Romans bore the legal responsibility for the execution. It would have been more accurate and more logical to blame the Romans. But the Christians did not do that.

In the same speech in which he expressed his ambivalence toward the Jews, on the one hand indicting them as Christ-killers, on the other forgiving them on the grounds of ignorance, Peter exonerated the Romans completely. According to him, Pontius Pilate had decided to release Jesus as an innocent man. It was only the Jewish mob and their threats of anarchy and riot that compelled Pilate to order the execution. In short, the hands that Pilate washed were clean and really needed no washing.

We recall that in the Gospel of John, Jesus gave Pilate a gratuitous exoneration for his role in the Messiah's destiny. Pilate was, then, twice judged guiltless, first by the Messiah during the trial, and then by Peter, pronouncing on his sect's foreign policy after the death of the Messiah. The Christians could not bring themselves to forgive the Jews, but as for the Romans, they were adjudged not guilty, and therefore they needed no forgiveness.[58]

Before the persecutions of Nero and Domitian brought out an anti-Roman bitterness of the Christians over the issue of necessary martyrdom, the attitude of the sect toward Rome was surprisingly complacent and submissive. In his first epistle Peter preaches cooperation and collaboration: "For the sake of the Lord, accept the authority of every social institution: the emperor, as the supreme authority. . . ."[59] Peter may have wanted to protect his charges from the fate of Zealots, proletarian revolutionaries, and rebellious slaves; but in his complacent submissiveness Peter backed off from the adversarial stance that was the appropriate one against idolatrous paganism.

The Master himself had equivocated on politics by giving his vague instructions to render to Caesar what was Caesar's and to

God what was God's. Some of his disciples would obey those instructions, but with the witty reservation that Caesar deserved nothing and so it was their religious duty to render nothing to him. Peter either misunderstood the noncommittal of his Master, or else he decided that changed times required a changed foreign policy. Peter told his charges exactly what was to be rendered to each: "Fear God and honor the emperor"[60] was his formula. As chief executive, Peter was working out the foreign policy. He seems to have concluded that political expediency would be of advantage to the sect.

In their political relatedness to the Jews and the Romans, the attitude of the Christians toward the first group was ambivalence and the grudge; toward the second, submission and collaboration. From the standpoint of religious values, the Christians chose to take on the wrong adversary. It was paganism, not Judaism, that was immoral and idolatrous. However, from the standpoint of political expediency, the Christians made the appropriate choice.

In their attempt to woo the Romans, we recognize that the Christians were trying to learn politics. They could free themselves from Jewish scruple. They could be expedient. It is an irony that they transposed ideological kin and ideological adversary in the process.[61]

The Roman Empire was a cosmopolitan society. The city of Rome itself was Cosmopolis, and the other great cities of the Empire, such as Alexandria, Antioch, and Ephesus, grew into cosmopolitan metropolises. Even Jerusalem, that citadel of tribal cult, attracted a cosmopolitan gathering. Since the imposition of world peace by the emperor Augustus, the peoples of the Mediterranean enjoyed free and safe travel throughout the Empire. Wherever they went, the travelers took their values with them.

In such an open society as was the Roman Empire, the Christians could exert little influence if they clung to the Jewish tradition of chauvinistic social separatism. If the Christian values were to make any headway in a cosmopolitan world, the consciousness of the Christians would have to become cosmopolitanized. Besides a foreign policy, the Christians needed a missionary strategy.

Early in the book of Acts there is the curious but highly significant episode of Pentecost. After the newest apostle had restored the apocalyptic mystic circle, the Twelve then sequestered themselves in a strategy session. They had to muster their courage to carry on the values revolution begun by their Master.

Suddenly the building reverberated with a roar from heaven.

Tongues of fire appeared in the room and came to light on the foreheads of all the apostles. Those tongues of fire are a metaphorical image for an inspiration that came to them. Enthusiastic in that inspiration, or "filled with the Holy Spirit,"[62] in the words of Acts, the apostles began to speak in foreign languages. Inflamed by a linguistic ecstasy, they received the *gift of speech* itself.

The apostles then went outside to proclaim the Good News to the cosmopolitan assemblies of Jerusalem, to each nationality, to each person, in an intelligible language. The listeners were astonished. They had come from all parts of the Empire, they spoke various languages, they held a multiplicity of values, and yet, all could understand the message proclaimed by this strange Galilean sect.

In the Old Testament tale of the Tower of Babel, the profusion of languages and cultures in the world was a curse put upon mankind by a tribal god jealous of his rights. The tale of the Tower of Babel is propaganda on behalf of tribal separatism. It is anticosmopolitan.

In Luke's story of the gift of speech on Pentecost, the profusion of languages was not a curse but a blessing, a grace from the Holy Spirit. The diversity of languages and cultures, an impediment to the Jews, was now an opportunity for the Christians. The Christians became polyglots. They could, and they would, speak to all the peoples of the cosmopolitan society around them.

Both in his gospel and in Acts, Luke promotes a cosmopolitan consciousness. In telling the Pentecost story, he repudiates the tribal chauvinism of the Jews, so overt in the story of the Tower of Babel. The descent of the tongues of fire is a vivid and memorable fiction meant to justify the increasingly cosmopolitan missionary strategy that the Christians were to adopt. Luke is a master propagandist on behalf of the cosmopolitanization of sectarian consciousness.

The apostles had been shut up tight in the building, just as the Jews were shut up tight in their tribal conceit and social separatism. The apostles had been suffocating from cultural claustrophobia. The roaring wind came as a breath of fresh air from the outside. The tongues of fire burned the cosmopolitan perspective into the minds of the apostles and so into the policy of the sect.

Luke reports that not all the listeners were convinced by the polyglot message that the apostles emerged to proclaim. Some laughed off the gift of speech as an alcoholic delirium. But cosmopolitanization does not come about all at once; it takes time. Pentecost was the occasion of the first inspiration. At that time the cosmopolitan voice of the Christians was not yet fully articulate. As infants stumble and struggle with newly learned speech, so, too, did the apostles.

Even if they did not succeed in becoming fully articulate all at once, the Christian leadership had opened their minds as well as their mouths. Their consciousness was becoming cosmopolitanized.[63]

A general inspiration needs to be articulated into the specifics of policy. Peter proceeded to transform the Pentecostal inspiration into a definite cosmopolitan policy. In characteristic New Testament style, the first policy decision of Peter is presented in the guise of a vision.

Praying on a rooftop under the sweltering midday sun, Peter was distracted by gnawing hunger. He fell into a dreamlike trance, which, like all true dreams, mingled mental and physical states into an image. The image that Peter saw was a huge tablecloth, covered with a promiscuous mix of all kinds of animal foods. His hunger, as a heavenly voice, directed Peter to eat something from the tablecloth.

Reacting like a Jew, Peter declined to eat anything that was "profane" or "unclean." In rebuttal the voice told Peter that God had made everything clean. The voice then repeated its directive. But Peter still held back, still clung to the traditional Jewish dietary scruples. The voice repeated its directive yet again. The order from heaven was now an unequivocal triple affirmation. Peter was forced to the conclusion that the Jewish dietary scruples, one aspect of their social separatism, had to be abandoned.

While Peter was pondering the implications of his vision, some messengers came to him with an invitation to visit a Roman centurion named Cornelius. The Jews would not profane themselves by stepping across the threshold of the home of a gentile. But if there was no unclean food, Peter thought, why should there be any unclean human beings? Deliberately violating the tribal taboo, Peter accepted the hospitality of Cornelius.

Peter had decided that, in light of the Pentecostal inspiration, the segregational stance of the Jews had become obsolete. Heaven itself, in its emissaries of tongues of fire, visions, and voices, was telling Peter that he could eat anything and associate with anybody. The traditional social separatism of the Jews, in its various aspects, had to be repudiated, in order for the Christians to make an effective cosmopolitan appeal to the peoples of the Empire.

"The truth I have now come to realize," said Peter in a momentous policy statement, "is that God does not have favorites, but that anybody of any nationality who fears God and does what is right is acceptable to him."[64] Peter went on to make a clear affirmation of a universalist ambition for his sect: "Jesus Christ is Lord of all men."[65]

Heaven immediately ratified Peter's decision. The Holy Spirit and even the gift of speech descended upon Cornelius and the pagans. Peter had no other choice but to recognize divine will. He had the pagans baptized, so that they could fully share in membership in the Christian community.

Whether it was Peter himself who pioneered Christian missionary strategy by dispensing with Jewish dietary scruples and the taboo on associating with gentiles, or whether the policy actually came about by gradual consensus, the significance of the historical event is the same. The consciousness of the Christians was becoming cosmopolitanized.[66]

Cosmopolitanization does not come about easily. Besides the inarticulateness of the first words to the world, as in the episode of Pentecost, there would be the drag of the old narrow tribal mentality. Peter had no sooner left the house of Cornelius, when he was challenged to justify his actions.

The rest of the apostles were still under the spell of the ingrained tribal scruples and taboos. There was an immediate backlash against the tentative first steps of cosmopolitan policy.

Peter justified himself on religious grounds, rather than on expedience. He recounted his vision of the tablecloth that descended from heaven laden with its promiscuous mix of food, and then told how the Spirit had directed him to consort with Cornelius and the pagans. "Who was I to stand in God's way?"[67] Peter argued. Presented in that way, as a heavenly directive, the new cosmopolitan policy overcame the resistance of the tribal mentality. The apostles were satisfied with Peter's explanation and justification. The vision and the Spirit were effective rebuttals to their objections.

Peter had taken the initiative in developing his sect's cosmopolitan missionary strategy and had successfully defended it against the backlash from the old tribal mentality. However, the potential proselytes, the pagans, would raise objections of their own. One of those was over circumcision.

The Mediterranean pagans considered circumcision an abhorrent sexual mutilation little different from castration. So steeped in eroticism was Mediterranean paganism that any anti-erotic practice, such as circumcision, aroused deep revulsion. When the pharisaical party of Christians insisted that pagan recruits undergo circumcision, in accord with the Mosaic Law, as well as Baptism, the Christian rite, they ran into an impasse. Pagan sensitivity reacted with disgust at the notion of sexual mutilation as a necessary initiation rite.

Peter dealt with the problem by appealing to the case of Cornelius. If God had already shown His approval of the uncircumcised pagan Roman by bestowing the Holy Spirit upon him, wouldn't it be impious of the apostles to demand the merely surgical initiation?

Once again Peter presented his own policy as a heavenly directive. His reasoning "silenced the entire assembly."[68] Circumcision, an impediment to any missionary work among the pagans, was not to be an essential sign of the New Covenant. One more characteristic of the social separatism of the Jews, one more drag of the tribal mentality, had been dispensed with.

Some accommodation did have to be made with the Jewish heritage from which the Christians had emerged. As we discover in the epistles, the issues were not resolved so easily as we would conclude from the account in Acts. In the egalitarian atmosphere of the brotherhood, the word of Peter was not *ex cathedra*.

Despite Peter's vision of the promiscuously laden tablecloth, for example, James pushed through a compromise on the issue of diet, a policy that would not be so offensive to the tenacious tribal scruples. The pagan recruits, James ruled, should abstain from any food that had been part of a sacrificial offering to a pagan deity, from any meat of strangled animals, and from blood. That ruling was a typically Jewish prohibition against idolatry and the eating of unclean products of nonkosher slaughtering and blood, which in the Jewish mind was identified with the life-force of the animal.[69]

If the Christians were to effectively preach their Good News in such cosmopolitan metropolises as Alexandria, Antioch, Ephesus, Corinth or Rome, they would have to free themselves from the scruples and taboos of the narrow tribal mentality of Jerusalem. The process of cosmopolitanization would be a complex mix of antitraditional initiatives, resistance and backlash, justifications, compromises, and accommodations.

After he had justified himself on his violation of dietary scruples and the taboo against consorting with pagans, Peter put his new policy into practice by sending Barnabas as an emissary to recruit pagans in Antioch. It was in Antioch that the first brotherhood of pagan recruits was established. It was in Antioch that the members of that brotherhood were first designated as "Christians," in an identification that fully distinguished them from the Jews. And it was from Antioch that the pagan resistance to circumcision first expressed itself.[70]

What had started as a breakaway Jewish sect in Palestine was now becoming a cosmopolitan religious organization. It was becoming a *Church.* According to tradition, Peter personally carried his cosmopolitan strategy to Rome, the capital of the world. He widened the scope of the values revolution, from Jerusalem, the closed tribal citadel, to Rome, the open Cosmopolis.

It was in Rome, too, that Peter embraced the ultimate aspect of the self-discipline of the brotherhood. He was martyred, crucified, like his Master, but upside down, in an *imitatio Christi* checked by a humility probably more personal than tactical.

The martyrdom of the Master had been the climax of his career and of a values revolution that had been directed against the religious Establishment of Jerusalem. For his part, Peter continued the campaign against Jerusalem. It was only a few years after the deaths of Peter and James that that city, repudiated and abandoned by the Christians, was utterly destroyed, just as the Master had prophesied. Jerusalem, the native city of the sect, would be fully supplanted by Rome, now destined to be the headquarters of a Universal Church. However, several centuries still lay between what Titus did to Jerusalem and what Constantine was to do in Rome.

The prophetic conclusion of Acts, like the tagged-on endings of the gospels, was an affirmation of the new cosmopolitan missionary strategy: "Understand, then, that this salvation of God has been sent to the pagans; they will listen to it."[71]

Jerusalem was a memory. It belonged to the sectarian past. Rome was a vision. It represented the opportunity for a cosmopolitan, a universal, even an eternal, future.

Antichrist

Peter may have taken the initiative in developing Christian missionary strategy, and his fellow apostles may have become persuaded that the future of their sect was to be a cosmopolitan one. However, the life experience of the twelve apostles was narrow. Born and raised in the restricted tribal atmosphere of Palestinian Judaism, lightly educated and little traveled, they were mostly ignorant of the great cosmopolitan world of the Roman Empire.

The Master had tried to liberate the apostles' consciousness from the straitjacket of tribal religious attitudes. He had told them that it was what came out of a man, not what went into a man's body, that made him *unclean*. He had readily granted a cure to a Syro-Phoenician gentile and to the servant of a centurion, an uncircumcised pagan.[1] Yet, after the Master was gone, Peter's initiatives on the issues of diet, consorting with pagans, and circumcision still encountered resistance and backlash from the other apostles.

During the Master's lifetime, the apostles had not attained even a full religious enlightenment. (Didn't the Master linger among them forty more days after his Resurrection, in order to help them along still further?) How much less, then, could be expected of the apostles in the way of cultural enlightenment. The apostles may have recognized the cosmopolitan necessity. But they were deficient in cosmopolitan sensitivity.

The task of carrying the Good News to all parts of the Roman Empire would have to be taken up by the recruits of the second generation, outsiders who lived in, and understood, the outside world. It so happened that such an outsider did appear. He was a genius and leader who managed to take hold of the mass psychology of both the Christian sectarians and pagan cosmopolitan urbanites. In experience and intellect he himself was fully cosmopolitan. He was to prove capable of taking up the task of cosmopolitanizing the sect.

The outsider was a Jew, but he had been born far from Palestine, in Asia Minor. He was well educated in Jerusalem itself, having learned rigorous Pharisaical Judaism from one of the most prominent rabbis in the city.

Although born into the tribal sectarianism of the Jews, the outsider was a fully cosmopolitan character. To the Jews he spoke Aramaic, and from the Jews he could command the respect that his Pharisaical learning merited. He was also fluent in Greek, the pagan cosmopolitan vernacular. He knew the pagan literature and the pagan mind; he was even adept at pagan philosophical argument. Finally, by accident of his birth, he was a Roman citizen, entitled to all the privileges of that citizenship. Jew, Greek, and Roman all at once, this outsider was to be the most valuable of all the recruits of the second generation.

The outsider had never met or even seen Jesus of Nazareth, the Master. He did encounter some believers in what was known as "the Way." At first the outsider let his Jewish self react against the followers of the Way. He saw them as blasphemers who deserved the prescribed punishment for that most capital of religious crimes.

The outsider participated in the execution of Stephen, the Christian protomartyr. He stood by and held the clothing cast off by those who flung the stones. He heard the words of Stephen's eloquent defense, his expressions of intimacy with the Deity, his resignation to death, and his strange, most strange, forgiveness of his executioners.

As the outsider stood by, performing the role of his Jewish sectarian self, he approved the execution of Stephen. But Stephen's eloquent words and his uncanny behavior penetrated the consciousness of the outsider. A short while later, something in the outsider's mind snapped.

He was on his way to Damascus, a city in Syria, a partly Jewish, mostly cosmopolitan city like Antioch, where the members of the Way were to establish their first foreign cadre. Just outside Damascus, on the cosmopolitan threshold as it were, the outsider collapsed to the ground and suffered a frightening hallucination.

A terrible voice from heaven spoke to him. It was the Master of the Way himself. He demanded to know why the outsider was persecuting him. The Master ordered the outsider to enter Damascus and await further instructions.

A brilliant light from heaven, a true *enlightenment,* had accompanied the terrible voice of the angered Master. The outsider was struck blind by that light. His blindness was guilt at his complicity in the murder of Stephen. He denied having witnessed that murder; he was just a blind man. Now, on the threshold of the cosmopolitan world, he realized that it was his old Jewish sectarian self that was blind; that, in fact, all the Jews were blind.

The outsider was led by the hand into Damascus, where he remained blind for three days, the same amount of time that the Master had lain dead in the darkness of the tomb. As if to re-create that temporary death in himself, the outsider neither ate nor drank anything for those three days.

The Master then took pity on the outsider, forgave him, and even called him to his service. The Master sent a healer to restore his sight. After the three days of the outsider's spiritual entombment came a resurrection of his soul, a new birth, a *conversion.* And so, the outsider, Saul, a cosmopolitan Jew, became an insider, Paul, a cosmopolitanizing Christian.[2]

Paul's experience on the road outside Damascus was a midday sunstroke,[3] a hallucination compounded of the model-image of Stephen, the guilt of complicity in his murder, and an anxiety about imminent retribution. Paul interpreted that hallucination as a vision and revelation. A heavenly power had appeared to him to bestow a mission, like those of the prophets of old. Out of his guilt and fear, rooted in the death of Stephen, Paul identified the heavenly power as the Master of Stephen's Way. He identified the mission bestowed upon him as a calling to that Way, and because it was the Master himself who recruited him, as a calling to leadership in the Way.

Such a conversion was, more likely, a self-calling. Paul had been impressed and unnerved by Stephen's courage and his self-sacrificing accomplishment. How could he make up for the crime of killing such a man? Just as the worst sinners become, upon conversion, the greatest saints (a behavioral about-face), so, too, do the most rabid adversaries become the most zealous partisans (an intellectual about-face). Paul was to become the most zealous of all the partisans of the Christian Way.

But how could he deal with the suspicion, even the grudge against him, of the friends of those who had suffered from his former persecutions? How could his conversion, which was a mere self-calling, become credible to the brotherhood? How could an outsider, a persecuting adversary, in fact, come to a position of leadership in the values movement?

The answer was in the vision and revelation. Peter had justified his policy initiatives on diet and consorting with pagans by telling of his own midday sunstroke-vision of the laden tablecloth and of heavenly directives from the Spirit. The truly religious mind cannot contradict or refute the reality and truth of visions or heavenly apparitions. So Paul, too, appealed to his own vision experience to gain, first, acceptance, then leadership, and, ultimately, a near preeminence in the movement.

Paul explained his change of mind and heart to his fellow Jews by recounting his conversion experience. In the telling, however, he got a few details mixeu up. In the narrative of the event, as given in Acts, the bystanders heard the voice, but could see no one. In Paul's telling, the bystanders saw the light, but did not hear the voice. By one account the bystanders were blind not deaf; by the other, deaf not blind. Such a test of consistency is not to be applied to reports of visions and apparitions. Paul justified himself in terms that the Jews could understand. He had had a vision and had been called by heaven to a prophetic role.[4]

Paul told the story of his conversion all over again, to King Herod Agrippa II.[5] In the original account of the incident, in Paul's telling to the Jews, and in his retelling to King Agrippa, we have a typical New Testament triple affirmation. Paul's threefold acknowledgment of the Master in Acts stands in counterpoint to Peter's threefold denial in the gospels as well as to Peter's threefold re-calling by the resurrected Master at the end of the Gospel of John. Like Peter, Paul too had been called to service by the resurrected Master.

The re-calling of Peter was meant only to rehabilitate Peter's reputation after his three denials of the Master during the time of crisis. Peter had, in fact, been called and chosen by the Master at the very beginning of the values revolution. Paul belonged to the second generation, to those who had neither seen nor known the Master. So Paul had a problem, the problem of legitimacy.

We might wonder what went through Peter's head when he heard the story of Paul's conversion. After all, Paul was a near contemporary of the apostles, and, had the Master needed him, he should have been able to draw Paul to him, somehow, during his lifetime.

It was almost as if the Master had been born just a bit too early to choose the mature Paul directly; at least that was Paul's own opinion: "Last of all," he writes, "he appeared to me too; it was as though I was born when no one expected it."[6]

Paul claimed membership in the apostolic brotherhood. Of the same generation, he was just slightly out of biographical synchrony with the Twelve. The Master remedied the lack by calling Paul, when Paul finally did mature to the stage of apostolic readiness. The Jews had been waiting for the Messiah. The Messiah, it seemed, had been waiting for Paul.

Peter and the other eleven may have had doubts and questions about Paul's right to membership in the apostolic brotherhood; but to his vision and to the heavenly directive, they could venture no contradiction or refutation. The apostles wanted to share their personal and religious experience of their Master. How could they deny anyone who had, no matter how strangely, already shared in that experience?

Paul's testimony to his conversion had to be believed, even if it was not convincing. If Paul showed, by his actions, that he had truly undergone a conversion, then he had to be accepted. Nonetheless, such an initiation into the apostolic brotherhood, as if by post-Resurrection afterthought, could only arouse suspicion and nagging doubt. The first-called, the directly called, would continue to have their doubts about this outsider who crossed the line from fanatic persecutor to zealous partisan. Paul was an upstart. Paul was an intruder.

The problem of legitimacy clung to Paul as a taint and suspicion throughout his life. He must have wearied at the many retellings of his Damascus vision to skeptical and fearful members of the persecuted Way. Was Paul, they must have wondered, a faker or a spy?

When Paul took up literary propaganda on behalf of the Way, he correspondingly propagandized on behalf of his own legitimacy. He did so again and again, in a desperate campaign to establish the authority for his teachings and for his ever more exalted status in the values movement.

Paul exhausted the possible formulas that express Christian legitimacy: He was called by Jesus; or he was appointed by God; or he was appointed by both Jesus and God the Father; or, finally, he was called by the Holy Spirit. Interpreted in terms of modern theological thinking, Paul's appointment, his authority, and his legitimacy were nothing less than trinitarian.[7]

In the gospels the legitimacy of Jesus was proclaimed by the Thunder-Voice of God the Father Himself and attested by the descent of the Spirit, in the scene of Jesus' baptism by John the Baptist. We would have expected such testimony to suffice, but were surprised to find that the devil, too, was enlisted to attest to the legitimacy of Jesus. Similarly, not even the trinitarian appointment was enough to establish the legitimacy of Paul. Once again the devil was enlisted.

There were some Jewish exorcists, in number seven (the same number as the stereotypical quota of devils), who were plying their trade in Ephesus. During the incantations of their exorcistic mumbo jumbo they happened to invoke the names of Jesus and Paul. At that the devil said, "Jesus I recognize, and I know who Paul is, but who are you?"[8] Then the devil, seven-in-one himself, attacked the seven imposters, stripped, and mauled them. The devil's words, "Jesus I recognize, and I know who Paul is," insinuated Paul into association with Jesus in an adversarial role against the devil. That insinuation, that association, was the devil's testimony to the legitimacy of Paul.

Jesus, as the Messiah, the Christ, the Resurrected One, as well as God the Father, as well as the Holy Spirit, as well as the devil—all those spiritual entities, in visions, revelations, and exorcisms, attested to the legitimacy of Paul as an apostle. The highest spiritual powers, both beneficent and maleficent, were appealed to by Paul in order to establish and assert his legitimacy as the outsider who deserved to be an insider, the last-arrived who deserved to be a first-respected.

In his epistles Paul deals with the suspicions and doubts about his legitimacy by means of ever more intimate associations with the Deity in all aspects of His person. Correspondingly, Paul resorts to an extreme on the subject of his late arrival and after-the-fact appointment. He goes back to his life before and beyond the incident at Damascus to an earlier, a much earlier, apostolic appointment. "God . . . had specially chosen me," he asserts, "while I was still in my mother's womb. . . ."[9]

That such intemperate rhetoric verges upon a parody of the Incarnation of the Master himself did not seem to deter Paul. His quest for legitimacy drove him to mystical and rhetorical extremes, to ever wilder formulas that should have been offensive to Christian, as well as to Jewish, religious scruple.

Among the Christians there could be as little contradiction of divine adoption as of visions and revelations. Those were the very religious experiences that the initiates themselves craved. If Paul could prove himself by his deeds, as well as by his zeal, then acceptance and even leadership were to be his. The early Christians were not critical. They were enthusiastic. They would be led along by anyone whose superiority was proved by an enthusiasm more intense than their own.

It had exasperated the Master to discover that the people would not believe him unless he proved the truth of his claims by *signs and wonders*. The Master did perform many signs and wonders, as did his apostles. To the religious mind, miracles are proof of truth, and of the honesty and goodness of the speaker. Like the Master and his chosen apostles, Paul was driven to work miracles as a demonstration and proof of his legitimacy.

Peter, the chief apostle, had cured a cripple on the steps of the Temple in Jerusalem. Paul, too, cured a cripple. He did so, significantly, not in Jerusalem, the stronghold of the Twelve, but in a town in Asia Minor near his own birthplace. And he did so not on the steps of the Jewish Temple, but virtually on the steps of a pagan temple of Zeus.[10]

The propaganda of legitimacy in that episode is clear: Peter could perform miracles, but his mission was only to the Jews of Jerusalem. Paul could perform miracles on a par with Peter, and his mission was to the pagans of the wider world. Paul worked his own territory.

In the early parts of the book of Acts certain biographical parallels are drawn between the apostles and their Master in various episodes of healing, preaching, and confrontation with the Establishment. In the later parts of Acts corresponding parallels are drawn to insinuate Paul into association with the Twelve, and beyond them, with the Master himself.

In the city of Philippi, in Macedonia, Paul and his sidekick Silas were thrown into jail. A timely earthquake broke their chains and liberated them. That miraculous escape is an obvious and propagandistic parallel to two earlier miraculous escapes from jail, by Peter, and by the apostles.[11]

The setting for Paul's escape is in a pagan cosmopolitan context; the escapes of Peter and the apostles take place in tribal Jerusalem.

Paul was delivered by an earthquake, a cosmopolitan prodigy; Peter and the apostles had been liberated by a Judaic angel. While Paul was confronting the civil authorities of the great Roman Empire, Peter and the apostles were still mired in petty confrontation with the Jewish religious Establishment of Jerusalem.

One task to which the Master had set his apostles was the expulsion of devils. Paul had to prove that he was not only legitimized by the devil's recognition, as in the incident of the seven Jewish exorcists at Ephesus, but that he could also wield power over any and every devil.

The Master and his apostles had exorcised devils from both men and women. While in Philippi, Paul was hounded by a hysterical woman, a fan who idolized him. Bothered by her attentions, Paul turned and drove the "devil" out of her. The woman was a slave and fortuneteller. That the loss of her devil caused a loss of income in the fortunetelling trade for her masters is given as a contributing cause of the imprisonment of Paul and Silas![12]

The Master and his apostles wielded power over the underworld and over death itself. The Master had raised to life Lazarus and the daughter of Jairus. Peter had raised to life a woman named Tabitha. Paul was able to accomplish even that supreme of all possible miracles by raising up a young man named Eutychus. The Master and his Twelve exercised their life-giving powers within the narrow sectarian boundaries of Palestine. Paul raised Eutychus in Troas, in Asia Minor, a setting in the very midst of the pagan cosmopolitan world of the eastern Mediterranean.[13]

Not only is Paul equal to Peter in these various miracle-episodes, but there is the implication that he might be, in fact, something and someone even greater than Peter.

Each act of Paul that paralleled those of the apostles and of the Master further insinuated him into acceptance and legitimacy. Equal to Peter and the apostles in deeds, Paul was to prove superior to them in words. Paul was a master propagandist, of such a subtle and calculating mind that he bewildered and, at times, bamboozled the more simple minds of the apostles.

Paul's desperate need for legitimacy drove him into a power struggle with the Twelve, the Jerusalem Christian Establishment. Paul even put himself into competition with Peter. In that competition Peter would be repeatedly robbed to pay Paul.

According to the Cornelius episode in Acts, it was Peter who had taken the cosmopolitan initiative. Paul tried to deprive Peter of any credit for that initiative. According to Paul, the Christians took their message to the pagans only as a last resort, because the Jews, for whom the message was intended, had rejected it.[14] That version of events served to spite both Peter, the first-chosen apostle, and the Jews, the first-chosen people. Even more characteristically, Paul claimed that it was the Master, appearing in a vision, not Peter in Jerusalem, who directed him to a mission among the pagans. Paul explicitly deprived Peter of the credit for the cosmopolitan initiative.[15]

Paul also took up the circumcision issue and once again presented himself as the advocate of the liberal and liberating policy. Hadn't Peter and James resolved the problem by dispensing with circumcision at the so-called Council of Jerusalem? Apparently not, because later in Acts Peter and James appeared as backsliders who did not grasp the full implications of their own policy.[16]

In his political pamphlet, the Epistle to the Galatians, Paul presents his own version of the Council of Jerusalem. By that version, it was Paul, not Peter, who had the *revelation* on the issue of circumcision. After working a full fourteen years independent of any control by the Christian Establishment of Jerusalem, Paul finally went to Jerusalem and carried the day in his confrontation with that Establishment. It was Paul, then, who had initiated and advocated the cause of the pagans.[17]

Later, "when Cephas came to Antioch . . . I opposed him to his face, since he was manifestly in the wrong,"[18] Paul boasts. (Note how Paul condescendingly refers to the chief apostle by the Aramaic tribal name, Cephas, rather than by the Greek cosmopolitan name, Peter, while Saul the Jew had become Paul the cosmopolite!)

What justified Paul's impudence to the chief apostle? How was it that Peter, reduced to Cephas, was "manifestly in the wrong"? Why, he had backslid on the issues of diet, consorting with pagans, and circumcision. According to Paul, Peter was an equivocating hypocrite. Paul gave Peter a dressing down and shamed him into returning to the right path of policy.

Paul's antagonism toward the Christian Establishment of Jerusalem is overt in his tract to the Galatians. The cause of that antagonism was the nagging question of legitimacy. "Not that their importance matters to me, since God has no favorites,"[19] is Paul's self-assertive putdown of the "acknowledged leaders." Paul refers to James, Peter, and John in a sarcastic tone as "these leaders, these pillars."[20] The word "pillar" is a spiteful pun directed at Peter, the "rock" of the Church.

Paul's epistles are all very self-serving, and Acts was written under his influence. Consequently, the roles of Peter and Paul in determining the various policies and issues of the early Church are quite muddled. The literary evidence, the only evidence that we have, is too tainted by competition, power struggle, and the propaganda of legitimacy for us to clear up the muddle.

Paul tried to take the credit for cosmopolitan policy away from Peter. He was also impudent and insolent toward Peter and toward the apostolic Establishment in Jerusalem. There was almost certainly a split between Peter and Paul. Some evidence for that is in a suspect passage in a suspect epistle, Second Peter, a passage that purports to indicate a mutual respect and harmony between Peter and Paul.

In that epistle, written long after the deaths of both men, Peter refers to Paul as "our brother . . . who is so dear to us" and whose writings are "scripture."[21] All the Church must have known, or sensed, the incompatibility, the split, between Peter and Paul. Paul's own epistles had put Peter and the other apostles in their place. Now some unscrupulous editor, a Pauline partisan, put words of reconciliation and approval into the mouth of the long deceased Peter. Paul, whose words are the earliest in the New Testament canon, was also to get in the last word of the political power struggle.[22]

When the first pagan cadre of the Church was established at Antioch, the Jerusalem apostolic Establishment sent Barnabas to supervise and manage the recruitment. Barnabas in turn recruited Paul to serve the pagan community. It was in the church in Antioch that the question of circumcision arose. After the Council of Jerusalem, the apostles sent Barnabas and Paul, along with Judas and Silas, to communicate their decision on that issue.[23]

By that time Paul had become dissatisfied with his role as junior partner. He took an opportunity to provoke a "violent quarrel"[24] with Barnabas, despite the fact that Barnabas was "a good man, filled with the Holy Spirit and with faith."[25] The pretext that Paul used was the "desertion" by John Mark.

We know from one of Paul's epistles that John Mark was a cousin of Barnabas, and from First Peter that Peter considered John Mark in the paternal warmth of "my son."[26]

What actually happened in the incident was probably this: Paul somehow drove off John Mark, then forced Barnabas to choose between his family loyalty to John Mark and his association with Paul. Paul's interpretation of John Mark's reporting back to Jerusalem as "desertion" and his "violent quarrel" pushed Barnabas to the desired decision. Paul's purpose was to rid himself of his sponsor and senior, a man of the apostolic Establishment, the one who was keeping tabs on him. At the same time Paul managed to snub a protégé, a "son," of Peter.[27]

Paul was playing power politics well. Free of his supervisor from the apostolic Establishment, Paul then assumed a senior role himself by wooing Silas as his assistant.[28] Paul next chose Timothy, his own man with no connection at all with the apostolic Establishment in Jerusalem. Timothy had a pagan father and a Jewish convert mother. Such parentage made him suitable for Paul's cosmopolitan propaganda campaign.

Inexplicably, in light both of the apostles' decision at the Council of Jerusalem and of Paul's own fanatic convictions on the subject, Paul had Timothy circumcised. He did so, according to Acts, merely so that he wouldn't offend the sensitivity of the local Jews. It seems that despite his fierce contentiousness on circumcision, Paul was not averse to stooping to political expedience on the issue. In any case, Paul was now a senior recruiting his own juniors. And Timothy was Paul's own Peter.[29]

Paul's calling of Silas and Timothy is reminiscent of the Master's callings of Peter and Andrew, and of James and John, in the gospels. When Paul was in Ephesus, he even recruited some followers of John the Baptist, who just happened to be twelve in number.[30] Such parallels approach parody. Was it the Master to whom John the Baptist had pointed, or was it beyond the Master, to Paul?

The synoptic gospelwriters dutifully list the names of the Master's twelve apostles, even though in the gospel narratives they are mostly mere names with no role other than that of supporting characters. Correspondingly, the names of Paul's disciples are noted for posterity, once again, a kind of supporting cast for the Main Character.

And so Paul chose Silas and Timothy, Titus and Erastus, Gaius and Aristarchus, Sopater and Secundus, Tychicus and Trophimus, Onesimus and Philemon. Paul was a Valuesmaster himself. He recruited disciples of his own. He established his own organization.

Paul carved out his own territory. Drawing a line of geographical and cultural demarcation, he divided the missionary world into two spheres of influence, and he himself laid claim to lordship over the larger half. Paul was to be the head of a pagan Mediterranean Church, just as Peter was the head of the Jewish Palestinian Church. Paul effected a political revolution within the Christian values revolution.[31]

What kind of man was this outsider, this upstart, this intruder, who so skillfully managed to insinuate himself into membership and even leadership in the Christian values revolution? In looking for the answer to that question, we are fortunate in having Acts, which is a documentation of his life, and Paul's own epistles, a documentation of both his life and his mind.

An incident in Acts reveals exactly what kind of man Paul was. Like Peter and John, Paul was summoned before the Sanhedrin to defend himself against the charge of blasphemy for teaching about the Resurrected One.

Unlike Peter and John, Paul had experience in the inner workings of religious politics. He knew that the Sanhedrin was composed of two factions, the Pharisees and the Sadducees, and he knew the specific doctrinal differences between them. In a brilliant maneuver of dividing the opposition, Paul identified himself not as a Christian, but as a Pharisee, who was on trial not for the blasphemy of proclaiming the Resurrected One, but for the doctrine of a general resurrection of the dead, a doctrine accepted by the Pharisees but repugnant to the Sadducees.

Paul pricked the sensitive nerve of Judaic dogmatism and faction. The Pharisees immediately rose to his defense, the Sadducees counterattacked, and Paul backed off to watch his opposition in opposition to itself. By an ingenious ploy Paul changed a trial into a debate and turned the decorum of a Sanhedrin session into the melee of a street mob. Here was a mind and a methodology very different from the simple conviction and honest stubbornness of Peter and John in their appearances before the Sanhedrin, or from the Master's submission and silence before Pilate![32]

Paul was a masterful psychologist. And he had no scruples about putting his insights into other men's minds to his own advantage, as he did in the Sanhedrin episode. At the opening of the Sanhedrin meeting, Paul had lost his temper when the high priest ordered him struck for false swearing. But he immediately regained his self-control and made a perfect kowtow to the high priest. When Paul was arraigned before Felix, the Roman governor, he opened his defense with flattery; he used the same tactic to the same success with King Herod Agrippa II.[33]

Paul refers to himself as "the cunning fellow that I am."[34] That self-characterization was meant as irony, but as we see in his behavior before the Sanhedrin and the high priest, before Felix, and before King Agrippa, there was a confession in the disclaimer, and some plain truth in the irony.

Paul was cunning. He admitted it, and he boasted of it. How different from the childlike simplicity that the Master had so insisted on from his disciples. Paul had little use for infancy as a moral ideal. Never mind what the Master had said. He, Paul, had put behind "childish ways."[35]

Paul writes, "I made myself all things to all men in order to save some at any cost."[36] That is the confession of a truly unscrupulous character.

The Master had never ever compromised himself or his integrity. Paul was nothing less than an antitype to the model of the Master.

As in his behavior, so in his epistles was Paul the slippery chameleon. He was a master of psychological manipulation. To the strong, to those with a high self-regard, he wrote words of honeyed flattery. To the weak, the lowly, Paul lashed out and administered a thorough browbeating. Or he followed up a browbeating with flattery and pleading.[37] He would be what it was to his advantage to be. He would say what it was to his advantage to say. No matter what it took, he would gain control and bend the minds and wills of others to his own mind and will. Cunning fellow! All things to all men!

Was the conscience of such a man, who was, after all, a religious leader, ever bothered by the unscrupulousness of his tactics? There is evidence that it was; but the truly cunning man can be cunning against himself, too. "I am speaking nothing but the sober truth,"[38] Paul insists with a disingenuous self-deception. In that claim Paul was, indeed, very much the stereotypical Pharisee. However *true* his words might have been, his inner heart was calculating, devious, *cunning,* and—should we say?—hypocritical. The Master had told the people to obey the words of the Pharisees, but under no circumstances should they imitate the Pharisees' behavior. The Master's directive would apply just as well with regard to Paul the Pharisee.

Just as the truly sincere do not affirm their sincerity—because the affirmation of sincerity casts doubt on one's sincerity—so, too, the truly honest do not affirm their truthfulness. Jesus of Nazareth had said that an honest man's yes is a yes, his no a no, and no more need be said. But Paul knew himself too well. In order to conceal from himself his own deviousness, Paul was driven to affirm and reaffirm his sincerity and his truthfulness.[39]

Paul had shown impudence toward Peter and a presumptuousness in his private visions and revelations of the Master. More than a dominant personality, there was a prodigious ego at work in Paul. What was the nature of Paul's ego?

The Master had often spoken in terms of "not I, but the Father." That sense of a greater, even if only one greater, than himself had checked the ego of the Master. Paul makes a similar disclaimer: "For it is not ourselves that we are preaching, but Christ Jesus as the Lord."[40] Paul follows up that seeming self-effacement with an indulgent self-promotion, in several epistolary chapters of *boasting*. The boasting was intended as mockery of Paul's opponents, in irony once again; but it was also boasting plain and simple.[41]

There was a lot of unchristian subtlety, sarcasm, and irony from the subtle mind of Paul the Pharisee. Such convoluted thinking bewildered his contemporaries. (Paul had to devote portions of his epistles to clearing up supposed misconceptions of himself and his ideas.) We moderns, who have more experience in psychology, can see the subtlety, sarcasm, and irony for what it actually was—the plain truth in a disclaimer.

"I have served the Lord in all humility,"[42] Paul says in another kowtow. But there was no humility in Paul at all, neither personal nor tactical humility. Paul's constant assertion was himself: He bragged and boasted, schemed and maneuvered, said whatever was necessary, did whatever was necessary, all for the sake, not of the Lord, but of his own self-advancement.

Paul's model was not the Master, with whom he had almost nothing in common, either intellectually or morally. As the model for his converts Paul presented . . . himself: "I wish before God that . . . all who have heard me . . . would come to be as I am."[43] Instead of the *imitatio Christi,* there was the *imitatio Pauli.* Paul was nothing so magnificent as a great egoist; he was just a petty solipsist.

Paul preached himself and himself only. And who was Paul? How should he be received? In his own words: "as if I were Christ Jesus himself."[44] That hypothetical phrase was a revelatory slip—not as an outsider, upstart, intruder, self-chosen latecomer, but (as if he were) Christ Jesus himself. There was Paul's ambition made overt in a slip. There was his megalomania.

The ego grows proportionally as all opposition to that ego is cut down and reduced to an inferiority. Self-righteous alienation is the necessary counterpart to egoism. Paul's alienation was twofold. As an outsider, an upstart, an intruder, he felt a keen alienation against the Twelve, the legitimate Christian apostolic Establishment of Jerusalem. Against them he claimed a private calling, a separate authority, and a special independence.

Paul was a subversive against the legitimate Christian Establishment. His goal was not to overthrow the apostles—an impossible task, certainly—but to be legitimized as one of them, as equal to them. Against the apostles it was not war; it was a power struggle. The outsider wanted to be an insider.

Paul's alienation against the Jewish Establishment was different. Against them it *was* war, against them the goal was destruction. The Sanhedrin had to be confounded, the Temple of Jerusalem toppled. Paul himself was very much the Jew, *inwardly a Jew*.[45] He was, he claimed, a Pharisee. In his relation to the Jews, Paul was an insider who craved to be an outsider.

Those were the two alienated stances that Paul took up. His peculiar alienation was to have ominous consequences for both the Christians, his chosen future, and for the Jews, his repudiated past.

The Master had directed his alienation against the religious Establishment of the Jews, not against the Jews as a people. After all, he saw himself as the Messiah who had come for the express purpose of saving and liberating that people. He had no wish to destroy those he had come to save.

The Master had taken up an alienated, subversive stance against the Establishment. It was not merely the persons of the Establishment that he meant to attack; it was their *values*. By exposing the hypocrisy and criticizing the contamination of the traditional values, and by promoting childlike simplicity and new, pure values, the Master had carried out his values revolution. By his self-sacrifice, he succeeded in overthrowing the values of the Establishment.

After the Master's death, his disciples persisted in the alienated stance that he had taught them, not yet realizing that the Master had, by his double triumph of martyrdom and Resurrection, accomplished his values revolution and so rendered alienation virtually obsolete. Worse still, misinterpreting his necessary martyrdom as unjust murder, the Christians succumbed to an ever more indiscriminate grudge against the Jews for the "crime" of "murdering" their Master and Messiah, the Just One.

Alienation, made obsolete by the self-sacrificing accomplishment of the Master, lingered on among his followers like a hangover or chronic infection. Instead of rising to the responsibilities of new citizens in the Kingdom of Heaven, the early Christians acted like delinquents in Israel. Their festering grudge got the better of them. They began to express their bitterness as much against the Jewish people as against the Jewish Establishment. Their alienation became less ideological, more racial. Somehow, they concluded, all the Jews were guilty.

As we have already recognized, the anti-Semitism of the early Christians was ambivalent. Peter expressed the ambivalence of the Christians toward the Jews when he first accused them of murdering the Messiah, then forgave them on the grounds of their ignorance of the gravity of the deed. Similarly, Stephen indicted the Jews for the murder of the prophets and of the Just One, but then forgave them for another provoked murder, his own. The Christians felt a grudge, a vindictiveness, but a forgiveness too—in short, an ambivalence.

In his epistles Paul picks up the refrain of Peter and Stephen. He characterizes the Jews as "the people who put the Lord Jesus to death, and the prophets too." He takes up the alienated stance: "And now they have been persecuting us, and acting in a way that . . . makes them the enemies of the whole human race."[46] For the crime of murdering the Messiah, killing the Christ, Paul demands retribution, for which we can read the word *revenge*.

For the "enemies of the human race" Paul nonetheless claims to feel the "warmest love."[47] Such "love" was an ambivalent love-hate. According to Paul, the Jews were the "enemies of God . . . with regard to the Good News . . . but as the chosen people, they are still loved by God. . . ."[48] With such tortuous logic did Paul the Christian, Paul the Pharisee, express his ambivalence toward the Jews.

Highly educated as an orthodox Pharisee, a fanatic Jewish persecutor of Christian blasphemers, then converted to the countervalues by a terrifying hallucination, becoming a zealous and compulsive partisan of Christian values, Paul was Jew and anti-Jew in the extreme. More than his coreligionists, Paul was deeply divided in mind and feeling in his attitude toward the Jews. The more he loved the Christ, the more he hated the Christ-killers. A man of extremes in both intellect and passions, Paul went to extremes in his ambivalence toward the Jews.

Peter had mustered up enough memory of his Master to extend

forgiveness to the Jews. Stephen, too, had shown a true grasp of the *imitatio Christi* by extending the same forgiveness. But Paul had no memory of, and nothing in common with, the Master. To the "enemies of the human race" and the "enemies of God," Paul would not extend forgiveness. He demanded vindictive *retribution.*

Paul could not forgive his own former self, that cruel blind self that had held the castoff clothing for those who murdered Stephen, a just one, whose only offense was to proclaim the Messiah, the Just One. Paul was too personally involved, too much infected by ambivalence in his own soul, to be capable of forgiveness and forgetting.[49]

The historical seedgerm of Christian anti-Semitism lay in the rhetoric of alienation that Jesus of Nazareth directed toward the Jewish Establishment of Jerusalem. Because it was the *Jews* who had *murdered* their Messiah, what had been germinal in the career of the Master, what had erupted in the destiny of the Master, now became explicit in values and doctrine. And of all the Christians the most virulent anti-Semite was Paul, the Pharisee-Christian, the insider-outsider, whose life and mind were so divisively at odds with themselves. Paul was the one who made Christian anti-Semitism explicit and therefore doctrinal. The Jews, *chosen people* though they were, were also the *enemies of the human race* and the *enemies of God.* For those enemies there could be no forgiveness; but there would be *retribution,* revenge. The Jews were under a curse.

And so anti-Semitism became a Christian value in itself. It is the only form of righteous alienation still felt by Christians today. It is now a kind of perpetual repetition-compulsion.

Jesus of Nazareth was, if anything, a Jew for the Jews. The New Testament propagandists, the chief among whom was Paul, turned Jesus into the nemesis of the Jews.

The most personally painful aspect of the Master's alienation, both in his own life and in the discipline that he imposed upon his followers, was estrangement from family. For the sake of the individual soul facing the imminent apocalypse, all ties, even intimate family ones, had to be severed. Instead of the biological family, the unit of the values revolution was to be the brotherhood of the alienated elect, an ideological family. And the economics of that family was to be the total sharing of communism and a social discipline of poverty.

It was the inextricable interrelatedness of family, tribe, and Establishment religion in the Jewish communities of Palestine that had made the Master insist on the either-or of loyalty to family or loyalty to him. Antifamilialism was a necessary proof of commitment to his values revolution.

Paul's world, a cosmopolitan one, was a heterogeneous mix. The cosmopolitan pagans lived in, and traveled throughout, a broader geographical and intellectual environment than did the people of Palestine. Pagan religion was not hereditary and tribal, as the Jewish religion was. Nor did pagan men live so much under the will and thumb of the family patriarchs, as the Jews still did. In the atmosphere of pagan tolerance, conversion to a new cult was not considered a catastrophe for the family. The Jews, the "chosen people," could never be free to abandon their traditional cult and choose another; but it was a pagan trait to dabble in religions and philosophies, without resistance from family or kin.

In the pagan cosmopolitan world antifamilialism offered no tactical advantage to the Christian sect; indeed it would succeed only in needlessly offending the ingrained Roman sense of family values. The extreme antifamilial stance of Jesus of Nazareth was not appropriate to the wider world. And so, in his turn as Valuesmaster, Paul dispensed with the values of antifamilialism.

When he recruited disciples to the peripatetic life, Paul did take them away from their families in a physical sense; but there is no indication in his epistles that he attempted to end their emotional ties to their families. On the contrary, the impression Paul gives is that he attached himself to the families of his disciples as an extra member, rather than set himself up as patriarch of a new, ideological family. His epistles contain many familial greetings.

Cosmopolitan culture induced Paul to dispense with the antifamilial discipline. Similarly, his peripatetic life necessarily led him to dispense with moneyless communism, the economics of antifamilialism.

Paul's territory and his way of life were different from those of the apostles in Jerusalem. Where the brotherhood lived a primarily sedentary life in a single community, it was practicable for them to pool their resources and share everything, even meals. But a man like Paul, who lived the peripatetic life, spent long periods of time separated from members of the brotherhood and those sympathetic to it. The pagans were not so dependable in their willingness to give handouts to transients as were members of the brotherhood. Where would Paul's next meal come from? To get *his* daily bread, Paul would have to have some cash in his pocket.

Paul needed to finance the extensive travels of both himself and his entourage. Despite the Master's directive to set forth without money or possessions, Paul claimed any fee he collected as the just wage due him. He had a right to that fee, whether or not he exercised that right. Like the modern peripatetic evangelist, Paul devoted a part of his preaching to the practical task of fundraising; he took while giving. Moneyless communism just did not accord with Paul's lifestyle. The economics of his missionary work had to be a cash-and-carry one.

The apostolic Establishment of Jerusalem, mindful of the directive of the Master, must have had scruples about handling money. And so they entrusted fundraising to Paul. They called upon him to collect cash from his scattered pagan churches and bring it as tribute to the apostolic Establishment in Jerusalem.[50] Whatever sensitivity Paul himself had on the issue was due not to the fact that the Master had told his followers to keep their hands clean of money, but to the doubt that some members of the pagan churches had about whether Paul's hands were clean enough to be trusted with their cash!

Besides collecting his fee as a preacher, Paul also continued to earn wages in his trade as a leather worker. Paul always suggested that his converts take him as their model. Because he was a full participant in the capitalist money economy, Paul was, understandably, "soft" on the issue of Christian poverty. He told Timothy, his own chief apostle, to take a moderate approach in his dealings with rich members of the sect. Timothy was to remind them that what mattered was spiritual wealth, and that they should invest some of their capital in generosity and sharing, so that they would reap a suitable spiritual profit.[51]

That revaluation of the Master's discipline of poverty, that most expedient revaluation, is pretty much the same as the approach of ministers in the affluent suburban churches even today. To Paul, the term "rich Christian" was not a paradox or an absurdity. Paul was as complacent on the issue of wealth as he was on the issue of family.

No such complacency characterized Paul's attitude toward another of the Master's values, namely, the eunuch ideal. If Paul devalued antifamilialism and communal poverty, he overvalued the eunuch ideal into nothing less than an all-pervading phobic antisexualism.

In Acts, it says that when Paul arrived in Athens, "his whole soul was revolted at the sight of a city given over to idolatry."[52] Very much the Jew in all things, Paul was very much the Jew in being revolted at the visual and erotic culture of the Greeks. Paul the Jew was fanatic both in his Jewish antivisualism and in the old patriarchal grudge against Eve.

The Roman emperors generally deferred to the Jewish antivisual scruple by refraining from setting up images of themselves or of any other idols within Jerusalem, the Holy City. The Jews of the dispersion, cloistered in the ghettoes of their social separatism, could avoid the temptations of visual erotic culture by living apart from them. They built walls around themselves, so that they would not have to shut their eyes against the alluring idols of the pagan world. By controlling their environment, the Jews controlled their inclinations to succumb to the allure of Eve.

Once again, Paul's lifestyle as a peripatetic required a different solution. As he traveled from pagan city to pagan city, Paul was barraged by the many images and idols of the pagan visual culture. Every moment of his life presented an unavoidable temptation. Besides the allure of Eve, he had to deal with the allure of Aphrodite and Artemis, the allure of a promiscuous harem of naked goddesses, each beckoning to him out of their gross physical attractiveness.

How could Paul deal with that overwhelming stimulation of the senses, that visual sensuousness, which, though normal culture to the pagans, was sin and damnation to the Jews? Paul dealt with the threat of stimulation as all the weak do. He developed a self-protective phobia.

In his notorious First Epistle to the Corinthians, Paul turns his personal phobic antisexualism into a general Christian sexual morality. First principle: "It is a good thing for a man not to touch a woman." Rationale in a parenthesis: "Sex is always a danger." First concession: "It is better to be married than to be tortured." Appeal to the role model: "I should like everyone to be like me." And finally, that divine sanction without which there can be no conviction: "I . . . have the Spirit of God, I think."[53]

Men should not look at or touch women, because sex was always a *danger*. Because of that danger, marriage existed, as a kind of lesser torture. "If you marry, it is no sin,"[54] says Paul; but the celibate life is more spiritual, preferable, even if reserved only for those fully capable of it. Paul, the celibate himself, should serve as the model, because he lived in, and expressed, the Spirit of God.

Paul reduced marriage to a kind of second-class state, a last resort for those who could not control their sexual urges. By that slander of marriage and by his identification of spirituality with celibacy,[55] Paul exerted a pernicious influence on Christian thinking about human sexuality, sexuality, our problem, but our fulfillment, too. What might have been an exemplary sexual morality among the Christians became a phobia, that self-righteous weakness that does them little credit. The pernicious influence of Paul's personal phobic antisexualism infiltrated the Christian Church and has lingered in doctrine and bias ever since.

One indication of the depth and intensity of Paul's personal sexual phobia is in his inability to drop the rhetoric and polemic over the issue of circumcision for converts. Because circumcision, a kind of sexual mutilation, was the initiation into Judaism, Paul's repudiated past, the issue fused his phobia and his alienation into a complex. In polemic he lashed out at the "cutters," the mutilators. In a counter-ideological metaphor arising out of his obsession, Paul urged Christians to be circumcised in their whole body and soul, rather than in just their minor members. Finally, in a deplorable lapse of good taste, he spited the circumcisers with the ardent wish that they slip up with the knife and cut off a truly vital part.[56]

Anything explicitly, or even symbolically, sexual was repugnant to Paul. He was as much revolted by the living human body as by idol-images of the body.[57] Every woman was a reincarnation of Eve, and therefore a renewal of the temptation to Adam. But Paul was astute enough to recognize that the real temptation was in sex, the force between men and women, rather than in women themselves.

Paul as a person appealed to women, as any man with a spiritual nature, a passion for a cause, and a belief in himself appeals to women. Paul aroused both the feminine devotion of Lydia and the female hysteria of the slave-girl soothsayer of Philippi.[58] Couldn't he put such devotion, such enthusiasm, to use? And hadn't the Master himself attracted female followers?

Paul's antisexualism did not prevent him from perceiving the romantic appeal that his doctrine (a romantic one, after all) would have on women. Paul decided to take his message to the women, as much as to the pagans. He could exploit the greater freedom of women in pagan society to the advancement of his cause. As the Roman moralists and satirists complained, the Romans ruled the world, but it was women who ruled the Romans. Paul's strategy was this: The way into a man's head could be through his wife's head and out of her mouth.[59]

Paul's phobic antisexualism was expressed in the dissonant themes of his First Epistle to the Corinthians. With other men, such as Barnabas and Peter, Paul suffered from dissonant relations. Indeed we must conclude from the evidence in his epistles that Paul managed to make enemies wherever he went. In dealing with women, however, he succeeded in establishing some consonant relations, at least with those women who could transmute their sexual passion into a nunnish religious enthusiasm. Paul took the Good News to the women. They listened eagerly, and they communicated that Good News to their husbands. Women proved very useful as propagandists.

Paul's appeal to the emotionality and enthusiasm of women did present him with certain problems, as when he had to fend off the slave-girl soothsayer of Philippi by exorcising her "devil." Anyone preaching a doctrine of indiscriminate spiritual love is bound to arouse some very discriminate, perhaps even grossly physical, love, and to draw that female feeling upon himself. The misinterpretation of philanthropy as eroticism must have been particularly common among the pagans, whose whole culture was erotic, whether philanthropic or not. Paul's sexual disclaimers might even have made him all the more attractive to his female fans.

Another problem with Paul's strategy was that a force, once unleashed, tends to be impelled by its own dynamics. If female enthusiasm became too assertive, it would threaten male power. Instead of mere agents in the dissemination of the Good News, the women would begin to see themselves as preachers and originators of some Good News of their own. Against that presumptuousness Paul resorted to the old Jewish patriarchal bias in the doctrine of the natural subservience of women. Paul wanted the women to listen to him. They were to repeat what they were told, but only if and when they were given permission to speak. A woman's voice could be a whisper into her husband's ear, but it was not to be a harangue from a pulpit.

Paul urged Timothy and Titus to keep women's religious enthusiasm from getting out of hand. The good woman was veiled and silent. The good woman, like the good slave, obeyed her master.[60]

Paul saw the strategic and tactical value of women, especially of those who could be recruited to the nunnish life of celibate service to the cult.[61] He was to become exasperated at the inherent spiritual inferiority of "silly women who are obsessed with their sins and follow one craze after another in the attempt to educate themselves."[62] Women could be useful, but they had to be kept under firm male control.

Paul claimed to be a spokesman of a cult of love. And so he had to preach love, of one kind or another. His contribution to the valuation of love is the thirteenth chapter of his First Epistle to the Corinthians. It is a somewhat attractive rhapsody on the indispensability and the primacy of love over all, even over faith and hope.

As an extract the passage is attractive; but it is set within an epistle blatant in its phobic antisexualism and irritating in its petty misogynism. In his catalog of the qualities of love, Paul includes two clanks discordant to our modern poetic ear. The phobia of sex and the religious rationale for the repression of women are not part of our modern catalog of the qualities and characteristics of human love.

The early Christians were as enthusiastic about death as they were about love. The willingness to martyrdom was the highest aspect of their discipline and the severest test of their commitment. As a self-appointed apostle who claimed leadership in the sect, Paul had to prove himself superior in enthusiasm, in discipline, and in commitment. He had to prove himself superior in the will to martyrdom.

"All I want," Paul proclaims, "is to know Christ and the power of his resurrection and to share his sufferings by reproducing the pattern of his death."[63] According to Acts, Paul tried to reproduce that pattern with a fidelity that seems like the acting out of a script.

Like the Master, Paul prophesied his own death as his destiny. Like the Master, Paul persisted in his resolve to go to Jerusalem and to his destiny, despite counsel to the contrary. As in the case of the Master, the mob of Jerusalem cried out for Paul's blood. And just like Pilate, Festus was reluctant to convict an "innocent man." In those biographical parallels it seems that Paul was, indeed, reproducing the pattern of the Master's death, at least in the preliminaries.[64]

In his epistles Paul proclaims his willingness to embrace martyrdom as an ideal in the ultimate imitation of the Master. But Paul reinterprets that ideal. To him, martyrdom did not take place at the end of one's life, but continued all through it. Martyrdom was not so much a fate as a state. "Always, wherever we may be, we carry with us in our body the death of Jesus."[65]

How could the death of the Master be carried in the body of the believer? The answer was in the marks that signified that death. "The marks on my body are those of Jesus,"[66] Paul boasts. If the word *marks* is interpreted literally, then Paul somehow bore on his own body the stripes of scourging, the crucifixion nail wounds on his hands and feet, perhaps even the lance wound on the chest. At the very least, Paul identified the scars of his own misadventures with the sacred marks of the Master's passion. Paul longed for the *stigmata.*

The stigmata, the pattern of the wounds of the crucified Master reproduced on the body of the believer, have appeared on the bodies of, or been self-inflicted by, mystics from St. Francis of Assisi to Padre Pio. The stigmata, real wounds that bleed real blood, are the perfect mystic symbol of the *pattern* of the martyrdom of the Master. They are the outward signs of the believer's total commitment to the *imitatio Christi.* Whatever Paul's own marks were, he thought of them as stigmata.

It is a short step from imitation to identification, one that Paul takes unhesitatingly. "I have been crucified with Christ,"[67] he boasts again. In that formula Paul insinuates himself into the redemptive act itself. Paul himself was crucified with Jesus of Nazareth; Paul himself participated in the redemptive act. Charges of outsider, upstart, intruder, latecomer all aside—Paul was there on Calvary, crucified together with the Master. Paul transformed the *imitatio Christi* into a megalomania.

The anticipation of an inevitable fate exacts a psychological toll. The chronic tension that the Master felt sometimes crumbled into a world-weariness. Paul, too, felt a world-weariness. "Life to me is not a thing to waste words on,"[68] is how he expresses it.

The dominant element in the Master's world-weariness was the disgust with the "faithless and perverse generation" that he had to put up with. Paul's world-weariness was a disgust with life itself. Life was a waste of words. It was martyrdom and death and resurrection that mattered.

The tension that produced the life-weariness in Paul was quite different from the tension that the Master had felt. The Master's tension was a suspense about whether he could, and would, succeed in the momentous values revolution that he had set in motion. His imminent death was just a means to the accomplishment of that revolution; it was not itself the cause of his tension and anxiety.

Paul's tension was much less purposive and significant; it was more diffuse and solipsist, detached from the real issues of the values revolution. Paul confessed that, on the one hand, he wished that he were dead, so that he could join the Master. But, on the other hand, he wanted to remain alive, so that he could carry on his career and meet his responsibilities to his converts. In short, Paul just did not know whether he wanted to live or die.[69]

Paul couldn't make up his mind on the question of martyrdom or mission. There were arguments for both sides. Paul felt impelled to his destiny but held back by his duties; on the whole, however, he leaned more toward his duties. How different from the Master's inflexible resolve and steady, straightforward march to *his* destiny!

However determined may have been his rhetoric, in his actions Paul vacillated and oscillated over the issue of martyrdom. He prophesied his destiny, he persisted in going to Jerusalem to face it; but then what did he do? He saved himself. He confounded the Sanhedrin; he flattered and tried to win over Felix, the imperial power, and King Agrippa, the tribal power. In his words Paul was all willingness, but in his acts all reluctance.

Unlike the Master, who had bowed his head to the high priest and to Pilate, in silence and full submission, Paul spoke up and resorted to all kinds of cunning tactics to save himself. At the critical moment he proved incapable of following the model of the Master. Paul was, as always, his own model. He would survive, and he would survive on his cunning.

One of Paul's self-saving tactics was to exploit the privileges of his Roman citizenship. When it seemed that a trial in Palestine might go against him, he entered an appeal to a higher court, that of the emperor himself in Rome.[70] According to tradition, it was in Rome that Paul finally did suffer his martyrdom. If so, then Paul might have attained the ultimate of Christian enthusiasm, discipline, and commitment to the Master, not by willful submission in imitation of the Master, but as a consequence of insufficient Pauline cunning, of an unsuccessful Pauline tactic. Paul's martyrdom was not a destiny. It was just bad luck.[71]

On the one hand, Paul proclaims, "I have been crucified with Christ." On the other hand, he shied away from making that mystical martyrdom actual and physical. He cries out in anguish, "What a wretched man I am! Who will rescue me from this body doomed to death?"[72]

We wonder how a man, blessed and specially chosen by Father, Son, and Holy Spirit, for the historically momentous mission of converting the entire world, could possibly describe himself as wretched. We wonder how a man who considered his body an alter-image of the crucified and gloriously resurrected Christ, a part of the mystical body of the Divine Incarnation itself, could refer to that body as doomed to death. Instead of wretched, Paul should have been joyous and ecstatic, above all men most blessed. Instead of doomed to death, he should have looked upon his body as glowing in the imminence of a glorious transfiguration. Why was Paul wretched? Why did he crave a rescue?

His own answer to that question is given just before that outburst on wretchedness and the doom of death. His problem, as Paul describes it, was this: "I cannot understand my own behavior. I fail to carry out the things I want to do, and I find myself doing the very things I hate."[73]

That self-description strikes a familiar chord in the modern mind. No psychiatrist could have given a better definition than Paul's words do of that very recognizable of pathologies. Paul's will and his actions did not correspond; his intentions and his behavior did not match up. In short, Paul was a neurotic.

One of his many enemies perceived Paul's neurosis when he observed that in his epistles, written from a distance, Paul was all fire and brimstone but when he appeared in person, Paul was only "half a man." Paul's mind was brilliant, but his character was suspect. His words carried conviction, but he himself was not convincing. Paul's personality was split. He was a man somehow divided against himself, not knowing whether he wanted to live or die. He couldn't bring his will and his actions into harmony.

In his own defense, Paul contradicted his enemy's criticism, claiming that his words and his deeds were one and the same.[74] In one of his rare simple and honest moments, however, Paul confesses that his critic's observation was, in fact, all-too-true: "Though the will to do what is good is in me, the performance is not, with the result that instead of doing the good things I want to do, I carry out the sinful things I do not want."[75]

The two formulations of Paul's confession to neurosis are in his Epistle to the Romans. On the one hand, that epistle is an intellectually brilliant work. It proceeds like a sustained philosophical argument, cunning both in its chain of logic and in its sequence of rhetorical questions and obvious answers. ("Does this mean . . . ? Of course not. Does it follow . . . ? Of course not. Is it possible that . . . ? Of course not.") On the other hand, the epistle is a case study of emotional morbidity. It is permeated throughout by a neurotic obsession with "conscience" and "sin" and "death."

Just as repeated affirmations of "sincerity" and "truth" make a man's sincerity and truthfulness suspect, so the refrain of "conscience . . . conscience . . . conscience" indicates neurotic obsession. "I swear that my conscience is clear,"[76] Paul insists in cunning self-deception. Like "sincerity" and "truth," "conscience" is a key word in Paul's vocabulary, as it is in the vocabulary of all religious neurotics.[77]

The Master had not permitted his disciples any self-indulgence over conscience; his concerns were social. He wanted his disciples to put values into action. But in Paul, a neurotic solipsist, the self-indulgent, self-centered, concept of conscience kept cropping up. Paul's own internal state and the internal states of his converts assumed more importance than external moral behavior. Paul and his followers wallowed in their own consciences.

Paul's good will only led to bad actions. He seemed a hypocrite, but that was only because neither he nor his contemporaries knew the word *neurotic*. Paul did know that something was terribly wrong with him and in him. "I know of nothing good living in me,"[78] he writes in a pathetic confession. All that Paul could find in himself and his conscience were *sin* and *death*. That is why he was "wretched," that is why his body was "doomed to death."

Paul looked to his new religion for therapy. But in the person of the Master, Paul could find no comfort. Jesus of Nazareth was a strong character. Despite his occasional very human self-doubts, his will and his actions were in purposeful harmony. There was nothing of the neurotic in Jesus of Nazareth.

Nor was there much sympathy for the equivocating weakness of the neurotic. Like all strong characters, Jesus felt contempt for those, like the stereotypical Pharisees, who were in one aspect one thing and in another aspect something else. The Master imposed the most severe of possible human disciplines, both upon himself and his followers. He had no sympathy or use for moral weaklings. He wanted single-minded and wholehearted commitment, as well as decisive action on behalf of his values revolution.

What Paul could not find, in the way of comfort, therapy, or rescue, in the person and teachings of the Master, he had to find somewhere in himself. He himself was a Valuesmaster. His own religious zeal could be therapeutic. A doctrine could be a cure.

It is in the Epistle to the Romans, the same work in which he confesses his pathology, that Paul conjures up the cure. He had been thinking about it for a long time; indeed, he had already made a tentative proclamation of the doctrine in his Epistle to the Galatians. And now, in a dogmatic manifesto, Paul pronounces the formula of his own cure: "A man is justified by faith."[79]

Paul's "justification by faith" was ostensibly meant as a formula to replace the old Judaic formula of justification by observance of the Law. Paul dispensed with the Law as well as with circumcision, the seal of obedience to that Law. Out of Paul's emotional and rhetorical complex of anti-Semitism, sex phobia, frustration of will, neurotic self-indulgence of conscience, and obsession with sin and death came the therapeutic eureka: "A man is justified by faith."

Twisting Old Testament texts to his purpose, arguing with the best of Greek philosophical logic, and uttering his oracle to the Romans, Paul the Jew-Greek-Roman delivered himself of his great contribution to Christian doctrine. No one can earn *justification. Grace* comes from God, as a *free gift.* If a man receives that grace and has faith alone, he can be justified and, therefore, saved. Love was not the answer, after all. Love was not prime. There were faith, hope, and love; but of those faith was now the most important. Faith was the prime value.

Paul's doctrine of justification by faith issued from both a recognition and a renunciation. The recognition—a self-recognition—was that "I act against my will." The renunciation was, "I am no longer trying for perfection by my own efforts."[80] Frustrated by his efforts, Paul renounced all effort. Faith was enough. By faith, and by faith only, he was justified.

The self-frustrated moral paralytic had found his cure and his rescue, justification by faith, a throwing-up-of-the-hands. But what a dangerous doctrine that was to the values revolution!

In the epistle attributed to James, one of those who had known the Master, the concept of justification by faith is emphatically contradicted. Harking back to the Master's directive to feed the hungry and clothe the naked, James insists that, "it is by doing something good, and not only by believing, that a man is justified."[81] James abruptly dismisses Paul's doctrinal innovation: "Faith is dead if it is separated from good deeds."[82] Whether the Epistle of James was written as a deliberate rebuttal to Paul's Epistle to the Romans or not, this is a fascinating case in which, no matter how ingenious the harmonizations, scripture contradicts itself

The great danger that Paul's doctrine of justification by faith posed to the Christian values revolution was that old bugaboo, hypocrisy. The Pharisees had faith, but they did little to prove it by good deeds. Were the Pharisees justified anyway, by their faith? If they were, then the entire values revolution set into motion by Jesus of Nazareth would have been undone. The Epistle of James is the voice of a good memory of the Master.

Faith without works is nearly indistinguishable from self-righteous hypocrisy. Worse yet, Paul's doctrine would go out as a siren-call to other neurotics. Instead of attracting men of character and commitment, the values revolution would attract frustrated weaklings and paralytics obsessed with their own consciences, their own inner emotional states, rather than committed to prosecuting the values revolution. Justification by faith was not an advance in religious spirituality. It was an innovation in psychotherapy.[83]

Whatever the inadequacies of the Christian concept of love, it was at least a social value. But Paul's faith is strictly personal and narcissistic. Paul promoted the religion of feeling against the religion of doing. Against that self-indulgence the Epistle of James and the spirit of the Master himself stand unalterably opposed.

An emphasis upon good deeds for salvation is susceptible to the misinterpretation that such deeds earn, or even buy, salvation. Despite such possible misinterpretation, a good deed done still does good. But, as James argues, what good is a faith that is nothing to anyone except he who has it?

Paul was trying to transform an in-the-world values revolution into a mere in-the-mind single-value overhaul. That attempt was subversive to everything that Jesus of Nazareth, the Master and Messiah, had lived and worked for.

In trying to save himself, Paul was corrupting Christianity into a narcissism and a neurosis. He must bear a good part of the blame for the deterioration in the quality of the recruits to the sect. It was Paul's version of Christianity and Paul's Christians—the "foolish," the "weak," the "common and contemptible," the "nothing at all"— who aroused the contempt of pagan society toward the sect.

Neurosis, however, is no bar to intelligence. Paul went on to his worldly success in spite of his neurosis. A masterful and cunning politician, he was able to hold his own against, and even to overcome, the apostolic Establishment of Jerusalem.

Paul was as masterful in propaganda as he was in politics. His epistles are the earliest Christian writings; the works of Paul and his impersonators constitute nearly half the books of the New Testament. Paul's charismatic personality, too, exerted its influence on impressionable others. Was Luke one of those impressionable others?

Luke gives over the entire second half of his Acts of the Apostles to the story of Paul's preaching and missions. By doing so, he attaches his general history of Church origins to a heroic biography of Paul. In thus advancing the reputation of the man who posed the most subversive of all dangers to the values revolution, Luke made a terrible error in judgment. How did that happen?

In his epistles Paul mentions Luke as one of his disciples. In his Second Epistle to Timothy, reputedly the last he wrote before his martyrdom in Rome, Paul complains that he had been deserted by everyone except—ominous words!—"only Luke is with me."[84]

If so, then Paul had Luke under his influence at the very time, at long last, that he was about to be glorified by martyrdom, the supreme test of commitment. Luke may have fallen fully under the influence of Paul during those last days. Whether Paul directed him to or not, Luke was to do more than anyone, save Paul himself, to secure Paul's lasting preeminence. Luke did that by casting Paul as the epic hero of the second half of Acts.

When we compare the Paul of Acts to the Paul of his own epistles, we conclude that Luke didn't know Paul very well. Not knowing him for what he really was, Luke made Paul better than he ever was.

In both his gospel and in his Acts of the Apostles we detected in Luke the cosmopolitan perspective. How much of that perspective was his own, how much had been inculcated in him by Paul, the cosmopolitan Jew-Christian-Greek-Roman, we can only speculate. But while serving the liberating cosmopolitan perspective, Luke served Paul as well. Deliberately selecting Paul as the heroic model of the cosmopolitan Christian, Luke inadvertently enhanced the reputation and authority of Paul the neurotic. Luke made a significant contribution to the values revolution. He also made an unfortunate error in judgment.

When we read the epistles of Paul, wading through all the politics and pathology, we are struck most of all by a lack and an absence.

Where in all that rhetoric and argument are the values or the historical person Jesus of Nazareth? Nearly nowhere.

In the thirteen Pauline epistles there is only one concrete allusion to the actual biography of Jesus of Nazareth. Paul devotes a mere three verses of his literary output to recalling an actual event in the life of Jesus of Nazareth, namely, the Last Supper that he shared with his apostles.[85] The language of those three verses echoes that in the narratives of the synoptic gospels, as if Paul were just rattling off an oral tradition learned by rote and there repeated.

A few other vague allusions to Jesus are so inaccurate as to cause us to wonder just how much Paul really knew about the life of the Master he claimed to serve.[86] In one place, he claims that Jesus was rich, but that he embraced poverty for the sake of his followers.[87] From the gospels we learn that Jesus' family origins were poor and humble. In another place, Paul urges Timothy to speak up for his faith just as Jesus "spoke up" to Pontius Pilate.[88] According to the synoptic gospels, far from speaking up to Pilate, Jesus submitted with a self-disciplined silence. Paul's version of the post-Resurrection apparitions, too, is at variance with the traditions represented in the gospels.[89]

The lack of definite references to the life of Jesus of Nazareth and the inaccuracies of his vague allusions make us wonder how much Paul did know about the life of Jesus of Nazareth and just how informed his knowledge was.[90]

Against such doubts, whether those of his contemporaries or our own, Paul makes his claim: "I am an apostle and I have seen Jesus our Lord."[91]

As a matter of fact, Paul was never chosen as an apostle by Jesus of Nazareth nor had Paul ever seen him. The claim was an outright lie. It was only from the experience of a hallucination that Paul could believe—in "sincerity," "truth," and with a "clear conscience"—that he had been chosen as an apostle and had seen Jesus of Nazareth, at least once, there outside the gate of Damascus. (What was to prevent any Christian from experiencing similar delusions and making similar claims?)

With Paul's claim there was a disclaimer: "The only knowledge I claimed to have was about Jesus, and only about him as the crucified Christ."[92] There Paul admits his ignorance of the life of Jesus of Nazareth. It was not that Jesus whom Paul knew; it was, rather, the crucified Christ, that is, the nonhistorical figure of a postmortem revaluation.

Despite the limitations of his latecoming and his essential ignorance, Paul could still claim that "we are those who have the mind of Christ."[93] Such was the impudence of the outsider, the upstart, the intruder. Paul could have known nothing about the mind of Jesus of Nazareth except what the eyewitnesses, the twelve chosen apostles, could have told him. But Paul would admit no dependence upon, or inferiority to, the Jerusalem Establishment. And so, ignorant of Jesus of Nazareth, Paul claimed special mystical intimacy with the mind of the *crucified Christ*. His mystical knowledge began at the point where the apostles' biographical knowledge ended.

Self-appointed as an apostle, a latecomer who never laid eyes on Jesus of Nazareth, legitimized only by his hallucinatory vision, Paul claimed to penetrate into the very mind of the crucified Christ. He claimed to be intimate and one with that mind. Paul was body in body with the mystical body, and mind in mind with the mystical mind.

When Paul carried his claims to the apostolic Council of Jerusalem, he said that he went there with a "revelation."[94] *Revaluation* is a more accurate description of what Paul did.[95] That revaluation was of the meaning of the person of the Master himself. Paul overthrew Jesus of Nazareth, replacing him with the crucified Christ, a mystical fantasy. Following Paul, the Church has embraced Christ, a title, a concept, forsaking Jesus of Nazareth, a person, a man. Metaphysics has won out over values-in-action.

Paul's crucified Christ was a reincarnation of sorts, a Second Incarnation. The apostles fought against Paul's revaluation, but time was against them. The eyewitnesses, those with biographical knowledge of Jesus of Nazareth, were aging. They were dying off. When it became apparent that the Second Coming, despite Jesus' apocalyptic prophecies, might not occur during the lifetimes of the Twelve, there was a frantic rounding-up of witnesses and a desperate scouring of the collective memory for every anecdote, every incident, every bit of biographical data about Jesus. The person of Jesus of Nazareth had to be saved from perishing with the deaths of those who had known him. The memory of him was preserved in the four gospels.

Against the gospels stand the epistles of Paul. In them, the person Jesus of Nazareth becomes a kaleidoscopic concept, and fantasy supplants memory. In forsaking the memory and the model for concepts and fantasy, the Christian literature of the past two millennia has been thoroughly Pauline.

Our biographical knowledge of Jesus of Nazareth is, and will always be, limited to the number of words in the four gospels. The mystical knowledge of the theological Christ, by contrast, is an ever-unfolding, ever-elaborated, limitless fantasy. Paul was a pioneer in that process of fantasy.

With so little biographical documentation, Christians have been secure in the certainty that the test of historical truth cannot be put to their notions. But inasmuch as they have been capable of feeling, they have administered to themselves a trial of love. As much as they loved, they thought, so much the more did they become intimate with the crucified Christ.

Christianity is *love*. It is fantasy and feeling. Love was one of the many aspects of the values revolution of Jesus of Nazareth; it is now the prime value of the organization in his name. Love was also, until neurosis found its cure in the primacy of faith, the professed prime value of the first of the antichrists.

The Revaluation

When Jesus of Nazareth was tempted by those who disbelieved in him, he resisted. But when he was tempted by those who believed in him, or who wanted to believe in him, he succumbed to the temptation.

Jesus had just made his resolve to undertake a values mission, when he was confronted by the devil in the desert. The devil would not believe who Jesus was, until he saw a demonstration of what Jesus could do. He tried to induce Jesus to fritter away his mana in tricks and stunts, so that the pretender-Messiah would be reduced to a mere magician. Jesus recognized the devil as a disbeliever and an adversary. And so, in a seesaw sparring match of wits, he thrice resisted the devil's temptation. He would not debase himself by a self-indulgent display of his own powers.[1]

While Jesus was prosecuting his values revolution, the Pharisees challenged him to perform a miracle as a proof of what he was. Jesus recognized the Pharisees as disbelievers and adversaries. Once again he resisted the temptation, this time with a blunt refusal.[2]

The devil and the Pharisees were skeptics. They tempted Jesus to a proof that they thought he would be unable to provide. But the common people, those who wanted to believe in Jesus, needed a proof to help along their belief. They would become believers, if only they could see a proof.[3] Jesus yielded to their want and to their need. He succumbed to their temptation. He gave them miracles.

Jesus' own methodology was to trap him in a dilemma. On the one hand, he despaired that the people would not believe him or believe in him, unless they saw him perform miracles. On the other hand, their disbelief, their lack of faith, rendered Jesus incapable of performing miracles. If there were no miracles, there would be no belief; but unless there was belief, there could be no miracles. It was a dilemma that Jesus of Nazareth never overcame.[4]

A similar dilemma faces every modern reader of the New Testament.

The basic argument of the New Testament biographies of Jesus is that the superiority of his magic proved the superiority of his person and, therefore, of his values. The same logic is applied to the persons and values of those who carried on Jesus' values revolution after his death. Philip's magic was more potent than that of Simon the Magician; Paul's magic was more potent than that of Bar-jesus and of the seven Jewish exorcists.[5]

To the question, What difference did Christianity make in the world? the answer given in Acts is that it was a magic more potent than any other. Christianity was a superior sorcery.

Acts presents the introduction of Christianity into the cosmopolitan pagan world of the ancient Mediterranean as a kind of Battle of the Superstitions, one that Christianity would eventually win: "Some believers, too, came forward to admit in detail how they had used spells, and a number of them who had practiced magic collected their books and made a bonfire of them in public. The value of these was calculated to be fifty thousand silver pieces."[6]

In those witch-trials, confessions, spells, magic, scrolls of arcane lore, book-burnings, and mysteries worth a fortune, we find ourselves deep within the subterranean labyrinth of the superstitious psyche. Such a passage is out of a primitive literature. These are not values but superstition. With Tacitus, we recoil.

The New Testament propagandists repeatedly resort to magic as an argument. Jesus had performed miracles as a proof of his legitimacy and of his values;[7] therefore, all those who follow him should also follow his methodology. As the gospel insists, believers should prove themselves by their ability to perform magic and miracles: "These are the signs that will be associated with believers: in my name they will cast out devils; they will have the gift of tongues; they will pick up snakes in their hands, and be unharmed should they drink deadly poison; they will lay their hands on the sick, who will recover."[8]

In the twentieth century of Christian belief there are no such signs. No one really casts out devils, except in Hollywood, for there seem to be no more devils to be cast out. No one has the gift of tongues, except for a few charismatic hysterics. No one molests venomous snakes or gulps down deadly poison in order to prove anything. No one treats illness by a laying-on of the hands, or at least no one succeeds in curing illness that way. If signs are indeed the test and proof of belief, then today there are no more believers.

All the values set forth in the New Testament are argued and *proved* by the cosmic attestation of magic and miracles. Of course we could try to ignore the miracles as irrelevant to the values, but they are not. We cannot take the miracle-stories of the New Testament as mere entertaining anecdotes separable from the values, because *superstition,* the belief in magic and miracles, is a value-in-itself.

More than a value-in-itself, superstition is a world view. As we discovered in the dreams on the very first pages of the New Testament, superstition is the world view of the Christians.

We might think that after the eighteenth-century Enlightenment and the nineteenth- and twentieth-century development of the scientific world view, that the Western world has long ago put behind the world view of superstition. But like the ancients, we are sometimes two-minded, scientific in our technology, but still superstitious in our religion.

Against that two-mindedness stands philosophy. Like the devil, the Pharisees, and Tacitus, the philosopher is skeptical; beyond them he aspires to be scientific. What is presented in the New Testament as proof seems to the philosophical mind to be a disproof. The common New Testament resort to magic as an argument works to prejudice against, rather than convince in favor of, the values that are presented there.

The very idea of philosophy is as incongruous to the world view of the New Testament as is Pilate's philosophical question, "What is truth?" The word *philosophy* does, in fact, appear in the New Testament, just once. In that sole occurrence, it is modified by the adjectives "secondhand," "empty," and "rational." The New Testament writers draw a line of demarcation between *the principles of this world* on the one side and *Christ* on the other.[9] The New Testament, then, is thoroughly obscurantist.

The Christian bond between mythology and ideology, between magic and values, is indissoluble. A philosophical distaste for superstition would incline us to reject the values, as we reject the basic argument for them. We do not want proof. We want reasoning.

Recognizing the incompatibility between the world view of Christianity and the critical skepticism of philosophy, we press ahead with the revaluation, anyway. What are we to make of the New Testament, then?

As we read through the books of the New Testament, we notice several major displacements of focus. In the synoptic gospels the great proclamation is the imminent arrival of the Kingdom of God upon earth. Men should adopt certain radical values and put them into action in preparation for that momentous event. Jesus of Nazareth was the man who made the great proclamation and taught the values. Then, in the Gospel of John, the Kingdom of God disappears,[10] and the values are reduced to a single prime value, love. The focus of attention has shifted from the values to the Valuesgiver, the Supreme Lover, toward whom one should render a spiritualized erotic homage. Finally, in the epistles of Paul, the Kingdom of God, the values, and the Valuesgiver are all gone, to be replaced by the believers' inner states. Radical values-in-action are now mere "good works." Love is relegated to a secondary virtue, following the new prime virtue, faith. The focus now is upon the subjective feeling of the believer.[11]

In the synoptic gospels, Jesus said, "Do this!" John said, "Love him." Paul said, "Feel this." These displacements of focus in the New Testament, from the values to the Valuesgiver to the believer, constitute further revolutions within the great values revolution known as Christianity.

Such displacements of focus subverted the values revolution. The test was not to be the synoptic command, "Do as he said and did!" The test was to be a mere affirmative answer to John's question, "Do you love him?" and to Paul's question, "Do you believe in him?"

"Do you love him?" To the recruits of the second generation the apostolic eyewitnesses could say, marveling, "You did not see him, yet you love him."[12] That paradoxical union of ignorance and eroticism has been characteristic of Christians of every generation since. They have never seen Jesus; they have not known him. But they have loved him. That the great, ruthless genius and values revolutionary, Jesus of Nazareth, would have accepted as tribute a love based on ignorance, may be doubted.

"Do you believe in him?" The Christians gradually abandoned the social task of an active, in-the-world values revolution in favor of a passive and socially useless self-indulgence in their own faith. Along with that self-indulgence went neurotic obsession with sin and conscience, in imitation of the model of Paul. The goal was no longer the great revolution on earth; it was petty personal salvation in heaven.

A values revolution is sabotaged by the easing of discipline. Jesus' great challenge, "Do this!" proved too difficult. Love and faith were much easier than the practice of the superstringent, nearly impossible, discipline of Jesus of Nazareth. Love and faith sabotaged the values revolution of Jesus of Nazareth.

Christian religious emotion was paradoxical. Christian religious thought became ever more useless. The Christians proved incapable of living out the discipline of their model and exemplar, but they still paid him homage as a Revered Person. That homage was theology, spiritualistic speculation into the possibilities of what Jesus meant in John when he said, "I am. . . ." As their ideal, Jesus was their idol, their god. Isn't that the grim fate of all values revolutionaries and geniuses who succeed too well? Don't they become gods and idols?

Like superstition, idolatry of a Revered Person is a value-in-itself. In Christianity it was that person who was the proof of the values, just as it was the magic and miracles that provided the proof of the person. There would be no Christian values without the Christ.

Backing off from the idolatry of the Revered Person, we take a reductionist view of the historical person Jesus of Nazareth. Perhaps the most we can know for sure is what Tacitus records about him, namely, that Jesus was the originator of a sect and that he was executed by Pontius Pilate sometime during the reign of the emperor Tiberius.[13] That is virtually all that the pagans have to say about Jesus.

The Jewish tradition about Jesus, no more historically reliable than the New Testament tradition, is, nonetheless, interesting as all polemic is. This is what the Jews have to say about Jesus: First, he was born illegitimate. (What to the Christians had to be interpreted in terms of miracle, the virgin birth, was to the patriarchal Jews the scandal of illegitimacy still.) Jesus' father, though, was no cipher named Joseph, but a Roman soldier named Panther. (The Jews would deny Jesus his Jewishness itself, as if that were possible!) The Jews recognized Jesus as a sorcerer, but that was no great distinction (as we discover in Acts) in a culture where sorcerers were common. About Jesus' mission the Jewish tradition says that he ridiculed the wise (the Establishment) and wooed and stirred up the common people. (So the Jews did recognize Jesus for what he was, then—a values revolutionary.) According to the Jewish tradition Jesus chose only five disciples, not the numerologically significant number of twelve. Finally, the Jewish tradition records that Jesus met an ignominious end on the cross during the Passover season.[14]

The Jewish tradition about Jesus is polemical and understandably hostile. But a greater damage was done to the person of Jesus by his followers than was ever done by his adversaries and enemies.

The followers of Jesus, those who tried to think the best of him— at least as far as they were capable of understanding what would be best in any human being—rendered Jesus four disservices. Taking Jesus' pacifist discipline as a psychological complex, they made Jesus seem harmless. Taking another discipline, the eunuch ideal, as another complex, they neuterized Jesus. Misconstruing his willful martyrdom and characterizing him as an *innocent victim,* they made Jesus pathetic. And directing love toward the teacher of love, they made Jesus into a love-object. That is what the Christians did to that formidable genius who turned the values of his society and of the ancient world upside down. They made him a harmless, neuter, pathetic, love-object.

No enemies of Jesus and of his values revolution could have done more to nullify everything he was and worked for than what the Christians did to him.

The proletarian riffraff who flocked to the sect found in Jesus of Nazareth their hero. They made him into one of their own. Even taking a reductionist view of Jesus, we still must regret the kind of reductionism practiced by the early Christians. In their misguided idolatry they reduced Jesus to the worst of themselves. And they turned all his disciplines into complexes.

That perverse reductionism persists in Christianity even today. Every reformed alcoholic, drug addict, or petty criminal who has "found Jesus" or been "born again" seems somehow entitled to assume a preaching role or even a position of leadership. The worst set themselves up as models, and the barely recovered minister to the still sick. Such a turnabout has corrupted, and still corrupts, the Christian values revolution.

The two New Testament propagandists who most influenced the redirections of the Christian values movement were John and Paul. If John bears much of the responsibility for shifting the focus away from practice of the values to an erotic idolatry of the Valuesgiver, Paul is to blame for the worse displacement, from the Valuesgiver to the self-indulgent feelings of the believers. Paul rendered the values revolution absurd.

Although John viewed Jesus through the rose-colored lenses of love and longing, as a mystical love-object, he did present Jesus as a historical human being whose life mattered. In Paul, however, Jesus of Nazareth lost his historicity altogether; there is no Jesus of Nazareth at all. There is only the *crucified Christ,* a concept not a man. The believer needed to feel the mystical presence of that crucified Christ. The life and teachings of Jesus did not matter; only the death and resurrection of the Christ mattered. If John was in love with a dead man, Paul was enamored of a ghost. For Paul, Jesus' person only acquired meaning after the man was dead. Jesus of Nazareth might as well never have lived.

We have noted in the New Testament the major displacements of Christian focus, away from the values to the Valuesgiver, and finally to the needs and feelings of the believers. In the gospel characterizations of Jesus there are the germs of the four disservices that were to be done to the historical person Jesus of Nazareth by his followers. And in Paul's epistles there is the ascendance of the "foolish," the "weak," the "common and contemptible," the "nothing at all."

If we could ignore the context of *superstition,* the displacements of focus, the idolatry of, and the disservices to, the Revered Valuesmaster, we would be left with . . . what? The values-in-themselves.

The New Testament was the manifesto of a values revolution in the ancient world, a values revolution that is, moreover, supposedly still operative in the world today. How are we to evaluate that manifesto?

We must take an inventory of the values-in-themselves and attempt their revaluation:

First of all, there is the self-righteous alienation expressed in the Christian formula, "in the world but not of it." If ever put fully into practice, as it once was by the Christian martyrs, that value would mean the total repudiation of all social and political responsibilities. To the ancient Romans the renunciation of social responsibilities was an intolerable subversiveness; that is why the Romans persecuted the Christian alienated ones. In the twentieth century our most pressing human problem has been the political problem. To save ourselves we need participation. Self-righteous alienation—the being "in the world but not of it"—would threaten not only our societies but human survival itself. Fortunately, the Christian value of self-righteous alienation is no longer put into full practice. Today's Christians are participators.

The nuclear age is no time for Christian pacifism or self-righteous masochism. Jesus never meant pacifism as a general social prescription; those of his followers who interpreted it as such would render society helpless against the criminals and the barbarians. The only ones capable of pure pacifism, anyway, are those rare souls of overdelicate feeling, like the Jainists, who think it a cosmic crime to kill the mosquito that is biting them. As the ancient Romans well understood, pacifism is subversive to security. We should dispense with the absurd paradox, "My power is at its best in weakness,"[15] once and for all. But there is very little of Christian pacifism evident in our modern world. The Christian churches are warlike enough. Communism, atheistic and militant, raised their hackles, so that they could in good conscience preach both the Bible and the Bomb.

The great age of Christian antifamilialism was the medieval millennium, when the Church siphoned off family wealth into the corporate coffers of its monasteries, cathedrals, and ecclesiastical landholdings. The Vatican stands today as the great monument to the Christian corporate plunder of family wealth, a plunder made possible by antifamilial doctrine. Europe's cure for that problem was the Reformation. Family wealth no longer flows into the Christian corporate coffers so plentifully as it once did. As for communalism, modern atheistic Communism has discredited that once-Christian value. And as for specifically Christian poverty, rather than just poor people who happen to be Christians, there is very little. In accord with the Protestant ethic, today's Christians are well-to-do.

The eunuch ideal, the virginity ideal, and sex-phobia are one Christian legacy that we are not yet free of. The notion that sexuality, the life-force, is inherently evil was one of the most pernicious doctrines in the history of human culture. It was a pathology, all the worse for being presented as a divine oracle.

We have had enough—in fact, too much—of the moral and sexual constipation of the eunuch ideal. We want to be healthy. We want to be fulfilled. We recognize the celibate as the freak, not as the model he has immemorially claimed to be. But just when it seems that we might overcome the Christian antisexual values, we succumb to another pathology. No longer phobic, we are pornographic. Sex is sin yet. Our *liberation* notwithstanding, we do not yet have our freedom, the freedom to be healthy.

There is nothing wrong with the Golden Rule, that philosophical platitude, inadequate though it is. But Christian indiscriminate love, the eroticization of philanthropy, is unhuman and antinatural. Their *love* as prime value was a love antifamilial, antisexual, paradoxical, a love imposed on anybody and everybody. We should have enough self-respect to resist that kind of love.

Living martyrdom as a value harms only those who suffer from it. The martyr's attitude toward the world is, like masochism and sex-phobia, a private pathology. As much as they might still consider both life and the world as evils, however, today's Christians no longer show such eagerness to end their lives and leave the world. Once again, the Christians do not practice a value they profess.

Apocalypticism can become a mass hysteria, as we observe in the various doomsday panics that have broken out from time to time since the Middle Ages. Apocalyptic suicidalism is still a dangerous value. Some Christians must secretly long for the nuclear holocaust as the fulfillment of their apocalyptic expectations. What would happen if a Christian true-believing apocalypticist had his finger on the trigger of the Bomb? "The earth and all that it contains will be burnt up,"[16] prophesies Second Peter. Nuclear holocaust would be the ultimate proof of the truth of the scriptures.

Finally, there is the value of dogmatism and intolerance, a Judeo-Christian value that has claimed its victims for many centuries. We have disarmed the Christian churches, so that no more heretics can be torched at the stake for a crime of thought. There is no longer any mortal danger in modern Christian dogmatism. However, there are plenty of dogmatists still around, those who would like to impose the rigor mortis of their own minds upon everyone else. We are fortunate in having the historical example of the ancient Romans to teach us the lesson of tolerance.

Those, then, are the values of the Christians as we find them in the New Testament, as they have affected the course of Western history, and as they persist in our own world. There are those who still think, despite the evidence of two millennia of experience with Christianity, that the Christian values, if fully put into practice, would do us some good, that Christian values are the *answer*. But after our revaluation we see that the Christian values are not the answer. They are only further problems.

We have tended to think of Christianity as a wave of truth, decency, and lovingkindness that swept into a world corrupt in error, perversion, and cruelty. As if the Greeks could have practically invented Western culture, as if the Romans could have achieved a world peace, while being corrupt to the core! As much as we might think of

Christianity as cure, it was, as the Romans recognized, an antisocial pathology. So would it be today too, if it were fully put into practice. That it is not is our good fortune.

It is also assumed that Christianity presented antitheses to the prevailing values of the ancient world and th t by presenting those antitheses, Christianity sharpened the sense of values. Christianity certainly did present antitheses, but those antitheses served as much to muddle, as to sharpen, values.

Five hundred years after the Greeks thought out the problems and principles of justice and while the Romans were still laboring to piece together an international law and a universal order, the Christians espoused turning the other cheek, an absurd and facile formula. Christian pacifism made a muddle of the concept of justice, the basic and most vexing political problem.

To the economic problem of the rights of property, the Christian solution was communism, another muddle. The Christians muddled the concept of family by setting up an ideological family against natural family. Their prescription for the human problems of sex and love was indiscriminate love, a muddle of the instincts.

The pagans used to cremate their dead in order to show their honest acceptance of the absolute schism between life and death. The Christians buried their dead and haunted the catacombs, mixing living and dead in a promiscuous necrophilic fellowship. The Christians muddled even the distinction between life and death.

In the world, the Christians wanted to be out of it; alive, they wanted to be dead and gone. They were the martyrs, the living dead. For them life was a death march, the *vita dolorosa* was a *via dolorosa*. The Christians wanted no part of society or its responsibilities. All that mattered was their personal salvation and the salvation of their alienated brotherhood. What was such an attitude, if not the be-nothing, become-nothing, do-nothing of the muddled mind?

Are we healthy enough, sensible enough, humane enough, to develop some modern counterideology to the Christian celibate valuation of love? "Whatever is done out of love always occurs beyond good and evil."[17] Will we ever grasp the depths of meaning in that great sentence?

It was the test of truth that was the unmaking of the Old Testament. Fossils and apes, the evidence of geology and biology, contradicted the Book of Genesis. Even though the preachers claimed that the fossils had been planted by Satan to deceive the believers and secure the ruin of their souls, and that relationship to apes was a blasphemous outrage, the rational nineteenth-century mind gradually came to accept scientific evidence over superstitious dogma. The Old Testament failed the test of truth. We now take Genesis for what it is, namely, myth, rather than for what it was long claimed to be, a cosmogony. Critical intellect revalued the Old Testament.

The test of love should be the unmaking of the New Testament. That is our twenty-first century task, if only we are capable of it. There is a need for critical intellect, still; but a rarer sensitivity is required, that is, the sensitivity of healthy human instincts. The sound good sense of the healthy human being is the greatest possible contradiction to the perversity of the pathological view of man. Are we healthy enough? Or could we become healthy enough?

As for the New Testament, we close its pages for the last time. In its story the characters mingled with phantasms in events that were, more often than not, hallucinations. It is a primitive literature. And in a book where attributions of authority and authorship are sometimes fraud, and where dogmatic *truths* are paradoxical fantasies, not all is as honest and holy as it purports to be.

There is a curious double meaning of the word *testament* in the titles Old Testament and New Testament. On the one hand, the word means a binding agreement between two parties, Yahweh and his chosen people in the Old Testament or the loving Father and the believers through the intermediary Jesus in the New. On the other hand, the word means a death-legacy, the last will and testament of a dying man.

In the New Testament, the testament in terms of binding agreement is *love,* as sign and seal of the covenant between Jesus and his believers. The testament in terms of a death-legacy is the death of Jesus of Nazareth, his martyrdom as saving act and example. The New Testament is love, and it is death. It is the love attached to the person of Jesus of Nazareth and the death, the last will and testament that person wrote in his own blood.

Love and death, then. But such love does not persuade us. And that death is neither proof nor argument. In our revaluation we see the values system of the New Testament as neither divine oracle nor absolute truth nor standard of human moral perfection. It is, rather, a romanticism, just another gothic romanticism of love and death.

LITERAE, JACTURA IN VACUO.

Notes

Preface, pp. 9–17

1. John 18:37-38, excerpted.
2. Pilate's judgment of Jesus' innocence: Matthew 27:23; Mark 15:10,14; Luke 23:4,14-15,22; John 18:38; 19:4,6. In Luke and John Pilate made a triple affirmation of Jesus' innocence. On the significance of triple affirmations in the New Testament see Context.
3. John 8:45, excerpted.

Context, pp. 19–42

1. "Gens superstitioni obnoxia [religionibus adversa]," Tacitus, *Histories,* 5.13.
2. The prophecy: Tacitus, *Histories,* 1.10; 5.13.
3. Vespasian's miracles: ibid., 4.81-82.
4. "Dedita superstitionibus gens," ibid., 4.81.
5. Compare Vespasian's healing of the blind man to Mark 7:32-37, Mark 8:22-26, or John 9:1-7; the healing of the man with the withered hand to Matthew 12:9-14, Mark 3:1-6, or Luke 6:6-11.
6. For the two-mindedness of Tacitus, compare *Histories* 1.10 to 4.81.
7. The *Kingdom* (of heaven, of God, of the Father, of the Son of Man): Matthew 3:2; 4:17,23; 5:3; 9:35; 10:6; 13:19,41,43; 16:28; 20:21; 24:14, passim; Mark 4:11; 11:10; Luke 12:32; 14:15; 23:41-42; 23:51. John 3:5.
8. The five dreams: Matthew 1:20-21; 2:12,13,19-20,22.
9. The Magi: Matthew 2:1-12.
10. Because Matthew is the most *Jewish* of the four gospels, it is in Matthew that the Jewish craving for retribution against historic enemies is at its most overt. The only other gospelwriter who tells the nativity story is Luke. Luke substitutes a benign Mediterranean symbol, the shepherd,

for the Magi, as the first to offer homage to the infant king. Similarly, Luke replaces the cold determinism of the Star by a nightwarming chorus of angels, who brighten the scene and fill the air with their music. In various other aspects of their treatment of the narrative, we will discover that Matthew is tribal-Jewish, Luke pagan-cosmopolitan.

11. Whatever the actual nationality of the Magi may have been, they symbolize the Persians and the Babylonians, the oppressor powers. The Magi came "from the East" (Matthew 2:1), that is, from Persia and Babylonia. The episode of the Magi is evidence of a Jewish historic grudge. When the Church became cosmopolitan, that old tribal grudge was forgotten. The Magi were depicted in art in a way to symbolize a more general international, or cosmopolitan, homage to Jesus. One Magus, for example, was painted as a black African. The propaganda of later Christian art was more diffuse on this subject than was the very specific, very pointed, anti-oppressor tribal grudge in Matthew.

12. Horace, *Tu ne quaesieris, Odes,* 1.11.

13. The *date:* Matthew 2:7,16.

14. The numerological genealogy: Matthew 1:1-17.

15. So fourteen generations after the humiliation of the deportation to Babylon there was the triumph of an *importation* from Babylonia, the Magi. The homage of the Magi was a historic turnabout.

16. Constantine's conversion actually occurred in A.D. 312. If we add fourteen generations to A.D. 310, we arrive at the year 590, where, once again, we find a significant person, this time Gregory I, the greatest pope of the early Middle Ages. The next year in the scheme would be 870, in which we find no significant person or event.

17. The parable of the talents: Matthew 25:14-30. This parable, incidentally, may serve as the Christian seal of approval on capitalism.

18. The three temptations in the desert: Matthew 4:1-11; similarly, but in different order: Luke 4:1-13. Mark treats the temptation episode in mere shorthand, John not at all.

19. The three prophecies: Matthew 16:21; 17:22-23; 20:17-19; Mark 8:31; 9:30-31; 10:32-34; Luke 9:22,44; 18:31-33. Peter's three denials: Matthew 26:69-75; Mark 14:66-72; Luke 22:54-62. The three prayers in Gethsemane: Matthew 26:36-46; Mark 14:32-42. Pilate's three judgments of Jesus' innocence: Luke 23:4,14-15,22; John 18:38; 19:4,6. Jesus' three questions and Peter's three answers: John 21:15-17.

20. The First Miracle of the Loaves: Matthew 14:13-21; Mark 6:30-44; Luke 9:10-17; John 6:1-15.

21. The Second Miracle of the Loaves: Matthew 15:32-39; Mark 8:1-10. In the Second Miracle the number of bodies fed was only four thousand, so Jesus had begun with more food, only to feed fewer bodies. The implication of diminishing potency, as well as the redundancy, might have been the

reason why Luke and John deleted the Second Miracle of the Loaves from their accounts. But why was there a second version in Matthew and Mark? Perhaps the second version was directed to doubt. Could such a thing happen? Yes, it was possible . . . because it happened twice! An event repeated becomes somehow more credible; repetitions and reaffirmations are intended to convince. In any case, Jesus himself said that the mystical numbers twelve and seven were the key to the meaning of the two miracles (see Matthew 16:8-11; Mark 8:19-21).

22. Devils in sevens: Matthew 12:45; Luke 11:26. Magdalene's seven devils: Mark 16:9; Luke 8:2. The sevenfold indictment of the Pharisees: Matthew 23:13-33. (Matthew also lists the number of vices as seven: Matthew 15:19.) Forgiveness not seven, but seventy-seven times: Matthew 18:21-22. (A variant reading of the text is "seventy times seven," instead of seventy-seven.)

23. The seven devilish exorcists: Acts 19:14.

24. Compare Matthew 4:2, Mark 1:13, and Luke 4:2 to Exodus 24:18; 34:28.

25. The forty days between Resurrection and Ascension: Acts 1:3.

26. The mystical numerology of the New Testament is not all so patent as in these examples. A number may be given opposite or contradictory moral valuations: devils came in sevens, but so did churches. Revelation contains seven letters to the seven guiding angels of the seven churches of Asia (Revelation 1:4-3:22). Revelation is the most numerological book in the New Testament.

A number may have nonrelated associations. Three is the number of speech, but it is also the number of privation. Before Jesus performed his First Miracle of the Loaves, the crowd had gone hungry for three days; Jesus himself was sealed up without food or water in the tomb for three days. The semantics of numerology is complex.

27. The Annunciation: Luke 1:26-38. The chorus of angels: Luke 2:13-14.

28. Luke, the author of Acts, was more cosmopolitan than Matthew. He even permits a pagan gentile to see an angel. See Acts 10:3-8.

29. The liberating angel: Acts 12:6-11.

30. See Matthew 26:53. Like angels, devils too came in legions, as in Mark 5:9 and Luke 8:30.

31. The early Christians were to add a new kind of temptation to the devils' repertoire, namely, the sexual temptation. Saint Jerome endured both temptations to hunger and to the *dancing girls of Rome*. When the devil became sexual, sexuality became diabolical. Modern Christians may be embarrassed by the bogeyman nonsense of devils, but they still think of sexuality as from the devil. That association has worked to corrupt both sexuality and religiosity. Hollywood even succeeded in luring a Jesuit, that

most educated of Christians, into collaborating in the diabolical pornography of *The Exorcist*.

32. Following Matthew; in Luke it was after the second temptation.

33. Mark 1:27; similarly, Luke 4:36.

34. Matthew 4:24, excerpted.

35. The Sheep Pool of Bethzatha: John 5:1-9.

36. Matthew 4:23, excerpted; also Matthew 14:34-36; 15:29-31; Mark 1:34; Luke 4:40; 5:15-16.

37. Jesus' cures: Of fevers, Matthew 8:14-15; Mark 1:29-31; Luke 4:38-39; John 4:43-54. Of the blind, Matthew 9:27-31; 20:29-34; Mark 8:22-26; 10:46-52; Luke 18:35-43; John 9:1-7. Of the deaf, Mark 7:32-37. Of hemorrhage, Matthew 9:20-22; Mark 5:25-34; Luke 8:43-48. Of dropsy, Luke 14:1-6. Of the crippled and paralytic, Matthew 8:5-13; 9:1-8; 12:9-14; Mark 2:1-12; 3:1-6; Luke 5:17-26; 6:6-11; 13:10-17. Of leprosy, Matthew 8:1-4; Mark 1:40-45; Luke 5:12-14; 17:11-19.

38. Jesus' cures of epilepsy/demonic possession: Matthew 8:16,28-34; 9:32-34; 12:22-23; 15:21-28; 17:14-20; Mark 1:23-28,32,34,39; 5:1-20; 7:24-30; 9:14-29; Luke 4:33-37,41; 8:26-39; 9:37-43; 11:14. As is evident from these references, the cure of epilepsy/demonic possession is the most reported kind of healing miracle that Jesus performed. The modern description "epileptic demoniac" is a curious one, at once scientific-medical and primitive-superstitious. Epilepsy is the modern diagnosis of some of the episodes of demonic possession in the New Testament; it was not the ancient Jewish understanding of the phenomenon. To the pagans epilepsy was just the "falling sickness;" from the time of Hippocrates, that is, four centuries before Christ, they understood it medically. Julius Caesar's epilepsy caused him no moral censure. To the Jews and early Christians, however, epilepsy was a moral, not a medical, pathology. The epileptic was "possessed by devils."

39. Jesus' raising of the dead: Matthew 9:18-19,23-26; Mark 5:21-24,35-43; Luke 7:11-17; 8:40-42,49-56; John 11:1-44.

40. Luke 6:19 and 5:17, excerpted, respectively.

41. The Transfiguration: Matthew 17:1-8; Mark 9:2-8; Luke 9:28-36.

42. Jesus' mana in ebb: Mark 6:5-6.

43. Weak mana: Mark 8:22-26.

44. Luke 8:46, excerpted; also, Mark 5:30.

45. See Matthew 10:1,8.

46. Illness as a symptom of hereditary guilt: John 9:1-3,34.

47. Mark 5:15, excerpted.

48. Matthew 8:34, excerpted; also Mark 5:17; Luke 8:37.

49. Matthew 9:8, excerpted.

50. The attempt to draw off Jesus' mana undetected: Matthew 9:20-21; also 14:35-36; Mark 5:25-34; 6:56; Luke 6:19; 8:43-48.

51. Idolatrous fetishism was to become a prominent characteristic of medieval Christianity. St. Paul was able to heal through the medium of handkerchiefs that had touched his body (Acts 19;11-12). Throughout the Middle Ages such handkerchiefs, *brandea,* were lowered down a shaft under the main altar of a church to touch the bones of some saint or martyr. Contact with the relics charged the *brandea* with healing mana. The main altar of St. Peter's in Rome, under which lay the reputed relics of Peter, Jesus' chief apostle, was the most renowned site of the fetishistic practice of charging objects with mana. Like his Master, Peter too had a potent mana; his mere shadow could cure (Acts 5:15).

52. Aramaic abracadabra: *Ephphatha,* Mark 7:34. *Talitha, kum,* Mark 5:41. The only other Aramaic words in the gospels are *Abba!* (Father!), Mark 14:36, and *Eloi, Eloi, lama sabachthani?* (My God, My God, why have you deserted me?), Mark 15:34 and Matthew 27:46, the words of Jesus' intimate address to Yahweh.

53. As noted above, Matthew and Mark report two Miracles of the Loaves, Luke and John only one. John tells the story of the Miracle at Cana, in which Jesus turned water into wine (John 2:1-11). The Miracle of the Loaves and the Miracle at Cana are as complementary as bread-and-wine. In the Gospel of John symbols and metaphors are richer than in the other three gospels.

54. The Nature miracles: The calming of the storm, Matthew 8:23-27; Mark 4:35-41; Luke 8:22-25. Walking on water, Matthew 14:22-33; Mark 6:45-52; John 6:16-21.

55. The Temple tax: Matthew 17:24-27. Matthew does not report that Peter did go fishing and catch the fish with its tiny treasure inside, but he does intend the reader to infer that a miracle did occur just as Jesus said it would.

56. The question of the Temple tax was more of an issue to the early Jewish Christians than it could have been to Jesus and his apostles. The episode is probably a retrojection of early Church policy back to the time of Jesus, as if such expedience were from the Master himself.

57. Earthquakes and zombies: Matthew 27:51-53.

58. Compare Matthew 28:1-2 to Mark 16:1-5.

59. On Jesus as superior to the angels see Hebrews 1;2.

60. Matthew 2:3, excerpted. Compare Matthew 2:2-4, the Messiah awaited, to Matthew 21:10-11, the Messiah arrived.

61. Luke 3:15, excerpted, applied to John the Baptist as a possible candidate for Messiah.

Legitimacy, pp. 43–59

1. The origins of Romulus: Livy, *History of Rome,* 1.3-4.
2. Moses as a foundling: Exodus 2:1-10.
3. Matthew 13:54, excerpted.
4. Matthew 13:55, excerpted; also Mark 6:3; for the variant, "Joseph's son," see Luke 4:22; John 6:42.
5. Matthew 1:2.
6. Matthew's genealogy: Matthew 1:1-17.
7. Luke's genealogy: Luke 3:23-38.
8. The numerological scheme in Luke is not explicitly stated in the text, but commentators have counted seventy-seven generations, or eleven sevens. Three significant persons—Abraham, David, and Enoch—each start one of the groups of seven. Matthew's scheme of fourteens may be interpreted as double sevens.
9. Luke is free of the Jewish historic grudge. Unlike Matthew, he doesn't even mention the Babylonian Captivity in his genealogy. Luke traces Jesus' lineage beyond Abraham the primal Jew to Adam the primal human being.
10. Some early Christians were left unconvinced by the argument of legitimacy by genealogy. See First Timothy 1:4 and Titus 3:9.
11. Luke 1:35.
12. Zechariah and Elizabeth: Luke 1:5-25. The Annunciation: Luke 1:26–38.
13. The Visitation: Luke 1:39-45.
14. Luke 1:66, excerpted. Compare Luke 1:66 and 3:15 (about John the Baptist) to Mark 4:41 and Luke 8:25 (about Jesus).
15. Compare Matthew 4:17 to 3:2.
16. Luke 1:37, citing Genesis 18:14.
17. Joseph, who was to be the biological link between his son Jesus and all the illustrious ancestors, becomes, by the tale of the virginal conception, the most awkward of all the characters in the New Testament. The embarrassment to logic makes Joseph an ambiguity, a doubt, a cipher, a nonentity. With poignant psychological realism Matthew reports that the mortified Joseph wanted to break off his engagement to his pregnant betrothed and hush up the scandal as best he could (Matthew 1:19)—a very human reaction under the circumstances. Matthew sends an angel into Joseph's dream to tell him of the virginal conception, thus putting the best possible interpretation upon the scandal of apparent infidelity and illegitimacy. Joseph, being a *man of honor,* duly accepted the angel's explanation. Joseph's fatherhood, such as it was, was out of a dream.
18. Luke 2:12, excerpted.
19. The child Jesus and the Temple savants: Luke 2:41-50. The Jewish

historian Josephus had the shameless impudence to tell a similar story . . . about himself!

20. The Baptist's premature witness: Luke 1:41.

21. John 1:30-34, excerpted. Repeated from John 1:15, repeated again in John 1:36. In the synoptic gospels the messiahship of Jesus is a secret, but in John it is an explicit affirmation.

22. Matthew 11:3; also Luke 7:19. In answer to the Baptist's question Jesus appealed to his miracles as proof of his legitimacy as Messiah. (See Matthew 11:4-5; Luke 7:21-22.)

23. Luke 3:16, excerpted; similarly, Matthew 3:11; Mark 1:7; John 1:26.

24. Jesus' retreat in sympathetic apprehension at the arrest of John the Baptist: Matthew 4:12; Mark 1:14. Jesus' identification of the opposition to John with the opposition to himself: Matthew 21:23-27,31-32; Mark 11:27-33; Luke 7:29-30; 20:1-8. John as the greatest and the least: Matthew 11:7-15; Luke 7:24-30. Jesus' solitude of grief at the death of the Baptist: Matthew 14:12-13; Luke 9:10.

25. Mark 8:27-28, excerpted; also Matthew 16:13-14; Luke 9:18-19.

26. Mark 6:16; also Matthew 14:2; but in Luke 9:9 Herod scoffs at the superstition. Note in Herod's remark how the resurrection of the dead was in the air.

27. John 1:31, excerpted; also John 1:33.

28. Mark 6:15, excerpted; compare to Matthew 21:10-11,46.

29. At the very least we must admit that John did not communicate his recognition of Jesus to all of his own disciples. Long after Jesus had come and gone there were still disciples of John the Baptist, whom the Christians had to try to convert (see Acts 19:1-7). The Gospel of John, written at the end of the first century, contains propaganda directed to the demotion of John the Baptist.

30. The testimonies of Simeon and Anna: Luke 2:25-38.

31. Mark 1:11, excerpted; also Luke 3:22. In the variant in Matthew, "This is my Son, the Beloved; my favor rests on him," (Matthew 3:17), the implication of the grammar is that the bystanders did hear, indeed, that they were the ones addressed. In John it was only the Baptist who witnessed the descent of the Holy Spirit upon Jesus (John 1:32-34); by that version the Baptist is made to add his own witness to that from heaven. The baptism of Jesus: Matthew 3:13-17; Mark 1:9-11; Luke 3:21-22. (John does not report the actual baptism of Jesus by the Baptist, perhaps because that event would imply Jesus' dependence upon, and therefore inferiority to, John the Baptist.)

32. Now that the paternity of Jesus has gone beyond the patriarchs to Yahweh Himself, the unfortunate Joseph becomes all the more a cipher and nonentity.

33. Matthew 17:5, excerpted; also Mark 9:7; Luke 9:35.

34. Matthew 8:29, excerpted; variants, Mark 5:7; Luke 8:28. How very like the devil to compliment while resisting!

35. Mark 3:11, excerpted; also Luke 4:41.

36. Mark 1:34, excerpted.

37. The devil's taunt: Matthew 4:3,6.

38. Matthew 4:3, excerpted. The devil tempted Jesus to turn stones into bread. John the Baptist claimed that Yahweh could turn stones into human bodies (Matthew 3:9). In the metamorphosis of stones into bread and bodies we detect the surreal hallucinations induced by desert asceticism.

39. Matthew 4:6.

40. Matthew and Luke report the three temptations in a different sequence. The psychology of the episode, with the devil first demanding proof—"If you are the Son of God"—twice, then becoming unconvinced and dropping his hypothesis, makes Matthew's the preferable sequence, from a dramatic standpoint at least. By the third temptation, as reported by Matthew, the devil has dropped both his skeptical qualifier and his appeal to Old Testament texts as argument.

41. Commentators recognize that the first two chapters of Matthew and the first two chapters of Luke, that is, the legitimizing chapters of each gospel, were the last parts of those gospels to be written. Correspondingly, the Prologue to the Gospel of John was a Christian hymn tacked on t o the beginning of that gospel in order to serve the purpose of legitimizing. It is not legitimacy that explains the subsequent career; rather, it is the remarkable career that explains the subsequent interest in theories of legitimacy.

42. Mark 1:12-13, excerpted.

43. The process of mythologizing a great man seems to proceed from his deeds and words to his being. In Mark, the earliest gospel, the focus is on what Jesus did. Luke and Matthew devote their attention to what Jesus said. Finally, in John, the latest gospel, there is an obsessive fascination with what Jesus was (or, better, *is*). The corpus of Jesus' deeds and words is closed; but to speculations on his being there will be no end.

44. Great attention has been paid to the parallelism and correspondences among the four gospels. Equally significant is what parts of any one gospel are missing from any of the others. The embellishments and the editing out reveal the editorial biases of the writers of each gospel. The gospels are not paintings; they are mosaics.

45. John 1:1.

46. John 1:14, excerpted.

47. The text of John's Prologue was later corrupted in order to accommodate the notion of the virginal conception. The clause "born not out of human stock or urge of the flesh or will of man but of God himself" (John 1:13) was probably written to modify "all who believe in the name

of him"; with a change of verb it was applied to Jesus himself, in order to lend support to the myth of the virginal conception and birth.

48. John 10:30.

49. John 10.38, excerpted.

50. John 14:10, asked as a rhetorical question, "Do you not believe . . . ?," then repeated as an affirmation, "You must believe me . . ." (John 14:11).

51. The early Christians followed Jesus' precedent (or, perhaps, attributed to him their own unscrupulous practice) of appropriation of the Old Testament. They plundered the Old Testament for its words and made all kinds of far-fetched associations and interpretations, all intended to show that the old words prefigured the Word, just as the old numbers prefigured the new numbers. (The epistles of Paul are models of such ingenious exegesis.) By the reductionism of interpreting the Old Testament not for what it was, but for what it previewed as *type,* the Christians succeeded in depriving the Jews of their own scriptures, all for the purpose of proving what to the Jews was a rank form of anti-monotheistic blasphemy. On the Christian method of typology, see Luke 24:27 and John 12:16.

52. Matthew 4:10, excerpted; Luke 4:8; quoting Deuteronomy 6:13. By *him alone* Jesus was not referring to himself!

53. John offers another proof of the legitimacy of Jesus, a psychological, rather than a theological one, namely, that Jesus was the Supreme Lover. John's characterization of Jesus belongs more to the problem of John than to the problem of Jesus. The problem of John will be taken up in the chapter, Love and Eroticism.

54. Matthew 27:54, excerpted; also Mark 15:39.

55. In his answer to John the Baptist's question, Jesus did cite his miracles as proof of his legitimacy. But the crowd's insatiable craving for signs also exasperated Jesus (see John 4:48).

Ego and Alienation, pp. 61-80

1. Matthew 5:17. But what a threat to Judaism, equally whether the Law was to be *abolished* or *completed!*

2. Or, in the translation of The Jerusalem Bible, "You have learnt how it was said to our ancestors. . . . But I say this to you. . . ." For instances of this refrain see Matthew 5:21-22,27-28,31-32,33-34,38-39,43-44.

3. Luke 6:5; also Mark 2:27-28; Matthew 12:8.

4. John 6:29, excerpted. (However, that statement may be from John about Jesus, rather than from Jesus about himself.)

5. Matthew 10:24-25, excerpted; also Luke 6:40. The disciple stood

in the same lowly relationship to his spiritual Master as the slave did in relationship to his economic master.

6. Matthew 11:6, emphasis added; also Luke 7:23.

7. Matthew 12:30, excerpted; also Luke 11:23. This quote is not in Mark. In Mark's early tradition the battle lines had not yet been drawn.

8. Revelation 3:15-16.

9. Mark 16:16.

10. The author of Revelation thought it necessary to pronounce a curse upon anyone who *adds* or *cuts anything* from his book. See Revelation 22:18-19. In addition to editorial tampering there were forgeries. Paul included his handwritten autograph as a seal of genuineness for his epistles. See Second Thessalonians 3:17; Colossians 4:18. Against forgeries, Second Thessalonians 2:2-3. But some think that Second Thessalonians and Colossians are forgeries themselves!

11. Mark 16:15-16.

12. Compare that universalist commission to the sectarian restrictions in Matthew 10:5-6.

13. In the Gospel of John the emphasized extreme is ego; in the Gospel of Matthew, it is alienation.

14. Jesus of lowly birth: Matthew 13:55-57; Mark 6:3; Luke 4:22. Jesus young: Luke 3:23; John 8:57. Jesus self-educated: John 7:15. The Jewish Establishment of Jerusalem also expressed a regional prejudice against Jesus as a native of Galilee, a region of mixed races and heterodox beliefs. See John 7:52; 8:48; also 1:46.

15. The Jewish Establishment of Jerusalem is portrayed in the gospels by a variety of terms. Besides *scribes and Pharisees,* there were *elders, rulers, chief priests, Sadducees,* and *the Sanhedrin.* In the Gospel of John the adversaries of Jesus are not those heterogeneous and overlapping members of the Establishment, but *the Jews* in general.

16. *Fools and blind:* Matthew 23:17. *Brood of vipers:* Matthew 3:8; 12:34; 23:33; Luke 3:7. *Whitewashed tombs:* Matthew 23:27. "Hypocrites" occurs thirteen times in Matthew, three times in Luke, only once in Mark, and in John not at all. It is in the Gospel of Matthew that Jesus is portrayed at his most alienated. In Matthew, the intemperate and abusive rhetoric of the sevenfold indictment of the Pharisees counterpoints and spoils the effect of the beatitudes of the Sermon on the Mount.

17. Acts 23:6, excerpted; also Philippians 3:5.

18. Luke 4:24, excerpted. For the significance of the variant phrasing of this proverb in Matthew and Mark, see the next chapter, Antifamilialism. John reports that Jesus had made such a statement, but Jesus was well received by the people despite his own expectatio st. See John 4:44-45.

19. Matthew 22:21, excerpted. Tribute to Caesar: Matthew 22:15-22; Mark 12:13-17; Luke 20:20-26. Note that Jesus had to ask the questioner

for a coin; his adversaries were the ones who possessed the hated tribute money with its idolatrous image of Caesar. Jesus himself was *clean*. He had no money; he rendered no tribute to Caesar. Some have interpreted Jesus' answer as a directive to render to Caesar, but that the answer was ambiguous is evident from Jesus' enemies' use of it in their accusations against him. See Luke 23:2.

20. The dilemma-question on John's baptism: Matthew 21:23-27; Mark 11:27-33; Luke 20:1-8.

21. John does not include these episodes in his gospel. If Jesus is divine, why bother to prove him merely humanly clever?

22. Each of the three synoptic gospels presents Jesus' question on John's baptism *before* the Pharisees' question about tribute to Caesar. If we were to interpret that sequence as accurate chronology, then we would draw a different, and worse, conclusion: Instead of stooping to his adversaries' methods, Jesus himself may have set the tone of the debate. In that case, the Pharisees stooped to *his* methods.

23. The devils' negotiations with Jesus: Matthew 8:30-32; Mark 5:10-13; Luke 8:30-33.

24. Mark 3:28-30. In Matthew 12:31-32, opposition to Jesus as the Son of Man may be forgiven, but opposition to the *Holy Spirit* as distinct from the person of Jesus will never be forgiven. Luke further censors the statement by dissociating Jesus' curse (Luke 12:10) from its context in the Pharisees' accusations of Jesus' intimacy with the devils (Luke 11:14-22).

25. How similar was the verbal sparring and one-upmanship between Jesus and the Pharisees to that between Jesus and the devil in the episode of the temptation in the desert! The Pharisees are portrayed as *devils*. The devils and Pharisees both quoted scripture wrongheadedly and with sinister intent. Such unscrupulous use of scripture was a diabolical, *Pharisaical* trait.

26. Matthew 10:32-33. Variant, Luke 12:8-9.

27. John 15:23.

28. We are familiar with many such cases of alienation in the arts, in economics, and in politics. Revolutionaries in religion are not so common in our religiously reactionary age.

29. The parable of the Pharisee and the publican: Luke 18:9-14.

30. The parable of the prodigal son: Luke 15:11-32. (Like Jesus later, the prodigal *died* and *came back to life* to be with his father. See Luke 15:31-32.) The son who had remained faithful to his father had a right to object to the big to-do at the prodigal's return. But Jesus was not a philosopher. As we discover in his parable of the vineyard laborers (Matthew 20:1-16), he had no interest in the abstraction of justice. Jesus' sympathies lay with the alienated and outcast, the publican and the prodigal.

31. Mark 2:15, excerpted.

32. Tax collectors were also reputed to be extortionate. We assume

that Matthew gave up his former occupation when he joined Jesus. Had Jesus permitted Matthew to continue working as a tax collector, he would have taken a definite and self-discrediting stand on the issue of tribute to Caesar.

33. Matthew 21:31, excerpted.

34. Mark 9:40; variant, Luke 9:50. Contrast with Jesus' statement of benign tolerance the fate of the seven Jewish exorcists who tried to heal in Jesus' name (Acts 19:11-17).

35. John 17:16; also 17:14.

36. John 15:18-19.

37. Matthew 24:9; also 10:22; Luke 21:17.

38. Jesus as a master psychologist: John 2:25; 6:64.

39. Luke 6:22-23; variant, Matthew 5:11-12.

40. Wasn't positively valued alienation a cultural trait of the Jews, the *chosen people?*

41. John 12:48; similarly, John 3:36.

42. Matthew 19:30; 20:16; Mark 10:31; Luke 13:30.

43. Luke 18:14, excerpted; also 14:11; Matthew 23:12.

44. Luke 19:26; also 8:18; Matthew 13:12; 25:29; Mark 4:25.

45. Luke 9:24; also 17:33; Matthew 16:25; Mark 8:35; John 12:25.

46. This refrain is sounded in Matthew 8:12; 13:42; 13:50; 22:13; 24:51; 25:30; Luke 13:28.

47. The spiteful righteousness of alienation: Matthew 10:14-15; Mark 6:11; Luke 9:5; 10:10-12; Acts 13:51; 18:6.

48. John 15:25, excerpted, quoting Psalms 35:19. There might have been no reason for hating Jesus the Supreme Lover of the Gospel of John, perhaps; but there existed plenty of reasons for the Establishment to hate Jesus the abusive subversive of the Gospel of Matthew.

49. Paul proclaimed his innocence. See Acts 25:8. All of the martyrs saw themselves as innocent victims.

50. Some cherished values of antiquity subverted by the Christians were the monotheism, Covenant rites, and observance of Law of the Jews; the aristocracy, pride, power, love of beauty and cult of excellence of the Greeks; and the sense of social responsibility of the Romans.

51. In choosing a Zealot named Simon as one of his apostles, Jesus did contribute to the misinterpretation of his mission as political.

52. See John 18:36.

53. The story of the slaughter of the innocents (Matthew 2:16-18) may represent an emerging humanitarian opposition to the male domination of the young inherent in patriarchal religion. In an attempt to kill the infant Messiah, Herod ordered all male children under two years of age to be slaughtered. The story is strongly reminiscent of Yahweh's practice of genocide in the murder of all the first-born of Egypt (Exodus 11:4-6; 12:29-

30). The story of the slaughter of the innocents indicts the cruelty of old men and sets the stage for Jesus, the antitype, the compassionate one.

54. "Up to this present time, the kingdom of heaven has been subjected to violence and the violent are taking it by storm." (Matthew 11:12, excerpted) The violent were the Herods, who murdered both male infants and the great prophet John the Baptist; the Romans, who murdered Jews; and the Jewish Zealots, who murdered Romans. Jesus' pacifism was a reaction against all that violence.

55. See Matthew 23:1-3. "Do as they say, but not as they do." But aren't those instructions a kind of hypocrisy, too?

56. Matthew 7:12, excerpted; also Luke 6:31.

57. Matthew 7:12, excerpted.

58. The Protestants of the Reformation tried the same thing against the Catholic Establishment. Religion, like politics, has its cycles of simplicity, elaboration, overelaboration, collapse, and simplicity once again.

59. Matthew 24:10, excerpted.

60. Matthew 26:52, excerpted.

61. Luke 6:27-29, excerpted.

62. Matthew 5:39, excerpted.

63. James 4:17.

64. In our own time the military cruelty of the Vietnam War evoked the pacifist movement of the 1960s and its theme of peace and love, antivalues to the war and hatred in Vietnam. (The love of the sixties' lovers was, however, more carnal than that of the Christian ideal.)

65. Matthew 10:16; also Luke 10:3.

66. Such a strategy was subversive, too. Compare Jesus' disciplinary parable about taking seats at a table (Luke 14:7-11) to his indictment of the Pharisees as the ones who assumed the places of honor (Luke 11:43; 20:46).

67. John 8:13, excerpted. The Gospel of John is a maze of contradiction on this subject. Jesus admitted that testimony on his own behalf was not valid (John 5:31). When the Pharisees ventured the same judgment, Jesus contradicted both them and himself, claiming that his testimony to himself was valid (John 8:14). Jesus also claimed that the Baptist's testimony proved his legitimacy (John 5:33), but that he really didn't need the Baptist's testimony (John 5:34). That combined appeal to, and standoffishness about, the Baptist's testimony makes the Baptist's historical witness to Jesus all the more suspect.

68. John 8:58, excerpted.

Antifamilialism, pp. 81-96

1. Mark 6:4, excerpted. In the variant of this in Matthew 13:57, the prophet's alienation is from his *own country* and *house*. In Luke 4:24, it is from only his *own country*. As usual, Luke censors and softens a harsh statement.

2. Matthew 1:21, excerpted.

3. Luke 1:32, excerpted.

4. Mark 3:21, excerpted.

5. Who was Jesus' family? There was Joseph, the nonbiological father; Mary, the mother of the human (but not of the divine) Jesus; and Jesus' brothers and sisters. Exploiting a linguistic ambiguity, Catholics have relegated Jesus' brothers and sisters to mere cousins. Which relatives tried to "take charge of" Jesus is not specified; but they must have been close relatives to feel such familial right and responsibility.

6. In Matthew, the Jewish-patriarchal gospel, the angel tells the father, while in Luke, the pagan-matriarchal gospel, the angel tells the mother.

7. Matthew 11:23, excerpted. Jesus' settlement in Capernaum: Matthew 4:13. His condemnation of the Galilean communities: Matthew 11:20-24; Luke 10:13-15. John's revisionism would deny Jesus' estrangement from his family. See John 2:12, but contrast John 7:5.

8. Luke 2:48, excerpted. This three-day loss and disappearance of the child Jesus prefigures the three-day loss and disappearance of the dead Jesus in the tomb.

9. Luke 2:49, excerpted.

10. Luke 2:50. Jesus among the Temple savants: Luke 2:41-50.

11. Because Josephus told the same story about his own childhood, we may surmise that the idea of a young boy discussing religion on terms of equality with his elders was a common fantasy of Jewish ambition.

12. Luke 2:51, excerpted.

13. John 7:5.

14. Matthew 12:46, excerpted.

15. Matthew 12:48-49, excerpted; also Mark 3:33-34. Luke softens the severity of the rebuff by eliminating the rude rhetorical question, "Who is my mother?" (see Luke 8:21). There are no insults to women in the Gospel of Luke. On Luke's treatment of women, see the chapter Dissonant Themes, Consonant Relations.

16. The sequence of ideas in Mark is as follows. 1) Jesus' family thinks that he is insane (Mark 3:21); 2) the scribes accuse him of being possessed by a devil (Mark 3:22); 3) Jesus contradicts the scribes and lashes back with his curse for their eternal sin (Mark 3:28-30); and 4) Jesus rejects his natural family (Mark 3:31-35). In this sequence we can detect a chiastic pattern; that is, 4) refutes 1), and 3) refutes 2). The bridge between the

accusations and refutations is provided by the saying about a house divided against itself (Mark 3:23-27).

17. John 19:26-27, excerpted.

18. In the Gospel of John theology and mysticism predominate over biographical facts. Whether or not a cross-side reconciliation did take place, some such reconciliation must have occurred, at least in Jesus' own mind, near the end of his life. When the struggle is over, the opponents may be absolved. Luke presents Jesus' abandonment of alienation, if not of antifamilialism: "Father, forgive them . . ." (Luke 23:34).

19. Mark 3:14, excerpted.

20. Matthew 24:38-39, excerpted; also Luke 17:26-30. Yahweh destroyed the world for its wickedness. Was, then, *eating, drinking,* and also *taking wives, taking husbands,* a kind of wickedness?

21. By our twentieth century, the end of the world has been prophesied too many times for us to be credulous. The prophet with the placard, REPENT, FOR THE END OF THE WORLD IS AT HAND, is an old subject of cartoon humor. But humor serves to ease anxiety. We may be skeptical of the prophets, but deep down we are still apprehensive about the prophecy. Nuclear War is our apocalyptic anxiety.

22. Luke 12:51-53.

23. Matthew 10:35, excerpted; compare Micah 7:6.

24. Matthew 12:25, excerpted.

25. Luke 14:26. Commentators like to explain away the shocking verb *hate* in this quotation as a Hebraic hyperbole. But in the context of an ultimatum, there can be no hyperbole. Jesus said what he meant and meant what he said.

26. Matthew 10:36, quoting Micah 7:6.

27. Matthew 19:27, excerpted.

28. Matthew 19:29; Mark 10:29-30; variant, Luke 18:29-30. This promise still stands for those—priests, nuns—who abandon their families to embrace a vocation.

29. Luke 21:16.

30. Matthew 10:37-38.

31. Matthew 8:21-22; Luke 9:59-60. In Luke, this is followed by an either-or ultimatum; it must be either family or the values revolution (Luke 9:61–62).

32. Matthew 10:21-22, excerpted.

33. See Matthew 10:34; variant, Luke 12:51; both reported in a context of antifamilial doctrine.

34. Luke 16:13, excerpted; Matthew 6:24.

35. Matthew 10:9-10.

36. The economic discipline of John the Baptist: Matthew 3:4; Mark 1:6.

37. Luke 14:33, excerpted.

38. The disciple who was rich: Matthew 19:16-22; Mark 10:17-22; Luke 18:18-23.

39. The blame for the historical corruption of the Christian poverty discipline goes to the emperor Constantine. In order to secure the tame allegiance of the Church to his imperial ambitions, Constantine bestowed both money and status upon it. He single-handedly killed off the Christian values revolution by incorporating the Church as an agency of the imperial Establishment. The Church became rich, powerful, and complacent. By the Middle Ages already, Christian poverty had become an antiquarian subject.

40. Matthew 5:42, excerpted; Luke 6:30.

41. As we discover in the history of the medieval monasteries or of the Vatican, the Church has preferred charity to poverty. If the people practiced charity, the clerics wouldn't have to endure poverty.

42. Acts 2:44-45; also Acts 4:32,34-35.

43. Jesus criticized the Pharisees' diversion of family wealth into religious coffers, to the dereliction of familial duty. See Matthew 15:3-6; Mark 7:8-13. But throughout the Middle Ages the Church siphoned off family wealth into the corporate coffers of its monasteries and churches. Of course compensatory rewards were promised.

44. Matthew 19:27, excerpted.

45. Luke 18:22; excerpted; similarly, Matthew 19:21; Mark 10:21.

46. In the famous beatitude, Luke 6:20.

47. Contortions with camels: Matthew 19:24; Mark 10:25; Luke 18:25.

The Eunuch Ideal, pp. 97-113

1. Luke 18:16, excerpted; also Matthew 19:14; Mark 10:14.

2. Matthew 11:25, excerpted. One thing hidden from *the learned and the clever* but revealed to *mere children* was the identity of Jesus as the Messiah. See Matthew 21:15-16.

3. Matthew 18:3, excerpted; similarly Mark 10:15; Luke 18:17.

4. Jesus as a romantic: Another aspect of Jesus' romanticism was his notion of divine Providence (see Matthew 6:25-34; Luke 12:22-31). The Heavenly Father might feed the birds of the air, but he also permits millions of them to starve in the harsh weather of winter. The experience of every individual in his own life, as well as the record of human history, contradicts the reality of any Providence watching over us. After our own twentieth-century experience of world wars and holocausts, we should be ready, at long last, to dispose of the notion of Providence once and for all. It is a romantic delusion. Or is God inept in his providential beneficence?

Jesus told his disciples not to be anxious about food, clothing, and shelter. But for that too-human economic anxiety Jesus substituted the much more intimidating apprehension of apocalyptic anxiety.

5. Matthew 22:30; Mark 12:25.

6. Luke 20:34-36.

7. Jesus and the Sadducees: Matthew 22:23-33; Mark 12:18-27; Luke 20:27-40. Perhaps because the Sadducees had already gone out of existence before the gospels were written, the Jesus of the gospels was not so hard on them as he was on the Pharisees. He would tell them, "You are wrong," (Matthew 22:29), but not "Hypocrites!" After his digression on the subject of marriage, Jesus did go on to straighten out the Sadducees on the issue of the resurrection of the dead.

8. Matthew 19:12.

9. Notice the sequence of thought in Matthew 19. There is 1) the problem of divorce (Matthew 19:1-9); 2) the eunuch ideal (Matthew 19:10-12); 3) infantilism as a moral ideal (Matthew 19:13-15); 4) the discipline of poverty (Matthew 19:16-26); and 5) antifamilialism and its rewards (Matthew 19:27-30). That sequence constitutes almost a full disciplinary charter for the disciples of Jesus.

10. Actually, Jesus bracketed his proclamation of the eunuch ideal by a double qualifier. See Matthew 19:11-12.

11. Because of the Protestant ethic, a revival of the Old Testament correlation of wealth and divine favor, it is not easy to come up with an example of the Protestant poor. Not the Mormons, certainly.

12. Martha and Mary: Luke 10:38-42.

13. Luke 7:36, excerpted.

14. Luke 7:38.

15. Luke 7:44-46, excerpted.

16. The anointing: Matthew 26:6-13; Mark 14:3-9; Luke 7:36-50; John 12:1-8 and allusion, John 11:2. Commentators take Luke's story as a different incident, rather than as a variant version. If so, then Jesus enjoyed repeated indulgences from women. What happened at the anointing may have been typical, not unique.

17. See John 8:46.

18. The seed that fell on bad ground and good ground: Matthew 13:4-9; Mark 4:3-9; Luke 8:4-8. The seed that grew spontaneously: Mark 4:26-29. Weeds among the wheat: Matthew 13:24-30. The mustard seed: Matthew 13:31-32; Mark 4:30-32; Luke 13:18-19. The grain of wheat that dies, in order to spring up: John 12:24.

19. Matthew 13:37, excerpted.

20. The curse of the fig tree: Matthew 21:18-22; Mark 11:12-14,20-24. According to Mark, the fig tree withered up the day after Jesus cursed it. Compressing the story for dramatic effect, Matthew reports that the fig tree withered immediately after Jesus' curse. Luke does not report the epi-

sode; he does, however, relate a parable about a barren fig tree, in which, instead of being cursed, the tree is spared (Luke 13:6-9). Again Luke censors out unattractive harshness in Jesus. In Luke 17:5-6, it is a mulberry rather than a fig tree, and the tree, rather than the mountain, is moved to the sea. The theme of that passage is the same as that of the episode of the curse of the fig tree, namely, the power of faith.

Because Israel was described in the Old Testament by such metaphors as "the vine" or "the tree and its branches," some commentators have taken the fig tree as a symbol for Israel. That interpretation of the episode of the curse of the fig tree is nothing less than anti-Semitic. The text says that Jesus was hungry. Therefore, it was privation in his own body, not alienation, that aroused his curse of the barren fig tree. According to John, Jesus' body was the vine.

Jesus also used the fig tree in his apocalyptic rhetoric, as warning sign of doom and destruction. See Matthew 24:32-33; Mark 13:28-29; Luke 21:29-31.

21. Mark 11:13, excerpted.

22. In Matthew 17:20, the image of moving mountains and the problem of lack of faith are related to the apostles' failure to cure an epileptic, that is, they are related to an impotence.

23. Luke 23:29, excerpted. Compare that to the implied beatitude on barrenness in Jesus' apocalyptic rhetoric (Matthew 24:19; Mark 13:17; Luke 21:23). When an enthusiastic woman pronounced a blessing on the fertile womb and nourishing breasts of Jesus' own mother, Jesus contradicted, or corrected, her by saying that the religious-minded were even happier. See Luke 11:27-28. Jesus' retort was both antifamilial and antisexual. Celibacy and the sterility ideal were linked to both antifamilialism and apocalyptic anxiety.

24. From the theological perspective, because Jesus' words were all divinely inspired, and therefore all equally and eternally applicable as absolute truth, no allowance is made for a mere impulsive outburst or intemperate rhetoric that might have been modified on balanced second thought. The dogmatic mind has no sense of fine discrimination. And so the theologians have done irreparable harm to Jesus of Nazareth as a *human being,* a human being inconsistent, contradictory, and paradoxical.

25. John 1:13, excerpted.

26. One theological text maintains that the infant Jesus shot through Mary's hymen like a ray of sunlight through a pane of glass!

27. Examples of antipagan stereotypes in the New Testament: Romans 1:26-32; First Peter 4:3.

28. The doctrine of Mary's Assumption, the last piece in the mosaic of desexualizing mythology, was proclaimed in 1950.

29. On the subject of catacomb sensuality and Christian necrophilia,

as well as the idolatrous fetishism of the cult of relics—referred to in note 51 of Context—see my forthcoming book, *Rome, The Values of Cosmopolis.*

30. The eunuch ideal is not dead yet. Shortly after this chapter was completed, Pope John Paul II reaffirmed celibacy as superior to marriage.

31. The clerical vow and ideal was actually poverty, chastity, and obedience. Obedience is pacifism in an institutional setting.

Dissonant Themes, Consonant Relations, pp. 115–128

1. Matthew 5:28, excerpted.

2. Significantly, no one has interpreted Jesus' magnification of lustful thought into adultery as a Hebraic hyperbole, comparable to Jesus' directive to *hate* one's father and mother when coming to him. We need an exegesis of the exaggeration in the New Testament.

3. Matthew 5:29, excerpted. This sentence directly follows the prohibition of lust.

4. According to the fourth-century Church historian Eusebius, the great theologian Origen actually did castrate himself in pursuit of the eunuch ideal. Eusebius, *Ecclesiastical History,* 6.8.

5. See John 8:3-11.

6. Jesus described lustful thought as adultery. It should be remembered that the Jews commonly drew parallels between sexual infidelity on the one hand—*adultery, fornication, harlotry*—and sectarian faithlessness on the other—*idolatry.* That metaphorical usage might be related to the fact that the very sign of the Jewish covenant with their god was circumcision, a sexual mutilation. In any case, the muddling of the terminology of sexual infidelity with that of religious faithlessness tended to take the rights and wrongs of sexual behavior out of the simple human sphere and relocate them in the theological, cosmic realm.

In the New Testament the Book of Revelation is the best example of the cosmic imagery of sexual metaphors: the Whore of Babylon, *fornication, harlotry,* and so on. See Revelation, 14; 17; 18.

7. Mark 10:11–12, excerpted. Jewish women had no right to divorce their husbands, but Mark's gospel was directed to Rome, a society in which women did have such a right.

8. Mark 10:5, excerpted.

9. See Mark 9:47. Mark does not specify lust as the sin meant, but he presents a series of necessary self-mutilations—cutting off the hand, cutting off the foot, plucking out the eyes—all castration imagery.

10. See Mark 9:42–10:16.

11. Matthew 5:32, excerpted.

12. Does fornication here mean that an adultery in the flesh by one's

spouse justifies divorcing that spouse, in other words, adultery as grounds? I take the fornication exception as an editorial interpolation, first because it does not occur in the other gospels, and second because Jesus rarely moderated his prohibitions or disciplinary impositions.

13. See Matthew 5:17–32. In Matthew the plucking out of the eye is explicitly associated with the problem of lust. The eye is susceptible to both lust and idolatry. And isn't sexual passion a kind of idolatry?

14. Matthew 19:9, excerpted.

15. In Mark, the Pharisees asked Jesus whether divorce itself was permitted, whereas in Matthew they asked about proper grounds. Compare Mark 10:2 to Matthew 19:3. Of course the Mosaic Law permitted divorce. Mark raised the issue as a member of his pagan audience would; Matthew presented the question as the Pharisees actually asked it.

16. See Matthew 19:1-15.

17. Luke 16:18.

18. In Luke's version, only the man is blamed, either the one who divorces and remarries, or the one who marries a woman divorced by her husband. In Matthew, the Jewish gospel, the grudge against woman is overt, but in Luke, the pagan gospel, there is no such grudge. Luke has no bad words to say about women.

19. Luke 16:17. This is an abbreviated version of Jesus' disclaimer in Matthew 5:17-19.

20. Luke 16 contains the parable of the crafty steward; advice on the use of money and a complementary indictment of the Pharisees; the cryptic saying about the storming of the Kingdom; the assertion of the immutability of the Law, followed by a repudiation of that part of it that regulates divorce; and, finally, the parable of the rich man and Lazarus.

21. Mark 10:6-8, citing Genesis 1:27; 2:24. In Matthew 5, there is no justification; Matthew 19 offers the same justification as in Mark, the source; in Luke 16, there is no context, and therefore no justification. Husband and wife might be *one body,* but from Jesus' answer to the Sadducees on the resurrection of the dead, we conclude that husband and wife are not *one soul.*

22. Mark 10:9, excerpted; also Matthew 19:6.

23. The eunuch ideal (Matthew 19:10-12) directly follows the prohibition of divorce (Matthew 19:1-9).

24. John 4:22, excerpted.

25. John 4:24, excerpted.

26. John 4:27, excerpted.

27. John 4:26, excerpted. Jesus and the Samaritan woman: John 4:1-42. In the Old Testament, the well was a common setting for a romantic encounter. The charm of Jesus in this scene might belong more to John than to Jesus. On John, see the following chapter, Love and Eroticism.

28. Women were extremely susceptible to Jesus' charms. Even Pontius Pilate's wife dreamt of him! See Matthew 27:19.

29. Luke 8:1-2, excerpted.

30. See, for example, Mark 5:18-20, 8:26; Luke 8:38-39.

31. It nowhere says that Mary Magdalene was a prostitute, but such is how she has been taken. Because Jesus drove seven devils out of her (Mark 16:9; Luke 8:2), Mary Magdalene, the fallen woman restored, stands as the symbol of the Christian sexualization of the devil and the diabolization of sexuality.

32. Luke 8:3, excerpted.

33. Luke 23:27.

34. Luke 23:49; similarly, Mark 15:41.

35. Luke 24:9-11.

36. Luke 24:22-24.

37. Peter's bewilderment: Luke 24:12.

38. See Luke 24:36-43.

39. This may not have been Luke's conscious intention. Nonetheless, the two great images of Italian matriolatrous Christianity—the *presepio* (nativity scene) and the Madonna—are right out of the Gospel of Luke. In Matthew and John, Jesus refers to Yahweh as *Father,* that is, in patriarchal terms. In Luke, however, the Father-Son relationship is not emphasized. Luke is not patriarchal.

40. The pagan mythologizing of Luke in the first two chapters of his gospel has had some beautiful effects. To Luke we owe the observance of Christmas and all its imagery of birth, infancy, and tender family feeling. The cult of Christmas is antithesis to the antifamilialism in Jesus' doctrine. Also, despite the fact that the Resurrection on Easter should be the prime event in the Christian ideology, we have taken Christmas instead. In our hearts we are pagan and familial, and so we love Christmas.

41. Following John 20:11-18. In Mark 16:9, Mary Magdalene was the first to see Jesus; in Matthew 28:9-10, it was the two Marys; in Luke 24:1-8, the women saw two men, or angels. According to First Corinthians 15:5, and implied by Luke 24:34, Peter was first.

42. John 20:17, excerpted; or, by one translation, "Stop clinging to me."

43. Erotic idolatry and fetishism: Matthew 9:20-22, 14:36; Mark 3:10, 5:27-28, 6:56; Luke 6:19, 8:44.

Love and Eroticism, pp. 129–149

1. Matthew 7:12, excerpted; also Luke 6:31.

2. Matthew 25:35-36.

3. Matthew 25:35-36, emphasis added.

4. Matthew 25:40, excerpted, emphasis added.

5. Matthew 25:45, excerpted, emphasis added.

6. Matthew 25:41, excerpted. On charity in the context of the Last Judgment, see Matthew 25:31-46.

7. John 15:17.

8. John 15:12.

9. John 15:9. In Mark, there is only one passage dealing with love, namely the reduction of the Law to love of God and neighbor (Mark 12:28-34). In Matthew and Luke, love means the Golden Rule.

10. The disciple Jesus loved: John 13:23; 19:26; 20:2; 21:7,20.

11. John 13:23-25, excerpted.

12. Mark 14:51-52.

13. See John 19:25-27.

14. According to Matthew, among the women standing at the foot of the cross was the mother of Zebedee's sons (see Matthew 27:56). Now, Zebedee's sons were James and John. If, therefore, "the disciple Jesus loved" was indeed John, then in the scene at the cross Jesus took John away from his own mother and gave him to Mary. Curiouser and curiouser! Was Jesus' last gesture an antifamilial one? That textual detail in Matthew casts doubt on the identification of "the disciple Jesus loved" with John, son of Zebedee.

15. See John 21:20-23.

16. John 11:33-38, excerpted. Mark portrays Jesus as a man of merely human emotion. Matthew and Luke both suppress any emotionalism in Jesus as unbecoming.

17. See John 11:3. Jesus and Lazarus: John 11:1-44. The similarity of the descriptions, "the man you love" and "the disciple Jesus loved" has led some commentators to identify the two, so that Lazarus was the anonymous author of the Gospel of John.

18. The Miracle at Cana: John 2:1-11. This miracle is not reported by the other three gospelwriters.

19. John 6:35, excerpted.

20. The "I am . . ." formula in John: John 6:35,41,48,51; 8:12,24,58; 9:5; 10:7,9,11; 11:25; 14:6; 15:1.

21. John 13:1, excerpted.

22. The "anointing" in John: John 12:1-8.

23. See John 13:14.

24. The washing of the apostles' feet: John 13:1-16. First Timothy 5:10 indicates that there might have been such a ritual in the early Church, practiced by women upon men. And the ritual continues every Holy Thursday when the pope washes the feet of the cardinals. In this the popes have assumed the title *servus servorum Dei,* or servant of the servants of God. Historically,

however, they have more frequently clung to the prerogatives of the role of Lord and Master.

25. See Matthew 26:67; 27:26; 27:30.

26. See Mark 14.65, 15:19.

27. See Luke 22:63.

28. See John 18:22; 19:3.

29. John 19:34.

30. John 20:27, excerpted. Doubting Thomas: John 20:24-29.

31. John 14:15; also, 14:21,23; 15:10. Compare Matthew 25:40, quoted above, on personal loyalty to, if not love of, Jesus as the rationale for philanthropy.

32. John 17:21-26, excerpted.

33. First John 4:16, excerpted. In his first epistle John makes his characteristic distinction between "the spirit" and "the flesh," but he shows a somewhat uncharacteristic concern about sin and conscience.

34. See Second John 3,5.

35. See Third John 12.

36. The Antichrist: First John 2:81,22; 4:3; Second John 7; under the guise of the Beast: Revelation 13; under the guise of the Rebel: Second Thessalonians 2:1-12.

37. John 6:63, excerpted.

38. The woman taken in adultery: John 8:3-11. This episode, considered an interpolation, is reminiscent of Luke in style. The question of interpolation aside, the episode accords with both Luke's favorable treatment of women and with John's notion of love as the solution to the problem of sin.

39. The Transfiguration: Matthew 17:1-8; Mark 9:2-8; Luke 9:28-36. I prefer to interpret this episode as an apotheosis, a becoming-divine of a human body, rather than a theophany or epiphany, an appearance of the divine to men. The Transfiguration is not reported in the Gospel of John, despite the fact that John, son of Zebedee, was one of the three witnesses to it. That lack casts further doubt on the identification of John as "the disciple Jesus loved," the author of the fourth gospel.

40. Besides the crucifix, another form of erotic idolatry on the theme of love-as-pathos is the bleeding Sacred Heart of Jesus, an imagery straight out of the Gospel of John.

41. John 2:21, excerpted.

42. Matthew 26:26, excerpted; also Mark 14:22; Luke 22:19. In Aramaic there would be no verb, so the "is" in the formula "this is my body" may be taken as "stands for" or "is like." The meaning may have been merely metaphorical or analogical, rather than anything about substance, being, or essence or other such concepts out of Greek philosophy.

43. Matthew 26:28, excerpted; also Mark 14:24.

44. Luke 22:19, excerpted.

45. Matthew 26:28, excerpted; variants, Mark 14:24; Luke 22:20.
46. John 13:15.
47. John 6:55-56.
48. John 6:60, excerpted.
49. Jesus himself gave "the cup" a funereal connotation, as a cup of blood. See Matthew 20:22-23; 26:39; Mark 10:38-39; 14:36; John 18:11. First Corinthians 11:26 likewise interprets the Eucharistic meal funereally.
50. John 6:53-54, excerpted.
51. John 10:30.
52. John 6:63.
53. Romans 12:5.
54. First Corinthians 6:15.
55. Luke 24:32, excerpted. In this scene, on the road to Emmaus, the resurrected Jesus taught his followers the methodology of typological exegesis of the Old Testament (see Luke 24:25-27). As if the Resurrection were not proof enough.
56. The corporate charter: Matthew 10; Luke 9:1-6; 10, *passim.*
57. John 13:34-35.

The Brotherhood of the Love Cult, pp. 151-170

1. Simplification is not that simple. The sixteenth-century Reformers only succeeded in setting up new Christian Churches, just as doctrinaire and intolerant as the Catholic one they broke away from. Although, in light of his apocalyptic expectations, it could not have been his intention, Jesus was to merely replace one Establishment by another.
2. Jesus expected as much of his twelve apostles as Yahweh had of his twelve tribes. Historically, there would be the same disappointment in both. The Christians would abandon many of their principles and values for the sake of power. But that development lay two centuries beyond the New Testament period. In the first century the Christian organization was powerless, adversarial, subversive, and righteous.
3. Mark 3:14-15, excerpted; similarly, Mark 6:7, 12-13; Matthew 10:1; Luke 9:1-2. The word "apostle" means someone sent as an emissary. In this discussion I limit the word to the Twelve. Besides the Twelve there was a broader group of "disciples" and "followers."
4. In the Miracle of the Loaves, for example, the apostles made the people sit down in parties of fifty (Luke 9:14-15) or in squares of hundreds and fifties (Mark 6:39-40).
5. Luke 22:49, excerpted. Jesus' acquiescence: Luke 22:36, 38.
6. On the armed resistance during the arrest, see Matthew 26:51-54; Mark 14:47, 49; Luke 22:49-50; John 18:10-11. With his typical succinctness

Mark reports simply that a bystander drew his sword and cut off the ear; Jesus then said that his arrest was necessary to fulfill the scriptures. Matthew adds the pacifist, anti-Zealot rebuke—"all who draw the sword will die by the sword" (Matthew 26:52) and Jesus' remark that he could appeal to twelve legions of angels, instead of twelve apostles, if he really wanted to be rescued. Luke mitigates the impression of violence in the scene by having Jesus heal the servant's ear. John identifies the swashbuckling apostle as Peter; he also gives the details of the name of the servant and that the ear cut was the right one. He has Jesus react with the characteristic Johannine metaphor about drinking the cup that his Father had given him.

7. Simon the Zealot: See Matthew 10:4; Mark 3:18; Luke 6:15.

8. Luke 9:6, excerpted.

9. Matthew 10:8, excerpted.

10. The episode of the epileptic demoniac: Matthew 17:14-20; Mark 9:14-29; Luke 9:37-43.

11. Luke 9:1, excerpted.

12. Mark 8:23, excerpted.

13. Episode of the blind man: Mark 8:22-26. An alternate explanation, proposed in Context, would be an ebb in Jesus' *mana.*

14. The inhospitable village: Luke 9:51-56. That it is John, the supposed "disciple Jesus loved," who lusted for the satisfaction of mass destruction makes us wonder once again about the traditional identification of "the disciple Jesus loved" with John, the son of Zebedee. The John of this incident is not the mystic lover of the Gospel of John, although he does bear resemblance to the fire-and-brimstone John of the Book of Revelation.

15. Matthew 10:5-6, excerpted.

16. Matthew 15:24, excerpted.

17. Matthew 28:19; compare Mark 16:15. Matthew 8:11-12 previews universalism in a context of alienation, Matthew 24:14 in a context of apocalypse.

18. Luke 2:32, excerpted.

19. The ten lepers: Luke 17:11-19. The Good Samaritan: Luke 10:29-37.

20. The Seventy-two: Luke 10:1-12; compare to Luke 9:1-6. A textual variant, "seventy," instead of "seventy-two," might signify tenfold power over the devils, seven being the devil's number. See Luke 10:17-18.

21. John 11:51-52, excerpted.

22. The apostles as lucky, special ones: Luke 10:23-24. The common gospel refrain, "Many are called, but few are chosen," also applies.

23. Luke 8:10, excerpted; also Matthew 13:11; Mark 4:11,34. Some commentators think that this esoteric nature of Jesus' teaching was only a Marcan misinterpretation. In the Gospel of John there is no in-group. An in-group is too narrow, too exclusive, too sectarian a concept for John,

the mystic lover. In John, Jesus can even claim, "I have said nothing in secret" (John 18:20).

24. Luke 10:16; see Matthew 16:19; 18:18 on *binding* and *loosing,* an authority expressed in authoritarian terms.

25. See Matthew 9:15; compare Matthew 25:1-13; also Mark 2:19-20; Luke 5:33-35. In John 3:29, the metaphor is put in the mouth of John the Baptist, a further indication of the confusion of identities between Jesus and John the Baptist.

26. The use of a marital metaphor to characterize loyalty is typical of the muddle of sexual and religious imagery in Jewish thinking.

27. Luke 22:28-29, excerpted. If the "kingdom" meant Jerusalem and Palestine, it was only forty years after Jesus' death that that kingdom was devastated and rendered valueless by the Roman legions of Vespasian and Titus. If the "kingdom" meant the Roman Empire, the Christians were indeed to acquire that, with the conversion of Constantine in A.D. 312; but that kingdom was to pass out of history, in A.D. 476. If the kingdom meant the earthly spiritual domain of the Catholic Church, well, that kingdom is still with us.

28. Matthew 19:28, excerpted; also Luke 22:30.

29. Luke 10:19, actually said to the Seventy-two; also Mark 16:17-18.

30. John 14:20, excerpted.

31. Selection of the Four: Matthew 4:18-22; Mark 1:16-20; Luke 5:1-11 is a variant tradition.

32. Selection of Matthew-Levi: Matthew 9:9; Mark 2:13-14; Luke 5:27-28. Matthew the tax collector has been taken as the author of, or at least the authority for, the Gospel of Matthew. However, for many of the books of the New Testament, attributions of authorship are suspect. The early Christians had no scruples about what we would consider literary fraud.

33. The lists of the Twelve: Matthew 10:2-4; Mark 3:13-19; Luke 6:13-16; Acts 1:13 (minus Judas).

34. Matthew 16:18-19, excerpted.

35. See Luke 22:8. Peter was supposedly Mark's principal informant; but Mark's gospel lacks both Peter's walking on the water and Jesus' investiture of Peter with executive authority, two episodes we might have expected Peter to convey to Mark.

36. The Inner Three were the Four, Andrew excluded. In his report of the selection of the Four, Luke doesn't mention Andrew's name, an omission that may have been due to Jesus' preference for the Inner Three. In writing that only Peter and John made the preparations for the Last Supper, Luke evidently thinks that towards the end of his life Jesus further reduced his companion group from the Inner Three to the Two. It does seem likely that Jesus systematically narrowed the scope of his social ties as his singular, very solitary, destiny approached. In the Gospel of John,

it is only "the disciple Jesus loved" who stood at the cross. But, by that time, psychologically speaking, Jesus was alone at last.

37. The Three: At the raising of the daughter of Jairus, Mark 5:37; Luke 8:51. At the Transfiguration, Matthew 17:1-8; Mark 9:2-8; Luke 9:28-36. At the agony in the garden, Matthew 26:37; Mark 14:33.

38. This device dramatizes the relationship between Jesus and the Baptist. By permitting two of his own disciples to leave him for Jesus, the Baptist gave approval to Jesus' mission. In John's gospel, the testimony of the Baptist to Jesus is at its most explicit, and the Baptist himself is demoted (see John 3:30).

39. John's version of Jesus' selection of his first apostles: John 1:35-51. In Nathanael's quick adherence we see how keen was the messianic expectation of the time.

40. Vague identifications in the Gospel of John: John 13:23; 18:15-16; 19:26; 20:2; 21:2,7,20.

41. By the time John's gospel was written, the Twelve were probably all dead and receding in memory; in any case, John is little concerned with historical exactitude.

42. See John 6:66.

43. Peter's faith versus Judas' betrayal: John 6:67-71.

44. See Mark 9:33-37; also Luke 9:46-48. Luke's version is repeated, out of context, in Luke 22:24-27, where it follows Jesus' prediction of betrayal. The question there should have been not "Who is the greatest?" but "Who is the traitor?" In another version, Matthew 18:1-4, the question is more impersonal.

45. John does not report these episodes of contentious wrangling among the apostles. However, in his brilliant scene of Jesus' washing of his apostles' feet, John makes Jesus give a demonstration of his teaching on the subject of rank and relationships.

46. The ambition of James and John: Matthew 20:20-28; Mark 10:35-45. Matthew's Jewish grudge against women comes out in this episode. He displaces the blame for this bit of impudent ambition from James and John onto their mother!

47. Matthew 16:22-23, excerpted.

48. The sequence: 1) Peter's profession of faith: Matthew 16:13-17; Mark 8:27-30; 2) the investiture ceremony: Matthew 16:18-19; 3) the rebuke: Matthew 16:23; Mark 8:31-33.

49. Luke 22:32.

50. Luke 22:61-62, excerpted.

51. Peter's threefold denial: Matthew 26:69-75; Mark 14:66-72; Luke 22:54-62; variant, John 18:25-27.

52. John 21:15, excerpted. Notice that in John love is the test for forgiveness.

53. John 21:15-17, excerpted.

54. John 21:19, excerpted. The rehabilitation and exoneration of Peter: John 21:15-17. Peter must have carried a burden of guilt for his denial all his life; his own missionary career was a long restitution for his sin.

55. "For Jesus knew from the outset . . . who it was that would betray him" (John 6:64, excerpted). Call it omniscience or manipulation, Jesus chose Judas expressly for the task of betrayal.

56. Luke 22:3, excerpted. Judas was paid for the betrayal, but that does not mean that money was his motive, as Matthew implies (Matthew 26:14-16). The money only sealed the bargain and made the contract valid.

57. John 6:70, excerpted (emphasis added). Jesus had also called Peter "Satan." It is ironic that both Peter, an obstacle to Jesus' destiny, and Judas, the means to that destiny, were branded with the same insult.

58. Compare John 12.4-6 to Matthew 26:8; Mark 14:4.

59. Judas as thief: John 12:6; as devil: John 6:70; as son of perdition: John 17:12. In The Jerusalem Bible translation the last description is softened to "who chose to be lost."

60. See John 13:26-27. In the synoptics, Judas is merely one who put his hand into a dish at the same time as Jesus (Matthew 26:23; Mark 14:20), or one who had a hand on the table (Luke 22:21).

61. Compare John 13:27 to 13:2.

62. John 19:11, excerpted. The exoneration of Pontius Pilate and the Romans of any blame relating to the death of Jesus was a position of political expediency for the early Church. More than Judas, it was the Jews who were to take on that blame. See the chapter, From Apocalyptic Sect to Cosmopolitan Church.

63. John 13:10, excerpted.

64. Mark 14:21; also Matthew 26:24; Luke 22:22. Luke softens the harshness by deleting Jesus' curse of the day of Judas' birth.

65. John 13:27, excerpted.

66. Matthew 27:3, excerpted.

67. The death of Judas: Matthew 27:3-10; variant tradition, Acts 1:18.

68. Luke 22:48, excerpted.

69. First Peter 5:14. The "holy kiss" is also referred to in Romans 16:16; First Corinthians 16:20; Second Corinthians 13:12; First Thessalonaians 5:26.

70. In Matthew and Mark, Judas walked straight up to Jesus, greeted him and kissed him (Matthew 26:49; Mark 14:45). In Luke, Judas was about to kiss Jesus, when he was stopped short by Jesus' challenging question about the intention behind the kiss (Luke 22:48). In John, both the kiss and even any intention to kiss are gone.

Martyrdom as Climax and Consequence, pp. 171–188

1. Luke 12:49-50.
2. John 7:6,8, excerpted.
3. Matthew 17:17, excerpted; also Mark 9:19; Luke 9:41.
4. John 10:17-18, excerpted.
5. Of course *conviction unto death* proves nothing about the truth of held beliefs, as any philosopher would agree. Martyrdom is not an argument. However, religion is an enthusiasm, and a contagious one at that. The willingness to martyrdom is at least proof of enthusiasm (commitment), if not of truth.
6. Luke 13:34, excerpted; also Matthew 23:37.
7. The parable of the wicked tenants: Matthew 21:33-46; Mark 12:1-12; Luke 20:9-19.
8. Luke 21:24, excerpted.
9. When the Apocalypse did not come, the early Christians succumbed to vindictiveness and the lust for vengeance for the deaths of the prophets, of Jesus, and of the martyrs. That vindictiveness was directed against both the Jews (*Jerusalem*) and the Romans (*Rome*). The New Testament specimen of Christian bitter vindictiveness is the Book of Revelation.
10. The first prophecy: Matthew 16:21-23; Mark 8:31-33; Luke 9:22. The prophecy is followed by the imposition of martyrdom as a discipline and then by the prophecies of Apocalypse: Matthew 16:24-28; Mark 8:34-38; 9:1; Luke 9:23-27.
11. The second prophecy: Matthew 17:22-23; Mark 9:30-32; Luke 9:44-45. In Luke's version reference to Jesus' death and Resurrection is deleted.
12. The third prophecy: Matthew 20:17-19; Mark 10:32-34; Luke 18:31-34. The third prophecy is more specific in vocabulary than are the first two. The contexts of the third prophecy are similar in all three synoptics, but not identical. The turnabout parable in Matthew, for example, is that of the vineyard laborers; in Luke, it is the Pharisee and the publican; in Mark, there is no parable. The eunuch ideal is only in Matthew. The general context in all three synoptic gospels is a disciplinary one. Willingness to self-sacrifice is the discipline to which all the other disciplines led.
13. John 2:21, excerpted.
14. See John 7:6,8 and John 10:17-18, quoted above.
15. John 7:33-34.
16. John 16:16.
17. John 7:20; also John 8:40.
18. John 7:25, excerpted.
19. John 8:22, excerpted.
20. John 12:27-28, excerpted.
21. John 12:30, excerpted.

22. John 12:36, excerpted. This scene is John's counterpart to the scene of the agony in the garden in the synoptic gospels.

23. Matthew 16:24, excerpted; also Mark 8:34. In Luke 9:23, the phrase "every day" is added, making Jesus' meaning merely metaphorical.

24. Matthew 10:38; similarly, Luke 14:27.

25. Matthew 16:25, repeated from Matthew 10:39; also Luke 9:24; 17:33. In Mark 8:35, the phrase "and for the sake of the gospel" is added, making the sacrifice more broadly ideological.

26. John 15:12-14, excerpted.

27. John 12:25, emphasis added.

28. Simon of Cyrene: Matthew 27:32; Mark 15:21; Luke 23:26.

29. The two criminals: Matthew 27:38; Mark 15:27; Luke 23:33; John 19:18.

30. The mockery: Matthew 27:39-44; Mark 15:29-32; Luke 23:35-38.

31. Matthew 27:46, excerpted; Mark 15:34. (It is interesting that Jesus' last words should be an old text, rather than a new revelation.)

32. Darkness: Matthew 27:45; Mark 15:33. The splitting of the Temple veil: Matthew 27:51; Mark 15:38; Luke 23:45.

33. Cosmic upheavals: Matthew 27:51-53.

34. Mark 15:39, excerpted; also Matthew 27:54.

35. Luke 23:46, excerpted.

36. See Luke 23:44. An eclipse is astronomically impossible during the passover season.

37. Luke 23:47, excerpted. By "great and good" the centurion was probably proclaiming Jesus' innocence of the political charges against him.

38. Luke 23:29, excerpted; compare to Luke 21:23.

39. Luke 23:34, excerpted. This verse is considered a scribal interpolation into the text. The editor may have taken his cue from Jesus' forgiveness of the "good thief" (Luke 23:43) and decided to extend that forgiveness to Judas, the Jews, and the Romans, all those in any way responsible for the death of Jesus. If only the rest of the textual tampering in the New Testament had been so constructive!

40. The *good thief:* Luke 23:39-43.

41. John 19:16-17, excerpted.

42. John 19:28, excerpted.

43. John 19:30, excerpted.

44. The actual Resurrection is not described in the gospels. In Mark, the earliest gospel, there is only the empty tomb. In the addendum to Mark and in the three later gospels, there are angelic announcements of the Resurrection and various post-Resurrection appearances by Jesus to women, to his apostles, and to other disciples.

45. See Luke 24:50-52; Acts 1:9-11. Unlike the Resurrection, the Ascension *is* described, as an apotheosis.

46. John 11:16.

From Apocalyptic Sect to Cosmopolitan Church, pp. 189–217

1. Matthew 24:21, excerpted. The destruction of Jerusalem: Matthew 24:15-22; Mark 13:14-20; Luke 21:20-24. In Matthew and Mark, the prophecy is directed at Judaea; in Luke, more narrowly at Jerusalem. There is no "disastrous abomination" in Luke.

2. Matthew 24:2, excerpted. Destruction of the Temple: Matthew 24:1-2; Mark 13:1-2; Luke 21:5-6.

3. See Luke 19:43-44; 21:24. Some interpret the description as mere stereotypes drawn from the Old Testament. In any case, the Gospel of Luke dates from after the destruction of Jerusalem in A.D. 70.

4. Matthew 24:29; also Mark 13:24-25; Luke 21:25-26.

5. In Second Peter the Transfiguration is cited as a preview of, and a type for, the Second Coming. See Second Peter 1:16-18. By the time of that epistle (ca. A.D. 90), skeptics had undermined the apocalyptic anxiety (Second Peter 3:3-4). The author presents a series of counterarguments to shore up the doctrine of the imminence of the Second Coming: Prophecy, if correctly interpreted, cannot be wrong (Second Peter 1:19-21); the Flood and Sodom and Gomorrah are types of the Last Judgment (Second Peter 2:5-9; 3:5-7); the divine conception and the human conception of time are different (Second Peter 3:8-9); and, finally, delay in the Second Coming only means that God is compassionate (Second Peter 3:9). Nonetheless, the End will come (Second Peter 3:10-12).

6. Matthew 16:27. The Second Coming: Matthew 16:27; 24:27,30; Mark 13:26; Luke 21:27. The Last Judgment: Matthew 16:27; 25:31-46. The Last Judgment in more positive terms, expressed as a gathering of the elect, without the damnation of the rest: Matthew 24:31; Mark 13:27; Luke 21:28.

7. Subsidiary events of the End-time: Pseudo-Christs, Matthew 24:4-5,11; Mark 13:5-6,21-23; Luke 17:22–24; 21:8. Disasters, Matthew 24:6-8; Mark 13:7-8; Luke 21:9-11. Persecutions, Matthew 24:9-10; Mark 13:9; Luke 21:12-19. Proclamation of the gospel, Matthew 24:14; Mark 13:10; Luke 21:13.

8. The time of the Apocalypse: Matthew 24:36; Mark 13:32. Apocalyptic expectancy: Matthew 24:32–33; 37-44; Mark 13:28-29, 33-37; Luke 21:29-31,34-36.

9. Matthew 16:28. In Mark 9:1 and Luke 9:27, it is the "kingdom of God," without the "Son of Man," a formulation that detaches the saying from its apocalyptic associations.

10. Matthew 24:34-35, excerpted; also Mark 13:30-31; Luke 21:32-33.

11. Exhortations to patience: James 5:7-8; Second Peter 3:13-15. Both epistles date from ca. A.D. 90.

12. See Matthew 24:29.

13. The Gospel of John lacks the apocalyptic rhetoric of the synoptics. To make up for that lack, the early Christians attributed the Book of Revelation, the Apocalypse, to John.

14. The Ascension: Acts 1:9-11.

15. The apocalyptic refrain: First John 2:18; First Peter 4:7; James 5:8; and Revelation 1:3 (repeated in Revelation 22:10), respectively, all excerpted. The two epistles to the Thessalonians, the earliest writings in the New Testament, are thoroughly apocalyptic, although in Second Thessalonians there is already some apocalyptic revisionism (Second Thessalonians 2).

16. First Corinthians 16:22, excerpted. The invocation "Lord, come!" is actually given as *Marana tha,* the Aramaic form. The Aramaic in the Greek text is a magical incantation, like the Aramaic *abracadabra* in the Greek text of the Gospel of Mark.

17. The election of the new twelfth apostle: Acts 1:15–26. Once elected, Matthias disappears from the story. That indicates the essential unimportance of his person.

18. Luke 24:52-53, excerpted.

19. Acts 2:46, excerpted; similarly, Acts 5:42. See also Acts 3:1; 5:12. The "breaking of the bread" here probably refers to a Christian communal meal, rather than a sacramental Eucharistic ritual.

20. The five thousand: Acts 4:4. As in the Miracle of the Loaves, five thousand is a number that needed to be *fed.*

21. The Seven: Acts 6:1-6. Concealed in this episode is a conflict between Hebraists and Hellenists, conservative-tribal and liberal cosmopolitan factions in the early Christian community.

22. Peter's miraculous cures: Acts 3:1-10; 9:32-35,36-42.

23. Peter's sermon: Acts 3:11-26.

24. Apostolic confrontations with the Jerusalem Establishment of the Jews: Acts 4:1-22; 5:21-33.

25. On the jealousy of the Establishment compare Acts 5:17 to Matthew 27:18 or Mark 15:10.

26. First Peter 1:8, excerpted.

27. See First Corinthians 1:27-31; 3:18-21.

28. Barnabas: Acts 4:36-37. Christian poverty and communism: Acts 4:32,34-35.

29. Acts 5:11, excerpted; similarly, Acts 5:5. Ananias and Sapphira: Acts 5:1-11.

30. See Matthew 19:16-26; Mark 10:17-27. In the variant of Luke 18:18-27, Jesus directed the saying to the reluctant rich disciple, and, we

might add, to types like Ananias and Sapphira. Luke valued poverty and correspondingly condemned the rich. See his parable of the rich man and Lazarus (Luke 16:19-31).

31. Acts 6.8, excerpted.

32. The story of Stephen: Acts 6:8-7:60. Stephen's Lucan words of forgiveness (Acts 7:60) parallel Jesus' Lucan words of forgiveness (Luke 23:34).

33. Acts 12:23, excerpted. The sequence: Peter's imprisonment and escape, Acts 12:1-19., the death of Herod, Acts 12:20-23.

34. Revelation 6:10, excerpted; also 16:6.

35. Jesus' hard stare: Luke 22:61; John 1:42 (but compare to 1:36, in which John the Baptist also has a "hard stare").

36. For these characterizations see: Second Corinthians 11:26; Second Corinthians 11:13; Galatians 1:7; Romans 3:8; Revelation 2:2; and First Timothy 4:2, respectively.

37. See First Thessalonians 5:14, "Warn the idlers," which had to be followed up by Second Thessalonians 3:6-12. Against the parasites: Titus 3:14.

38. Gluttony at the sacrament: First Corinthians 11:17-34.

39. See Second Peter 3:17. Christianity as a secret society: Second John 12: Third John 13. Paul had to disclaim a code in his epistles (Second Corinthians 1:13) after he claimed special knowledge of secret mysteries (First Corinthians 15:51-53). "Uneducated and unbalanced" people distorted the meaning of Paul's letters (Second Peter 3:15-17).

40. The adulteration of the Good News: The citations are from Hebrews 13:9 (similarly First Timothy 1:3); Second Timothy 2:23; First Timothy 4:7; Second Timothy 2:14; First Timothy 6:20; Acts 20:30, and First Timothy 4:1.

41. Acts 4:32, excerpted.

42. Second Corinthians 12:20, excerpted, and James 4:1, excerpted, respectively. See also Galatians 5:20; First Timothy 6:3-5.

43. The spirit of faction: First Corinthians 1:10-16; 3:3ff.; 11:18; Second Corinthians 11:3-4,13-15; 12:20; Galatians 1:6-9; 4:17; 5:9-12,15; Ephesians 4:14; Philippians 1:15-17; 3:2; First Timothy 1:3ff.; 4:1-7; 6:3ff.;, Second Timothy 2:14ff.; Titus 1:10ff.; Second Peter 2:1-3., Jude 4-16; Revelation 2:6,9,14-16,20-25; 3:9; Acts 20:30.

44. Schism: First John 2:19. Heresy: Second John 7-11. Power struggle: Third John 9-11.

45. Simon the Magician: Acts 8:9-25.

46. The Catholic Church managed to read the episode of Simon the Magician with blindfolds on. Simony, or the buying and selling of Church offices, spiritual dignities, favors and dispensations of all kinds, came to be a conspicuous organizational vice in the Catholic Church, one that

continued well beyond the Reformation. However, the episode of Simon the Magician in Acts indicates that it was a corruption that arrived early, as well as lingered long.

47. First Thessalonians 2:5, excerpted. On money scandals see First Corinthians 9:3-18; Second Corinthians 2:17; 7:2; 8:20-21; 11:7-9; 12:14-18; First Timothy 6:5; First Peter 5:2. Second Corinthians 8 and 9 could serve as a manual of strategy for ecclesiastical fundraising. All the manipulative psychological techniques are there. "God loves a cheerful giver" (Second Corinthians 9:7).

48. Accusations against the elders: First Timothy 3:3, 8; 5:17-20; Titus 1:7, 11.

49. James 1:21 and Romans 6:17, respectively, both excerpted.

50. Doubt as a moral evil: James 1:6-8.

51. Shunning imposed: Second Thessalonians 3:6,14-15; seemingly lifted: Romans 14:10; re-imposed: Romans 16:17. Shunning on strictly moral grounds: First Corinthians 5, especially 5:11-13. Shunning on ideological grounds: Titus 3:10; Second John 10. Shunning of personal enemies in a power struggle: Second Corinthians 2:6. Excommunication is a more formal kind of shunning (see Matthew 18:17).

52. First Corinthians 16:22, excerpted.

53. Acts 3:14-15, excerpted.

54. Acts 3:17.

55. Compare Acts 3:17 to Luke 23:34.

56. Compare the Jewish complaint—"You . . . seem determined to fix the guilt of this man's death on us" (Acts 5:28, excerpted) to the self-curse put into the mouths of the rabble at Jesus' trial: "His blood be on us and on our children!" (Matthew 27:25). That last sentence is the most ominous in the New Testament, containing within it the concept of hereditary racial guilt and therefore a rationale for righteous Christian anti-Semitism.

57. See Acts 2:23; 3:13-15; 5:30; 7:52.

58. Exoneration of Pilate: By Peter, Acts 3:13; by Jesus, John 19:11.

59. First Peter 2:13. Paul too urged submission to Rome: see Romans 13:1-7 and Titus 3:1. The Christians should even pray for the civil Establishment: First Timothy 2:1-2.

60. First Peter 2:17, excerpted.

61. The Christian policy of political expedience was to fail, due to a recrudescence of the old Jewish scruple over "idolatry," in this case the statues of the divinized emperors and the patriotic sacrifice-ritual that the state could require of citizens. When the Christians refused to sacrifice, their refusal was interpreted by the Roman civil authorities as disloyalty to the state.

Both the Jews and the Romans were to rebuff and persecute the Christians, each group for different reasons. To the Jews, the Christians were outrageous blasphemers who insinuated their candidate for Messiah, a mere human, into association with Yahweh Himself. To the Romans, the Christians were suspect subversives who renounced social responsibilities and deadbeats who eagerly awaited a fiery cosmic cataclysm.

The values of the Christians were antitheses to both the values of Jerusalem and the values of Rome. That there could be no ultimate religious or political accommodation between the Christians on the one hand, and Jerusalem and Rome on the other, was to be disastrous for both the Jews and the Romans.

62. Acts 2:4, excerpted.

63. Pentecost: Acts 2:1-13. The enthusiasm of the "gift of speech" spread throughout the sect. Luke interprets the Pentecost episode as a kind of simultaneous translation, like that in the United Nations. The speeches made by those in the hysterical trance of the gift of speech were, more probably, mostly unintelligible babble (First Corinthians 14:2-25). The spontaneous eruptions of those under the influence, fakers many of them, tended to throw Christian meetings into an unseemly and rowdy disorder (First Corinthians 14:26-40). What had begun as an inspiration ended up as a nuisance that needed to be regulated.

64. Acts 10:34-35, excerpted.

65. Acts 10:36, excerpted.

66. Peter's dietary vision, the visit to Cornelius, and the baptism of the first pagans: Acts 10. In an editorial interpretation of one of Jesus' teachings (see Mark 7:19), there is the assertion that the Master himself had dispensed with Jewish dietary scruples. But those scruples must have been tenacious, if the dispensation had to be stated afresh, as if in an original decision by Peter.

67. Acts 11:17, excerpted. Peter's justification: Acts 11:1-18.

68 Acts 15:12, excerpted. The issue of circumcision: Acts 15:1-12.

69. This so-called apostolic decree is given a typical New Testament triple affirmation: Acts 15:19-20,28-29; 21:25. The James who made the decision was not the apostle James (who, we learn in Acts 12:2, was executed by Herod), but the James, "brother of the Lord," that is, a blood-relation, a cousin or brother, of Jesus. Evidently, Jesus' family, who had opposed him during his ministry, joined the sect and assumed leadership in it after Jesus was dead. Even Jesus' mother joined the cult of her own son (see Acts 1:14).

70. The church at Antioch: Acts 11:19-26.

71. Acts 28:28.

Antichrist, pp. 219-251

1. On "clean" and "unclean": Matthew 15:10-20; Mark 7:14-23. That is directly followed by the cure of the Syro-Phoenician gentile: Matthew

15:21-28; Mark 7:24-30. The cure of the centurion's servant: Matthew 8:5-13; Luke 7:1-10; variant, John 4:46-53.

2. Paul's conversion: Acts 9:3-9; and allusions in Galatians 1:11-16; First Corinthians 9:1; 15:8; Second Corinthians 4:6. The cure of Paul's blindness: Acts 9:10-19. In a clever variation on the theme of "all the Jews are blind," Paul later struck blind a Jewish magician and, imposter named, significantly, bar-Jesus (Acts 13:6-12). Paul struck him blind to impress a Roman. There was the familiar Christian strategy of an attack upon the Jews and subservience to Roman political authority.

3. ". . . at midday . . . a light brighter than the sun . . ." (Acts 26:13)

4. Paul's first telling of his conversion experience: Acts 22:1-16. Compare Acts 9:3-9.

5. Paul's second telling of his conversion experience: Acts 26:12-18.

6. First Corinthians 15:8.

7. Paul's legitimacy: Called by Jesus, Acts 9:15; 20:24; 22:21; 23:11; 26:16-17; Galatians 1:11-12; Romans 1:4-5; First Timothy 1:12. Appointed by God, First Thessalonians 2:4; Galatians 1:15; Romans 15:15-16; First Corinthians 1:1; Second Corinthians 1:1; Colossians 1:1; Ephesians 1:1; Second Timothy 1:1; Titus 1:3. Appointed by both Jesus and by God the Father, Galatians 1:1-2; First Timothy 1:1. Called by the Holy Spirit, Acts 13:2.

8. Acts 19:15, excerpted. The seven exorcists: Acts 19:13-17.

9. Galatians 1:15, incorporating phraseology of Isaiah 49:1.

10. Paul's cure of the cripple: Acts 14:8-18. Compare to Peter's cure, Acts 3:1-10.

11. Paul's jailbreak: Acts 16:23-40. Compare to Acts 12:4-11 and Acts 5:17-21.

12. Paul's exorcism: Acts 16:16-18.

13. Paul's raising of Eutychus: Acts 20:7-12. The episode is unintentionally funny. Paul was preaching to a group in a second-story room. Eutychus was sitting on the windowsill. Paul's longwindedness put Eutychus to sleep, and he tumbled out the window. So Paul had to raise to life a man whom he himself had killed off for that very purpose!

14. Cosmopolitanization as a last resort: Acts 13:46; 18:6.

15. Paul's vision of Jesus: Acts 22:17-21. Notice the sequence of ideas: The Jerusalem Establishment of the Twelve oppose Paul (Acts 22:18); his former persecutions of the Christians are the reason for their distrust (Acts 22:19-20); and so Paul will go to the Gentiles and carve out his own territory (Acts 22:21). Galatians 2:7-9 and Romans 11:13 contradict Peter's claim in Acts 15:7.

16. Peter and James as backsliders: Acts 21:17-26. The Council of Jerusalem: Acts 15.

17. Paul's revelation: See Galatians 2:2. His fourteen years of autono-

mous preaching: See Galatians 2:1. Paul's account of his meeting with the apostolic Establishment: Galatians 2:1-10.

18. Galatians 2:11.

19. Galatians 2:6, excerpted.

20. Galatians 2:9, excerpted.

21. See Second Peter 3:15-16, excerpted.

22. Peter on behalf of Paul: Second Peter 3:15-16. First Peter too is a very Pauline epistle, perhaps due to Silvanus (Silas) (see First Peter 5:12), a Pauline agent. So in both the epistles attributed to Peter, Peter was robbed to pay Paul.

23. Barnabas' recruitment of Paul: Acts 11:22-26. Paul as emissary: Acts 15:22.

24. See Acts 15:39.

25. See Acts 11:24.

26. John Mark and Barnabas cousins: Colossians 4:10. John Mark a "son" of Peter: First Peter 5:13.

27. The split between Paul and Barnabas: Acts 15:36-39. First Peter is not so suspect as Second Peter, and the merely incidental nature of the inclusion of Mark's name might indicate the reference as genuine. (However, accepting New Testament statements as "facts" is often a naive interpretation.) According to Colossians 4:10, Second Timothy 4:11, and Philemon 24, Paul eventually won over John Mark to his service; but the first two of those three epistles are of uncertain authorship.

28. See Acts 15:40.

29. Paul's recruitment of Timothy: Acts 16:1-3. Immediately after the report of Timothy's circumcision there is the assertion that Paul went about enforcing the decisions of the Council of Jerusalem, a non sequitur if ever there was one! See Acts 16:4. Paul could be expedient. He feigned a vow to placate the Jews of Jerusalem (Acts 21:17-26).

30. Paul's Twelve: Acts 19:1-7.

31. Paul's territory: See Romans 15:20; Second Corinthians 10:15-16.

32. Paul before the Sanhedrin: Acts 23:6-10; recounted, Acts 24:20-21; 26:8.

33. Paul's kowtows and flatteries: Acts 23:1-5; 24:10; 26:2-3.

34. See Second Corinthians 12:16.

35. Paul's renunciation of childlike simplicity: First Corinthians 13:11.

36. First Corinthians 9:22, excerpted.

37. For Paul's epistolary flatteries (called *thanksgivings* by the commentators), see the two epistles to the Thessalonians. Galatians is a browbeating. Second Corinthians is a mix of flattery, browbeating, and pleading (perhaps derived from several different epistles edited into one).

38. Acts 26:25, excerpted.

39. Paul's truthfulness: Second Corinthians 1:23; 11:31; Galatians 1:20;

Romans 9:1; First Timothy 2:7. Compare those protestations to Jesus' directive in Matthew 5:33-37.

40. Second Corinthians 4:5, excerpted.

41. Paul's boasting: Second Corinthians 10;11;12. Much of the boasting was directed against the "archapostles," that is, the Christian Establishment of Jerusalem. Against them Paul cites his own miracles, his own revelations, and his own sufferings as proof of his legitimacy.

42. Acts 20:19, excerpted.

43. Acts 26:29, excerpted. Those are Luke's words, but First Corinthians 7:7 is similar. On Paul as model, see First Corinthians 4:16; 11:1; Philippians 3:17; 4:9.

44. Galatians 4:14, excerpted. Not Jesus of Nazareth, notice, but *Christ Jesus,* the glorified one.

45. Romans 2:29, excerpted.

46. First Thessalonians 2:15.

47. See Romans 10:1.

48. Romans 11:28, excerpted.

49. Paul's ambivalence toward the Jews: Romans 9; 10; 11; also Romans 2; 3:1-8. Galatians, *passim.*

50. Paul as fundraiser: Acts 11:30; 24:17; First Corinthians 16:1-4; Second Corinthians 8; 9; Galatians 2:10; Romans 15:25-31; Philippians 4:10-20.

51. Paul's expedience: First Timothy 6:17-19. The two epistles to Timothy and the epistle to Titus were written by an impersonator of Paul, rather than by Paul himself; but compare to Second Corinthians 8:11-15.

52. Acts 17:16, excerpted. Paul himself makes the connection between idolatry and sexual immorality in Romans 1:18-27.

53. The sequence of these excerpts: First Corinthians 7:1; 7:2; 7:9; 7:7; 7:40.

54. First Corinthians 7:28, excerpted.

55. The identification of spirituality with celibacy: See First Corinthians 7:32-35.

56. Against the "cutters:" Philippians 3:2. Spiritual circumcision: Colossians 2:11. The castration curse: Galatians 5:12. In First Corinthians 7:18-19, circumcision is brought up in the context of sexual morality.

57. See First Corinthians 12:23-24. In Philippians 3:19, "shame" is the euphemism Paul uses for the penis.

58. The devotion of Lydia: Acts 16:14-15,40. The female hysteria of the slave girl of Philippi: Acts 16:16-18.

59. See Acts 16:13; 17:4,12,34. Taking the gospel to the women: First Corinthians 7:14,16. That passage parallels First Peter 3:1-3. Once again we wonder whether Paul or Peter was the innovator. It should be observed here that letting women act as religious propagandists was an affront to traditional Jewish patriarchal values.

60. The good woman: Veiled, First Corinthians 11:2-16. Silent, First Corinthians 14:34-35; First Timothy 2:11-13; 5:13. On the respectful and obedient slave as the model for a good woman, compare First Timothy 6:1-2 to First Timothy 2:9-15, or Titus 2:9-10 to Titus 2.4-5.

61. See First Timothy 5:3-16 on the subject of the recruitment of nuns (*widows*). Notice that they should be old, beyond any capacity for sexual temptation.

62. Second Timothy 3:6-7, excerpted. Female waspishness must also have been a problem; see Philippians 4:2-3.

63. Philippians 3:10; also Romans 6:5.

64. Paul's prophecy: Acts 20:25. Like Jesus, Paul was "proclaiming the kingdom." Paul made his prophecy to the elders of Ephesus. If those elders are the same men as the twelve disciples that Paul lured away from John the Baptist (Acts 19:1-7), then he would be even closer to the pattern of the Master's prophecy to his own disciples, his Twelve. Paul's resolve: Acts 21:10-14. The bloodlust of the mob: Acts 21:35-36. (The shout of the mob, however, was not "Crucify him!" but "Kill him!" As a Roman citizen, Paul could not be executed by the ignominious method of crucifixion.) Festus in the role of Pilate: Acts 25:25; 26:31.

65. Second Corinthians 4:10, excerpted.

66. Galatians 6:17, excerpted.

67. Galatians 2:19, excerpted.

68. Acts 20:24, excerpted.

69. See Philippians 1:21-26.

70. Paul's appeal to Caesar: Acts 25:11-12.

71. That was Agrippa's appraisal of the situation: See Acts 26:30-32.

72. Romans 7:24.

73. Romans 7:15; similarly, Galatians 5:17.

74. See Second Corinthians 10:10-11.

75. Romans 7:18-19, excerpted. To those commentators who interpret this "I" in a collective sense, we answer that Paul speaks only for himself in his confession of neurosis.

76. Acts 20:26, excerpted.

77. Paul's "conscience": Acts 18:6; 23:1; 24:16; First Corinthians 4:4 and eight more times in chapters 8 and 10; Second Corinthians 1:12; 4:2; 5:11; Romans 2:15; 9:1; 13:5; 14:22. "Conscience" is also a key word in the vocabulary of the impersonators of Paul. See First Timothy 1:5,19; 3:9; 4:2;, Second Timothy 1:3; Titus 1:15; Hebrews 10:22; 13:18. Paul as the greatest of all sinners: First Timothy 1:15.

78. Romans 7:18, excerpted.

79. Romans 3:28, excerpted. On "justification by faith," see Romans 3; 4; 5. Although Jesus claimed that he did not come to abolish the Law, Paul insisted that he did do that very thing (see Romans 10:4; Ephesians

2:15). Paul would make the Master as devious and deceptive as he himself was.

80. The recognition: Romans 7:20, excerpted. The renunciation: Philippians 3:9, excerpted. Paul the sick one: Second Corinthians 12:7-10; Galatians 4:14. One wonders what Paul's "disease," his "thorn in the flesh," was. Could it have been epilepsy, malaria, or some other kind of affliction that the Jews would call "unclean," thus driving Paul to the pagans, who had no such moral prejudices against disease?

This discussion suggests a new test of the genuineness of the Pauline epistles, namely, the test of neurosis. Any impersonators of Paul could plagiarize his ideas, appropriate his vocabulary, even imitate his style; but it is unlikely that they would manifest his symptoms. Where the symptoms are, then (see the quotations in the previous discussion), there is Paul.

By the test of neurosis, Romans, First and Second Corinthians, Galatians, and Philippians are certainly genuine. Ephesians, Colossians, First and Second Timothy, and Titus—all free of symptoms—are probably not genuine. Hebrews lacks the Pauline solipsism. In First and Second Thessalonians, the point of view oscillates between "I/me" (Paul) and "we/us" (Paul, Silas, and Timothy), indicating collaboration and joint authorship; it is not possible to diagnose one who speaks as three. Philemon is too brief for any appraisal on the basis of the test of neurosis.

Interestingly, the division that results from applying the diagnostic test of neurosis to the Pauline epistles corresponds fairly well to the general critical judgments on which epistles are by Paul and which not, judgments made on the basis of textual criticism.

81. James 2:24, excerpted.

82. James 2:26, excerpted. James' rebuttal to Paul: James 2:14-26. The rebuttal is actually a quadruple contradiction and affirmation: James 2:17, 20, 24, 26.

83. A millennium and a half later, Paul's doctrine effected its cure on another neurotic of similar self-frustrated temperament. While sitting on the toilet in the monastery at Wittenberg, Martin Luther, constipated in will and deed, suddenly experienced a great outpouring of religious insight:— It was Paul's doctrine of "justification by faith" that was the true key to Christianity. The ghost of Paul appeared and cured Luther.

Unfortunately, the ghost of James made an appearance, too. Luther dealt with him by high-handedly dismissing the Epistle of James as an "epistle of straw." (Luther, with his taste for coprophilic imagery, probably meant "of straw" to signify not only "insubstantial," but also suitable for the deposits of the barn animals.)

Good deeds and papal indulgences would never earn, and could not buy, salvation, Luther realized. Grace was a free gift from God, and it was faith and faith alone that justified. A man is saved when he stops trying.

And so Protestantism was born out of a reincarnation of Paul the neurotic and a reenactment of Paul's cure.

84. Second Timothy 4:11, excerpted. Even if Second Timothy was written not by Paul but by a Pauline impersonator, it still might contain accurate biographical information. Luke as a disciple of Paul: Colossians 4:14; Philemon 24.

There are many contradictions between the biography of Paul as presented by Luke in Acts and the autobiography of Paul as presented in his own epistles. Most commentators deal with the contradictions by accusing Luke of ignorance, mistakes, or free invention to explain some event the true nature of which he could only guess at. As for Paul, the commentators have taken everything he wrote at face value. But when we consider Paul's many protestations of his truthfulness, his solipsism, his polemical power-struggle against the apostolic Establishment, his self-deceptive mind, his fanaticism, and his neurosis, we must wonder how much of Paul's version of events was a self-serving distortion.

85. The Last Supper, according to Paul: First Corinthians 11:23-25.

86. First Corinthians 7:10-11 seems to show a knowledge of Jesus' divorce doctrine, but Paul refers to that doctrine as "from the Lord," rather than from Jesus of Nazareth. Romans 12:14 preaches pacifism, but once again Jesus is not credited. Romans 12:20 urges philanthropy, but with unchristian spite. In Acts 20:35 Paul quotes Jesus as saying, "there is more happiness in giving than in receiving," but it is unlikely that Jesus of Nazareth ever uttered such a watery platitude. Jesus' directive was the absolute, "Give it all away, and do it right now!"

87. See Second Corinthians 8:9. This occurs in a context of a discussion about money, so "rich" and "poor" cannot be taken as metaphorical and metaphysical.

88. See First Timothy 6:13. Paul himself "spoke up" in longwinded self-defense in his trial before Felix (Acts 24). But Paul was always urging his disciples to follow an *imitatio Pauli,* rather than an *imitatio Christi.*

89. The post-Resurrection appearances, according to Paul: First Corinthians 15:3-7.

90. Commentators have generally claimed that Paul knew about Jesus, but just didn't tell. It is more natural to assume that he never told because he just didn't know much.

91. First Corinthians 9:1, excerpted,

92. First Corinthians 2:2, excerpted.

93. First Corinthians 2:16, excerpted.

94. Paul's *revelation:* See Galatians 2:2.

95. Paul's revaluation: From time to time, it has been suggested or affirmed or even argued that it was Paul who *invented* Christianity. Or, because his epistles are the oldest Christian documents we possess, some

have considered his notions as the *original* Christianity. Contrary to those assertions of the primacy of Paul, I consider his Christianity a hodgepodge of Judaism, Greek philosophy, and mystery religion grafted onto the person Jesus of Nazareth, in short, a warped and idiosyncractic muddle. By now it should be clear that I believe that the *original* Christianity was the values revolution of the rabbi ("the Master") Jesus of Nazareth. That Christianity was not a mere faith (at least not a faith beyond traditional Judaism). It was, rather, a *discipline,* a severe ascetic discipline of values-in-action. If so, then the *original Christians* were Jerusalem-based ascetic sects, like the Ebionites, who were decimated and scattered by the destruction of Jerusalem in A.D. 70 and ostracized by the orthodox Church as heretics (because they claimed so little about Jesus f Nazareth). They ultimately vanished into the oblivion of the Palestinian desert, mingling with the ghosts of John the Baptist and Jesus of Nazareth.

The Revaluation, pp. 253–263

1. The devil's temptations: Matthew 4:1-11; Luke 4:1-13.
2. The Pharisees' temptation: Matthew 12:38-39; 16:1-4; Mark 8:11-12; Luke 11:16,29-30. In the basic version of the incident, in Mark, Jesus fends off the Pharisees with a blunt refusal. In the embellished versions of Matthew and Luke, Jesus does promise a sign, "the sign of Jonah," that is, Jesus' own three days and three nights in the cavern of the tomb, a parallel to Jonah's three days and nights in the cavernous belly of the sea monster. That editorial embellishment may be taken as a typical Christian exercise in typology, retrojected into the mouth of Jesus. In Luke 11:29-30, it is the general crowd, rather than the Pharisees, who look for a sign.
3. The father of the epileptic boy answered Jesus' challenge to faith with the plea, "I do have faith. Help the little faith I have!" (Mark 9:24, excerpted).
4. Jesus' dilemma: No miracles, no faith, see John 4:48. No faith, no miracles, see Mark 6:5-6. Also, no belief despite miracles, see John 12:37; 15:24.
5. Philip versus Simon the Magician: Acts 8:5-13. Paul versus Bar-jesus: Acts 13:6-12. Paul versus the seven Jewish exorcists: Acts 19:11-17. In Paul's confrontation with Bar-jesus, he struck the adversary magician blind. Like Peter's slaying of Ananias and Sapphira, that "black magic" introduced the element of fear and force into the miracle stories, very different from the beneficent "white magic" of Jesus' healing miracles.
6. Acts 19:18-19.
7. On miracles as proof, see, for example, John 5:36; 10:25,37-38; 14:11; Acts 2:22.

8. Mark 16:17-18.

9. "Philosophy" in the New Testament: See Colossians 2:8.

10. The expression "Kingdom of God" occurs only once in John, in John 3:5.

11. This is not, of course, the actual chronological sequence of the displacements. Paul's epistles antedate John's gospel by about forty years.

12. First Peter 1:8, excerpted.

13. Tacitus on Jesus: See *Annals,* 15.44.

14. This summary of the Jewish tradition about Jesus is derived from the article "Jesus Christ," in *Encyclopaedia Britannica,* fifteenth edition.

15. Second Corinthians 12:9, excerpted.

16. Second Peter 3:10, excerpted.

17. Nietzsche, *Beyond Good and Evil,* section 153.

Bibliographical Note

"A book lives as long as it is unfathomed. Once it is fathomed, it dies at once."

—D. H. Lawrence, *Apocalypse,* p. 5

In the days of my youth, the Bible was generally available in English only in the Revised Standard Version of the King James Version and in the Douay-Rheims Version. The former was from a poor Greek text, the latter from the Latin Vulgate, and so a translation of a translation. In the King James and the Douay-Rheims versions, the Bible, the reputed sourcebook of Western culture, was locked in a time-capsule date 1610/11.

During the past half-century, while archeological findings have enriched our understanding of the biblical milieu, analytical advances have been made in philology, source criticism, form criticism, textual criticism, redaction criticism, and other bibical disciplines. The consequent and subsequent publication of many accurate, faithful, modern-English versions of the Bible has been nothing less than a literary (if not a cultural) revolution.

In order to undertake a philosophical revaluation, it is necessary to go directly to the primary source. The Bible as primary source is now, at last, fully accessible.

I chose *The Jerusalem Bible* (Darton Longman & Todd, Ltd., and Doubleday & Co., Inc., 1966) for my own revaluation, because it is intended as a study Bible, is recognized for its accuracy of translation, and attains a high standard of modern literary English. In *The New Jerusalem Bible* (Darton Longman & Todd, Ltd., and Doubleday & Co., Inc., 1985), the introduction and notes have been updated and revised, reflecting scholarly progress since initial publication.

If the criteria for selection of an English translation of the Bible are the best available scholarship, the most accurate translation of meaning, and good modern English, then other versions to be recommended are the following: *The Catholic Study Bible, New American Bible* (Oxford University Press, 1990, update of 1970); *The Revised English Bible* (Oxford University Press, Cambridge University Press, 1989, update of *The New English Bible,* Oxford University Press, 1970; 1961); *The New International Version* (Zondervan, 1984, from earlier editions); and, with a translation more vernacular than literary, *The Good News Bible, Today's English Version* (American Bible Society, 1976 and earlier editions).

To consult various translations at once, there is *The Eight Translation New Testament* (Tyndale House, 1974), in which the versions (including *The Jerusalem Bible, The New English Bible, The New International Version,* and *Today's English Version*) are laid out together on facing pages.

I have also used volumes in *The Anchor Bible* (Doubleday & Co., Inc.), well described as "the most painstaking and exhaustive edition of the Bible ever undertaken." Sixteen volumes of the New Testament are now available from that series. In some of the most recent volumes, however, the exegesis, exposition, and commentary get mired in minutiae.

The Interpreter's Bible (12 volumes, Abingdon Press, 1952) is based on the Revised Standard Version, but is still valuable for its introductory articles, maps, and general information.

The Modern Concordance to the New Testament (Doubleday & Co., Inc., 1976) is designed for use with *The Jerusalem Bible,* but serves the other modern versions as well.

At one step remove from the primary source is the commentary, which provides historical orientation, literary criticism, and a guided tour through the books of the Bible. Massive one-volume commentaries as useful to the revaluator as to the student are: *The New Jerome Biblical Commentary* (Prentice-Hall, 1990); *Harper's Bible Commentary* (Harper & Row, San Francisco, 1988), and the older *The Interpreter's One-Volume Commentary on the Bible* (Abingdon Press, 1971).

A survey of modern criticism of the New Testament is conducted by Stephen Neill in *The Interpretation of the New Testament, 1861–1961* (Oxford University Press, 1964). Of further secondary sources, there is such an exhaustive and exhausting proliferation that we fear that the prophecy of D. H. Lawrence is about to come to pass.

Index